Brian J. Arnold
Justification in the Second Century

Brian J. Arnold

Justification in the Second Century

—

BAYLOR UNIVERSITY PRESS

Arnold, Brian J.: *Justification in the Second Century*
© 2017 Walter de Gruyter GmbH Berlin/Boston.
All rights reserved.

This work is a reprint edition of the original work from De Gruyter, *Justification in the Second Century*, Brian J. Arnold, ISBN 978-3-11-047677-4.

The work may not be translated or copied in whole or part without the written permission of the publisher (Walter De Gruyter GmbH, Genthiner Straße 13, 10785 Berlin, Germany).

The ISBN for this 2018 Baylor University Press paperback edition is 978-1-4813-0898-4.

Baylor University Press Cover Design by Savanah N. Landerholm.

Library of Congress Cataloging-in-Publication Data
A CIP catalog record for this book has been applied for at the Library of Congress.

Bibliographic information published by the Deutsche Nationalbibliothek. The Deutsche Nationalbibliothek lists this publication in the Deutsche Nationalbibliografie; detailed bibliographic data are available online at http://dnb.dnb.de.

Printed in the United States of America on acid-free paper.

To Lauren,
my heart's captor

Acknowledgements

I am indebted to many professors, colleagues, pastors, friends, and family who all played a special role in the completion of this work. Without the careful guidance, meticulous editing, and constant encouragement from Michael Haykin, this project would have never taken flight. I spent years studying the fathers under him and learned more than anything else to love them. Jonathan Pennington has stretched my thinking more than any other person, pushing me to reflect on every angle, which has always served to sharpen my own thoughts. This is the greatest gift a professor can bestow. And Brian Vickers's work on justification and imputation informed my own views on these critical doctrines. He reminds me that justification by faith is not primarily academic, it is missional. These men served on my dissertation committee, which is where this work began, and have shaped me far beyond the pages of this book.

I am thankful to the members of Smithland First Baptist Church who called me as pastor when I had no experience and afforded me the time to write, even as I was learning to preach. Their tender love and tireless patience allowed me to spend countless hours away from church business as I completed this arduous task. The leadership of Bubbie Martin, Kenny Martin, Philip Orr, Garrick Ramage, and Mike Ramage made this possible. They are men of gold.

Between completing the dissertation and revising the work for publication, I took a post teaching theology and history at Phoenix Seminary. I have been overwhelmed by the kindness and encouragement of my colleagues—particularly, John DelHousaye, Wayne Grudem, John Meade, and Justin Smith—as well as my dean, W. Bingham Hunter. John Meade has been a friend for over a decade and he is a large reason why I am at Phoenix Seminary. Additionally, his help on chapter five was invaluable. The depth of my gratitude to him is bottomless. The library staff—Doug Olbert, Jim Santeford, and Mitch Miller—deserve more than an honorable mention. They combed over my bibliography and secured the sources I needed. Also, they do not seem to mind that my books never make it back by their due date.

Writing a book is filled with many highs and many (perhaps more) lows. There were countless times when I needed friends who were willing to encourage me, prod me, and act as sounding boards when I was stuck. Adam Smith is a first-rate friend. He received daily phone calls and kept me from capping the pen on numerous occasions. He also provided me with advice on how to reframe this work for publication. But if these changes are not well-received, I blame him. J. Ryan West pushed me all through the doctoral program and kept me accountable to write as often as possible. Brad Henson was a providential gift who distracted me, in a good way, and gave me countless pieces of advice on finishing strong. And Charles Loder came through for me in a pinch by providing a thorough index for this book.

Family has also been a constant source of encouragement. My parents, Gary and Chris Arnold, have relentlessly pushed me to do my best. As a child, I hated how my mom refused to give me easy answers but would instead force me to look up whatever it was that had piqued my curiosity. I did not know at the time that I was making my first forays into research. And my dad always wanted me to receive the education that was unavailable to him. Even though I became a different kind of doctor than he had hoped, his pride for me always beamed. I also had another set of parents who encouraged me through this process, my in-laws David and Gail Black. For the past decade, they have provided for us in countless ways, and I cherish the time we have spent at their home in the lazy river town of Hickman, which is a haven to me.

My wife Lauren deserves the most credit, for she endured not only the long, demanding dissertation process, but the constant strain of school and work even before we exchanged vows. Her sacrifice as a mother and longsuffering as a wife have bound our family together when the need to read, write, and think stole me away to the study for hours on end. This work is her accomplishment as much as it is mine. I gladly dedicate this labor to her.

Brian J. Arnold
Phoenix, Arizona
Fall 2016

Contents

List of Abbreviations —— XIII

1 Introduction —— 1
1.1 Paul and the Second Century —— 6
1.2 Torrance and the *Doctrine of Grace* —— 12
1.3 Justification in the Fathers —— 13

2 "But Through Faith": Clement of Rome —— 18
2.1 The Background —— 19
    Authorship —— 19
    Date —— 20
2.2 Summary of *1 Clement* —— 22
2.3 Translation and Commentary —— 24
    Translation of 32.3–4 —— 25
2.4 Objections and Responses —— 29
2.5 Conclusion —— 34

3 "Faith and Love": Ignatius of Antioch —— 36
3.1 Background —— 37
    Manuscripts —— 38
    Antioch —— 42
3.2 The Negative: What Justification is not —— 44
    Ignatius's Opponents —— 45
    "We Love the Prophets" —— 48
    "Parting of the Ways"? —— 48
    Jewish Practices —— 50
    Ignatius, Paul, and Judaism —— 53
3.3 The Positive: Justification in Ignatius —— 55
    Faith and Love —— 55
    The Gospel —— 57
    Justification —— 60
    Excursus: Prayer and Justification —— 64
    Ignatius and Paul? —— 67
3.4 Martyrdom —— 73
3.5 Conclusion —— 75

4 "O Sweet Exchange!": *Epistle to Diognetus* —— 77
- 4.1 Background —— 78
  - Genre —— 79
  - Authorship —— 80
  - Date —— 84
- 4.2 The Text: Summary, Translation, Commentary —— 86
  - Summary —— 87
  - Translation —— 89
  - Commentary —— 90
- 4.3 Theological Considerations: Atonement and Justification —— 96
  - Atonement —— 96
  - Justification —— 100
- 4.4 Conclusion —— 102

5 "My Chains Were Cut Off": *Odes of Solomon* —— 104
- 5.1 Background —— 105
  - Manuscripts and Languages —— 106
  - Authorship and Influences —— 107
  - Dating and Provenance —— 111
- 5.2 The Text —— 112
  - The God of Salvation —— 113
- 5.3 Justification in the *Odes* —— 114
  - *Ode* 17 —— 115
  - *Ode* 25 —— 128
  - *Ode* 29 —— 142
- 5.4 Conclusion —— 152

6 "Δικαιοπραξιας Εργον": *Dialogue with Trypho* —— 154
- 6.1 Justin and Paul —— 156
- 6.2 Rhetorical Device or Genuine Interlocutor? —— 159
- 6.3 Structure of the *Dialogue* —— 163
- 6.4 Exegesis of Selected Passages —— 164
  - *Dialogue* 8 —— 165
  - *Dialogue* 10 —— 171
  - *Dialogue* 23 and 92 —— 172
  - *Dialogue* 137 —— 180
- 6.5 Conclusion —— 181

7 Conclusion —— 183

Bibliography —— 189
    General Works —— 189
        Books —— 189
        Articles —— 191
        Dissertations —— 193
    1 Clement —— 193
        Books —— 193
        Articles —— 194
        Theses —— 195
    Ignatius of Antioch —— 195
        Books —— 195
        Articles —— 197
    Epistle to Diognetus —— 198
        Books —— 198
        Articles —— 200
    Odes of Solomon —— 201
        Books —— 201
        Articles —— 203
        Dissertations —— 205
    Dialogue with Trypho —— 205
        Books —— 205
        Articles —— 206
        Dissertations —— 207

Index of Authors —— 208

Index of Scripture References —— 212

Index of Ancient Sources —— 215

Topical Index —— 221

List of Abbreviations

AB	Anchor Bible Commentary
ATDan	Acta theological danica
ATR	*Anglican Theological Review*
AusBR	*Australian Biblical Review*
BBR	*Bulletin for Biblical Research*
BDAG	Walter Bauer, *A Greek-English Lexicon of the New Testament*, ed. and trans. Frederick W. Danker, William F. Arndt, F. Wilber Gingrich, 3rd ed. (Chicago: University of Chicago Press, 1979)
BDF	Friedrich Blass and Albert Dubrunner, *Greek Grammar of the New Testament and Other Early Christian Literature*, trans. Robert Funk (Chicago: University of Chicago Press, 1961)
BECNT	Baker Exegetical Commentary on the New Testament
BFCT	Beiträge zur Förderung christlicher Theologie
BHT	Beiträge zur historischen Theologie
CBQ	*Catholic Biblical Quarterly*
CH	*Church History*
CTJ	*Calvin Theological Journal*
DBI	*Dictionary of Biblical Imagery*
DBSJ	*Detroit Baptist Seminary Journal*
DLNT	*Dictionary of the Later New Testament*
EQ	*Evangelical Quarterly*
ExpT	*Expository Times*
HeyJ	*Heythrop Journal*
HNT	Handbuch zum Neuen Testament
HTR	*Harvard Theological Review*
JAC	*Jahrbuch für Antike und Christentum*
JBL	*Journal of Biblical Literature*
JCR	*Journal of Communication and Religion*
JECS	*Journal of Early Christian Studies*
JEH	*Journal of Ecclesiastical History*
JETS	*Journal of the Evangelical Theological Society*
JSNT	*Journal for the Study of the New Testament*
JSNTSup	Journal for the Study of the New Testament Supplement Series
JTS	*Journal of Theological Studies*
Lampe	G. W. H. Lampe, *A Patristic Greek Lexicon* (Oxford: Clarendon Press, 1961)
LCL	Loeb Classical Library (Cambridge, MA: Harvard University Press; London: William Heinemann, 1912–)
LNTS	Library of New Testament Studies
LSJ	Henry George Liddell and Robert Scott, *A Greek-English Lexicon*, rev. Henry Stuart Jones, 9th ed. (Oxford: Clarendon Press, 1996)
LXX	Septuagint
NICNT	New International Commentary on the New Testament
NICOT	New International Commentary on the Old Testament
NIGTC	The New International Greek Testament Commentary

NovT	*Novum Testamentum*
NovTSup	Supplements to Novum Testamentum
NTOA	Novum Testamentum et Orbis Antiquus
NTS	*New Testament Studies*
OCP	*Orientalia Christiana Periodica*
OrChr	*Oriens Christianus*
Payne Smith	Robert Payne Smith, *Syriac Thesaurus or Thesaurus Syriacus*, 3 vols. (Oxford: Clarendon Press, 1879; repr., Piscataway, NJ: Gorgias Press, 2007)
PNTC	Pillar New Testament Commentary
PP	Philosophia patrum, Leiden
RB	*Revue biblique*
RevQ	*Revue de Qumran*
RHPR	*Revue d'histoire et de philosophie religieuses*
SBEC	Studies in the Bible and Early Christianity
SBLDS	Society of Biblical Literature Dissertation Series
SC	Sources chrétiennes
SHAW.PH	Sitzungsberichte der Heidelberger Akademie der Wissenschaften: Philosophischhistorische Klasse
SNTS	Society for New Testament Studies
ST	*Studia Theologica*
TDNT	Theological Dictionary of the New Testament
ThStK	*Theologische Studien und Kritiken*
TSAJ	Texts and Studies in Ancient Judaism
TU	Texte und Untersuchungen
TübZTh	*Tübinger Zeitschrift für Theologie*
TynBul	Tyndale Bulletin
VC	*Vigiliae christianae*
VT	*Vetus Testamentum*
WUNT	Wissenshaftliche Untersuchungen zum Neuen Testament
ZNW	*Zeitschrift für die neutestamentliche Wissenschaft*

1 Introduction

With a hammer in one hand and a list of grievances in the other, Martin Luther nailed his ninety-five theses to the door of All Saints' Church on All Hallows' Eve 1517. Luther's theses served as the precursor to his belief that justification is on the basis of faith alone. He then placed this doctrine at the epicenter of the Reformation "because if this article stands, the Church stands; if it falls, the Church falls."[1] John Calvin echoed this thought when he said that justification is "the main hinge on which religion turns."[2] Justification by faith has stood at the center of Protestantism since that time.

The traditional Lutheran reading of Paul understands that justification is forensic, which means that the sinner is declared righteous in God's sight by faith and found not guilty of sin.[3] Over the past century or better, an impressive number of scholars have challenged this definition, suggesting that Protestants have misunderstood Paul for centuries.[4] The purpose here is not to get bogged down

---

[1] This popular phrase is most often repeated as *articulus stantis et cadentis ecclesiae*, which seems to have originated in the writings of Johann Heinrich Alsted (*Theologia scholastic didacta* [Hanover, 1618], 711). See Alistair McGrath's helpful discussion of the genesis of this phrase in *Iustitia Dei: A History of the Christian Doctrine of Justification*, 3rd ed. (Cambridge: Cambridge University Press, 2005), vii.

[2] John Calvin, *Institutes of the Christian Religion*, ed. John T. McNeill, trans. Ford Lewis Battles (Louisville: Westminster John Knox Press, 1960), 1:726.

[3] Any subsequent reference to the "traditional" reading of justification refers to the Lutheran understanding of justification as defined above.

[4] A painfully brief history of Paul's recent interpreters may be given. Though by no means the first to dissent from the traditional view of Paul's doctrine of justification, Albert Schweitzer famously said, "The doctrine of righteousness by faith is therefore a subsidiary crater, which has formed within the rim of the main crater—the mystical doctrine of redemption through being-in-Christ" (*The Mysticism of Paul the Apostle*, trans. W. Montgomery [Baltimore, MD: John Hopkins University Press, 1998], 225, originally published in 1930 as *Die Mystik des Apostels Paulus* [Tübingen: J. C. B. Mohr]). According to Schweitzer, justification should not be thought of as Paul's central idea. W. D. Davies followed and reminded everyone that Paul was influenced more by Judaism than Hellenism in his revered work *Paul and Rabbinic Judaism: Some Rabbinic Elements in Pauline Theology*, 4th ed. (Philadelphia: Fortress, 1980), originally published in 1948. These important works helped set the stage for the seismic shift in Pauline studies that occurred in the second half of the twentieth century. E. P. Sanders, one of Davies's doctoral students, wrote the seminal work in his 1977 *Paul and Palestinian Judaism: A Comparison of Patterns of Religion* (Philadelphia: Fortress), wherein he rehabilitated the Judaism of Paul's day, demonstrating that Judaism was not legalistic. James D. G. Dunn first gave this diverse movement the title the New Perspective on Paul (NPP) (James D. G. Dunn, "The New Perspective on Paul," *Bulletin of the John Rylands Library* 65 [1983]: 95–122; reprinted in *Jesus, Paul and the Law: Studies in Mark and Galatians* [London: SPCK, 1990], 183–214). N. T. Wright has somewhat adopted this po-

in the quagmire of Pauline studies by asking who has interpreted Paul rightly. Such a task should be left to Pauline scholars. This book enters the discussion on justification from a historical vantage point, seeking to understand how justification was received in the earliest era of the church.

Justification has not always been approached with enough historical sensitivity. There are two particular errors regarding Luther that need to be cleared up. The typical narrative is that Luther either rediscovered or created the doctrine

---

sition and further nuanced it in his books *What Saint Paul Really Said: Was Paul of Tarsus the Read Founder of Christianity?* (Grand Rapids: Eerdmans, 1997) and *Paul in Fresh Perspective* (Philadelphia: Fortress Press, 2009). These scholars have made great strides in our understanding of the Judaism of Paul's day, and there is much to be commended in their works. Responses to the so-called New Perspective are just as numerous. For the most thorough, scholarly response, see D. A. Carson, Peter O'Brien, and Mark Seifrid, eds., *Justification and Variegated Nomism: The Complexities of Second Temple Judaism*, WUNT, 2 vols. (Grand Rapids: Baker Academic, 2001). The best general introductions can be found in Stephen Westerholm, *Perspectives Old and New on Paul: The "Lutheran" Paul and His Critics* (Grand Rapids: Eerdmans, 2004), and Guy Prentiss Waters, *Justification and the New Perspectives on Paul: A Review and Response* (Phillipsburg, NJ: P&R Publishing, 2004). Waters's use of "perspectives" in his title signals the diversity of those who espouse the NPP and there does not appear to be an end to the splintering. This book may have implications for the NPP, but any sustained interation with the NPP would swell this project to unmanageable proportions.

Two recent studies have landed like bombshells in Pauline studies, each of them massive in size and argument. The first is N. T. Wright's *Paul and the Faithfulness of God*, 2 vols. (Minneapolis: Fortress, 2013), which comes in around 1700 pages, wherein Wright has the space to lay out his mature view of Paul's theology. Wright always does a fine job of providing a holistic picture of Paul, who was influenced both by his background in Judaism (monotheism, election, and eschatology) and his new life in Christ and the Spirit. Wright defies any established camp of Pauline interpreters, forging his own path. Regarding justification, Wright seems to be either in contradiction to his previous views (*What Saint Paul Really Said*) or to have evolved, for now he speaks of justification as a declaration that constitutes a new status (946), while still maintaining that justification is what includes one in the covenant community. Justification still does not signal the moment when a person becomes a Christian in Wright's view. The second study is Douglas Campbell's *The Deliverance of God: An Apocalytpic Rereading of Justification in Paul* (Grand Rapids: Eerdmans, 2009), which is more than 1200 pages. Campbell attempted to summarize this work in a brief article, "An Apocalyptic Rereading of 'Justification' in Paul: Or, an Overview of the Argument of Douglas Campbell's *The Deliverance of God*—by Douglass Campbell," *ExpT* (2012): 382–93. A full-scale review of Campbell's work is not possible here. Suffice it to say that he rebuffs what he calls "Justification Theory," which he sees as the predominant Protestant reading of Paul. He believes this stems from modern European thought (*The Deliverance of God*, 7). However, if the argument presented in this book is correct, then the so-called "Justification Theory" that focuses on a forensic/retributive notion of justification is not modern or European (in the sense that we think of European), but ancient and represented in the East (Ignatius and the *Odes of Solomon*) and the West (*1 Clement* and Justin Martyr).

of justification by faith.[5] As this book will show, the problem with the narrative that Luther *created* this view of justification is that several second-century fathers spoke of justification in a similar way, meaning that Luther was not the first one to suggest that justification is by faith or that justification is forensic. And the story that Luther *rediscovered* justification by faith leads us to believe that the doctrine went into hibernation immediately after the apostles and stayed dormant until the Reformation.[6] But is this account historically accurate? Alistair McGrath already amended this tale when he argued that justification by faith was not altogether absent in the years preceding Luther. Tracing this doctrine from the dry sands of the ancient Near East to the towering cathedrals of medieval Europe, McGrath posits that justification played a significant role in the formation of western Christianity. However, despite his great care of the sources from Augustine on, he argues like many before him that the early patristic period has little to offer on this doctrine, which leaves a noticeable gap between Paul

---

[5] Luther has been accused of reading his own historical situation into the doctrine of justification (see Krister Stendahl, "The Apostle Paul and the Introspective Conscience of the West," *HTR* 56 [1963]: 199–215). The difficulty of such a claim is that it ignores the fact that the Reformers were steeped in the fathers. Though *sola scriptura* was their mantra, this slogan did not interfere with their dependence on their forerunners, from whom they were happy to glean. (See, for instance, Heiko Oberman, *Forerunners of the Reformation: The Shape of Late Medieval Thought* [Cambridge: James Clarke & Co., 1966]. Oberman shows how there were rumblings on doctrines like justification by faith prior to Luther. His study traces those rumblings back through the Middle Ages.) On the centrality of the fathers for the Reformers, D. H. Williams has acutely recognized, "Without the Christological and soteriological doctrinal formations of the patristic age, the sixteenth-century formulation of justifying faith could never have been produced" (D. H. Williams, "Justification by Faith: A Patristic Doctrine," *JEH* 57 [2006]: 651). It was to the fathers, in addition to the Scriptures, that the Reformers looked for guidance. The most important work in this regard is *The Reception of the Church Fathers in the West: From the Carolingians to the Maurists*, ed. Irena Backus, 2 vols. (Leiden: Brill, 1997). These masterful volumes go a long way in showing the doctrinal dependence the Reformers had on the fathers. It may be added that even in the eigthteenth century, John Wesley looked back to the fathers for confirmation of his view of justification by faith. He writes, "And [that we are] justified only by this true and lively faith in Christ speak all the ancient authors, especially Origen, St. Cyprian, St. Chrysostom, Hilary, Basil, St. Ambrose and St. Augustine, by which they take away clearly all merit of our works and wholly ascribe our justification unto Christ only" (John Wesley, "The Doctrine of Salvation, Faith and Good Works, Extracted from the Homilies of the Church of England," in *John Wesley*, ed. Albert C. Outler [New York: Oxford University Press, 1964], 126–27). The Reformers and Wesley believed that the fathers endorsed a view of justification by faith apart from works.
[6] This was the theory that T. F. Torrance proposed, which suggested that the Apostolic Fathers turned aside from Paul's doctrine of justification by faith. Torrance's view will be discussed below.

and Augustine.⁷ The question is whether this gap is one of scholarship or one of history. That is to say, is there a gap between Paul and Augustine because the earliest fathers disregarded the doctrine of justification, or is the gap a result of scholars who have not given due attention to the earliest sources, or have even misinterpreted them? The gap, I suggest, is one of scholarship.

There are two possible ways to close this gap. First, a diachronic study could start with Luther and trace his view of justification backward in time. The problem is that this approach places too much emphasis on Luther and ends up reading justification through the lens of his writings and historical situation.⁸ The second option, and the approach used here, is to assess the doctrine of justification from the perspective of those who immediately followed the apostles. By opening one's ear to the texts and listening to words and phrases that others have overlooked, it will be apparent that the fathers were concerned with the doctrine of justification, and that they looked to the Apostle Paul for their argument, though they presented it in their own words.

This book seeks to answer the following question: how did the second-century fathers understand the doctrine of justification? It is argued that the fathers sampled in this period believed in justification by faith, and that their view was consistent with the so-called "traditional" reading of Paul.⁹ At times they present their view of justification forensically and they often contrast justification with works righteousness. Additionally, they use other doctrines associated with Paul, such as imputation and substitutionary atonement. A few caveats, though, are in order. First, this does not mean that the fathers are correct about Paul's view of justification. All this affirms is that the second-century fathers examined below held to a view of justification that was in large measure congruent with

---

7 McGrath actually gives Augustine the epithet "fountainhead" of justification (*Iustitia Dei*, 38). It is telling that Westerholm also begins with Augustine in his discussion on the history of justification. This would be true of many authors who set out to study the history of justification.
8 Jordan Cooper's recent work, *The Righteousness of One: An Evaluation of Early Patristic Soteriology in Light of the New Perspective on Paul* (Eugene, OR: Wipf and Stock, 2013), does just this. He reads the second century in light of Luther instead of in continuity with Paul. See my review of this book in *Themelios* 39.1 (2014): 125–27.
9 Nick Needham asks what justification means in the fathers and answers, "Although it does not always have the same precise connotation, it seems clear that there is a very prominent strand of usage in which it has a basically forensic meaning. That is, it means something like 'to declare righteous,' 'to acquit,' 'to vindicate'" ("Justification in the Early Church Fathers," in *Justification in Perspective: Historical Developments and Contemporary Challenges*, ed. Bruce L. McCormack [Grand Rapids: Baker Academic, 2006], 28). The crystal-clear examples that he uses come from later fathers like Origen and Chrysostom, but there are many instances in the second century where justification means a declaration of righteousness.

the Lutheran reading of Paul. Second, we must be careful not to exaggerate the evidence. To suggest that the fathers were monolithic in their view, or to say that their views are expressed with the clarity of the Reformers, would be to overdraw the bow.[10] Doctrines are not forged until they have passed through the furnace of controversy and been pounded out on the anvil of debate. Justification did not enter the white-hot intensity of this furnace until the Reformation.[11]

Answering this question is more complicated than it may appear. Typically a work of this nature would examine the δικ- word group to determine how various authors viewed justification. While each chapter will certainly incorporate the δικ- words, it is imperative to look below the surface at conceptual links as well. Even though a particular author may not use δικαιόω or δικαιοσύνη, the concept of justification may still be present. James Barr has decisively shown that bare etymological studies are insufficient.[12] It is no problem, then, to hunt for justification's tracks even where the word itself is absent.

Justification was a central issue to the Apostle Paul.[13] But what happened to the doctrine of justification in the second century? Was it abandoned? Was it ig-

---

[10] Needham cautions on this point as well. He expresses his skepticism that the fathers were in harmony on justification, or any doctrine for that matter, with this thought: "I am not convinced that these [fathers] formed a monolith, and doubt whether the 'consensus of the fathers' over that period extended much beyond the Apostles' Creed" (Needham, "Justification in the Early Church Fathers," 27). Still, there is remarkable dependence on Paul and striking similarities between many second-century fathers on the doctrine of justification.

[11] For this reason, even viewing Augustine as the "fountainhead" of justification is a misnomer. Augustine may have waded into this issue more than his predecessors, but he was still not able to give it the same attention as the Reformers because it was not as significant of an issue, despite the pressure of the Pelagian debate. David Wright opens an essay on justification in Augustine saying, "It is a frustrating business writing on a subject that Augustine did not write on—at least did not write on in the manner we would assume of a modern writer who had 'written on justification'" (David Wright, "Justification in Augustine," in *Justification in Perspective: Historical Developments and Contemporary Challenges*, ed. Bruce L. McCormack [Grand Rapids: Baker Academic, 2006], 55). This frustration would be true of all of the fathers since none of them set out to write a treatise on justification.

[12] See James Barr, *The Semantics of Biblical Language* (Oxford: Oxford University Press, 1961). See also Moisés Silva's introduction in *Biblical Words & Their Meanings* (Grand Rapids: Zondervan, 1983), 17–32. Silva comments, "When a discussion depends primarily or solely on the vocabulary, one may conclude either that the writer is not familiar with the contents of Scripture or that Scripture itself says little or nothing on the subject" (22). Of course, Silva's concern is primarily the Bible, but this comment could extend to the fathers as well.

[13] Mark Seifrid spends nearly eighty pages spelling out the dangers of trying to identify justification as the center of Paul's theology. He writes that "attempts to employ 'justification' as the conceptual center from which the whole of Paul's theology may be explained, have failed to produce satisfactory results" (Seifrid, *Justification by Faith* [Leiden: Brill, 1992], 75–76). Justification

nored? Neither of these is the case. These chapters demonstrate that Paul's influence extended into the second century, even when these fathers do not cite the Apostle directly.

1.1 Paul and the Second Century

A steady stream of scholarship has been produced over the past few decades that sufficiently demonstrates Paul's place among the early fathers. The three years between 1979 and 1981 proved to be particularly fruitful on the subject of the reception of Paul in the second century. Four dissertations, two of which became monographs, were produced during this brief period, all challenging nineteenth-century, higher-critical scholarship that claimed that Paul was subsumed by Gnostics and considered suspect by the proto-orthodox.[14] F. C. Baur popularized this nineteenth-century view in his *The Church History of the First Three Centuries*.[15] Each commentator after him had his own phrase to articulate what he saw as an abandonment of Paul. For E. J. Goodspeed it was the "Pauline Eclipse,"[16] for Hans Conzelmann the "Pauline School,"[17] for Donald Penny the "Pauline Fragmentation,"[18] and, most notably, for Walter Bauer the "Pauline Captivity."[19]

---

was certainly at the center of Paul's thinking but to say that it is *the* center is to overburden just one pillar of Paul's doctrine.

[14] See Andreas Lindemann, *Paulus im ältesten Christentum: Das Bild des Apostels und die Rezeption der paulinischen Theologie in der frühchristlichen Literatur bis Marcion*, BHT 58 (Tübingen: Mohr, 1979); Donald N. Penny, "The Pseudo-Pauline Letters of the First Two Centuries" (Ph.D. diss., Emory, 1980); Ernst Dassman, *Der Stachel im Fleisch: Paulus in der frühchristlichen Literatur bis Irenäus* (Münster: Aschendorff, 1979); David K. Rensberger, "As the Apostle Teaches: The Development of the Use of Paul's Letters in Second-Century Christianity" (Ph.D. diss., Yale University, 1981).

[15] F. C. Baur, *The Church History of the First Three Centuries*, trans. Allan Menzies, 3rd ed., 2 vols., Theological Translation Fund Library (London: Williams and Norgate, 1878–79).

[16] E. J. Goodspeed, *The Formation of the New Testament* (Chicago: University of Chicago Press, 1926), 56.

[17] Hans Conzelmann, "Die Schule des Paulus," in *Theologica crucis—signum crucis: Festschrift für Erich Dinkler zum 70. Geburtstag*, ed. Carl Andresen and Günter Klein (Tübingen: J. C. B. Mohr, 1979), 85–96.

[18] Penny, "The Pseudo-Pauline Letters of the First Two Centuries," 5. Penny discusses these aforementioned people and renders these characterizations of Paul in the second century.

[19] Walter Bauer, *Orthodoxy and Heresy in Earliest Christianity* (Philadelphia: Fortress Press, 1971). See Benjamin L. White, "*Imago Pauli*: Memory, Tradition and Discourses on the 'Real' Paul in the Second Century" (Ph.D. diss., University of North Carolina, 2011), 66, which was subsequently published as *Remembering Paul: Ancient and Modern Contests over the Image of the*

Paul was captive to the Gnostics, exiled from the thoughts and theology of the proto-orthodox, not to make his return to orthodoxy until a later juncture in history.

This view held surprising sway for a century until the revolutionary work of Andreas Lindemann, *Paulus im ältesten Christentum*. This massive tome is a comprehensive guide to Paul's theology in the second century up until the time of Marcion.[20] His thesis, that Paul was a central figure in the rise of orthodox Christianity in the second century, was intended to overcome the previously entrenched view that "Paulus habe in der nachpaulinischen Kirche nur einen sehr geringen Einfluss besessen."[21] Moreover, Lindemann sought to correct the view that has dominated since the time of Adolf von Harnack that Paul was the Apostle to the heretics.[22] Along the way Lindemann highlights various tenets

---

Apostle (Oxford: Oxford University Press, 2014). White's most recent and thorough history of the reception of Paul in the second century is invaluable. I am indebted to him in this section. See especially, *Remembering Paul*, 43–49.

20 David Rensberger makes a fair assessment of Lindemann's work that he frequently examines documents that come in the late second century, generations after Marcion's death. See Rensberger, review of *Paulus im ältesten Christentum: Das Bild des Apostels und die Rezeption der paulinischen Theologie in der frühchristlichen Literatur bis Marcion*, by Andreas Lindemann, *JBL* 101 (1982): 289.

21 Lindemann, *Paulus im ältesten Christentum*, 1.

22 Before Lindemann challenged the field, it was the common assumption that Paul was the apostle of heretics. According to C. K. Barrett, throughout most of the second century, "Paul was the heretics' apostle and it was wise to be cautious about using him" (Barrett, "Pauline Controversies in the Post Pauline Period," in *On Paul: Essays on His Life, Work, and Influence* [New York: T&T Clark, 2003], 167). Because heretics used Paul, the orthodox were suspicious about using him, or so goes the theory. "The mistrust is reflected in the disuse of Paul by second-century figures nearer to the mainstream of Christian thought" (Barrett, "Pauline Controversies," 165). These comments Barrett makes actually predate Lindemann. This chapter originally appeared as C. K. Barret, "Pauline Controversies in the post-Pauline Period," *NTS* 20 (1974): 229–45. The theory that Paul was the apostle of the heretics is typified in Adolf von Harnack who famously said that Marcion was the only one in the early church who really understood Paul (See Adolf von Harnack, *History of Dogma*, trans. Neil Buchanan, vol. 1 [Boston: Little, Brown, and Co., 1902], 89 and *Marcion: The Gospel of the Alien God*, trans. John E. Steely and Lyle D. Bierma [Durham, NC: Labyrinth Press, 1990]). Marcion understood Paul's doctrine of justification by faith but the orthodox wanted to distance themselves from Marcion and so they distanced themselves from Paul. Therefore, in von Harnack's mind, Marcion was the only true disciple of Paul and he alone rightly understood the connection of faith and justification (see Adolf von Harnack, *History of Dogma*, 266–81 where von Harnack expands this idea). This misunderstanding of the second-century fathers is largely responsible for the confusion about justification by faith in this period. Among many others who argue that Paul was used only by heretics, see Albrecht Ritschl, *The Christian Doctrine of Justification and Reconciliation: The Positive Development of the Doctrine*, trans. and ed. H. R. Mackintosh and A. B. Macaulay, 2nd ed. (Edinburgh:

of Pauline theology to demonstrate just how closely those in the second century followed Paul. In his review of Lindemann's work, Eric Osborn states, "The substance of Paul's theology especially on justification is not found in early Christian writers, but says [Lindemann], these writers use their own words to say the same thing and their success or failure is not settled out of hand."[23] Lindemann is to be credited with the realization that justification is present but that it is repackaged for a different context, an idea that will become apparent as we survey the primary sources. Though Lindemann is exhaustive, and at times "tedious" and "repetitive,"[24] a fresh look at the sources reveals more dependence on Paul for their view of justification than even he noticed. As much as he tried to rescue Paul from the exclusive hold of the Gnostics, Lindemann was still not willing to see that these fathers looked to Paul for their doctrine of justification. He writes, "Die theologische Substanz der Paulus-Tradition, insbesondere die Rechtfertigungslehre, ist in der ältesten Kirche selten gesehen und ausgesprochen worden; bei Marcion und bei den Gnostikern fehlt sie freilich

---

T&T Clark, 1902), J. Knox, *Marcion and the New Testament: An Essay in Early Christian History* (Chicago: University of Chicago Press, 1942), 115 ff, Elaine Pagels, *The Gnostic Paul: Gnostic Exegesis of the Pauline Letters* (New York: Continuum International, 1992), and Anne Pasquier, "The Valentinian Exegesis," in *Handbook of Patristic Exegesis*, by Charles Kannengiesser (Leiden: Brill, 2004), 1:459, who said, "Paul's Letters, especially Galatians and Romans, had an important influence on [Gnostics]. The history of interpretation of Paul's Letters during the second century, it has been said, is essentially the history of Gnostic exegesis." In response, Eric Osborn has brought to the fore the valuable insight that "only those who were concerned with the central issues of Pauline theology could have felt so intensely and written so persistently against Marcion" (Eric Osborn, "Origen and Justification: The Good is One," *AusBR* 24 [1976]: 26). Against those who suggest that only the Gnostics used Paul and only Marcion understood the apostle, Osborn points out the obvious that early Christian authors fought ruthlessly against their opponents because they held tightly to Paul's theology.

Though it seemed that one could no longer argue a "Pauline Captivity" narrative in the wake of these four studies, Jason Scarborough did just that in his 2007 dissertation, "The Making of an Apostle: Second and Third Century Interpretations of the Writings of Paul" (Ph.D. diss., Union Theological Seminary, 2007). He rehashes much of the same ground as von Harnack and company, believing that "Paul's theology was all but absent from the writings of the apostolic period" (277). Irenaeus is the hero who rescues Paul from his captors, like Marcion and Valentinus. Cf. Calvin Roetzel, "Paul in the Second Century," in *The Cambridge Companion to St. Paul*, ed. James D. G. Dunn, Cambridge Companions to Religion (Cambridge: Cambridge University Press, 2003), 228, and idem, *Paul: the Man and the Myth* (Minneapolis: Fortress Press, 1999), 152–57. See White, "*Imago Pauli*," 68–69.

23 Eric Osborn, review of *Paulus im ältesten Christentum: Das Bild des Apostels und die Rezeption der paulinischen Theologie in der frühchristlichen Literatur bis Marcion*, by Andreas Lindemann, *AusBr* 28 (1980): 59–60.

24 David Rensberger, review of *Paulus im ältesten Christentum*, 289.

ganz."²⁵ Lindemann's aim is broad, encompassing a number of doctrines as they relate to Paul, whereas this work narrows on one particular doctrine.²⁶ Justification was seen and spoken of more frequently in the second century than Lindemann realized.

The focus of David Rensberger's dissertation, "As the Apostle Teaches: The Development of the Use of Paul's Letters in Second-Century Christianity," is almost entirely dedicated to the reception of Paul's letters and not his theology.²⁷ His purpose is to discredit the captivity theory propounded by those in the Tübingen School. Silence does not equate to rejection in Rensbeger's reckoning, and he is right on this score.²⁸ This idea is central to this book because three of the sources examined (*Diognetus*, *Odes of Solomon*, and *Dialogue with Trypho*) make no mention of Paul and yet bear the marks of Pauline influence.

Donald Penny's dissertation is less helpful for our purpose because he addresses what he considers pseudo-Pauline letters, such as the Pastorals, 2 Thessalonians, Ephesians, *3 Corinthians*, and *Laodiceans*. His attention remains on Pauline pseudepigraphy and the contribution of pseudepigraphy to the legacy of Paul. Again, this matters little because the second-century fathers were not asking questions about pseudepigraphy. Many of them assumed that Paul was the author of thirteen epistles, and so to trace Pauline influence means to see how all the letters ascribed to him were appropriated.²⁹

---

25 Lindemann, *Paulus im ältesten Christentum*, 403. He ends his work on this note.
26 Lindemann's work is critical for all work done on Paul and the second century. He laid much of the foundation that not only challenged previous scholarship on this matter, but also provided a new way for broaching the subject. Because of this, Lindemann had to exercise extreme caution in not overstating his case. Lindemann more or less wanted to show that Paul was well-known to those who are considered orthodox. Osborn notes on Lindemann's work, "nearly all the writers who are considered orthodox maintained a dependence on Paul, if not in his major theological tendencies, at least in familiarity with his writings and use of his works" (Osborn, review of *Paulus im ältesten Christentum*, 58). The issue taken up here, which is still a lacuna on the scholarship, is whether or not these fathers followed Paul's theological tendency on the doctrine of justification, a matter not settled in Lindemann.
27 Rensbeger also has an article that condenses his dissertation. See David K. Rensberger, "The Second Century Paul," in *The Writings of St. Paul*, ed. Wayne A. Meeks and John T. Fitzgerald, 2nd ed. (New York: Norton, 2007), 341–51. See also David Warren, "The Text of the Apostle in the Second Century: A Contribution to the History of Its Reception" (Th.D. diss., Harvard University, 2001). Similar to Rensberger, Warren is preoccupied with the nature of the text more than the theology of Paul.
28 Rensberger, "As the Apostle Teaches," 332.
29 Regardless of whether Paul genuinely authored the letters attributed to him is of no consequence for the chapters that follow. What does matter is that those in the second century believed Paul wrote them. See Andreas Lindemann, "Paul in the Writings of the Apostolic Fathers,"

More than Rensberger or Penny, Ernst Dassman came closer to the present aim, that is, the discovery of Pauline theology in the second century. Dassman's dissertation, published as a monograph, *Der Stachel im Fleisch: Paulus in der frühchristlichen Literatur bis Irenäus*, explores a wide assortment of literature, from the New Testament (e.g., Acts, what he considers pseudo-Pauline literature, 1 Peter, and Hebrews) to second-century documents (e.g., Apostolic Fathers, Marcion, Apologists, and Irenaeus). Dassman does not want to ascribe too much weight to Paul over and above other pertinent voices, like Peter and the other apostles. Paul was an authority, but by no means the only authority.

These four works have forever changed the approach to Paul's influence in the second century. They challenged the prevailing winds of scholarship and plotted a new course for the reception of Paul that flew directly in the face of received knowledge. The Apostle was not hijacked by either the proto-orthodox or the Gnostics—he was used by every group despite their varying theological persuasions. Without the groundwork laid by these scholars, this present work would have no foundation on which to build. It first had to be shown that Paul was pivotal to the construction of second-century Christianity before individual points of doctrine could be argued.

A fifth book has entered the discussion on the so-called "real Paul" that examines how the communities of the second-century remembered the Apostle. Benjamin White, in his monograph *Remembering Paul: Ancient and Modern Contests over the Image of the Apostle*, contends that "by the second century Paul had become a traditioned figure,"[30] meaning that he comes down to us only through the reshaped memory of those in history. Since the beginning, various communities had sought to get Paul on their side, "each of whom needed the 'real' Paul for the sake of larger theo-political contests."[31] The study of Paul in the second century must contain images of Paul, that is, what is said of Paul when an author mentions him, and the "particular lines of textual interpretation."[32] More than anything, White offers a new methodology aimed at exploring "how Pauline traditions (written and oral) develop and make their way into early Christian rhetoric about the 'real' Paul."[33] Just as was the case with Rensberger's

---

in *Paul and the Legacies of Paul*, ed. William Babcock (Dallas: Southern Methodist University Press, 1990), 25.

30 White, *Remembering Paul*, 13.
31 White, *Remembering Paul*, 7.
32 White, *Remembering Paul*, 13.
33 White, *Remembering Paul*, 10. White's project is well-worth considering. Social-scientific study, and in particular 'social memory' theory, has its place and can contribute to the overall portrait of Paul. My goal here, however, is to recolor a portion of the picture that was erased or

work, White's book does not seem to account for Pauline lines of argument or theology that appear when there is no explicit mention of Paul or his writings. As will be seen, several authors base their case for justification by faith on Abraham, which must have derived from Paul since he coined this argument. Thus, Paul's theology is used even when there is no other hint of his presence in the text.

Several other important volumes are worth mentioning, two of which contain articles by Lindemann on Paul in the Apostolic Fathers. The first, edited by William Babcock, is *Paul and the Legacies of Paul*.[34] The scope of this book reaches to the fifth century and covers Pauline themes in Augustine and Chrysostom, though it begins with articles on the Apostolic Fathers, Irenaeus, and Tertullian. The other book that has made significant inroads into the understanding of the reception of Paul is *Trajectories through the New Testament and the Apostolic Fathers*, edited by Andrew Gregory and Christopher Tuckett.[35] Though it is not entirely dedicated to Paul's influence, it does contain a handful of essays that contribute to correcting this previous oversight.

Finally, Michael Bird and Joseph Dodson have edited a pertinent monograph, *Paul and the Second Century*, which examines the way Paul was received in the century after his death.[36] Painting with a broad brush, the scope of the book extends beyond just the proto-orthodox writers and includes chapters on Marcion and Valentinianism, covering many different ways in which the Apostle was interpreted. However, the book only rarely touches on justification by faith.

This resurgence of scholarship devoted to the reception of Paul in early Christianity is long overdue. Paul has cast an enormous shadow over the entirety of church history, not just in Augustine, the Reformers, and modern evangelicals. Those who were left to take up the reins after the apostles were martyred looked to their predecessors and consciously tried to imitate their doctrines, their devotion, and at times, their deaths. Since it is difficult to deny that justification was

---

painted over in the past century or two by those who saw discontinuity between Paul and his sucessors.

34 William Babcock, ed., *Paul and the Legacies of Paul* (Dallas: Southern Methodist University Press, 1990). Lindemann's article in this volume is "Paul in the Writings of the Apostolic Fathers," in *Paul and the Legacies of Paul*, 25–44.
35 Andrew F. Gregory and Christopher M. Tuckett, eds., *Trajectories through the New Testament and the Apostolic Fathers* (Oxford: Oxford University Press, 2005). See especially, Andreas Lindemann, "Paul's Influence on 'Clement' and Ignatius," 9–24, David M. Reis, "Following in Paul's Footsteps: *Mimēsis* and Power in Ignatius of Antioch," 287–306, and Harry O. Maier, "The Politics and Rhetoric of Discord and Concord in Paul and Ignatius," 307–24.
36 Michael Bird and Joseph Dodson, eds., *Paul and the Second Century*, LNTS 412 (New York: T&T Clark, 2011).

near the heart of Paul's theology, then the question of how his successors understood that doctrine reveals much about the theological makeup of the early church.

1.2 Torrance and the *Doctrine of Grace*

T. F. Torrance has shaped the discourse for how the second-century fathers received Paul's doctrine of justification, having written the standard work on this matter. Torrance studied under Karl Barth at the University of Basel over a half-century ago and his dissertation was later published under the title *The Doctrine of Grace in the Apostolic Fathers*.[37] In this landmark work Torrance argued that the doctrine of grace which received such eloquent expression in Paul's letters was lost in the writings of those who came in the next generation. Scholars across the theological spectrum readily accepted this thesis, from his *Doktorvater* Barth who first supplied him with the idea,[38] to F. F. Bruce, who wrote a glowing endorsement for the book when it was first published. Torrance's belief that the Apostolic Fathers misunderstood the Pauline doctrine of grace has permeated the literature on these Fathers. According to Torrance, the Apostolic Fathers may use the word grace but they mean something entirely different by it. He sees an infusion of works righteousness in these Fathers and thus a decisive turn from Paul. The implication is that this sent the church on a downward spiral of works righteousness that became so abused during the late Patristic and Medieval period, that it took a fresh look at the New Testament during the Reformation to recover grace. Though his theory may not be entirely without credence, it is certainly overstated and misses important expressions of grace in the early church. If it be granted that salvation by faith implies grace, as it seems to in Paul, then Torrance's thesis suffers a fatal blow.[39]

---

[37] Thomas F. Torrance, *The Doctrine of Grace in the Apostolic Fathers* (Grand Rapids: Eerdmans, 1959).
[38] Torrance, *The Doctrine of Grace in the Apostolic Fathers*, v.
[39] Tashio Aono has also studied Pauline doctrine in the Apostolic Fathers. See Tashio Aono, *Die Entwicklung des paulinischen Gerichtsgedankens dei den Apostolischen Vätern*, Europäische Hochschulschriften Theologie 137 (Las Vegas: Lang, 1979). His work is a major step away from the old guard but he has not come far enough. He does look at justification by faith and other issues pertaining to salvation, even suggesting that many of the Apostolic Fathers picked up on Paul's use of imperative and indicative. Yet he is still reticent to see a strong connection to Paul. One wonders if his book would have been altered had he had access to the four dissertations produced within a few years of his publication.

Some helpful correctives to Torrance, and others who deny a Pauline understanding of justification in the second century, have started to trickle into scholarship. Jaroslav Pelikan has issued the best critique:

> To condemn the doctrine of grace in the apostolic fathers, for example, for not being sufficiently Pauline greatly oversimplifies the development both within the first century and between it and the second. There is a continuity in the doctrinal development from one century to the next, and there is a unity within any particular century; neither the continuity nor the unity can be identified with uniformity.[40]

To suggest that the fathers departed at once from a central tenet of Pauline Christianity grossly overstates the case. Yet, Pelikan is careful to assert that continuity does not mean uniformity. While the writings investigated in this book do contain a Pauline view of justification, this does not mean that they always conform exactly to Paul's approach. The fathers might not explicitly connect justification by faith to Christology, the atonement, or sin as Paul does, but this does not therefore mean they are presenting justification in ways antithetical to Paul. Room must be left for these authors to express themselves with their own voice in their own context.

1.3 Justification in the Fathers

While conducting a brief historical sketch on justification in the early church for *Justification: Five Views*, the editors comment, "No one doubts that Pauline-like statements on justification are scattered throughout the early church writings."[41] The problem, as the editors put it, is that justification in the fathers is "a significant point of debate today."[42] Several important inroads into the fathers' understanding of justification have been made and are worth mentioning, if nothing else than to demonstrate that the thesis put forth in this book is not entirely novel.

Thomas Oden, for instance, put forth in *The Justification Reader* that "there is indeed a textually defined consensual classic Christian teaching on salvation

---

[40] Jaroslav Pelikan, *Development of Christian Doctrine: Some Historical Prolegomena* (New Haven: Yale University, 1969), 65.
[41] Paul Rhodes Eddy, James K. Beilby, and Steven E. Enderlein, "Justification in Historical Perspective," in *Justification Five Views*, ed. James K. Beilby and Paul Rhodes Eddy (Downers Grove, IL: IVP Academic, 2011), 16.
[42] Rhodes Eddy, Beilby, and Enderlein, "Justification in Historical Perspective," 15–16.

by grace through faith."[43] Oden clarifies what he means a few sentences later, saying,

> My intent is simple: I will show how the classic Christian exegetes, mostly of the first five centuries, dealt with Paul's justification teaching. In doing so I will ask whether there is already formed in the first millennium a reliable, clear, central core of the classic Christian teaching of salvation by grace through faith.[44]

He answers in the affirmative. Nick Needham, whose own work on justification in the fathers is discussed below, calls Oden's thesis "intrepid," because few venture such a bold assertion.[45] Oden desires his reader to see that "there is a full-orbed patristic consensus on justification that is virtually indistinguishable from the Reformer's teaching."[46] Oden's work is fine as far as it goes, but it is brief and provides only a flyover of most sources—dense, exegetical work in the primary literature is lacking. I make a similar claim to Oden but narrow the focus to the second century and take a sustained look at only five sources.

Others have also raised the issue of justification in the fathers. Nick Needham's article "Justification in the Early Fathers" effectively argues for the prevalence of justification language in the fathers up to and including Chrysostom.[47] Needham gives several points of warning before launching into his investigation, warnings that should be heeded in the following pages. First, one must avoid making exhaustive claims about justification in the fathers. When one considers the sheer volume of sources, many of which are untranslated, it would be pretentious to assert a definitive answer when new evidence could surface. All that can be claimed is that the ancient authors presented here are consistent with Paul's doctrine of justification by faith. The second warning, which is similar to the first, deals with the expanse of time under investigation. For Need-

---

43 Thomas Oden, *The Justification Reader* (Grand Rapids: Wm. B. Eerdmans, 2002), 16.
44 Oden, *The Justification Reader*, 16.
45 Needham, "Justification in the Early Church Fathers," 25. Needham observes that the thesis that the fathers subscribed to Paul's doctrine of justification goes back to George Stanley Faber, *The Primitive Doctrine of Justification*, 2nd ed. (London: Seeley and Burnside, 1839).
46 Oden, *The Justification Reader*, 49.
47 An article remarkably similar to Needham's is Robert Eno, "Some Patristic Views on the Relationship of Faith and Works in Justification," *Recherches augustiniennes* 19 (1984): 3–27. He understands the fathers to promulgate justification by faith and that works come into play only after the individual is justified. However, the bulk of his article focuses on Origen, Marius Victorinus, Ambrosiaster, Pelagius, John Chrysostom, and Augustine, sources from the third century and beyond. However, the second half of the article moves through other church fathers in rapid succession, and includes brief comments on Clement and Justin Martyr. Brief in this case means a single quotation from their writings—no extensive work is done on either author.

ham, this is a span of five centuries during which massive changes in the ecclesial and political spheres took place.[48] This book examines a much briefer time, but it does account for sources from all across the Empire. Cultural differences can certainly have an impact on a writer's theology, which is why care is taken to situate each author in his historical context.

In addition to Needham, the works of D. H. Williams[49] and Eric Osborn[50] are significant for their confirmation that justification by faith was at least present by the fourth century in the writings of Hilary of Poitiers and Origen, respectively. Williams is also incredulous of the notion that justification was not rediscovered, or as some would claim discovered, until the sixteenth century.[51] For Williams, Hilary "is the first Christian theologian explicitly to have formulated what Paul left implicit by referring to God's work of grace in the phrase, 'fides sola iustificat.'"[52] Striking about Williams's superb study is that Hilary of Poitiers articulated a clear doctrine of Pauline justification by faith from his Matthew commentary, demonstrating that Hilary was familiar with Paul's doctrine and that he let his understanding of Paul influence his reading of the Gospel. The exception taken to his thesis is his assertion that justifying faith is present in Latin theology, and not, by implication, in the Greek fathers. This book represents Greek fathers (except for the Syriac *Odes of Solomon*), and shows that they too were concerned about preserving Paul's theology.[53]

---

[48] Needham, "Justification in the Early Fathers," 27.
[49] Williams, "Justification by Faith."
[50] Eric Osborn, "Origen and Justification," 18–29. Rowan Williams claims that Origen is "very close to Pauline thinking in his commentary on Romans" (Rowan Williams, "Justification," in *Encyclopedia of Christian Theology*, ed. Jean-Yves Lacoste [New York: Routledge, 2005], 2:844), even though Osborn maintains, "The evidence on justification in Origen's commentary on Romans is inconclusive" (Osborn, "Origen and Justification," 20). See also I. T. Holdcraft, "The Parable of the Pounds and Origen's Doctrine of Grace," *JTS* n.s. 24 (1973): 503–04. In step with Origen's tenacious conviction of free will, there was something lacking in grace that needed to be overcome with human will and effort.
[51] Williams, "Justification by Faith," 649.
[52] Williams, "Justification by Faith," 660.
[53] This sentiment is also made by Ben Blackwell who, though speaking of Irenaeus, makes a broader statement about the Greek fathers. He writes, "Like many Greek fathers, Irenaeus does not use the language of justification frequently, nor does he find it necessary to explain it in depth when he does" (Ben Blackwell, "Paul and Irenaeus," in *Paul and the Second Century*, ed. Michael Bird and Joseph Dodson, LNTS 412 [New York: T & T Clark, 2011], 205). I agree that statements on justification may not be frequent and the authors may not spend much time explaining them, but what they do mean when they speak of justification remains our focus. The Greek fathers were not oblivious to justification and, since they were writing in the same language as Paul, they had a good handle on the terms.

Osborn has performed a similar service in the writings of Origen. Using Matt 19:17 as his guide, Osborn argues that Origen did hold to Paul's doctrine of justification (though perhaps with a Platonic vocabulary), concluding, "The gospel of justification by grace was still his chief concern; this is confirmed by his obsession with Marcion."[54] Thomas Scheck has also made significant headway in the doctrine of justification in Origen with his dissertation turned monograph *Origen and the History of Justification: The Legacy of Origen's Commentary on Romans*.[55] Origen's mammoth Romans commentary, his second longest work after *Contra Celsum*, has largely been ignored. Scheck, desiring to remedy this omission, has dusted off this long-neglected volume in order to see how Origen interpreted justification in what may be considered Paul's greatest letter. One interesting observation he makes is that "Origen's discussions cleared a path for later theologians who likewise attempted to demonstrate harmony between the ideas of Paul and James."[56] For this reason, Origen was picked up by many who came later, even those represented by diverse and even contradictory viewpoints. The best example of this is how Pelagius and Augustine both were able to point to Origen for support on their stance on justification.[57] Nevertheless, by the third century, there emerged a much clearer portrait of justification, as has been adequately argued from Hilary and Origen. The goal here is to push back the question to the second century to see if they too held a doctrine of justification by faith.

The chapters that follow survey an array of genres. These chapters examine apologists who defended nascent Christianity against many forms of heresy, a bishop who wrote epistles to various churches exhorting them to continue in their faith, a pastor who contended for unity in the church, and even a hymnal from which one can listen in on churches as they gathered together in corporate worship. The main approach taken is an evaluation of these primary source materials. The early fathers have received a lot of attention throughout church his-

---

[54] Osborn, "Origen and Justification," 26. Osborn uses Origen's exegesis of Matt 19:17 as a test case because Origen must deal with Jesus' comment that "God alone is good," which touches on the issue of justification, and because it would force Marcion, or more precisely Marcion's heirs, to wrestle with the fact that Jesus calls the Father alone good.

[55] See also Kathy L. Gaca and L. L. Welborn, eds., *Early Patristic Readings of Romans* (New York: T & T Clark, 2005). The focus of this work is the late second and early third centuries, mostly on Irenaeus, Clement of Alexandria, and Origen, sources that are later than those considered here.

[56] Thomas Scheck, *Origen and the History of Justification:The Legacy of Origen's Commentary on Romans* (Notre Dame, IN: University of Notre Dame Press, 2008), 6–7. See the discussion on James and Paul in the next chapter.

[57] Scheck, *Origen and the History of Justification*, 63–103.

tory, but the sources considered here have never received a thorough treatment regarding their beliefs on justification, the possible exception being *1 Clement*.

Each chapter begins with a brief introduction followed by a section covering the historical background. While the historical background does not directly pertain to the doctrine of justification *per se*, it is nonetheless important. In order to argue that the fathers of the second-century held particular views of justification, it must first be shown that these individuals and documents come from this time period. Thus a brief word on these issues will help locate these documents and their authors in the second century. Following the background concerns is the exegesis of the relevant passages and a discussion of the theological issues the text raises.

Returning to Pelikan's quotation given above, one must keep in mind that continuity and uniformity are not the same thing. The documents under review in the chapters that follow display continuity with the so-called "traditional" view of Paul's doctrine of justification by faith, but this does not mean they are uniform with each other or with Paul. The second-century fathers may not have held to a view of justification with the same precision as the sixteenth-century Reformers, yet they nonetheless held to a doctrine of justification by faith, as shall be shown.

2 "But Through Faith": Clement of Rome

The writings of the Apostolic Fathers are among the most important extra-biblical documents in the history of the church, with several of them, including *1 Clement*, almost achieving canonicity.[1] Coming on the heels of the apostles, these men give valuable insights into the doctrines of the early church, whether early sacramental theology or the occasional glance into their ecclesiology. Their writings also contain some of the earliest references to justification, using this doctrine both as an apology of what Christians believed regarding salvation (e.g., *The Epistle to Diognetus*) and as a way to teach those in the church about their faith. Clement of Rome is a representative of the latter group, writing as a shepherd to the wayward flock of Corinth reminding them, amongst other things, of their righteous standing before God.

Soteriology in *1 Clement* has produced significant controversy because Clement appears to speak of important doctrines like justification in varying and seemingly contradictory ways. While it can be difficult to untangle the complex web, it will be shown that instead of confusion in Clement, there is coherence. In other words, Clement never strays from New Testament language or concepts but rather he captures aspects of this doctrine from different vantage points. *First Clement* teaches justification by faith, despite Clement's heavy emphasis on morality and works.

To understand justification in *1 Clement*, it is essential first to get a feel for the entire document. Because of the complicated nature of faith and works in Clement, it is easy to overemphasize either faith or works above the other and lose the delicate balance that he maintains. His unambiguous statement on justification in *1 Clement* 32 is inserted between two sections that appeal to the necessity of good works. The broader context, then, must be taken into account in order to understand the argument that Clement makes. But first a brief digression into authorship and dating is in order especially since *1 Clement* contains the earliest discussions on justification after Paul.

---

[1] For instance, Clement of Alexandria introduces a quotation from *1 Clement* by calling Clement of Rome an Apostle (*Strom.* 4.17). Also, he cites this along with other Scriptures in this passage without making a distinction between them, thus giving the impression that he held *1 Clement* on the same level as the documents that would later make up the New Testament. Even more telling is the inclusion of *1 Clement* in *Codex Alexandrinus*, an important fifth-century manuscript.

2.1 The Background

As with most documents of antiquity, controversy surrounds the traditional background materials of *1 Clement*. Both the authorship and the dating of this book have recently come under scrutiny, and for good reason. But the list of potential authors remains short and the date, although not as concrete as was once assumed, remains fairly certain.

Authorship

Determining the author of *1 Clement* is difficult because there is no explicit claim of authorship made. The letter opens with a salutation from the church which sojourns in Rome to the church which sojourns in Corinth, without ever mentioning a single author. Complicating the matter further is that it is written in the first person plural giving the impression that it was the collective voices in Rome authorizing this letter and not a particular individual.[2] It is more likely, however, that there was a single voice behind this text, especially when one considers the fluidity of the letter. The fathers are unanimous in their attribution of this letter to Clement.[3] However, several Clements have been put forward as the potential author.

The once popular suggestion that Flavius Clemens, the cousin of Emperor Domitian, wrote *1 Clement* has fallen out of favor. This theory purported that members Domitian's family had converted to Christianity which drove the megalomaniac Emperor to rage. He charged Clement with atheism (ἀθεότης) and Jewish superstition and had him put to death and exiled his wife Domitilla.[4] This Clement was attractive because it meant that there was a significant leader in the Church of Rome who was near the Emperor. There is no reason, however, to assume that this Clement wrote anything, let alone the book which now bears his name.

Origen, the great theologian from Alexandria, endorsed the Clement of Phil 4:3 as the author.[5] There Paul mentions a Clement in passing as one who labored

---

[2] Clayton Jefford makes the argument for multiple voices through one secretary (*The Apostolic Fathers and the New Testament* [Peabody, MA: Hendrickson, 2006], 17).
[3] See, for example, Eusebius, *The Church History*, 3.38; 4.23, trans. Paul L. Maier (Grand Rapids: Kregel, 1999), 126; 159 (respectively).
[4] Dio Cassius, *Roman History*, trans. Earnest Cary, LCL, vol. 8 (Cambridge, MA: Harvard University Press, 1925), 67.14.1–2.
[5] Origen, *Commentary on John*, 6.36.

by his side. This suggestion is also appealing because it links Clement with the Apostle Paul, thus adding weight to his teaching. The problem is that he based this theory upon the shared name, a name that was common in first-century Rome.

The most likely Clement is the one Irenaeus records as the third bishop of Rome. Of this Clement Irenaeus said, "he had seen the blessed apostles, and had been conversant with them, [and] might be said to have the preaching of the apostles still echoing [in his ears]."[6] It is true that the author of *1 Clement* writes with an authority that one would expect from the leader of such an influential congregation. Interestingly, Eusebius connects the Clement of Philippians 4:3 with the Clement whom Irenaeus lists as the third bishop of Rome, which is a possibility.[7] Perhaps Paul met Clement in Rome and trained him for the role he would undertake later in his life. Though nothing decisive can be said about which Clement is the author, the field can be narrowed down to one of these three as the most probable candidate. Regardless of which Clement wrote this letter, the important thing to note is that these different Clements were contemporaries.

Date

First Clement is generally dated to the final years of Domitian's reign, specifically 96 CE. This date is based on the obscure line in 1.1 which reads, "Because of the sudden and repeated calamities and experiences that have happened to us ... we have been rather tardy in giving attention to the matters in dispute among you."[8] The calamities (συμφοράς) and unpleasant experiences (περιπτώσεις) are thought to speak of the persecution that Domitian inflicted on the church during the last decade of the first century. Leslie Barnard, a representative of this view,

---

[6] Irenaeus, *Against Heresies*, III.3.3, trans. by A. Roberts and W.H. Rambaut, in *The Apostolic Fathers with Justin Martyr and Irenaeus*, Ante-Nicene Fathers. American ed., vol. 1 (Buffalo: Christian Literature, 1885; repr., Peabody, MA: Hendrickson Publishers, 2004). It is important to note that there is no suggestion of a monarchial episcopacy in *1 Clement*, despite the testimony of Irenaeus. See James S. Jeffers, *Conflict at Rome: Social Order and Hierarchy in Early Christianity* (Minneapolis: Fortress, 1991), 95.

[7] Eusebius, *The Church History*, 3.15.

[8] For critical editions, see Bart D. Ehrman, *The Apostolic Fathers*, vol. 2, LCL (Cambridge, MA: Harvard University Press, 2003); A. Jaubert, *Épître aux Corinthiens*, rev. ed., SC 167 (Paris: Cerf, 2000); G. Schneider, *Epistola ad Corinthios*, Fontes Christiani 15 (Firbourg, Switzerland and NewYork: Herder, 1994). The text used here is taken from Michael W. Holmes, *The Apostolic Fathers*, 3rd ed. (Grand Rapids: Baker, 2007). All translations are my own unless otherwise noted.

has confidently asserted, "1 Clement was written just after the reign of Domitian when the Church was not sure how the new Emperor, Nerva, would react. Or it could perhaps be fitted into a lull a year or two before Domitian was assassinated."[9]

While it is possible that this is the case, there are problems with this theory. First of all, this is not enough evidence to conclude definitively that this letter was written during that time. The language itself is hardly suggestive of persecution. Neither the New Testament authors nor the authors after them shied away from recounting their persecution. It would seem strange for Clement to use such veiled language if the Roman church was enduring harsh persecution. Secondly, Clement does not speak of persecution anywhere else in this book, even in his closing prayers and requests. In fact, L. L. Welborn has observed that the letter is characterized by a positive attitude toward the Empire.[10] Therefore, if Clement was writing during the persecution of Domitian, he certainly did not think it necessary to make much mention of it.

Though the case for this letter being written just after Domitian's persecution is weak, a date in the 90s CE is nonetheless very strong. There are several clues in the text itself which help pinpoint a date in the 90s. Michael Holmes identifies three pieces of evidence in support of a date sometime during the last two decades of the first century: (1) chapters 5 and 6 recount the Neronian persecution as a past event,[11] (2) 63.3 references those "who from youth to old age have lived blameless lives among us," and (3) 44.3–5 states that some leaders whom the apostles appointed were still living.[12] When these arguments are assessed together, the likelihood of a date near the close of the first century is very plausible.

---

[9] Leslie Barnard, "St. Clement of Rome and the Persecution of Domitian," in *Studies in the Apostolic Fathers and their Background*, ed. Leslie Barnard (New York: Schocken, 1966), 12. This article first appeared as Leslie Barnard, "Clement of Rome and the Persecution of Domitian," *NTS* 10 (1964): 251–60.

[10] L. L. Welborn, "On the Date of First Clement," *Biblical Research* 29 (1984): 36. However, of all the examples he lists (37.2–3; 21.1, 6; 60.2, 4; 61.1–2), only 61.1–2 seems to support his case. Even this example is simply a prayer for those whom the Lord has placed in leadership over the Empire, a prayer similar to that of 1 Pet 2:13–17, which was written during persecution. Welborn understands the "calamites" and "experiences" to be problems within the Roman church (48). Although Welborn may overstate his case, his argument is bolstered by the surprising lack of rhetoric against the Empire, especially if the church in Rome was bearing the brunt of Domitian's persecution.

[11] *Pace*, A. E. Wilhelm-Hooijberg, "A Different View of Clemens Romanus," *HeyJ* 16 (1975): 266–88, who argues for a date c. 70 CE. This view is unpersuasive because it fails to account for the way the author speaks of the Neronian persecution as though it happened many years before. Clement's account does not read like a recent memory.

[12] Holmes, *The Apostolic Fathers*, 35.

The external evidence for a date in the 90s is equally strong. J. B. Lightfoot has provided sufficient proof that Polycarp used *1 Clement*, spending four pages in his classic *Apostolic Fathers* comparing the Greek texts of both works in order to demonstrate the many linguistic parallels that exist between the two.[13] If Lightfoot is correct and Polycarp employed *1 Clement* in his own writings, then the letter must have a *terminus ad quem* of 120 CE.[14] Furthermore, *1 Clement* was established well enough that when Hegesippus came to Corinth in 150 CE, he became familiar with a "long and wonderful" letter which was addressed to the Corinthian church from Rome.[15] All things considered, the letter of *1 Clement* was likely known in the early years of the second century.[16]

2.2 Summary of *1 Clement*

Clement's letter to the Corinthians is reminiscent of Paul's epistles to that church in many ways, both in doctrine and style.[17] Like Paul, Clement wrote an occasional letter to the church in Corinth because of specific problems within the congregation.[18] In chapter 47 Clement actually mentions Paul's letters to their

---

13 J. B. Lightfoot, *The Apostolic Fathers: S. Clement of Rome. A Revised Text, with Introductions, Notes, Dissertations, and Translations* (London: Macmillan, 1890), 149–52, 348.

14 *Pace*, Welborn, "On the Date of First Clement," who dates *1 Clement* as late as 150 CE. Welborn can suggest such a late date because he denies any connection between Polycarp and Clement.

15 Eusebius, *The Church History*, 3.16; 4.22.

16 See Holmes, *The Apostolic Fathers*, 36, who makes these aforementioned claims as to the use of *1 Clement* by later second-century writers.

17 Hubertus Drobner helpfully outlines the work as follows: Proem (1–3), exhortations against jealousy and envy (4–39), acknowledgement of the ecclesiastical issues in Corinth (40–58), and the conclusion which consists of a closing prayer, a summary, a commendation, and a salutation (59–65) (*The Fathers of the Church: A Comprehensive Introduction*, trans. Siegfried S. Schatzmann [Peabody, MA: Hendrickson, 2007], 48).

18 The fullest discussion on the genre of *1 Clement* can be found in W. C. van Unnik, *Studies over de zogenaamde eerste brief van Clemens*, vol. 1 of *Het litteraire genre*, Mededelingen der Koninklijke Nederlandse Akademie van Wetenschappen, Afd. Letterkunde 33.4 (Amsterdam: N. V. Noord-Hollandsche Uitgevers Maatschappij, 1970). For an English translation, see W. C. van Unnik, "Studies on the so-called First Epistle of Clement: The Literary Genre," in *Encounters with Hellenism: Studies on the First Letter of Clement*, ed. Cilliers Breytenbach and Leslie L. Welborn, trans. L. L. Welborn, Arbeiten zur Geschichte des Antiken Judentums und des Urchristentums 53 (Leiden: Brill, 2004), 115–81. See Barbara Ellen Bowe, *A Church in Crisis: Ecclesiology and Paraenesis in Clement of Rome*, Harvard Dissertations in Religion 23 (Minneapolis: Fortress Press, 1988), 61–74 for a helpful discussion of van Unnik's work. Van Unnik classifies *1 Clement* as a symbouletic letter, that is, he is giving advice to the church, advice meant to warn against

congregation, citing the factions which had torn them apart a half century before. Strife had now once again threatened their "well-established and ancient church" because one or two people had rebelled against the presbyters (47.6), even usurping their authority (44.6). The reason for their rebellion is not given but this has not stopped speculation as to what caused this faction to depose their leaders.[19]

What is clear is that Clement believed the root of their revolt was jealousy. Within the first few chapters Clement cites examples both ancient and recent of jealousy and its detrimental consequences. He recounts the stories of Cain and Abel, Jacob and Esau, Joseph and his brothers, and several more from the Old Testament as warnings to the fractured congregation. He also reminds them of Peter and Paul whose deaths he attributes to the jealousy of unrighteous men (5.4–5). For Clement, jealousy is out of place for Christians, which is why he calls them to repentance by inciting them to "fix [their] eyes on the blood of Christ and understand how precious it is to his Father, because, being poured out for [their] salvation, it won for the whole world the grace of repentance" (7.4; ἀτενίσωμεν εἰς τὸ αἷμα τοῦ Χριτοῦ καὶ γνῶμεν ὡς ἔστιν τίμιον τῷ πατρὶ αὐτοῦ, ὅτι διὰ τὴν ἡμετέραν σωτηρίαν ἐκχυθὲν παντὶ τῷ κόσμῳ μετανοίας χάριν ὑπήνεγκεν).[20]

Beginning in chapter 9 Clement shifts his focus from negative examples of jealousy and the call of repentance, to positive examples of men and woman who "perfectly served his magnificent glory" (τοὺς τελείως λειτουργήσαντας τῇ μεγαλοπρεπεῖ δόξῃ αὐτοῦ). Illustrations of Noah, Abraham, Lot, and Rahab abound as those who lived obedient lives, culminating in the quintessential example, Jesus Christ (chap 16). Interjected into his long section on right behavior is the plea for humility. This entreaty is made in sharp contrast with those who

---

quarrels and divisions. This is made clear in Clement's stated purpose of the letter: "Receive our counsel (συμβουλή), and there shall be nothing for you to regret" (58.2). For another work on the genre and purpose of *1 Clement*, see Odd Magne Bakke, *Concord and Peace*, WUNT 143 (Tübingen: Mohr Siebeck, 2001).

19 Bowe claims that too much attention is given to church hierarchy in the letter and not enough attention is given to the community itself. She reasons, "Far from being exclusively dominated by a concern for undergirding the hierarchical order in the Church, *1 Clement* contains a strong and urgent appeal for unity and solidarity based not on hierarchical agendas but on the conviction that Christians form a common ἀδελφότης which must be preserved" (Bowe, *A Church in Crisis*, 4).

20 Edmund Fisher wrongly sees an early appeal to the Eucharist in this verse. For him it is the blood of Christ poured out in the Eucharist that saves ("Let us look upon the blood-of-Christ" [*1 Clement* 7:4], *VC* 34 [1980]: 218–36). But *1 Clement* 7:4 concerns the blood of Christ poured out at his crucifixion, not the metaphorical blood that fills the Eucharistic cup.

"set themselves up as leaders in abominable jealousy" (14.1; τοῖς ἐν ἀλαζονείᾳ καὶ ἀκαταστασίᾳ μυσεροῦ ζήλους ἀρχηγοῖς ἐξακολουθεῖν). Once again Clement draws from his extensive knowledge of the Old Testament to find copious examples of people who exhibited godly character and humility.[21] He spends an exorbitant amount of time on morality in order to shame those who had caused the faction as well as to exhort those who remained in the church to live in harmony with Scripture.

2.3 Translation and Commentary

Living in accordance with biblical morality could be considered the main theme of *1 Clement*.[22] As a result, it is often presumed that Clement held to justification by works because of the sheer amount of weight he places on morality in this letter, not to mention that he says in 30.3 that people are "justified by works and not by words" (ἔργοις δικαιούμενοι καὶ μὴ λόγοις), a phrase that will be examined later in this chapter. While it is true that the vast majority of *1 Clement* is taken up with Clement urging the people at Corinth to live in a godly manner, this never eclipses his unmistakable declaration of justification by faith. Moral living is the result of the Corinthians' justified standing, not a means by which they earn God's favor.

It is hermeneutically wise to find the clearest passage on a given topic within a document and then explain the remainder of the occurrences which may be more ambiguous. Thus, the discussion will commence in chapter 32 because it

---

[21] Donald Hagner has commented on Clement's impressive knowledge of the LXX, observing that nearly a quarter of *1 Clement* is drawn from the Old Testament (*The Use of the Old and New Testaments in Clement of Rome*, NovTSup 34 [Leiden: Brill, 1973], 21).

[22] Andreas Lindemann stresses the paraenetic nature of the letter (*Paulus im ältesten Christentum* [Tübingen: Mohr Siebeck, 1979], 198–99). Again, the importance of this cannot be overemphasized for the argument that follows. He is addressing a particular problem in the congregation and calls them to live by their profession of faith. Accentuating morality does not overshadow justification by faith in this particular instance. See also Heikki Räisänen, "'Righteousness by Works': An Early Catholic Doctrine? Thoughts on 1 Clement," in *Jesus, Paul, and Torah: Collected Essays*, trans. David E. Orton, JSNTSup 43 (Sheffield: Sheffield Academic Press, 1992), 206. Räisänen observes, "So it is clear from the outset that [Clement] has to appeal strongly to the individual; the question of a person's behaviour has to be in the forefront of the discussion. It is not the purpose of the letter to instil [sic] faith in the readers." Commentaries on justification in Clement run astray when this is not remembered. *First Clement* must be appreciated first and foremost for what it set out to accomplish—a change in behavior amongst those who had rebelled.

contains the most straightforward exposition of justification in *1 Clement*, or what Lindemann calls the "dogmatic aspect of the doctrine of justification."[23] From here, other passages that touch on justification throughout the remainder of the letter will be examined, all while keeping in mind the clarity with which Clement speaks of justification by faith alone in chapter 32.

Translation of 32.3 – 4

> Therefore, all were glorified and magnified, not through themselves or through their own works or through righteous actions[24] that they did, but through his will. Therefore we too, having been called through his will in Christ Jesus, are not justified through ourselves nor through our own wisdom or through our understanding or through our piety or through our works which we did in holiness[25] of heart, but through faith, through which the Almighty God justified all who existed from the earliest times; to whom be glory forever and ever. Amen.

Chapter 32 is one of the more famous passages in *1 Clement* and there is no shortage of commentators who have tried to determine how this apparently clear reference to justification fits in the broader context of the book.[26] For the better part of the letter Clement gives a wealth of examples of those who lived morally exemplary lives in the Old Testament. In chapter 32 Clement suddenly breaks from this approach to comment on justification, as though he realized that his previous remarks could be mistakenly used to promote a works based salvation, a message he did not want to communicate to an already confused congregation.

The οὖν that connects this verse to the previous section refers specifically to the quotation from Gen 15:5 which Clement recites in 32.2 that "your seed will be as the stars of heaven" (ἔσται τὸ σπέρμα σου ὡς οἱ ἀστέρες τοῦ οὐρανοῦ). For Clement, this promise made to Abraham was fulfilled in those whom God has

---

23 Andreas Lindemann, "Paul in the Writings of the Apostolic Fathers," in *Paul and the Legacies of Paul*, ed. William S. Babcock (Dallas: Southern Methodist University, 1990), 33.
24 The noun δικαιοπραγίας is a *hapax legomenon* in the New Testament and early Christian literature (see BDAG, s.v. "δικαιοπραγίας"). It is evident that this neologism is a fusion of δίκαιος (righteous) and πρᾶγμα (deed). Though this genitive is singular in form, it is to be translated in the plural. It is strikingly similar to a phrase that Justin Martyr uses. See chap. 6.
25 The word Clement uses for holiness is ὁσιότητι, which means "state of proper attitude toward God as exhibited in action" (BDAG, s.v. "ὁσιότητι").
26 Even Adolf von Harnack, who does not otherwise think that Clement is Pauline, is forced to admit that the Pauline echo comes as a surprise (*Einführung in die alte Kirchengeschichte: Das Schreiben der römischen Kirche an die korinthische aus der Zeit Domitians (1. Clemensbrief)* [Leipzig: Hinrichs, 1929], 112).

justified and he indicates that "all" (πάντες) people have entered into salvation in this manner. He goes on to say that these individuals have been "glorified and magnified" (ἐδοξάθησαν καὶ ἐμεγαλύνθησαν), which simply means that they have attained the outcome of their faith.

When discussing how one is justified in this passage, Clement begins with the negative, describing the various ways a person is not justified. He says that it was "not through themselves or through their own works or through righteous actions" (οὐ δι αὐτῶν ἤ τῶν ἔργων αὐτῶν ἤ τῆς δικαιοπραγίας ἧς κατειργάσαντο).[27] Such an argument only makes sense and is rhetorically effective if there were those who thought they could receive God's favor through their efforts. Clement wants his readers to know that there is nothing they can do in themselves to merit salvation, whether good works or righteous actions. Not even those whom he has just praised for their right behavior and humility earned salvation because of their deeds. They too were saved on the basis of faith alone.

Clement says that these people have been glorified, not through these works, "but through his will" (ἀλλὰ διὰ τοῦ θελήματος αὐτοῦ). Not only are individuals justified through faith, as he will articulate it in the next verse, but they are saved "through [God's] will." If this were not the case, then an individual could boast of his faith, which could then be conceived of as a work. Instead, Clement attributes salvation to the call and will of God. In 59.2 Clement writes, "But we will be innocent of this sin, and we will ask, by making earnest prayer and supplication, that the Creator of the universe might carefully guard the specified number of his elect in the whole world" (ἡμεῖς δὲ ἀθῷοι ἐσόμεθα ἀπὸ ταύτης τῆς ἁμαρτίας καὶ αἰτησόμεθα ἐκτενῆ τὴν δέησιν καὶ ἱκεσίαν ποιούμενοι ὅπως τὸν ἀριθμὸν τὸν κατηριθμημένον τῶν ἐκλεκτῶν αὐτοῦ ἐν ὅλῳ τῷ κόσμῳ διαφυλάξῃ ἄθραυστον ὁ δημιουργός). In 32.3 and 59.2 there is mention of God's sovereign will in salvation, a recurring theme in *1 Clement*.

Much of verse 4 is simply a reiteration of what Clement had already said in verse three. He begins verse four by saying, "Therefore we too, having been called through his will in Christ Jesus, are not justified through ourselves nor through our own wisdom or through our understanding or through our piety or through our works which we did in holiness of heart." Just as with those who came before, Clement and his fellow believers have been called to salvation, not through anything within themselves, but through God's will. In this verse he expands the list of good works to include wisdom (σοφίας), piety (εὐσεβείας), and works done in holiness of heart (ἔργων ὧν κατειργασάμεθα ἐν ὁσιότητι καρ-

---

[27] The διὰ is elided after each ἤ but it is implied. This has been brought out in the translation in order to show the emphasis Clement is making on each of these works.

δίας). Wisdom is raised because of the supreme importance placed on this virtue in the Greco-Roman world. After all, it was the love of wisdom (i.e., philosophy) which propelled ancient Greek society. For centuries philosophy was the path toward true knowledge, and thus a type of salvation in itself. Clement may also have had in mind an early form of Gnosticism and their emphasis on Sophia.[28] But not even wisdom adorned in all her beauty can ensure salvation in Clement's reasoning.

Another common perception is that a pious individual will merit salvation on the basis of her devotion to God. A pious Jew would have offered up animal sacrifices to God for the remission of his sins. Although sacrificial offerings were never meant to function apart from faith, a Jew might still be inclined to believe that his sacrifice was a sufficient act of piety irrespective of the condition of his heart. This attitude, of course, is contrary to the Old Testament's view of true piety (1 Sam 15:22; Ps 51:16–17).

Similarly the Romans had their own forms of worship that focused on worshipping the Emperor's *genius*, paying homage to the traditional Greco-Roman pantheon, or participating in a mystery religion, like the cults of Mithras or Isis.[29] Even the word piety (*pietas*) had a significant and nuanced meaning to the Roman ear. As James Jeffers observes, "*Pietas* ... refers to the Romans' unqualified acceptance of their obligation to the gods, to the state and to their elders," and the pursuit of piety was for the *paterfamilias* alone.[30] Through *pietas* a father would connect his family to the gods of the state and to his ancestors, seeking their protection and fortune. However, for Clement it does not matter how pious an act is, it still constituted a work in his mind and was thus not acceptable as a means to salvation.

Finally Clement breaks through with a positive response, using only four words to answer how a person is justified: ἀλλὰ διὰ τῆς πίστεως.[31] The adversa-

---

28 Deirde J. Good, *Reconstructing the Tradition of Sophia in Gnostic Literature* (Atlanta: Scholars Press, 1987). Good draws out the prominent place that Sophia had in the Gnostics.
29 For a helpful introduction to Greco-Roman religions, see Everett Ferguson, *Backgrounds of Early Christianity*, 3rd ed. (Grand Rapids: Eerdmans, 2003), 148–318. For a more thorough study, see Hans-Josef Klauck and Brian McNeil, *The Religious Context of Early Christianity: A Guide to Graeco-Roman Religions* (London: T&T Clark, 2000).
30 James S. Jeffers, *The Greco-Roman World of the New Testament Era: Exploring the Background of Early Christianity* (Downers Grove, IL: InterVarsity, 1999), 92. Cf. Cicero, *De haruspicum responsis* IX.8–9.
31 Whether or not the justification spoken of by Clement is forensic or ethical is also a point of debate. Carey Newman argues the former ("Righteousness," in *DLNT*, ed. Ralph P. Martin and Peter H. Davids [Downers Grove, IL: InterVarsity Press], 1057), Räisänen the latter ("'Righteous-

tive ἀλλά is used to contrast sharply these two ways of salvation—the one through works, which is no salvation at all, and the other that comes through faith.[32] The fact that this statement comes without qualification demonstrates that Clement is espousing an early form of *sola fide*. Faith, for Clement, is the only means "through which the Almighty God justified all who existed from the earliest times" (δι ἧς πάντας τοὺς ἀπ αἰῶνος ὁ παντοκράτωρ θεὸς ἐδικαίωσεν). Thus all those who have ever been justified were justified *through* faith. There was no one in the Old Testament who was justified through her works, regardless of how noble or pious she was.

The idea that even those in previous times were saved through faith is made explicit when Clement speaks of Abraham. In the previous chapter Clement beckons his reader to think back with him to former times saying, "Let us call to mind again the things which happened from the beginning. Why was our Father Abraham blessed with grace? Was it not because he attained righteousness and truth through faith?" (31.1–2).[33] Once more he uses the prepositional phrase διὰ πίστεως in order to demonstrate that δικαιοσύνη comes only through πίστις. He also mentions Abraham's faith in 10.1 where he acknowledges that Abraham, "was found faithful when he became obedient to the words of God" (πιστὸς εὑρέθη ἐν τῷ αὐτὸν ὑπήκοον γενέσθαι τοῖς ῥήμασιν τοῦ θεοῦ). Abraham proved himself to be full of faith through his works of obedience. Works, in Clement, serve to evidence faith not to garner salvation. To those in Corinth who were disrupting peace and concord, Clement calls into question their justification by faith on account of their works of disunity. They must look at the Old Testament examples of people who had faith in God and then showed this faith through their obedience. For Clement, as for Paul, Abraham serves as the prototype of justification of those in former times, proving that God has always saved his people through faith.

---

ness by Work,'" 212). Considering the entire letter, with the emphases on repentance, sin, and the cross, it does seem better to side with Newman and see justification in *1 Clement* as forensic.

32 Herbert Smyth makes the following comment concerning the strength of ἀλλά: "ἀλλά marks opposition, contrast protest, difference, objection, or limitation; and is thus used both where one notion entirely excludes another and where two notions are not mutually exclusive." See Herbert Smyth, *Greek Grammar*, rev. by Gordon M. Messing (Cambridge, MA: Harvard University Press, 1984), §2775. In this passage, it is necessary to see this ἀλλά marking two options that stand diametrically opposed to one another.

33 I am following Holmes on the translation of ποιήσας as "attain" instead of the normal sense of "do." This better captures the meaning which Clement is conveying. If it were taken as "do," it would read, "Was it not because he did righteousness and truth through faith?" Either way the emphasis is on his faith, not the accomplishing of righteousness. Even if Abraham "does righteousness," it is righteous actions flowing from his faith.

2.4 Objections and Responses

Though Clement's statement that justification comes through faith may seem self-evident, it has not been without its many skeptics. The most prominent objection has come from T. F. Torrance, who has also influenced the way others have read *1 Clement*.[34] Regarding *1 Clement*, Torrance holds, "Salvation thus conceived by Clement is thought of as issuing from a radical good-will in God, and as being based on His βούλησις."[35] When specifically addressing justification in chapter 32, Torrance writes, "There can be no doubt that this is Pauline language, but it cannot be understood in a Pauline fashion. It is quite consistent with Clement's whole position, particularly the disclaimer about self-justification which really means self-abasement as a righteous act."[36] He acknowledges that Clement refers to justification in a Pauline manner, but then denies that Clement meant something similar to Paul. Instead of reading Clement in his context, Torrance seeks to pierce through Clement's language "to look for other meanings in his use of traditional language."[37]

The section Torrance finds most troubling, which is in fact the greatest challenge to justification by faith in *1 Clement*, is found in 30.3 where Clement exhorts the Corinthians to clothe themselves in harmony and to keep away from gossip and slander, "because we are justified by works, and not by words" (ἔργοις δικαιούμενοι καὶ μὴ λόγοις).[38] This simple phrase appears to sound the death knell of justification by faith in *1 Clement*, since Clement plainly states that justification is on account of works. On this verse Torrance says the following:

> And so Clement can say that we are 'justified by works, not by words' ἔργοις δικαιούμενοι, μὴ λόγοις, and insists that we are not justified by πίστις alone but by πίστις and εὐσέβεια, by πίστις and φιλοξενία by πίστις and ἀληθεία. *This means that Clement is well on the way to the legalism of later times*, as is evidenced also by his almost liturgical use of δικαιώματα and προστάγματα.[39]

---

34 See also Richard Parvo, *The Making of Paul: Contructions of the Apostle in Early Christianity* (Minneapolis: Fortress, 2010). Righteousness in Clement "was not justification by faith but proper conduct" (18).
35 Thomas F. Torrance, *The Doctrine of Grace in the Apostolic Fathers* (Grand Rapids: Eerdmans, 1959), 48.
36 Torrance, *The Doctrine of Grace in the Apostolic Fathers*, 50.
37 Torrance, *The Doctrine of Grace in the Apostolic Fathers*, 50.
38 The adverbial participle δικαιούμενοι is causal.
39 Torrance, *The Doctrine of Grace in the Apostolic Fathers*, 49. Emphasis added.

For Torrance, the very essence of religion in Clement is self-abnegation which in turn becomes the meaning of faith in *1 Clement*. The people used as illustrations from the Old Testament were in fact justified by faith, but this faith is redefined by Clement to be self-abasement as a righteous act.[40] In fact, Clement did not even "aim at speaking of justification by faith; he wished rather to show how by repentance, humility, and good conduct, including an obedient faith, the Corinthians might please God."[41] Therefore, faith becomes a posture of humility that one must display as a work of righteousness in order to obtain justification. It is a subtle shift from the traditional understanding of justification by faith. While humility is often deemed to be a necessary prerequisite to justification, Torrance understands Clement to argue that humility is a work that pleases God.

This understanding of works righteousness in *1 Clement* is not unique to T. F. Torrance. Others have made similar claims that Clement is advocating high morality as the means of salvation. Johannes Weiss observed that a "strong moralism runs through all its expressions from the first page to the last."[42] Charles Nielsen, though not entirely agreeing with those who say Clement lapsed into moralism, makes the argument that Clement was inconsistent, teetering between justification through faith and works righteousness.[43] In the end Nielsen concludes that Clement was a "theologian of paradox," who did not take the time to consider carefully the ramifications this letter would have.[44] Accusing Clement of inconsistency is just one one way to handle the conundrum.

J. B. Lightfoot offers a second way to solve the discrepancy between 30.3, where justification is on the basis of works, and 32.4, where justification is through faith, which does not depend on accusing Clement of contradiction.[45]

---

[40] Torrance, *The Doctrine of Grace in the Apostolic Fathers*, 50.

[41] Torrance, *The Doctrine of Grace in the Apostolic Fathers*, 54.

[42] See, for example, Johannes Weiss and Rudolf Knopf, *The History of Primitive Christianity*, ed. Frederick C. Grant (New York: Wilson-Erickson, 1937), 2:853. Räisänen distinguishes between morality and moralism saying, "There is thus a strong emphasis on morality, but there is little sign of 'moralism' and none at all of casuistry and the like; it is completely misleading to speak in this context of such things as anthropocentric piety or the decisive soteriological significance of meritorious works" (Räisänen, "'Righteousness by Works,'" 211).

[43] Charles M. Nielsen, "Clement of Rome and Moralism," *CH* 31 (1962): 131–50. This article is invaluable for the issue of justification and morality in *1 Clement*. His argument is lucid and he draws from a vast amount of secondary literature, but it is not ultimately convincing.

[44] Nielsen, "Clement of Rome and Moralism," 148.

[45] Lightfoot, *Apostolic Fathers*, 96. Lightfoot is probably correct in assuming Clement's reconciliation of the two apostles was "coincidentally affirmed." Pace, W. K. Lowther Clarke who, critiquing Lightfoot, says, "To conclude that Clement was deliberately reconciling the teaching of St. Paul and St. James would not be a historical judgment" (W. K. Lowther Clarke, *The First Epis-*

The solution is to see *1 Clement* as a practical guide for bridging the gap between Paul and James.[46] Harmony is sought by suggesting that Paul and James are looking at justification from two distinct vantage points. Paul viewed justification from the side of un-conversion and argued that people are justified on the basis of faith alone. James, on the other hand, was looking back on salvation and making an argument that justification is not a reality if works are absent.[47] In a similar fashion, Clement contends in 32.3–4, along with the Paul, that the only way a person is justified is through faith. Nothing is added here to this prescription because he is arguing for the doctrine of justification by faith alone. In 30.3 Clement took up the mantle of James to argue that words are not sufficient in themselves—they must be accompanied by works, such as the works he had

---

tle *of Clement to the Corinthians* [London: Society for Promoting Christian Knowledge, 1937], 39). This misrepresents Lightfoot who argues for an unintentional bridging of the two Apostles.

[46] On the problem of Paul and James, Dale Allison has commented, "the relevant books, chapters, and articles are as the sands of the sea," and that the "exegete here confronts an overgrown, entangled mess beyond sorting" (*A Critical and Exegetical Commentary on the Epistle of James*, ICC [New York: Bloomsbery, 2013], 426). Allison posits six solutions that have been given for this age-old enigma: "(i) James and Paul wrote independently of each other, so neither was concerned with the other; and if one did know what the other taught, he was not consciously being oppositional. (ii) Paul responded to James or to followers of James in order to correct or rebut him or them. (iii) Paul agreed with James but sought 'to prevent a mischievous use' of his words, which the apostle 'thought likely to be perverted by the Judaisers who were corrupting the Gospel of Christ.' (iv) James responded to Paul in a polemical fashion. (v) James responded to Paul but sought to clarify his teaching, not counter it. A recent variant of this last position is the thesis that James is a second-century, canonically conscious pseudepigraphon composed in part to stave off heterodox interpretations of Paul. (vi) James reacted negatively not to Paul but to some form of (distorted) Pauline antinomianism, a view Augustine already had" (Allison, *James*, 427–28). For another discussion of how James and Paul can be read together in harmony, see Douglass Moo, *The Letter of James*, PNTC (Grand Rapids: Eerdmans, 2000), 36–43, 118–84. Others, such as Peter Davids, also believe that there need not be a problem with reading these apostles together but his solution is to argue that Paul used δικαιόω to mean "declare to be just" whereas James used it to mean "show to be righteous" (Peter Davids, *The Epistle of James*, NIGTC [Grand Rapids: Eerdmans, 1982], 51). Of course there are those who suggest that the fissure between Paul and James is too wide and they cannot be brought together. See, for example, G. Luedemann, *Opposition to Paul in Jewish Christianity* (Minneapolis: Fortress, 1989), 144–49.

[47] *Pace*, Siegfried Schulz, *Die Mitte der Schrift: d. Frühkatholizismus im Neuen Testament als Herausforderung an d. Protestantismus* (Berlin: Kreuz-Verlag, 1976), 286. Schulz argues that James posits justification by works and merit. Not only does he pit James against Paul, but he also thinks that Hebrews and the Pastorals (which he sees as deutero-Pauline) to be out of step with the apostle. For Schulz, Clement is just another example of departure from Paul, not the first one.

been advocating through his many examples.⁴⁸ Robert Eno makes the sweeping claim that the Fathers in general "supplemented Paul with James," and that this was not unique to Clement.⁴⁹

A third position, which is the best way forward, avoids bringing James into the coversation. In this view, Clement used Paul exclusively. Räisänen makes this point with an eye towards *1 Clement:* "The notion that justification through faith should lead to works of love is of course fully compatible with the theology of Paul."⁵⁰ In short, Clement employs Paul's interplay between the indicative and imperative.⁵¹ Paul often lays the groundwork of his theology by declaring what is already true of his readers (indicative) before he constructs ethical standards for how they should live in light of this reality (imperative). Lindemann notes that Clement "formulates the theme in almost classic fashion," when he argues that "Christians ... must realize their status of 'holiness' by doing works, not merely speaking words."⁵² Paul made use of the imperative only when the indicative was established; Clement gave the imperatives first be he still seems to ground the imperative in the indicative. Once more Lindemann argues, "The righteous produce good works, that is, works according to righteousness (cf. 33.8: 'let us work the work of righteousness'), not the other way around."⁵³

This solution seems clear when one takes into account the opening verse of chapter 33. In response to the declaration that one is saved through faith, he says, "What then shall we do, brothers? Shall we idly abstain from doing good, and forsake love?" He answers insistently: "May the Master never allow this to happen." Immediately after claiming that justification is by faith alone, he asks what the reader should do in response, much like Paul does in Romans

---

48 *Pace*, Newman, who maintains, "It is clear that Clement embraced 'justification by faith' as the way to obtain salvation ... . It is also clear that Clement understood good works as the means to maintain salvation" (Newman, "Righteousness," 1057). Newman claims that in *1 Clement* one 'gets in' by faith but one 'stays in' through works. "Clement thus evinces a twofold soteriological pattern," writes Newman (1057). See also Carey Newman, "Righteousness/Justification Language in 1 Clement: A Linguistic and Theological Enquiry" (M.Th. thesis, University of Aberdeen, 1985).
49 Robert Eno, "Some Patristic Views on the Relationship of Faith and Works in Justification," *Recherches augustiniennes* 19 (1984): 4.
50 Räisänen, "'Righteousness by Works,'" 212.
51 For this theme in Paul, see among others Michael Parsons, "Being Precedes Act: Indicative and Imperative in Paul's Writing," *EQ* 88 (1988): 99–127, and William D. Dennison, "Indicative and Imperative: The Basic Structure of Pauline Ethics," *CTJ* 14 (1979): 55–78.
52 Lindemann, "Paul in the Writings of the Apostolic Fathers," 33.
53 Lindemann, "Paul in the Writings of the Apostolic Fathers," 33.

6 after expounding justification by faith in Romans 3–5.⁵⁴ It is essential to see that Clement's appeal for good works comes after the statement on justification through faith. Good works, then, are the appropriate response to the work of God in salvation, not the foundation of their justification. This is similar to Ephesians 2:8–10 where Paul follows his statement of salvation through faith with an appeal for "good works which God prepared beforehand that we should walk in them." Salvation, though by faith alone, must be accompanied by works as evidence. Options two and three do justice to Clement's letter and offer the most promising way forward in understanding the relationship between faith and works in Clement.

One final objection ought to be addressed. Carey Newman has argued that Clement drifted from Paul's doctrine of justification by faith because he failed to tie justification to the person, work, and resurrection of Christ.⁵⁵ Also missing for Newman is the indwelling of the Holy Spirit that empowers believers to pursue the holy life, a doctrine that Paul never omitted.⁵⁶ It is true that Clement has surprisingly little to say about the Spirit's transforming presence, just as it is true that he does not connect the person and work of Jesus to statement on justification in chapter 32. But this does not, therefore, mean that the letter is bereft of Christ's work on behalf of the elect. Quite the opposite is the case.

Räisänen points out that Jesus is of great importance to Clement, both in his person ("high priest") and in his work ("our sacrifice"). After weighing Clement's remarks that appear to teach human effort, he states:

> But does this demand, which emphasizes a person's own efforts, perhaps neutralize the statement in 35.1–2, formulated in the indicative, concerning the beauty of the gifts of salvation which we are able to grasp with our understanding? In 36.1, at any rate, it says that salvation was already 'found' in Jesus Christ: Christ is called 'the high priest of our sacrifice' and 'the protector and helper in our weakness'; through him the eyes of our hearts are opened, our darkened mind perceives something of his light, through him the Lord let us

---

54 Lindemann says of 33.1, "'Clement' is here using the style of diatribe, as Paul had done in the transition from Rom. 5 to Rom. 6" ("Paul's Influence on 'Clement' and Ignatius," 13–14). However, Lindemann does continue, "But, unlike Paul, 'Clement' does not put his argument in *Christological* but rather in *theological* terms" (14). This later statement is evaluated in the following paragraphs. On the comparison of Clement's argument of works and justification to Paul in Romans 5–6, see Rudolf Knopf, *Die apostolischen Väter* (Tübingen: Mohr, 1920), 98, and Räisänen, "'Righteousness by Works,'" 213.
55 Newman has made this critique in several personal correspondences we have had. Newman believes that a line can be drawn from Wisdom, to Jesus, to James, and finally to *1 Clement*. For Newman, Clement is within the apostolic faith, but he does not stand in harmony with Paul.
56 Carey C. Newman, "Saved by Faith, Kept by Peace: The Shape of Clement's Ecclesial Ethic—A Response to Father Denis Farkasfalvy," unpublished paper.

'taste the immortal knowledge', and so forth (36.2). Jesus is both the way to salvation and the mediator of salvation. His significance is seen above all from an intellectual point of view: through him gnosis came. But the initiative lies clearly on God's side.[57]

Salvation is found in Christ, according to Clement, and not in the will or works of man. Jesus is the mediator of salvation and through him one can have his mind enlightened and his sins atoned. Clement already made the connection between salvation and atonement patent in 7.4: "Let us fix our eyes on the blood of Christ and understand how precious it is to his Father, being poured out for our salvation, it won for the whole world the grace of repentance." This one verse captures many facets of salvation that cannot be ignored when contemplating soteriology in Clement. Christ's blood, poured out for salvation, "won" the "grace of repentance" for the whole world.[58] Grace is not redefined or misapplied here. The atonement, which stems from the grace of God, makes repentance possible and, in turn, won salvation for those who "repented of their sins" (7.7). So while the person and work of Christ may be missing from the immediate context of chapter 32, it is not outside of Clement's purview, which is apparent when the entire letter is taken into consideration.

One might ask, after all, in what or in whom did Abraham place his faith in chapter 32? Since Clement most likely derived his argument from Paul, given that Paul developed the argument of justification by faith alone from Gen 15, the answer is Christ. Faith has a referent in Clement—it is not a generic faith in God. He makes this abundantly clear in 36.1: "This is the way, dear friends, in which we found our salvation, namely Jesus Christ, the high priest of our offerings, the benefactor and helper of our weakness." One is justified by faith in Jesus Christ.

2.5 Conclusion

Räisänen brings out a point that commentators on Clement and Paul would do well to remember: "If all Pauline statements were measured with equally strict yardsticks as those used on poor Clement's, we should read much more often of the apostle's latent, or not quite subdued, synergism or the like."[59] Clement is not the harbinger of works righteousness in church history as he is often thought to be. He admired Paul and used Paul's arguments, issuing both indicatives and imperatives, and although he is not as particular as some would like, it

---

57 Räisänen, "'Righteousness by Works,'" 209.
58 Repentance is a "central concept" in *1 Clement* (Räisänen, "'Righteousness by Works,'" 210).
59 Räisänen, "'Righteousness by Works,'" 213.

is essential to keep in mind his own context, his specific occasion for writing, and the fact that there is only one letter by which his theology can be judged.

In Clement there is a clear declaration that justification is on the basis of faith alone, while there is also an equally clear declaration that justification is on the basis of works. Is Clement, then, hopelessly adrift in a sea of confusing doctrine? No, he is firmly planted in apostolic soil, understanding well the interplay between faith and works. Clement was neither confused nor contradictory when he wrote to the believers in Corinth—his emphasis on morality flowed from his belief of justification by faith and had the immediate purpose of changing the immature behavior which threatened to destroy their church.

3 "Faith and Love": Ignatius of Antioch

The iconic image of Ignatius of Antioch portrays him as he is best remembered—a bold martyr standing tall while two lions feast on his flesh, one devouring his shoulders, the other his feet.¹ For this bishop, martyrdom was a fitting end to a life of Christian service and it was a final testimony to the churches scattered about Asia Minor of what whole-hearted devotion to Christ must look like. And while his grotesque martyrdom, his advanced ecclesiology, and his robust Christology have received the lion's share of the scholarship, Ignatius also had a great deal to say about soteriology, particularly how salvation relates to Judaism, the Gospel, and martyrdom. His writings show a remarkable dependence on the New Testament and he appeals to Paul twice by name as an example of godly living.² Paul informed Ignatius's mature ecclesiology, gave him the appropriate weapons in his fight against Judaizers and Docetism, and emboldened him as a witness for Christ, even unto death.

Ignatius's soteriology, in particular his view of justification, is compatable with Paul's view. Ignatius adds his own emphasis, however, suggesting that one is justified by faith in and love for Christ.³ "Faith and love" is a formulaic

---

1 That is, the icon of the martyrdom of St. Ignatius.
2 *Eph.* 12.2 and *Rom.* 4.3. The connection to Paul runs much deeper than a few uses of the Apostle's name. Ignatius drew from Paul's writings as well. See Carl Smith, "Ministry, Martyrdom, and Other Mysteries: Pauline Influence on Ignatius of Antioch," in *Paul in the Second Century*, LNTS 412, ed. Michael Bird and Joseph Dodson (New York : T&T Clark, 2011), 37–56; David M. Reis, "Following in Paul's Footsteps: *Mimēsis* and Power in Ignatius of Antioch," in *Trajectories through the New Testament and the Apostolic Fathers*, ed. Andrew Gregory and Christopher Tuckett (New York: Oxford University Press, 2005), 287–306; Harry O. Maier, "The Politics and Rhetoric of Discord and Concord in Paul and Ignatius," in *Trajectories through the New Testament and the Apostolic Fathers*, ed. Andrew Gregory and Christopher Tuckett (New York: Oxford University Press, 2005), 307–24; Andreas Lindemann, *Paulus im ältesten Christentum: Das Bild des Apostels und die Rezeption der paulinischen Theologie in der frühchristlichen Literatur bis Marcion,,* BHT 58 (Tübingen: Mohr, 1979), 82–87, 199–221. Albert Barnett speculated that Ignatius had access to the majority of the Pauline epistles: "It is clear that Ignatius knew 1 Corinthians, Romans, and Ephesians and that he probably knew Galatians, Philippians, and Colossians. He may also have known 2 Corinthians, 1 and 2 Thessalonians, and Philemon" (*Paul Becomes a Literary Influence* [Chicago: Chicago University, 1941], 170).
3 The aim of this chapter is not to suggest that either justification or soteriology was the primary aim of his letters. Willard Swartley, criticizing Theodore Preiss's work ("La mystique de l'imitation du Christ et de l'unité chez Ignace d'Antioche," *RHPR* 17 [1938]: 197–241), said, "Ignatius' theology is not shrunken into the kernel of a quest for personal redemption" (Willard Swartley, "The Imitatio Christi in the Ignatian Letters," *VC* 27 [1973]: 102). It is hard to shrink Ignatius's theology down to any one thing. Suggestions have been made as to what unifying theme

expression that occurs frequently in Ignatius and summarizes his view of salvation. His letters are peppered with other salvific phrases throughout and, even if soteriology is not his chief aim, it is a doctrine that he more or less assumes. Moreover, it is his confidence that he will attain God in his death that sustains him on his journey.

Primarily, this chapter will examine the letters themselves. Because the δικ- word group is infrequently used, the scope will broaden to investigate other ways that Ignatius spoke of salvation with regard to justification. First, Ignatius gave a negative response to justification, that is, what justification is not. He had much to say about the so-called "parting of the ways" that occurred between Judaism and Christianity in the early church and his invective against Jews is well-documented. Second, the positive response is evaluated, looking mostly at Ignatius's use of the word Gospel, the phrase "faith and love," and the meaning of justification in his writings. Finally, Ignatius's martyrdom is examined as the means by which he thought his salvation would be completed.

3.1 Background

Were it not for a small collection of letters written in the twilight of his life, Ignatius would have passed into oblivion.[4] His only preserved writings came while he was chained to ten Roman soldiers, or leopards as he called them (*Ig. Rom* 5.1), en route to his execution. The little data that surfaces about his life or his background in these letters is frustrating. Michael Holmes captures this point well saying, "Just as we become aware of a meteor only when, after traveling silently through space for untold millions of miles, it blazes briefly through the atmosphere before dying in a shower of fire, so it is with Ignatius, bishop of Antioch in Syria."[5] Ignatius shined brightly at the end of a life that is otherwise concealed in darkness.

Little can be pieced together from the limited internal evidence in the letters themselves and not much more is gleaned from what other ancient authors wrote about Ignatius's life. Eusebius recorded that Ignatius was the second after Peter

---

might be found. If pressed, "unity" or "attaining God" could probably serve as the one theme to which the others attend.

4 On his opaque origins, Christine Trevett cleverly quipped, "Ignatius of Antioch, bishop, letter-writer and martyr, appears on the scene like Melchizedek ... without father, mother, genealogy or beginning of days" (*A Study of Ignatius of Antioch in Syria and Asia*, SBEC 29 [Lewiston, NY: Edwin Mellen, 1992], 1).

5 Michael W. Holmes, *The Apostolic Fathers*, 3rd ed. (Grand Rapids: Baker, 2007), 166.

to hold the bishopric in Antioch and that he "became food for wild animals because of his witness for Christ."[6] Jerome, who is probably just echoing Eusebius, wrote, "Ignatius third bishop of the church of Antioch after Peter the apostle, condemned to the wild beasts during the persecution of Trajan, was sent bound to Rome."[7] Even these details are suppositions based on tradition. All that remains are letters that bear the essentials of what Ignatius wanted to communicate in his final weeks, a sort of last will and testament for the churches that he cared about deeply.[8] Very few have challenged that the Ignatius who wrote these epistles was in fact the bishop of Antioch.[9] The question is which of these letters are authentic to him. This uncertainty presents one of the largest problems in Ignatius scholarship, namely which letters belong to Ignatius's hand and which letters belong to later editors.

Manuscripts

The letters of Ignatius are preserved in numerous manuscripts and languages.[10] The *Manuscript of the Greek Original* (G) does not contain the *Epistle to the Ro-*

---

6 Eusebius, *The Church History*, 3.36, trans. Paul L. Maier (Grand Rapids: Kregel, 1999), 123.
7 Jerome, *On Famous Men*, 16. On the dating of Ignatius's martyrdom to the time of Trajan.
8 The question of why Ignatius was condemned as a criminal has vexed scholars for years. If he was condemned as a Christian, then why was he not executed in Antioch? Why the parade to Rome? Was he a citizen making an appeal to Caesar? Nothing seems to suggest that he was. Moreover, if he was a citizen, then why was he thrown to beasts? Citizens were beheaded, not subjected to the more barbaric forms of torture and death. Allen Brent has put forth the most probable theory, suggesting that it was inner politics in the church and not external persecution that led to his arrest and sentence for the capital crime of disturbing the peace. "The answer," Brent replies, "would appear to be that it was normal practice to transport condemned criminals from the provinces in order to offer spectator sport in the Colosseum at Rome" (*Ignatius of Antioch: A Martyr Bishop and the Origin of the Episcopacy* [New York: T&T Clark, 2007], 15). Some have objected to this theory, claiming that individuals were not brought in from the periphery of the Empire for fodder in the Colosseum until Marcus Aurelius (Robert Joly, *Le dossier d'Ignace d'Antioche*, Université Libre de Bruxelles, Faculté de Philosophie et Lettres 69 [Brussels: Éditions de l'Université, 1979], 50–51). Brent calls upon Cicero for proof that from time to time this practice did happen before it became commonplace at the end of the second century (Brent, *Ignatius of Antioch*, 15).
9 Those who do take the minority position that Ignatius was not the author of any of the epistles will be discussed in the following section.
10 The following paragraph borrows heavily from J. B. Lightfoot, *The Apostolic Fathers*, ed. J. R. Harmer (Whitefish, MT: Kessinger, 2003), 99ff. All modern studies take their orientation from Lightfoot's groundbreaking discoveries on Ignatius, and even those who disagree must give a serious account for their departure from Lightfoot's hypothesis.

mans and dates to the medieval period. The *Latin Version* (L) "holds the first place" in regard to its formal equivalent translation. Now lost, the work was likely translated by Robert Grosseteste in the thirteenth century. Should the *Syriac Version* (S) have been preserved intact, it would have provided a helpful "check" against the Greek and Latin versions. Lightfoot claims that this manuscript cannot date later than the fourth or fifth century and that it would have "exhibited the text much nearer to the fountain-head than either the Greek or the Latin."[11] The Syriac is the oldest extant manuscript, not to mention that Ignatius's native tongue could very well have been Syriac, though he most definitely would have been proficient in Greek and probably Latin as well. As it stands, the *Syriac Version* remains in four fragments, hardly able to render an accurate depiction of the originals. Finally, the *Coptic Version* (C) contains only the first six chapters of the *Epistle to the Smyrnaeans*. Lightfoot contends that this is an early manuscript, but because of its limitations, it offers little assistance in determining the original script. The real question concerns what letters are authentic to Ignatius.

There are three recensions of Ignatius's letters: the short recension that contains an abridgment of *Polycarp, Ephesians, Romans*, and a brief passage from *Trallians*; the middle recension that contains *Ephesians, Magnesians, Trallians, Romans, Philadelphians, Smyrnaeans*, and *Polycarp*; and the long recension that contains the seven aforementioned letters with additions as well as six additional letters—to Ignatius from Mary of Cassobola, from Ignatius to the same Mary, to the Tarsians, to the Antiochenes, to Hero, and to the Philippians.[12] The short recension, preserved only in the Syriac, appears to be a truncated version of the authentic letters.[13] The long recension includes six spurious letters that cannot be attributed to Ignatius. These additional letters could be compared to the counterfeit gospels and pseudonymous epistles that arose long after the

---

11 Lightfoot, *Apostolic Fathers*, 99.
12 William Schoedel, "Are the Letters of Ignatius of Antioch Authentic?" *Religious Studies Review* 6 (1980): 196–201. Idem, *A Commentary on the Letters of Ignatius of Antioch*, Hermeneia (Philadelphia: Fortress, 1985), 3–5, has a brief summary of this article. Cf. Mikael Isacson, *To Each Their Own Letter: Structure, Themes, and Rhetorical Strategies in the Letters of Ignatius of Antioch*, Coniectanea Biblica New Testament Series 42 (Stockholm: Almqvist & Wiksell International, 2004), 12–14, for a succinct discussion of authenticity.
13 William Cureton published the short recension in 1845, arguing that the Syriac "most nearly represents what St. Ignatius himself wrote" (*The Ancient Syriac Version of the Epistles of Saint Ignatius* [London: Rivington, 1845], xl). Cf. idem, *Vindiciae Ignatianae* (London: Rivington, 1846). Fairy von Lilienfeld made the case that these letters were abridged for monastic use ("Zur syrischen Kurzrezension der Ignatianen: Von Paulus zur Spiritualität des Mönchtums der Wüste," *Studia Patristica VII*, TU 92 [Berlin: Akademie-Verlag, 1966], 233–47).

death of the apostles. The additional letters supposedly from Ignatius are not accepted by anyone who undertakes the study of Ignatius. It is the middle recension that has garnered the most attention.

Theodor Zahn[14] and J. B. Lightfoot[15] have left an indelible imprint in Ignatian scholarship by arguing almost conclusively that the middle recension is authentic to Ignatius. Though they worked independently of each other, they amassed a strong case for the middle recension that centers on the textual evidence itself.[16] The manuscript evidence is overwhelming with texts having been preserved in Greek, Latin, Syriac, Armenian, Arabic, and Coptic. Snippets of these letters are also quoted by the fathers as early as Irenaeus[17] and Origen[18] and all corroborate the tradition of Ignatius's martyrdom. Aside from the potential anachronism in *Magn.* 8.2,[19] there is nothing within the letters that fit outside the timeframe that Eusebius gives of Ignatius dying under Emperor Trajan in 117 CE.[20]

---

[14] Theodor Zahn, *Ignatius von Antiochien* (Gotha, Germany: F. A. Perthes, 1873).
[15] J. B. Lightfoot, *S. Ignatius, S. Polycarp*, 2 vols. in 3, pt. 2 of *The Apostolic Fathers*, 2nd ed. (London: Macmillan, 1889–90).
[16] Holmes, *Apostolic Fathers*, 172.
[17] Irenaeus nearly quotes from *Rom.* 4.1 in his *Against Heresies:* "Wherefore a certain one of ours said when he had been condemned to the beasts on account of his testimony to God: Because I am grain of Christ, and am ground through the teeth of beasts, so that I may be found to be the pure bread of God" (5.28.4).
[18] Writing in the prologue of his commentary on the Song of Songs, Origen defended a much disputed passage in *Rom.* 7 saying, "Indeed, I remember that one of the saints, by name Ignatius, said of Christ: 'My Love is crucified,' and I do not consider him worthy of censure on this account." In a homily on Luke 6:4 he wrote, "I have found it written beautifully in one of the letters of a certain martyr—I am referring to Ignatius, second bishop of Antioch after St. Peter, who is a persecution fought at Rome with wild beasts" and then goes on to cite *Eph.* 19.1: "the virginity of Mary escaped notice of the ruler of this age" (*Hom. in Luc.* 6.4).
[19] *Magn.* 8.2 reads, "λόγος ἀπὸ σιγῆς προελθών." The "Word coming from silence" has been taken to be a response to Valentinianism. Lightfoot and Zahn both take *Magn.* 8.2 as a corruption in the text. See Schoedel, *Ignatius*, 5. Recently, Thomas Lechner devoted an entire monograph to the theory that the Ignatian corpus dates to the latter half of the second century (*Ignatius Adversus Valentinianos? Chronologische und theologiegeschichtliche Studien zu den Briefen des Ignatius von Antiochien*, Supplements to Vigiliae Christianae 47 [Leiden: Brill, 1999]). He doubts Eusebius's claim that Ignatius was martyred under Trajan, which then allows him to move the middle recension to the time he sees fit based on the internal evidence. Allen Brent gives a very good critique of Lechner's work, taking him to task on Eusebius's chronology, the middle recension postdating the succession list of Hegesippus, and challenging Lechner's supposition that Ignatius's letters reflect a late form of Valentinianism (*Ignatius of Antioch*, 119–34).
[20] Eusebius chronicled that Ignatius suffered his martyrdom under Emperor Trajan (3.36), which would provide a *terminus ad quem* of 117 CE, the year Trajan fell ill and died. There is no good reason to challenge this dating.

Though the majority view is not without its detractors, the middle recension remains the most likely body of authentic letters.[21]

This chapter follows Zahn, Lightfoot, and the myriad of other modern scholars who support the middle recension.[22] There is good reason to think that these seven letters flowed from Ignatius's pen, but these letters do have their limitations. Thomas Robinson, in a word of caution against over reading Ignatius's letters, reminds that "although seven of Ignatius's letter have survived—a fairly rich body of literature from any person of that time—they represent only one glimpse, not several, into his life, for all the letters were written within days of each other (perhaps four of them on the same day) and they address the same concerns."[23] Nevertheless, these seven letters do open a portal into the mind of Ignatius and

---

21 The case that Zahn and Lightfoot so convincingly presented was essentially closed for the better part of a century, but it was reopened in the 1960s and 1970s. (See Allen Brent for a careful critique of each of these attacks on the middle recension [*Ignatius of Antioch*, 95–143]). Reinoud Weijenborg brought the first attack, arguing that the middle recension is nothing more than a shortened version of the long recension (Weijenborg, *Les lettres d'Ignace d'Antioche* [Leiden: Brill, 1969]). Then Joseph Rius-Camps speculated that there were only four original letters (*Rom., Magn., Trall.*, and *Eph.*) with the other letters coming from a later forger (*The Four Authentic Letters of Ignatius, The Martyr*, Orientalia Christiana Analecta 213 [Rome: Pontificium Institutum Orientalium Studiorum, 1980]). The next attack, and the most significant one, was issued by Robert Joly, who believed that all seven letters were later forgeries (*Le dossier d'Ignace d'Antioche*. Note that Rius-Camps's original argument surfaced in 1977 thus predating Joly's). Joly is troubled by a number of anachronisms he finds in the letters, such as the possible use of the *Shepherd of Hermas*, the use of technical terms like Χριστιανισμός, καθολική, and ἐκκλησία, Gnostic influence, and the borrowing of *4 Maccabees*. While these critiques to a greater or lesser degree are worth mentioning, it should be noted that the evidence supporting the middle recension is difficult to overcome. Holmes has rightly noted that these proposed solutions actually raise more problems than they solve (*Apostolic Fathers*, 173). Schoedel, in agreement with Holmes, comments that "the critics ... damaged their own cause by the unduly speculative character of much of their work" (*Ignatius*, 5). And again, "there is nothing in the middle recension of Ignatius clearly anachronistic and ... the cumulative weight of arguments against its authenticity is insufficient to dislodge it from its place in the history of the early church" (*Ignatius*, 7).
22 Schoedel accurately calls the middle recension the "modern consensus" (*Ignatius*, 4).
23 Thomas Robinson, *Ignatius of Antioch and the Parting of the Ways: Early Jewish-Christian Relations* (Peabody, MA: Hendrickson Publishers, 2009), 3. Recently this practice of lumping together all of Ignatius's letters has come under scrutiny. In his work *To Each Their Own Letter*, Isacson sets out to "widen Ignatian research and to point out the individual character of each letter by comparative analysis of the structure, the (main) themes, and the rhetorical strategies employed" (12). His burden is to study each of the letters in their own right. While commendable, it is important to keep in mind the close proximity of time in which these letters were written, which does not give much time for variation in views, much less writing style. If anyone's letters from antiquity could be lumped together and studied as a unit, it would be the letters of Ignatius.

give substantial insight into the life of the church at the dawn of the second century through the eyes of Antioch's bishop.

Antioch

Josephus reports that Antioch "is the metropolis of Syria, and without dispute deserves the place of the third city in the habitable earth that was under the Roman empire, both in magnitude, and other marks of prosperity."[24] The city of Antioch thus had a privileged position in the early church, even though not much is known of the city itself.[25] Raymond Brown and John Meier called Antioch, along with Rome, the "cradles of Catholic Christianity,"[26] and speculated that it was up to individuals like Ignatius to blend the Petrine tradition he had received in Antioch with the Pauline tradition that was already flourishing in western Christianity, particularly in Rome.[27] This perhaps overstates the isolation of the traditions, especially since Ignatius clearly knew of and used Paul,[28] but these authors are correct to highlight the prominence of Antioch in the development of early Christianity. Antioch was the seedbed from which eastern

---

24 Josephus, *Jewish War*, 3.2.4. Antioch was third behind Rome, of course, and Alexandria.
25 For a good treatment of Antioch during this time, see J. H. W. G. Liebeschuetz, *Antioch: City and Imperial Administration in the Later Roman Empire* (Oxford: Clarendon, 1972). See also the recent, thoroughly researched volume by Robinson, *Ignatius of Antioch*, 1–39, which contains a wealth of up-to-date information on the city itself from recent archeological finds, as well as the brand of Judaism that was likely found in the city. But Robinson is quick to point out that Antioch is not a "data-rich environment," which is surprising given the fact that it was one of the most important cities in Ignatius's day (6–7).
26 Raymond E. Brown and John P. Meier, *Antioch and Rome: New Testament Cradles of Catholic Christianity* (New York: Paulist Press, 1983). It is noteworthy to remember that Ignatius is the first to use the phrase "catholic church" (ἡ καθολικὴ ἐκκλησία; *Smyr.* 8.2).
27 Brown and Meier's supposition that the "eastern thrust (about which the NT is totally silent) would have had little or no contact with Paul's thought" must be rejected (*Antioch and Rome*, vii). F. C. Baur was the first to popularize the split between Peter in Paul as seen in the second half of the title of his article "Die Christuspartei in der Korinthischen Gemeinde, der Gegensatz des petrinischen und Christentums in der ältesten Kirche, der Apostel Petrus in Rom," *TübZTh* 4 (1831): 61–206. (See James D. G. Dunn, *The Partings of the Ways: Between Christianity and Judaism and the Significance for the Character of Christianity* [London: SCM Press, 1991], 1–2). To sustain his thesis, Baur had to assert that Acts was written later than is usually assumed in order to smooth over the Peter and Paul schism. Dunn has provocatively said, "The dispute between the Petrine and Pauline parties was thus a dispute between *Jewish particularism* and *Christian universalism*" (*Partings of the Ways*, 2, emphasis original).
28 See n. 2 of this chapter.

Christianity germinated—out of Antioch came many treasured thinkers and pastors, the first of whom was Ignatius.

Determining the composition of the church in that critical hub helps one appreciate Ignatius's theological framework.[29] Robinson conjectures that "perhaps most members of Ignatius's assembly converted to Christianity from paganism—perhaps even Ignatius himself."[30] And yet, given the fair amount of invective against Judaism in his writings, it is safe to assume that there was a fairly large Jewish population in the region, and that he perceived them to be a threat to the believers in the cities where he wrote letters, especially in Philadelphia and Magnesia in Asia Minor, where Judaizers come under his indictment. While it is widely acknowledged that there was a significant Jewish representation in Antioch and in neighboring cities, the consensus is far less certain as to the composition of these Jews. Many scholars have been quick to point out that first- and second-century Judaism was not homogenous.[31] Complicating the issue even further was the new breeds of Jewish-Christians that were emerging all throughout the Mediterranean. These Jewish-Christians ranged from those who entirely jettisoned the Mosaic law to those who maintained large sections of the Torah and imposed these beliefs on others in the church.[32] In Antioch and

---

[29] The discussion is even murkier because Ignatius's view of Judaism in Asia Minor would have been influenced and tainted by his interactions with Jews and Judaizers in Antioch. Yet, the only surviving evidence comes from letters written to churches in Asia Minor. There is nothing explicitly stating his view of Jews in his bishopric. Thus, it cannot be safely assumed that these letters uncover the situation in Antioch—this goes beyond the evidence. However, to think that his prior dealings with the Jews did not color the letters he did write to other congregations would be just as wrong. The setting in Antioch is important for understanding his response to Judaism that is extant.

[30] Robinson, *Ignatius of Antioch and the Parting of the Ways*, 17.

[31] Dunn asserts, "In short, the concept of an orthodox or normative Judaism for the period prior to 70 CE is, to say the least, very questionable" (*Partings of the Ways*, 18). The diversity of Judaism continued well after the Temple lay in ruins. See also Richard Bauckham, *The Jewish World Around the New Testament* (Tübingen: Mohr Siebeck, 2008), 175–92.

[32] Brown and Meier give these four possibilities: group one consists of Jewish Christians and their Gentile converts who insisted on full observance of the Mosaic law; group two consists of Jewish Christians and their Gentile converts who did not insist on circumcision but did require the keeping of some Jewish observances; group three consists of Jewish Christians and their Gentile converts who did not insist on circumcision or observance of the Jewish food laws; and group four consists of Jewish Christians and their Gentile converts who did not insist on circumcision, food laws, or a significance of the Jewish cults and feasts (*Antioch and Rome*, 2–8). In reality, there are likely more perspectives possible along this spectrum.

Asia Minor it would seem that the Jewish Christians were insisting on keeping at least a portion of the law, much to the chagrin of their bishop.[33]

3.2 The Negative: What Justification is not

Ignatius reveals a lot about his positive view of justification in his negative response to Judaizers. He has become a crucial player in the debate of the so-called "parting of the ways" because of his close proximity to the apostles and because he makes several stark comments about Judaism. C. K. Barrett has said that one might suppose that Ignatius "is fruitful ground for those who would study the interrelation of Judaism and Christianity in and just after the New Testament period," but he gives a word of caution because of the complexity of these issues, particularly pinpointing the false teaching(s) that he was combating.[34] The relevance of Ignatius in this debate has less to do with how accurate he was in portraying his opponents and much more to do with *his perception* of them.[35] There are two things in play for Ignatius as it regards Judaism—first, there was Judaism of the Old Testament which had prepared the way for Christianity, and second, there were Judaizers who tried to mix former Jewish

---

[33] It is important to remember that even within certain cities one would not find homogeneity in thought or practice. Simply because there were large numbers of Jewish-Christians in a given town would certainly not mean that they were of one accord as to the place of the Mosaic Law. Still, the aim here is not to assert dogmatically the makeup of the Christians, but rather to try to uncover Ignatius's attitude towards Judaism in relation to Christianity.

[34] C. K. Barrett, "Jews and Judaizers in the Epistles of Ignatius," in *Jews, Greeks and Christians: Religious Cultures in Late Antiquity—Essays in Honor of William David Davies* (Leiden: Brill, 1976), 220.

[35] Judith Lieu's volume *Image and Reality* is immensely helpful in this regard. She maintains that there is disparity between the way that the second-century authors imagined their Jewish counterparts and the reality of what those Jews believed and practiced (*Image and Reality: The Jews in the World of the Christians in the Second Century* [Edinburgh: T&T Clark, 1996]). "The image," says Lieu, "is the presentation, that which each text projects concerning Jews or Judaism; the reality is the actual position of Jews and Jewish communities in the context from which the literature comes, both in themselves and in relation to the Christian contemporaries" (2). The argument goes even a further step: "the 'image' they project ... in turn becomes part of the 'reality' for the next generation" (12). The second-century authors had a concept of Jews and Judaism that is found in their works. Regardless of how accurate this image was, it became a reality as it was projected to their followers. Even if Ignatius was wrong about the Judaizers he opposed, he is still giving a wealth of information about his perception, and his warnings to the believers in these churches reveal both a positive and negative affirmation of what he believes.

practices with their new Christian faith. He is far more favorable to the former than to the latter, even though he sometimes speaks of Judaism in general when he seems to be referring to Judaizers in particular (e. g., *Phld.* 6.1). His comments unveil, at least to some extent, the Jewish-Christian communities he was writing. To overlook the influence of Judaizers in Ignatius's writings would be a mistake because Ignatius reveals a lot about what he affirms about Christian doctrine in his brief polemic against them.

Ignatius's Opponents

A perennial debate in Ignatius scholarship concerns what group or groups provoked such sharp rhetoric from Antioch's bishop. There is wide agreement that Ignatius vehemently opposed Judaizers and Docetism. The question is this: were these two separate groups he was warning against or were these antagonists Jewish-Docetists? While most people who work on Ignatius fall under one of these broad categories, no consensus has been reached.[36] Given the fact that there is no overlap between these two groups in his letters, the scales

---

[36] Many scholars from a previous era opt for one group: J. B. Lightfoot, *The Apostolic Fathers II. S. Ignatius, S. Polycarp* (London: Macmillan, 1889), calls it "Doceto-judaism"; Theodor Zahn, *Ignatii et Polycarpi epistulae martyria fragmenta* (Leipzig: Hinrichs, 1876); Walter Bauer, *Die Apostolischen Väter*, HNT 18 (Tübingen: Mohr, 1920); Barrett, "Jews and Judaizers in the Epistles of Ignatius"; Leslie W. Barnard, *Studies in the Apostolic Fathers and their Background* (New Haven: Yale University, 1966), 24–26. Many modern scholars hold to two groups: P. J. Donahue, "Jewish Christianity in the Letters of Ignatius of Antioch," *VC* 32 (1978): 81–93; P. Meinhold, *Studien zu Ignatius von Antiochen*, Veröffentlichung des Instituts für Europäische Geschichte 97 (Wiesbaden, Germany: Franz Steiner, 1979); Charles Munier, "Où en est la question d'Ignace d'Antioche?" *Aufstieg und Niedergang der Römischen Welt II* 27 (1993): 404–13; Matti Myllykoski, "Wild Beasts and Rabid Dogs: The Riddle of the Heretics in the Letters of Ignatius," in *The Formation of the Early Church*, ed. Jostein Ådna, WUNT 183 (Tübingen: Mohr Siebeck, 2005), 344. Christine Trevett offers a unique third position. She postulates that Ignatius battled three groups: Docetism, Judaism, and a charismatic group that was protesting episcopalianism ("Prophecy and Anti-Episcopal Activity: A Third Error combated by Ignatius," *JEH* 34 [1983]: 1–13). Myllykoski summarizes the debate well: "The countless different readings of the Ignatian polemics against false teachings have led to frustrating results. Strictly speaking, there is no agreement on anything. There are several possible labels that may be attached to the group or groups of Christians that Ignatius opposed: Gnostic Docetists, Cerinthians or Ebionites, Judaizing Docetists, Judaizing Gnostics, Docetists who debated on the basis of the Old Testament, Judaizers, zealots for Mosaic Law and so on" (Myllykoski, "Wild Beasts and Rabid Dogs," 351).

tip in favor of there being two distinct groups that received his rebuke.[37] Docetism bears the brunt of his attack in *Eph.* (7–8, 18), *Trall.* (9–10), and *Smyr.* (1–7), whereas Judaism is assailed in *Phld.* and *Magn.*

Docetism was not a new heresy in the early second century. There are traces of Docetism in the New Testament, meaning that the apostles also had to combat misconceptions of Christ's flesh. The Johannine corpus gives special insight into the prevalence of docetic views in the early church (1 John 4:1–6; 2 John 1:7), and Docetism may account for the inclusion of Jesus eating the fish in John 21.[38] Paul also had to correct deviant Christologies in the church at Colossae (Col 1). As a result of a docetic heresy in churches he had visited or heard reports of, Ignatius gave a strong statement affirming that Jesus came from a human and divine lineage and that his flesh was real:

> I glorify Jesus Christ, the God who made you so wise, for I observed that you are established in an unshakable faith, having been nailed, as it were, to the cross of the Lord Jesus Christ in both body and spirit, and firmly established in love by the blood of Christ, totally convinced with regard to our Lord that he is truly of the family of David with respect to human descent, Son of God with respect to the divine will and power, truly born of a virgin, baptized by John in order that all righteousness might be fulfilled by him, truly nailed in the flesh for us under Pontius Pilate and Herod the tetrarch (from its fruit we derive our existence, that is, from his divinely blessed suffering), in order that he might raise a banner for the ages through his resurrection for his saints and faithful people, whether among Jews or among Gentiles, in the one body of his church (*Smyr.* 1.1–2).[39]

The overuse of adverbs intentionally highlights the reality of the incarnation. The triple repetition of "truly" (ἀληθῶς) emphasizes the legitimate humanity of Christ. The person of Jesus Christ as God and man animated Ignatius's life

---

[37] It cannot be, as some suggest, that Ignatius was confused about Judaism to the point that Judaism was just an imprecise synonymy for heresy in general (see Wilhelm Lütgert, *Amt und Geist im Kampf: Studien zur Geschichte des Urchristentums*, BFCT [Gütersloh: Bertelsmann, 1911], 163–64).

[38] John's authorship of 2 and 3 John is hotly contested. Nevertheless, even a late date of these epistles would make them near contemporaries with Ignatius's letters. Both the Ignatius and Johannine corpuses testify that Docetism was present by the turn of the second century.

[39] Holmes, *Apostolic Fathers*, 249. Cf. *Trall.* 9. Quotations from Ignatius in this chapter are taken from Holmes, *Apostolic Fathers*. Other critical editions include *Lettres*, ed. P. T. Camelot, 4th ed., SC 10 (Paris: Cerf, 1969) and Bart Ehrman, *The Apostolic Fathers*, vol. 1, *I Clement. II Clement. Ignatius. Polycarp. Didache*, LCL 24 (Cambridge, MA: Harvard University Press, 2003).

and ministry.⁴⁰ As Torrance makes plain, "Christ fills the whole field of vision, and it is only through Christ that the Father is known."⁴¹

For the purpose of this chapter, it should be noted that Ignatius's harangue against Docetism was primarily salvific. If Jesus did not have a body, then his crucifixion was a charade and vicarious atonement was not achieved. It was necessary for Jesus to suffer and die in the flesh, an idea he likely drew from 1 Peter (3:18, 4:1). Ignatius's harshest language usually came when he perceived that someone had tampered with matters of salvation. For this reason he also tussled with the Judaizers.⁴²

Of the seven letters, only two of them contain significant interactions against Judaizers—*Philadelphians* and *Magnesians*.⁴³ Ignatius became aware of the problems in these churches on his death march to Rome and he did not mince his words when he charged them, "if anyone expounds Judaism to you, do not listen to him" (*Phld.* 6.1).⁴⁴ Judaism, for Ignatius, was now antithetical to Christianity—the two faiths stood as polar opposites to one another. Christians could not dabble in Judaism, and Jews could not retain their Judaism and assent to Christianity. These faiths may share a common heritage but only insofar as Judaism recognized that Christianity is the anticipated hope of the Jews.

---

40 Larry Hurtado thinks that these Christological statements in Ignatius laid the groundwork for the Apostle's Creed. He says, "[Ignatius's] penchant for confessional catenas of events of Jesus' human existence prefigures and probably influenced the sort of creedal tradition that received classic expression in the Apostles' Creed" (*Lord Jesus Christ: Devotion to Jesus in Earliest Christianity* [Grand Rapids: Wm. B. Eerdmans, 2003], 640).
41 Torrance, *The Doctrine of Grace in the Apostolic Fathers*, 57.
42 The word Ignatius uses is ἰουδαΐζειν (*Magn.* 10.3).
43 Schoedel identifies the opponents of Ignatius in these letters as "Judaizing Christians," saying, "*Phd.* 5–9 has many affinities with *Mag.* 8–10. Both passages are concerned with the problem of Judaizing Christians" (Schoedel, *Ignatius of Antioch*, 200). Michael Goulder detects an element of Judaizing in more than just *Phld.* and *Magn.* He thinks, for instance, that Ignatius's praise of the church in Ephesus (that no αἵρεσις resides there) refers to their freedom from Judaizing (Goulder, "Ignatius' 'Docetists,'" *VC* 53 [1999]: 17). Another example comes from *Trall.* 6 where Ignatius "implies that the 'heretics' have been bragging about their visions of the angels and principalities in heaven." The visions are "the stuff of all Jewish visions," according to Goulder, "from 1 Enoch to the Hekhalot writings" (18). Goulder admits that the evidence in *Eph.*, *Trall.*, and *Smyr.* rests on inference, but the threat of Judaizing was certainly ubiquitous in the early church as is overwhelmingly clear from the New Testament and early church fathers. While a hint of Judaism may legitimately be found in these other letters, the statement above stands that only in *Phld.* and *Magn.* does Ignatius significantly cross swords with Judaism.
44 Schoedel says, "The verb 'expound' (ἑρμηνεύῃ), however, suggests that such 'Judaism' is seen as the result of a misinterpretation of the prophets, that is, scripture (cf. *Phd.* 8.2; 9.1)" (*Ignatius of Antioch*, 202).

"We Love the Prophets"

Despite his railings against Judaism, Ignatius did acknowledge that Christianity sprang out of Judaism, even though he did say, "Christianity did not believe in Judaism, but Judaism in Christianity" (*Magn.* 10.3).[45] By this phrase he shows the superiority of Christianity over and above Judaism. How, then, did Ignatius find any continuity in what he thought were vastly different faiths? Most notably, Ignatius spoke favorably of the prophets:

> And we also love the prophets, because they anticipated the gospel in their preaching and set their hope on him and waited for him; because they also believed in him, they were saved, since they belong to the unity centered in Jesus Christ, saints worthy of love and admiration, approved by Jesus Christ and included in the gospel of our shared hope (*Phld.* 5.2).[46]

The prophets link Judaism in the Old Testament and Christianity in the New Testament. They foresaw the coming of Jesus Christ and they "set their hope on him," "believed in him," and "they were saved" because "they belonged to the unity centered in Jesus Christ."[47] It was their "anticipation of the gospel," namely the coming and work of Jesus (*Phld.* 9.2), and their faith in this Christ, that secured their salvation and made them "saints worthy of love." Together the faithful Jews of old and the Christians of late had a "shared hope" in the gospel and in this way shared a common faith. His praise of Judaism stops here, however.

"Parting of the Ways"?

James D. G. Dunn made famous the rift between Jews and Christians in the early church with the memorable phrase "the partings of the ways."[48] He contends

---

[45] Virginia Corwin thinks that Ignatius is responding to the "slogan" of his opposition who would say that "Christianity bases its faith on Judaism" (*St. Ignatius and Christianity in Antioch* [New Haven: Yale University Press, 1960], 58).

[46] Holmes, *Apostolic Fathers*, 241. Cf. *Phld.* 9.2, *Magn.* 8.2.

[47] Note well that belief is the only condition listed for the prophets' salvation. Even though they were Jews, Ignatius does not list any Jewish distinctive (e.g., circumcision) as a prerequisite necessary for their salvation. The Jews were saved, according to Ignatius, because they believed in the coming Savior, Jesus Christ. In *Magn.* 8.2 he said, "For the most godly prophets lived in accordance with Christ Jesus."

[48] Dunn, *The Partings of the Ways*. Discussion, really debate, over Jewish-Christian relations in the early church is endless. Library stacks are full of books on this issue and there is no sign of

that "Christianity's origins within second Temple Judaism and its emergence from within that matrix was the central issue for our understanding of the beginnings of Christianity."⁴⁹ In order to understand Christianity, one must first appreciate the historical milieu from which it emerged, which in the case of Christianity, was Judaism. Christianity, then, is to be defined and delimited against a backdrop of Judaism, though it is important to reiterate that Judaism was not monolithic at this time, and neither was Christianity for that matter.⁵⁰

Dunn focuses his attention almost solely on the New Testament and does not venture out into church history to wager a hypothesis as to when the ways finally parted.⁵¹ No one has yet been able to identify a particular moment when Christianity and Judaism finally split, and some contend that the ways never truly parted.⁵² At best the lines are blurred. But as far as Ignatius was concerned, the ways were not parting, they were parted. "It is utterly absurd," said Ignatius, "to profess Jesus Christ and to Judaize" (ἄτοπόν ἐστιν Ἰησοῦν Χριστὸν λαλεῖν καὶ ἰουδαΐζειν; *Magn.* 10).⁵³ Ignatius was not combating Judaism so much as he had

---

this discussion abating. Because of the complicated nature of the debate, Anders Klostergaard Petersen has called for an end of the "partings" metaphor ("At the End of the Road—Reflections on a Popular Scholarly Metaphor," in *The Formation of the Early Church*, ed. Jostein Ådna, WUNT 183 [Tübingen: Mohr Siebeck, 2005]). Petersen outlines the history of the metaphor and finds that James Parkes was the first to use the "partings" metaphor in a manner similar to modern scholarship. See James W. Parkes, *The Conflict of the Church and the Synagogue: A Study in the Origins of Antisemitism* (London: Soncino, 1934). Cf. Judith Lieu, "'The Parting of the Ways': Theological Construct or Historical Reality?" *JSNT* 56 (1994): 101–19.
49 Dunn, *Parting of the Ways*, xi.
50 Robinson, *Ignatius of Antioch and the Parting of the Ways*, 17.
51 Dunn did edit a follow-up volume to *Parting of the Ways* with *Jews and Christians: The Parting of the Ways A.D. 70–135*, ed. James D. G. Dunn (Tübingen: Mohr Siebeck, 1992). Remarkably, not a chapter in that volume is devoted to Ignatius. This oversight is surprising given the fact that Ignatius fits snugly in this timeframe and had an important perspective on Judaism.
52 See Adam H. Becker and Annette Yoshiko Reed, eds., *The Ways that Never Parted: Jews and Christians in Late Antiquity and the Early Middle Ages* (Tübingen: Mohr Siebeck, 2003). The contributors to this volume contend that the split between Judaism and Christianity is "a far messier reality than ... the Parting model" allows (2). Even well into the Middle Ages there was often not a clear demarcation between the two. The problem of Christians proselytizing to Judaism would continue for centuries, even in Antioch. John Chrysostom chastised this practice in his *Discourse against Judaizing Christians*. See Robert L. Wilken, *John Chrysostom and the Jews: Rhetoric and Reality in the Late Fourth Century* (Berkeley: University of California Press, 1983).
53 In the case of *Magn.* 10.3, BDAG defines ἄτοπος ἐστιν as "it is wrong, absurd" (s.v. "ἄτοπος"). Holmes's translation of this phrase as "utterly absurd" captures the tone of Ignatius well (*Apostolic Fathers*, 209). Reed and Becker comment that this phrase in *Magn.* 10.3 often serves "as the representative example for those who claim that 'Jew' and 'Christian' became clear-cut and mutually exclusive religious identities in the first century CE. However, counter-examples abound,

locked horns with Judaizers. Christianity was of little value to the person who, after becoming a believer, turned aside to Judaism or added Jewish practices to his faith. Thus, as Robinson has remarked, "The definition of the boundaries separating one religion from another was a pressing and necessary business for him. His reflection on these issues is perhaps his most important contribution to the development of the Christian movement."[54]

Jewish Practices

Debates over circumcision had deep roots in Ignatius's hometown of Antioch. When addressing the topic of circumcision, Dunn, relying on Josephus, remarked, "in Syria, of which Antioch was the capital, many Gentiles had 'judaized' and become 'mixed up' with the Jews during the first century."[55] The first century saw many Gentiles "judaized" and there is a fair amount of New Testament witness that Gentile Christians were encouraged to keep portions of the Old Testament law in Antioch (Gal 2:11–14). Thus, Ignatius was no stranger to ongoing quarrel between Jews and Christians, but he was adamant that Christians did not need to adhere to Jewish practices. A lingering question is whether or not these problems persisted in the churches of Asia Minor as well.

Ignatius had surprisingly little to say about circumcision given the fact that the Apostle Paul spent a fair amount of time discussing circumcision and other "works of the law" (ἔργα νόμου).[56] In fact, direct reference to the Mosaic law in Ignatius is scarce. Myllykoski notes, "if Mosaic Law was the issue, it is very difficult to understand why Ignatius, a keen admirer of Paul, does not refer at all to any question concerning the practice of the Torah."[57] Yet circumcision does ap-

---

both from this period and well beyond" (Becker and Reed, *The Ways that Never Parted*, 2 n. 6). Counter-examples may abound, but they do not lessen *Ignatius's belief* that the two were indeed "clear-cut and mutually exclusive."

54 Robinson, *Ignatius of Antioch and the Parting of the Ways*, 18. Perhaps he overstates his case. Not to detract from the importance of Ignatius's role in defining Christianity apart from Judaism, but his ecclesiology and Christology are certainly more important to the formation of nascent Christianity. Nevertheless, Robinson is correct to assert that "the distinction between Judaism and Christianity is sharper than the trends in the current debate have admitted, and that Ignatius's pointed assessment of Judaism is much more dismissive and uncompromising" (Robinson, *Ignatius of Antioch and the Parting of the Ways*, 6).
55 Dunn, *Parting of the Ways*, 125. He is citing Josephus, *Jewish War*, 2.463 ff; 7.45.
56 This phrase, highly contested amongst scholars, is found eight times in Paul (Gal. 2:16 [3x], 3:2, 5, 10; Rom 3:20, 28).
57 Myllykoski, "Wild Beasts and Rabid Dogs," 354 n. 44.

pear in one of the most controversial lines in all his letters: "But if anyone expounds Judaism to you, do not listen to him. For it is better to hear about Christianity from a man who is circumcised than about Judaism from one who is not" (Ἐὰν δέ τις Ἰουδαϊσμὸν ἑρμηνεύῃ ὑμῖν, μὴ ἀκούετε αὐτοῦ. ἄμεινον γάρ ἐστιν παρὰ ἀνδρὸς περιτομὴν ἔχοντος Χριστιανισμὸν ἀκούειν ἢ παρὰ ἀκροβύστου Ἰουδαϊσμόν; *Phld.* 6.1).

What, then, is to be made of his comment in *Phld.* 6.1? Was there a problem with circumcision in Philadelphia as there had been in Antioch?[58] Shaye Cohen singles out this verse in his article "Judaism without Circumcision and 'Judaism' without 'Circumcision' in Ignatius"[59] in which he seeks to "rebut the claim that Philadelphians 6:1 is evidence for the presence of foreskinned men within the Jewish community of the city."[60] Cohen is probably right that this verse yields little about the Jewish community there.[61] Nevertheless, Ignatius's point remains. Circumcision does not matter and is not necessary for salvation. The circumcised man, presumably a Jew, who expounds Christianity should be heard because he is no longer relying on his circumcision as necessary for his salvation. However, the Gentile in their midst who expounds Judaism but is not himself circumcised, is entirely confused. He does not understand either Christianity or Judaism. But the circumcised man, who was probably born a Jew, can become a Christian and accurately portray his new faith, regardless of his circumcision.

Circumcision, in other words, could be a sign that someone was headed in the wrong direction—towards Judaism and away from Christianity. Schoedel provides the best solution for this verse, stating, "What Ignatius is saying is this: Any entanglement with Judaism is unfortunate, but how much better to have moved—as especially the apostles did (cf. *Mag.* 9.1)—from Judaism to Christianity

---

[58] Of possible note is Rev 3:9, "Behold, I will make those of the synagogue of Satan who say that they are Jews and are not, but lie—behold, I will make them come and bow down before your feet and they will learn that I have loved you" (ESV). If a date of 90s CE is taken for Revelation, then there would be a mere two decades separating *Philadelphians* and Revelation.
[59] Shaye J. D. Cohen, "Judaism without Circumcision and 'Judaism' without 'Circumcision' in Ignatius," in *The Significance of Yavneh and Other Essays in Jewish Hellenism*, TSAJ 136 (Tübingen: Mohr Siebeck, 2010). This article originally appeared as "Judaism without Circumcision and 'Judaism' without 'Circumcision' in Ignatius," *HTR* 95 (2002): 395–415.
[60] Cohen, "Judaism without Circumcision," 473. He offers four possible interpretations. First, the Judaism Ignatius speaks of is not Judaism at all—"Ignatius' 'Judaism' is what we would call 'Christianity.'" Second, it is "far more likely that [the foreskinned man] was a gentile member of the Christian community." Third, "circumcision" and "foreskin" were metaphors for "Judaism" and "not-Judaism" respectively. Fourth, both preachers in Ignatius's creation were "invented for the sake of an effective antithesis" (473–74).
[61] Cohen, "Judaism without Circumcision," 475.

than in the reverse direction."[62] The key for Ignatius was movement away from Judaism, to the point where all ties were severed. The reason he makes little reference to the Mosaic law is because his readers were themselves confused about the law, which is why an uncircumcised Gentile could expound Judaism without realizing his inconsistency. Ignatius did not want Christians to mix with Judaism at all and he made the most obvious connection he could think of—circumcision.

The real point behind this enigma comes in the next verse. "But if either of them fails to speak about Jesus Christ, I look on them as tombstone and graves of the dead" (ἐὰν δὲ ἀμφότεροι περὶ Ἰησοῦ Χριστοῦ μὴ λαλῶσιν, οὗτοι ἐμοὶ στῆλαί εἰσιν καὶ τάφοι νεκρῶν; *Phld.* 6.1). The critical thing for Ignatius was to speak of Christ. Circumcision muddied the waters and distorted the nature of Christianity. Anything that sets itself apart from salvation in Christ was to be rejected. For the believers in Philadelphia, this seems to have been a form of Judaism, albeit a skewed form, that would distract them from grace. Christ is the centerpiece of salvation and not circumcision.

Circumcision may not have played a frontline part in Ignatius's attack against Judaism but another aspect of the Mosaic law did—Sabbath keeping. Observing the Sabbath was another unique boundary mark of the Jews that set them apart from the Gentile neighbors in every city. The signal that a person moved from Judaism to Christianity was that they no longer kept the Sabbath but they now observe the Lord's day.[63] Ignatius said, "If, then, those who had lived according to ancient practices came to the newness of hope, no longer keeping the Sabbath but living in accordance with the Lord's day … (then) how can we possibly live without him, whom even the prophets, who were his disciples in the Spirit, were expecting as their teacher?" (*Magn.* 9.1–2). The argument is that one will know that a person has moved from "ancient practices" (παλαιοῖς πράγμασιν), that is Jewish practices, to the "newness of hope" (καινότητα ἐλπίδος), that is Christianity, because of their allegiance to the Lord's day. Worshipping on the Lord's day shows that they "came to believe" the "mystery" of Jesus' death and resurrection and are "found to be disciples of Jesus Christ," just as "the prophets … were his disciples in the Spirit" long before his advent (*Magn.* 9.1–2). Disregard for the Lord's day in order to worship on the Sabbath is more than just the difference in a day–at the heart is one's belief in the death and resurrection of Jesus.

---

[62] Schoedel, *Ignatius of Antioch*, 202–3.
[63] Smith makes the point, "For Ignatius, observing the Sabbath was tantamount to departing from the faith (*Magn.* 9–10)" ("Ministry, Martyrdom, and Other Mysteries," 48).

If one statement sums up Ignatius's position that Judaism is antithetical to the Gospel, it is the comment he makes in *Magn.* 8.1: "For if we continue to live in accordance with Judaism, we admit that we have not received grace" (εἰ γὰρ μέχρι νῦν κατὰ Ἰουδαϊσμὸν ζῶμεν, ὁμολογοῦμεν χάριν μὴ εἰληφέναι). Assent to Jewish practices nullifies Christianity because it adds to salvation by grace. For those in Magnesia, Sabbath observance was the issue. In Philadelphia, there does seem to be some problem with circumcision and the appeal to the authority of the "archives." Ignatius could not be clearer—one cannot Judaize and profess that he had received grace.

Ignatius, Paul, and Judaism

One major concern remains. Was Ignatius following Paul in his critique of Judaism? This question has raised much debate and many scholars think that there is quite a bit of discontinuity between Paul and Ignatius on their handling of Judaism and Christianity. Carl Smith, for instance, has said, "Paul writing nearly a half century earlier, seems to portray a situation of greater continuity between Judaism and Christianity."[64] And again, Ignatius "evidences an unrestrained supersessionism."[65] This may be so. Ignatius may not have rummaged through the Old Testament for theological proof and his arguments against Judaism were not as sophisticated as the Apostle's (which should come as no surprise given that Paul was a Jew and Ignatius was most likely a Gentile), but both of their arguments move in the same direction. Paul warned against Jewish practices as a means of earning salvation; Ignatius, in a similar vein, chastised Christians who partook in Jewish practices and advised them that continuing on that path would signal that they have never received grace (*Magn.* 8.1).

Scholars drive too sharp of a wedge between Paul and Ignatius.[66] Judith Lieu, one of the finest scholars on the interrelations of Judaism and Christianity in the early church, claims, "Ignatius opposes not law and grace but *Judaism* and

---

[64] Smith, "Ministry, Martyrdom, and Other Mysteries," 48.
[65] Smith, "Ministry, Martyrdom, and Other Mysteries," 44. Adding to this, C. K. Barrett writes that for Ignatius, "Christianity has now replaced Judaism." He also states, "We must not assume that for Ignatius 'to judaize' meant exactly what it did for Paul" (Barrett, "Jews and Judaizers in the Epistles of Ignatius," 221).
[66] A notable exception to those who pit Ignatius against Paul is Donahue, who argues rightly, "Ignatius is the product of a line of development which goes directly back to Paul and to his law-free gospel" (Donahue, "Jewish Christianity in Ignatius' Letters," 92).

grace."⁶⁷ It is unlikely that Ignatius would have made such a differentiation. He is aware of Jewish particulars (circumcision and Sabbath), and he makes no qualms about highlighting these aspects of the Jewish law when strictly forbidding his readers from following Judaism. For him, Judaism and law are inseparable—to follow Judaism was to practice the law.⁶⁸ Just before this quotation Lieu states, "To continue to *live according to Judaism* is not just to misunderstand the implications of the Gospel, it is to put oneself outside the compass of the salvation it offers."⁶⁹ Lieu is correct that living according to Judaism places one outside the compass of salvation for Ignatius. It is not clear, though, that Ignatius would have thought that Judaism meant something other than following the law.⁷⁰

At the heart of the issue, then, is justification, even if it not explicitly stated. How, in Ignatius's mind, were individuals saved? How could people become Christians, a term coined in Antioch (Acts 11:26)? The answer was most definitely not by becoming a Jew or by blending Jewish practices in with the Christian faith. Donahue is correct to say, "For both Ignatius and Paul, salvation comes either from the law or from Christ. The Christian who accepts obedience to the law as the path to salvation has, from the perspective which Paul and Ignatius share, deserted Christ."⁷¹ Not only are people not justified by obedience to the law, but practicing Judaism could actually prevent salvation (*Magn.* 8.1). Why else did Ignatius warn, "If anyone expounds Judaism to you, do not listen to him"? (*Phld.* 6.1). Why did he say that following Judaism demonstrated that a person has not received grace? (*Magn.* 8.1). And why is it "utterly absurd to profess

---

67 Lieu, *Image and Reality*, 29, emphasis original. Schoedel comments, "It is more debatable whether the Judaizers of Philadelphia were interested in the observance of Jewish laws and customs. I shall suggest that it was the idea of Judaism rather than its practice that appealed to them and that this manifested itself principally in a display of exegetical expertise" (Schoedel, *Ignatius*, 200–01).
68 Charles Thomas Brown rightly identifies these Judaizers saying, "It is reasonable to assume that these opponents are those favoring judaizing interpretations *and practices* over the faith in the gospel" (Brown, *The Gospel and Ignatius of Antioch*, Studies in Biblical Literature 12 [New York: Peter Lang, 2000], 22, emphasis added).
69 Lieu, *Image and Reality*, 29, emphasis original.
70 It is possible, one supposes, that following Judaism could have ethnic ramifications. But this could not be said of Gentiles. In order for a Gentile to become a Jew, to Judaize (which is at the heart of Ignaitus's condemnation of Judaism in his letters), they would have to comply with aspects of the Mosaic law. He speaks of "practicing Judaism" (ἰουδαΐζειν). Holmes's translation of ἰουδαΐζειν as "practice Judaism" expresses the idea (Holmes, *Apostolic Fathers*, 209). BDAG defines ἰουδαΐζω as to "live as one bound by Mosaic ordinances or traditions" (s.v. "ἰουδαΐζω"). Ignatius would not permit this.
71 Donahue, "Jewish Christianity in Ignatius's Letters," 85–86.

Jesus Christ and to practice Judaism"? (*Magn.* 10.3). What was it about Judaism that worried Ignatius to the point that he wanted Christians to turn a deaf ear to those attempting to Judaize? For Ignatius, the Judaizers were harmful because they tainted Paul's message of grace, which formed the basis of his doctrine of justification. Salvation for them entailed some allegiance to Judaism through adherence to at least portions of the law. This flew in the face of salvation by grace that was based on the imperishable, finished work of Christ (*Phld.* 9.2). Ignatius did not just spend his time arguing with the churches he visited about what salvation is not—he also said a great deal in the affirmative.

3.3 The Positive: Justification in Ignatius

Ignatius's polemical tone against Judaizers was fueled by his passion for Christian doctrine, and in particular his doctrine of salvation.[72] Soteriology was constantly at his pen's tip and all the major themes in Ignatius can be traced back to his conception of salvation, from martyrdom to the bishopric. Obedience to the bishop was about obedience to God and martyrdom was a means of completing one's salvation. He is also at times overt about soteriology, speaking of justification, belief, and the Gospel. These soteriological motifs find a summary statement in a common phrase he liked to use—faith and love.

Faith and Love

To the Smyrnaeans Ignatius wrote: "for faith and love are everything" (τὸ γὰρ ὅλον ἐστὶν πίστις καὶ ἀγάπη; *Smyrn.* 6.1). Faith and love form the basis for Christianity as far as Ignatius was concerned and nothing is preferable to them

---

[72] Many scholars do not see doctrinal cohesion in Ignatius. Richard Bower, however, demonstrates with great skill how seemingly diverse streams of thought converge into one main river in Ignatius's writings ("The Meaning of ΕΠΙΤΥΓΧΑΝΩ in the Epistles of St. Ignatius of Antioch," *VC* 28 [1974]: 1–14). The one idea under which all the others coalesce is "attaining God" (ἐπιτυχεῖν/τυχεῖν). He argues, "ἐπιτυχεῖν and τυχεῖν have in Ignatius a pronounced soteriological focus. God himself is the reward and prize" (4). Bower convincingly shows how union, martyrdom, ecclesiology, and a host of other ideas in Ignatius fit under the notion of "attaining God," an idea rich with soteriological overtones. As Bower says, "It is important to note that the linking of grace and mercy to 'attaining to God' bring 'attaining' closer to the realm of redemption. Whatever 'attaining to God' means for Ignatius, it is in some way made possible through divine grace and mercy" (3).

(*Magn.* 1). Everything could be summed up in these two things—faith in and love for Jesus Christ and others. This he makes plain in *Eph.* 14.1:

> None of these things escapes your notice, if you have perfect faith and love toward Jesus Christ. For these are the beginning and the end of life: faith is the beginning and love is the end, and the two, when they exist in unity, are God. Everything else that contributes to excellence follows from them.[73]

Faith is the ἀρχή and love is the τέλος. Of the sixty-four occurrences of "love" in Ignatius, sixteen are joined together with "faith."[74] Faith and love were even allegorized in the elements of the Eucharist—faith corresponded to the body, and love to the blood (*Trall.* 8.1). His emphasis on faith and love probably reveals his dependence on 1 Cor 13 where Paul says "now these three remain: faith, hope and love" (νυνὶ δὲ μένει πίστις, ἐλπίς, ἀγάπη, τὰ τρία ταῦτα).[75] Or, perhaps, this stock phrase derived from 2 Tim 1:13: "What you heard from me, keep as the pattern of sound teaching, with faith and love in Christ Jesus" (ἐν πίστει καὶ ἀγάπῃ). This would also explain the role of the bishop. It is the duty of the bishop to "guard the good deposit" (τὴν καλὴν παραθήκη φύλαξον; 2 Tim 1:14), that is the teaching of the apostles, and he is to do this with faith and love.[76] Faith and love are nearly always tied to the message of the gospel for Ignatius.

---

[73] Holmes, *Apostolic Fathers*, 195.
[74] Schoedel, *Ignatius*, 24.
[75] It is certain that Ignatius knew 1 Corinthians. Robert Grant identifies forty-six allusions to 1 Corinthians, some clearer than others. He says, "It is very clear that he knew 1 Corinthians practically by heart" (Grant, *After the New Testament* [Philadelphia: Fortress, 1967], 39). Cf. *Eph.* 16.1 and 1 Cor 6:9–10; *Eph.* 18.1 and 1 Cor 1:23; *Rom.* 5.1 and 1 Cor 4:4; *Rom.* 9.2 and 1 Cor 15:8–9; and *Phd.* 3.3 and 1 Cor 6:9–10. Hope was also a prominent theme in Ignatius, though never occurring with faith and love. It appears eleven times most often in connection to Christ as the hope for Christians (Schoedel, *Ignatius*, 27).
[76] John Meier, pondering how such an advanced ecclesiology could exist so quickly in the church, hits the nail on the head: "It seems that some further crisis or crises at Antioch had demanded a tightening up of church structures so that a united church could meet a common enemy. The most likely candidate for the role of catalytic crisis is the rise of Gnosticism, especially in its docetic tendencies" (Brown and Meier, *Antioch and Rome*, 75). The authority of the bishop was central for Ignatius. Wherever poisonous plants of heresy grow, it was up to the bishop to uproot them. Safeguarding doctrine fell to the highest ranking member of the church, the top of the tripartite hierarchy, the bishop. So high was his view of bishops that he would tell the Philadelphians, although professing it to be a word from the Spirit, "Do nothing apart from the bishop" (7.2). To be a genuine Christian, and not just a Christian in name only, means submission to the bishop (*Magn.* 4). Schoedel correctly points to the various heresies that had sprouted up during this time that Ignatius specifically had in mind when encouraging com-

The Gospel

The word Gospel appears eight times in Ignatius's writings, all of them coming in his letters to the *Philadelphians* or *Smyrnaeans* (*Phld.* 5.1, 2 [twice], 8.2, 9.2 [twice]; *Smyr.* 5.1, 7.2). It is quite telling that εὐαγγέλιον appears only in two of the seven authentic epistles, and the significance of this fact must not be ignored. Charles Hill raises the right question concerning Ignatius's use of "Gospel," namely, why is the word Gospel found only in *Philadelphians* and *Smyrnaeans*, which were two of his last three letters?[77] Briefly, the answer is that Ignatius was countering the claims of some in the churches who claimed the authority of the "archives" over and against the Gospel. Hill has shown that each time the word Gospel is used, it is accompanied by either the prophets, the archives, or the law of Moses.[78] In each case Ignatius juxtaposed the Old Testament with the Gospel in order to show that the prophets were actually on his side in anticipating the coming of Christ. Thus, the Gospel trumps the Old Testament. Ignatius stressed the importance of the Gospel to these churches because of the particular problems each congregation was facing. As has been pointed out, the Philadelphians were confronted with Judaizers and the Smyrnaeans with Docetists. In both of these cases, comprehending the Gospel rightly was the antidote to these heterodoxies.

What does Ignatius have in mind when he speaks of the Gospel? He was not referring to any of the canonical Gospels when he wrote this[79]—in fact, he was

---

plete allegiance to the bishop (Schoedel, *Ignatius*, 12–13). Likewise, Torrance says, "One of the main functions of the Ignatian Bishop is the preservation of theological unity, for heresy destroys ἕνωσις, therefore the union with Christ, and that means estrangement from His passion and so from all the blessings of the Father" (Torrance, *The Doctrine of Grace in the Apostolic Fathers*, 81). Unity under the bishop kept one on the path to attaining God.

77 Charles Hill, "Ignatius, 'the Gospel,' and the Gospels," in *Trajectories through the New Testament and the Apostolic Fathers*, ed. Andrew F. Gregory and Christopher M. Tuckett (Oxford: Oxford University Press, 2005), 270–71.

78 Hill, "Ignatius, 'the Gospel,' and the Gospels," 269. Hill gives a helpful reminder to the students of Ignatius's letters: "As a prisoner in transition, he probably did not have any, let alone all, of these with him as he wrote, and thus had to rely upon memory, as seems evident even from his Old Testament parallels and citations" (269). To approach his letters expecting an exact replication of any portion of Scripture is an exercise in futility.

79 Just because Ignatius used the term gospel to refer to something other than the written Gospels does not mean that he was ignorant of the canonical Gospels. To the contrary, there is broad scholarly consensus that Ignatius knew Matthew's Gospel, which flourished in Antioch. Of the early sources known to have their provenance in Antioch, many of them show a remarkable dependence on the first Gospel (e.g., *Didache*). For Ignatius's knowledge and use of Matthew, see Brown, *The Gospel and Ignatius of Antioch*, 1–6, 78–81; Brown and Meier, *Antioch and Rome*,

not referring to the written word at all.⁸⁰ When Ignatius used τὸ εὐαγγέλιον he was speaking of the content of the Gospel, that is, the Christ event, specifically the death and resurrection of Jesus. Schoedel rightly states, "It is most unlikely that Ignatius has in mind written gospels and the letters of the apostles or is thinking of the gospel as put in the form of written documents by the apostles. The term 'gospel' in Ignatius seems regularly to refer to the good news about Jesus Christ."⁸¹

Charles Thomas Brown, in his monograph on the use of τὸ εὐαγγέλιον in Ignatius, identifies several key themes, or "gospel motifs," that are tied to his use of τὸ εὐαγγέλιον, specifically, παρουσία, σταυρός, θάνατος, πάθος, and ἀνάστασις.⁸² Ignatius drew his conception of the Gospel from Paul.⁸³ As Brown notes, "for Paul τὸ εὐαγγέλιον thus becomes a term that sums up the salvation accomplished by God through Jesus. The εὐαγγέλιον no doubt is at the heart of

---

45–72; Édouard Massaux, *The First Ecclesiastical Writers*, in vol. 1 of *The Influence of the Gospel of Saint Matthew on Christian Literature before Saint Irenaeus*, trans. N. J. Belval and S. Hecht, New Gospel Studies 5.1 (Macon, GA: Mercer University Press, 1990); Christine Trevett, "Approaching Matthew from the Second Century: The Under-Used Ignatian Correspondence," *JSNT* 20 (1984): 59–67; idem, *A Study of Ignatius of Antioch*, 22–23, although Trevett cautions saying, "I remain to be convinced that he would have known it in its present form" (22); Virginia Corwin, *St. Ignatius and Christianity in Antioch*, 94 ff; J. Smit Sibinga, "Ignatius and Matthew," *NovT* 8 (1966): 262–83; Grant, *After the New Testament*, 37–54. Grant claims, "We conclude that there is no reason to suppose that Ignatius did not know the Pauline epistles and the gospels of Matthew and John" (43). The extent to which Ignatius knew another Gospel, particularly John, is more debatable. See P. Dietze, "Die Briefe des Ignatius und das Johannesevangelium," *ThStK* 78 (1905): 563–603, and especially C. Maurer, *Ignatius von Antiochien und das Johannesevangelium* (Zürich: Zwingli Verlag, 1949). On Maurer's work, Grant says, "The thesis that Ignatius used the Gospel of John seems highly probable" (Grant, *After the New Testament*, 41). *Pace* Helmut Koester who, though acknowledging that Ignatius shared many similarities with John's Gospel, concludes that "it cannot be demonstrated that he knew and used this gospel" (Koester, *Introduction to the New Testament: Volume Two: History and Literature of Early Christianity* [Philadelphia: Fortress, 1984], 282).

80 Some have actually argued that Ignatius did have a written Gospel in mind. Instead of landing on either side of this issue, Hill argues that it is both/and. "Gospel" was on its way from being a kerygmatic proclamation of good news to an authoritative writing. He remarks, "Alongside its original meaning of the good news of salvation in Christ (*Phld.* 5.2), the word 'gospel' is already being used as a convenient form of reference to the content of an authoritative Christian writing or set of writings containing that good news, the coming, birth, baptism, death, and resurrection of the Lord and faith through him" (Hill, "Ignatius, 'the Gospel,' and the Gospels," 284). Ignatius was caught in a time when there was no technical term for the canonical gospels.
81 Schoedel, *Ignatius*, 201.
82 Brown, *The Gospel and Ignatius of Antioch*, 23–41.
83 Brown is correct to suggest that "we can say that in general Ignatius' idea of the gospel is most like Paul in that the εὐαγγέλιον is preached" (*The Gospel and Ignatius of Antioch*, 79).

Paul's theology."[84] When Paul spoke of the εὐαγγέλιον he too had something other than a written Gospel in mind. The Gospel came to be a solidified message in Paul's thinking, centered on the person and work of Christ. In other words, "τὸ εὐαγγέλιον is a technical term in Pauline Christianity … . Paul assumes that his readers know the content of the gospel message."[85]

Ignatius picked up on Paul's understanding of the Gospel message and gave it a similar shape. Again, Brown is helpful: "Ignatius' εὐαγγέλιον is specifically defined by the salvific παθός and ἀνάστασις of Jesus. For Ignatius, Jesus is the content of the εὐαγγέλιον."[86] Ignatius defines his understanding of the Gospel in *Phld.* 9.2:

> But the gospel possesses something distinctive, namely, the coming of the Savior, our Lord Jesus Christ, his suffering, and the resurrection. For the beloved prophets preached in anticipation of him, but the gospel is the imperishable finished work. All these things together are good, if you believe with love.[87]

The εὐαγγέλιον, appearing twice in this passage, is the entire story of redemptive history. It is the coming of the Savior whom the prophets promised and anticipated, along with his "imperishable finished work" (τὸ εὐαγγέλιον ἀπάρτισμά ἐστιν ἀφθαρσίας). Given what he says just before this in the first half of 9.2, the "imperishable finished work" is the suffering and resurrection of Christ. And how is one to respond to the εὐαγγέλιον? "All these things together," (i.e. the Gospel message), "are good, *if* you believe with love" (πάντα ὁμοῦ καλά ἐστιν, ἐὰν ἐν ἀγάπῃ πιστεύητε, emphasis added). The apodosis is somewhat nondescript simply saying that "all these things together are good," but the protasis of this conditional sentence makes clear that the Gospel is only good for those who "believe with love" (ἐὰν ἐν ἀγάπῃ πιστεύητε).[88] For Ignatius, salvation is contingent on belief, which plays a very significant role in his conception of justification.

---

[84] Brown, *The Gospel and Ignatius of Antioch*, 54.
[85] Brown, *The Gospel and Ignatius of Antioch*, 57.
[86] Brown, *The Gospel and Ignatius of Antioch*, 79. Torrance adds, "It is quite clear that salvation has as much to do with the death of Christ as with the Incarnation" (Torrance, *The Doctrine of Grace in the Apostolic Fathers*, 60).
[87] Holmes, *Apostolic Fathers*, 245.
[88] This phrase is very similar to Ignatius's favorite phrase, "faith and love."

Justification

While justification is the focal point of this chapter, there is only one relevant use of δικαιόω in Ignatius's letters.[89] *Philadelphians* 8.2 reads:

> But for me, the 'archives' are Jesus Christ, the inviolable archives are his cross and death and his resurrection and the faith that comes through him; by these things I want, through your prayers, to be justified.[90]

The crux of the Gospel message is present in this verse, not to mention that this statement comes in the broader context of an Ignatian reference to the Gospel. This verse comes sandwiched between three important uses of εὐαγγέλιον (*Phld.* 8.2 and 9.2 [twice]). Therefore, there is no leap to make a strong connection between justification and his understanding of the Gospel. On this connection Brown observes: "in *Phld.* 8.2 as in *Phld.* 5.1, Ignatius connects his own ultimate goal (in 8.2 to be justified, and in 5.1 the 'lot in which I attain mercy') with the εὐαγγέλιον (as well as the prayer of the Philadelphian church). It is the present faith in the past events of Jesus' life, death and resurrection that is the locus of justification for Ignatius."[91] Justification, in Brown's reckoning, is the "ultimate goal" for Ignatius and he explicitly binds this to the Gospel. The last part of the quotation is essential for the purpose of this chapter. The Gospel is defined, even by Ignatius, in terms of Jesus' life, death, and resurrection and this Gospel is "the locus of justification for Ignatius."

A closer look at this verse draws out important Pauline themes.[92] Christine Trevett, commenting on this passage, perceives Paul's influence: "Ignatius, the

---

89 The other reference, from *Rom.* 5.1, offers little help in uncovering Ignatius's understanding of justification. While recounting his journey to Rome, Ignatius writes to the church in that city about the harsh treatment he has received. He says, "But by their mistreatment," that is the mistreatment from the guards, "I am becoming more of a disciple; nevertheless I am not justified by this" (*Rom.* 5.1). In all likelihood, Ignatius is quoting from 1 Cor 4:4 because he finds himself in a similar situation of persecution but believes he will not be acquitted on account of his good treatment of the guards.
90 Holmes, *Apostolic Fathers*, 243.
91 Brown, *The Gospel and Ignatius of Antioch*, 18.
92 Koester makes several interesting comments about Ignatius's use of Paul (*Introduction to the New Testament*). He said Ignatius "was deeply influenced as a theologian by the letters of Paul" (281), and that "elements from the Pauline letters are consciously adopted in these passages, and the many allusions to the Pauline correspondence demonstrate that Ignatius repeatedly returned to those letters to find guidance and instruction" (284). However, he goes on to say that some may accuse Ignatius "of frequent misunderstandings of Pauline terminology" (284). Koester does not mention which terms Ignatius supposedly misunderstood.

imitator of Paul, dealt with these judaizers very much with a backward glance at the Pauline emphases on faith and justification."[93] It must be kept in mind that this positive statement of justification comes in the same letter as his harshest critiques against Judaizers (along with *Magn.*), in fact right in the middle of his argument. The immediate context of *Phld.* 8.2 is the Judaizers who want to pit the "archives," or the Old Testament, against the Gospel, contending, "'If I do not find it in the archives, I do not believe it in the gospel.'"[94] Schoedel believes this to be the primary battle Ignatius encountered in Philadelphia, that is, their unhealthy fascination with the Old Testament Scripture.[95] The Judaizers were contesting Christian doctrine by appealing to the Old Testament. They wanted proof from the archives, but Ignatius is saying that Jesus Christ is the true archive. In the broader polemic about the archives, Ignatius's thoughts turn to the issue of circumcision. Schoedel claims that Ignatius "probably speaks of circumcision in particular under the influence of the Pauline polemic in Galatians and Romans and elsewhere."[96] If he is correct, which he seems to be, then Ignatius had in mind justification apart from works of the law.[97]

Ignatius is consciously opposing the Judaizers whose "concept of righteousness and justification may well have been less Pauline."[98] He was opposing Jewish practices with a Gospel of justification on the basis of faith.[99] In the passage under review, Ignatius states that he wants to be justified by "these things" (ἐν οἷς). What are "these things" by which he "wants to be justified"? It must be the Gospel message.[100] Not only is it the cross, death, and resurrection, which have been mentioned at length above, but he goes a step further to speak of the "faith that comes through him." Faith, then, is an aspect of the "unalterable archives"

---

93 Trevett, *A Study of Ignatius*, 176.
94 Holmes, *Apostolic Fathers*, 243.
95 William R. Schoedel, "Ignatius and the Archives," *HTR* 71 (1978): 105.
96 Schoedel, "Ignatius and the Archives," 103. He goes on to say, "Whether a person is circumcised or uncircumcised makes no difference; if he does not speak of Jesus Christ, he is doomed. We are reminded of Paul's statement that 'neither circumcision counts for anything nor uncircumcision ... ' (1 Cor 7:19; Gal 5:6; 6:15)" (103–04).
97 Grant, along the lines of Schoedel, senses Paul's influence: "Ignatius then proceeds ... in a Pauline fashion (cf. Gal 2:14–15)" (*After the New Testament*, 38).
98 Trevett, *A Study of Ignatius*, 176.
99 Trevett accuses the Judaizers with legalism. In a sentence very similar to that of Judith Lieu's mentioned above, Trevett avers that "what Ignatius held in contrast were not grace and Law (as Paul did) but rather grace and 'Judaism'" (Trevett, *A Study of Ignatius*, 177; Lieu, *Image and Reality*, 29). She goes on to state, "It does seem to me that Ignatius did find them overly-legalistic" (Trevett, *A Study of Ignatius*, 177). Following Judaism is, at least in some measure, tantamount to keeping the Jewish law in Ignatius's mind.
100 See the excursus below on the significance of prayer in Ignatius.

that comes through Jesus Christ. In this verse faith is the response to the Gospel, and it is faith in the person and work of Christ that results in his justification. Thus, not only is Ignatius repudiating Judaizers within these chapters of *Philadelphians*, but he also giving them the Gospel message of justification by faith in the person of Jesus Christ.

Turning to the other passage that Brown calls the "locus of justification" (*Phld.* 5.1) in Ignatius, the issue is not overtly a matter of justification but the parallel can be easily made without reading into the text, for a strong conceptual link is present. Ignatius confesses,

> Though I am in chains for his sake, I am all the more afraid, because I am still imperfect. But your prayer to God will make me perfect, so that I may attain the fate by which I have received mercy, since I have taken refuge in the gospel as the flesh of Jesus and in the apostles as the council of presbyters of the church.[101]

Ignatius recognizes that he has not yet been made perfect, but his hope is that he will be made perfect. Here again he appeals to the prayers of those in the church to see him through his martyrdom. He recognizes that perfection is needed for the goal he desires, namely to attain to God, yet he also understands that his perfection will come about because God has shown him mercy (ἠλεήθην). The necessity of perfection is at the core of justification in Ignatius, as is also the inability of man to gain perfection.[102]

The next clause gives the reason why he has received mercy. Ignatius has taken refuge (προσφυγὼν)[103] in the Gospel and in the apostles' council. The

---

101 Holmes, *Apostolic Fathers*, 240–41.
102 Schoedel's thoughts on justification in Ignatius are worth reviewing. "Similarly the bishop's present sufferings are dealt with as teaching him to become a disciple (cf. *Rom.* 4.2) and readying him for his 'justification.' Ignatius speaks of his justification in terms that are directly dependent on 1 Cor 4:4 (echoed again in *Tr.* 5.2); but 'justification' for Ignatius is apparently nothing other than becoming a disciple (cf. *Tr.* 5.2) and gaining perfection (cf. *Phd.* 8.2) through martyrdom; Paul's words serve to emphasize the fact that Ignatius' justification is still future and thus to discourage the Roman Christians from interfering with his attaining it" (Schoedel, *Ignatius*, 179). Schoedel reads against the grain of *Phld.* 8.2 when he lumps the two texts together just because they share a common word (δικαιόω). The point Ignatius is making in *Rom.* 5.1 is that suffering might make him more of a disciple (Col. 1:24), but he is not expecting acquittal because of his kindness, a point he similarly makes in *Trall.* 5.2. The comparison to *Phld.* 8.2, on the other hand, is unfounded. It would be analogous to comparing Rom 3:28, for instance, and 1 Tim 3:16 on the basis that both use a form of δικαιόω. The context in both cases demands a different definition of the word.
103 I take this as an adverbial participle of cause. Thus, "I have received mercy, *because* I have taken refuge in the Gospel."

phrase "taken refuge" has the idea that he has sheltered himself under the protection that the Gospel offers. Since he understands the Gospel as the Christ event, then he believes that he will receive mercy on account of his belief in the coming, the suffering, the death, and the resurrection of Jesus. By the council of the apostles he means the tradition that he has received from them through the church, much like the Gospel tradition that he has received.[104] In other words, the Gospel is the only source of his hope (*Phld.* 5.2).[105] Ignatius finds mercy in the Gospel and ultimately is justified by his belief in the Gospel. These two verses from *Philadelphians* demonstrate well the explicit connection that Ignatius makes between the Gospel and salvation.

Though many more passages could be adduced, one final one is especially worth mentioning. In the midst of telling the Smyrnaeans about how God has heard their prayers in Antioch, he tells them (*Smyr.* 11.1),

> I am not worthy to be from [Antioch], for I am the very least of them. Nevertheless in accordance with the divine will I was judged worthy, not because of the witness of my own conscience, but by the grace of God, which I pray may be given to me in perfection, so that by your prayer I may reach God.[106]

His opening phrase echoes a frequent Pauline sentiment, that he is the most unworthy of all of God's people (1 Cor 15:9). Yet, even as the least of these, he was still "judged worthy" (κατηξιώθην) to attain God (ἐπιτύχω). The verb καταξιόω means to "consider worthy" and is used by Ignatius eight times.[107] Ignatius declares that he is considered worthy, not by the witness of his own conscience, but by the grace of God.[108] His ability to "attain God," an eschatological reality in his theology, depends not on what he has done (or else his conscience could bear

---

104 Grant notes that "in almost every case ... it is possible to hold either that Ignatius was relying upon memories of what he had read (scripture) or that he was relying upon memories of what he had heard (oral tradition)" (Grant, *After the New Testament*, 42). Going a step further, Grant argues, "In Ignatius's life, tradition almost certainly came to be crystallized as scripture" (44). This sums up nicely the twofold witness of Ignatius. He clearly had and used the written word but he also does rely on tradition that he had received from the apostles who lived just a generation or two before.
105 Ignatius concludes *Philadelphians* with a word of praise for the brothers and sisters in Troas who sent their love. Then he writes, "The Lord Jesus Christ will honor them; on him they set their hope in body, soul, and spirit with faith, love, and harmony. Farewell in Christ Jesus, our shared hope" (*Phld.* 11.2). Twice in this verse Ignatius points to Jesus as the foundation of hope.
106 Holmes, *Apostolic Fathers*, 259.
107 BDAG, s.v. "καταξιόω." See *Eph.*20.1, *Magn.* 1.2, *Trall.* 12.3, *Rom.* 2.2, *Phld.* 10.2, *Poly.* 1.1, 7.2. Ignatius uses ἀξιόω numerous times as well.
108 See the use of ἀξιόω in *Epistle to Diognetus* 9.1.

him witness), but rather on the grace of God. Καταξιόω is analogous to δικαιόω in that both words testify to the inability of the person—καταξιόω referring to the need of a person to be worthy of something that he or she is not inherently worthy of, and δικαιόω referring to the need of a person to be declared righteous on a merit not his or her own. In both cases the individual must thrust himself on the mercy of God so that he might be considered worthy of attaining God—the very thing Ignatius does here.

The only use of καταξιόω in Paul comes in 2 Thessalonians 1:5 where the Apostle writes, "This is the evidence of the righteous judgment of God, that you may be considered worthy of the kingdom of God, for which you are also suffering" (ἔνδειγμα τῆς δικαίας κρίσεως τοῦ θεοῦ εἰς τὸ καταξιωθῆναι ὑμᾶς τῆς βασιλείας τοῦ θεοῦ, ὑπὲρ ἧς καὶ πάσχετε). The similarity of Ignatius's *Sitz im Leben* to this verse is remarkable. Ignatius too is suffering persecution for his faith, and like the Thessalonians, he wants to be considered worthy of the kingdom, or in Ignatius's words, which could be seen as a synonym for the kingdom, to attain God. Ignatius wants more than anything to be considered worthy when he faces divine judgment, which for him, means an unflinching spirit in the prospect of martyrdom.

Excursus: Prayer and Justification

The three passages cited above in support of the argument that Ignatius appealed to Paul's view of justification (*Phld.* 5.1, 8.2; *Smyr.* 11.1) all have a curious phrase about the prayers of his readers embedded in them, and these phrases could leave the impression that prayer is actually the catalyst of his salvation. The most difficult of the three is *Phld.* 8.2: "by these things I want, through your prayers, to be justified." The inclusion of the prepositional phrase ἐν τῇ προσευχῇ ὑμῶν could be construed, if the preposition is taken as means, as saying that their prayers are the vehicle for his justification.[109] But surely Ignatius does not think that his justification hinges on the prayers of people he had just met! The passage in *Phld.* 5.1 has a very similar phrase. There he states, "But your prayer to God will make me perfect" (ἀλλ' ἡ προσευχὴ ὑμῶν εἰς θεόν με ἀπαρτίσει).[110] Once more, is it conceivable that Ignatius would be plac-

---

[109] It is perhaps better to take the ἐν preposition as "reference/respect" (Daniel Wallace, *Greek Grammar beyond the Basics* [Grand Rapids: Zondervan, 1996], 372). It is the exact same prepositional phrase used in *Smyr.* 11.1.

[110] With an eye on *Phld.* 5.1, BDAG translates ἀπαρτίζω as "complete." Ignatius uses this verb multiple times and in *Poly.* 7.3, at least, the idea is "to perfect." Here, though, "complete" is prob-

ing his eternal destiny in the prayers of strangers? Does he think that he will be completed in a soteriological sense by their prayers for him? It would seem not. Much of Ignatius's soteriology would have to be reconsidered if this were so.

It is important to note that it is not the prayers that justify him. The prayers do not add to his justification, nor is his justification contingent on their prayers. Ignatius was simply pleading with them to continue their intercession on his behalf, so that his faith might be genuine. As in all of his epistles, his impending death weighed heavily on his mind because at any moment the caravan leading to Rome would move on and the day of testing would arrive. Ignatius believed his justification would only be complete at his martyrdom.[111] Thus, the beasts that awaited him would test the reality of his faith—if he failed, then his faith was not real. He coveted their prayers, pleading with them to pray for his resolve. He made this point in *Eph.* 1.2: "[I] was hoping through your prayers [ἐλπίζοντα τῇ προσευχῇ ὑμῶν] to succeed in fighting with wild beasts in Rome—in order that by so succeeding I might be able to be a disciple."[112] Successful martyrdom would result in him becoming a disciple. This is how prayer ties into Ignatius's view of salvation.[113]

Returning now to the discussion of justification in Ignatius, it is needful to show what happens to those who do not believe. Writing to the Smyrnaeans, Ignatius gave this word on judgment (6.1):

---

ably best with the idea that the prayers of the people will see him through to the end, so that with his final breath he will have completed his mission.

111 Due to the fact that there is a future sense to his conception of justification, some have argued that Ignatius's notion of justification was not Pauline. However, Paul too could look towards a salvation yet to come (Rom 5:9–10, 13:11; Eph 1:13–14). Bower states, "the eschatological tension between present and future is negligible in Ignatius. Final salvation is not linked to the future, historical unfolding; rather, it can be realized in an immediate way" (Bower, "ΕΠΙΤΥΓΧΑΝΩ," 14). In some ways, then, Ignatius is Pauline in keeping an eschatological tension of the already/not yet. Salvation could be a present realization, but for Ignatius, his martyrdom was to play a part (see the final section on martyrdom). Pace, Schoedel who understands "attaining God" only to refer to a future hope. "In any event, 'attaining God' represents a future possibility and most characteristically a *post mortem* possibility" (Schoedel, *Ignatius*, 29).

112 The prayers of fellow believers played a major role in his thinking. See *Eph.* 10.1, *Magn.* 14.1, *Rom.* 8.3, and *Smry.* 11.1. See Bower, "ΕΠΙΤΥΓΧΑΝΩ," 3. Further study is needed on exactly how prayer connects to his soteriology.

113 Willard M. Swartley interprets the phrase "by your prayers" as a "subtle appeal for church unity" (Swartley, "The Imitatio Christi in the Ignatian Letters," 103). Surely he is right to see this element of unity present in Ignatius's insatiable appeal for prayers. Collective prayers demonstrate the unity of the church, and when these prayers are undertaken by the church and the bishop, they are even more powerful (*Eph.* 5).

Let no one be misled. Even the heavenly beings and the glory of angels and the rulers, both visible and invisible, are subject to judgment if they do not believe in the blood of Christ. Let the one who can accept this accept it. Do not let a high position make anyone proud, for faith and love are everything; nothing is preferable to them.[114]

Divine judgment was a reality for Ignatius and this judgment could only be avoided through belief in the blood of Christ. Belief in Christ's atonement is the one condition given in this clause to escape God's wrath.[115] Those who

---

114 Holmes, *Apostolic Fathers*, 253.
115 Many who comment on Ignatius's letters are troubled by the lack of "sin" language. Corwin, for instance, observes, "Although Ignatius' understanding of the world was conventional, his analysis of the plight of men in somewhat more individual. His conception differs sharply from that of Paul, for the lively awareness which Paul has of the sinfulness of human beings is almost lacking" (*St. Ignatius and Christianity*, 160; see also Schoedel, *Ignatius*, 241 n. 10). Once more, the reader must pick up on some of the finer points Ignatius makes. Numerous times he calls for repentance, such as in *Eph.* 10.1: "Pray continually for the rest of humankind as well, that they may find God, for there is in them hope for repentance." The believers are to pray that unbelievers will come to God through repentance. Repentance seems at least to imply sin. Ignatius knows that their salvation is contingent on them repenting of their sins. In *Phld.* 8.1 reminds them, "The Lord, however, forgives all who repent, if in repenting they return to the unity of God and the council of the bishop. I believe in the grace of Jesus Christ who will free you from every restraint." God grants forgiveness to all who repent. His admonition comes with the stipulation that they return to God and the bishop. Submission to the bishop marks the genuineness of their repentance, because Ignatius cannot conceive of a truly repentant person who does not submit again to the bishop. Notice too that Ignatius follows this with a statement on the grace of Jesus Christ that releases them from restraint (δεσμόν), which introduces a forensic element. Then comes the comment on justification immediately after this in *Phld.* 8.2 and then only a few chapters later Ignatius writes, "may those who dishonored them be redeemed by the grace of Jesus Christ." Those who stirred up trouble can also be redeemed, or purchased, by grace. Redemption, as Ignatius makes clear in all of his comments on the Gospel, is possible through the death and resurrection of Christ.

In regard to redemption, Ignatius seems to have held to a substitutionary view of the atonement, which also implies sin. The Docetists are said to abstain from partaking of the Eucharist which is "the flesh of our savior Jesus Christ, which *suffered for our sins* and which the Father by his goodness raised up" (*Smyr.* 6.2, emphasis added). Jesus Christ, the savior, died for (ὑπὲρ) our sins (ἁμαρτιῶν). He may not refer to sins often, but when he does he makes an explicit connection to Christ's vicarious work on the cross. Also to the Smyrnaeans he states, immediately after his strong Christological statement in chapter 1, "For he suffered all these things for our sakes, in order that we might be saved" (*Smyr.* 2). Likewise, Ignatius declared, "Him I seek, who died on our behalf; him I long for, who rose again for our sake" (*Rom.* 6.1). Of particular note as it pertains to sin, justification, and salvation, Ignatius said that he lives in accord with "Jesus Christ, who died for us in order that by believing in his death you might escape death" (*Trall.* 2.1). By believing in Christ's substitutionary death, a person is able to escape death (cf. *Trall.* 9.2: the "Father will likewise also raise up in Christ Jesus us

spurn the blood of Christ through unbelief are liable to God's judgment. Thus, "let the one who can accept it" refers to the one who accepts the blood of Christ, not the part on judgment. And finally he tied this into his favorite theme—faith and love. The condition is belief in the blood and this belief stems from faith in and love for Jesus, and then in turn for others, lest someone be proud. Faith and belief play a central role in his soteriology, which he had learned from Paul.

Ignatius and Paul?

Not everyone is convinced that Ignatius had a Pauline view of justification. Rudolf Bultmann, for instance, thinks that Ignatius touched upon many Pauline themes, but that justification was not one of them.[116] For Bultmann, Ignatius comes closest of all the fathers to Paul in his understanding of the Christian life as eschatological existence.[117] Though not entirely present, Ignatius had a conception of the "already" and "not yet" and he "recognized the unity of indicative and imperative that for Paul characterizes Christian existence."[118] But Ignatius did not follow his favorite Apostle when it came to righteousness and justification. Bultmann declares, "It is symptomatic that the concept of 'righteousness' loses its Pauline meaning and, in general, seldom appears in the forensic sense, but it mostly used with a moralistic meaning. The consequence is that a perfectionism develops."[119] Bultmann supplies few examples of perfectionism, resting almost entirely on the fact that Ignatius perceived justification as an "exclusively future" event.[120] When Bultmann comes to *Phld.* 8.2

---

who believe in him. Apart from him we have no true life"). Torrance acknowledges, "Without doubt there is some notion of vicarious atonement here" (Torrance, *The Doctrine of Grace in the Apostolic Fathers*, 62. Torrance has a very helpful paragraph on the atonement).

116 Rudolf Bultmann, "Ignatius and Paul," in *Existence and Faith: shorter writings of Rudolf Bultmann*, ed. Schubert M. Ogden (New York: Meridian Books, 1960), 267–77. Originally published as Rudolf Bultmann, "Ignatius und Paulus," in *Studia Paulina, in honorem Johannes de Zwaan septuagenerii*, ed. J. N. Sevenster and W. C. van Unnik (Haarlem, Netherlands: De Erven F. Bohn N.V., 1953), 37–51.
117 Bultmann, "Ignatius and Paul," 267.
118 Bultmann, "Ignatius and Paul," 268. Though later he claims, "The thought that dominates Ignatius' mind is not the striving for righteousness, but the longing for life" (271).
119 Bultmann, "Ignatius and Paul," 269.
120 Bultmann, "Ignatius and Paul," 269. He too is bothered, among other things, by "the almost complete absence of the concept of sin" and the missing connection between "righteousness" and "life" (270). Bultmann completely misses the manifold passages that touch on vicarious atonement, which speak to the issue of sin.

he dismisses the idea that a Pauline doctrine of being "rightwised" is present because Ignatius connects faith to "cross," "death," and "resurrection," which he claims is a "co-ordination that, to be sure, is hardly possible for Paul."[121]

Ignatius, though, never connects salvation or justification to personal righteousness. Quite the opposite is true. Trevett notes, "Ignatius wrote that the saving acts of Christ brought justification (*Phld.* 8.2) and in *Magn.*12 Ignatius praised the Christians for Magnesian Christians' modesty and lack of an undue sense of personal righteousness."[122] The Magnesians were embarrassed when Ignaitus praised them for their righteousness (*Magn.* 12), which would hardly be possible if he thought personal righteousness necessary for their salvation. His praise would either come with a comment on how they are attaining God through their righteous deeds, or he would encourage others to emulate them if they too wanted to gain salvation. To the contrary, they are not conceited at all by their good works, because Jesus Christ is within them. He simply encourages them to be "firmly grounded in the precepts of the Lord and the apostles, in order that in whatever you do, you may prosper, physically and spiritually, in faith and love, in the Son and the Father and in the Spirit" (*Magn.* 13.1). Faith and love in the Triune God are the means to prospering both physically and spiritually. Bultmann, however, is not alone in perceiving a bent towards works righteousness and away from grace in Ignatius.

The most serious critique comes from T. F. Torrance. Not all of his arguments can be taken up in this chapter but the most substantial ones directly relating to justification and moralism beg exploration. In a section on justification in Ignatius, Torrance states, "The word δικαιοῦμαι is only twice used in these epistles, and in neither case is it used in the Pauline sense. Like *1 Clement* he approaches St. Paul on the negative side of the doctrine, but when we enquire what the positive meaning of justification is, we find it to be that of becoming just. In other words, justification is a process that is not wholly independent of man."[123] Torrance is correct to say that Ignatius paints the negative side of justification in Pauline hues, in particular how he handles Judaizers, but it is imperative to also see that Ignatius does communicate a positive side of the doctrine, even if these comments occur less often.

It may come as a surprise to learn that Torrance argues precisely that which is argued in this chapter, that "faith and love" summarize Ignatius's soteriology. The issue at hand is what is meant by "faith" and "love" and whether or not they

---

121 Bultmann, "Ignatius and Paul," 270.
122 Trevett, *A Study of Ignatius of Antioch*, 178.
123 Torrance, *Doctrine of Grace in the Apostolic Fathers*, 67.

constitute an act of works righteousness. In a telling sentence Torrance states, "In the end to be justified means to be perfected, and this justification is a matter of faith and love, or of faith and works."[124] In response to the first part of that claim, that justification means to be "perfected," is Ignatius not touching upon a Pauline theme? Does not the sinner in Paul need to be perfected by the righteousness of Christ (2 Cor 5:21; Phil 3:9)? Ignatius may not make a direct corollary in his writings to the imputed righteousness of Christ, but he does not say anything that would negate this possibility either, and at times says things that tend in the direction of imputation.[125] The perfection of which Ignatius speaks is a perfection of faith and love. He tells the Ephesians, "None of these escapes your notice, if you have perfect faith and love toward Jesus Christ. For these are the beginning and the end of life: faith is the beginning and love is the end, and the two, when they exist in unity, are God" (14.1). The goal is perfect love and faith, not perfectionism through works.

Torrance, it would seem, is right to connect the idea of perfection to "faith" and "love." But he insists that love amounts to works in Ignatius, on the basis that love is the "principle of new life" that "works immanently within the actions of the believer."[126] His argument is worth citing at considerable length because of his emphasis on love as a work:

> For the most part love is a power given by God through the passion of Jesus Christ, and has to do most frequently with the relations between believers. It concerns the harmonious life of the church in faith and practice. Faith is not perfect unless it is exercised in love, but the union of these two is divine. In this sense, then, love is the principle of new life, of πίστις, and, we can even say, of justification. Certainly it is regarded as a gift, but a power that works immanently within the actions of the believer, producing in him the likeness to God. Here Ignatius comes close to identifying ἀγάπη with χάρις, both being thought of as the principle of new life, the former more in respect of its association with faith, the latter more in its connexion with the giving of God, which also includes γνῶσις. The point that concerns us here is that this principle is imparted to the Christian and works within him as a power such that it practically becomes identified with his own nature. This means that ἀγάπη passes over into a moral quality closely concerned with doing rightly, both in respect of actions and beliefs. It is easy to see how such a position leads to a subtle moralism. Ignatius is admittedly less moralistic than the other Fathers, but in principle his position is

---

124 Torrance, *The Doctrine of Grace in the Apostolic Fathers*, 68.
125 *Smyr.* 4.2: "Only let it be in the name of Jesus Christ, so that I may suffer together with him! I endure everything because he himself, who is the perfect human being, empowers me" (Holmes, *Apostolic Fathers*, 253). Christ is the τελείου ἀνθρώπου. *Eph.* 11.1: "only let us be found in Christ Jesus, which leads to true life" (Holmes, *Apostolic Fathers*, 193). Ignatius's view of imputation may be wrapped in his understanding of union.
126 Torrance, *The Doctrine of Grace in the Apostolic Fathers*, 69.

much the same. Associated with love in this way, faith is turned into faithfulness or endurance with a view to salvation. Suffering and repentance and even love itself are looked upon as helpful and necessary means in the effort to attain unto God ... . Therefore it is up to men to make their choice, be renewed in baptism and by depositing good works ensure the back-pay due to them. They are rewarded by grace! These last words show us how little a New Testament understanding of grace is present in these epistles. From the uncalculating, sovereign, free grace of St. Paul's letters this χάρις which is correlative to human credit is a μετάβασις εἰς ἄλλο γένος.[127]

His argument runs thus: in Ignatius, love is the basis of all things, even faith and justification. Love is the "principle of new life," a phrase Torrance repeats twice, and this love is imparted to believers. The point he is trying to make is that for Ignatius love is infused into the believer, no doubt by God, and it becomes equated with the new nature. Love is thus measured as a "moral quality" and subtly leads to moralism. The degree to which a person loves, as calculated by his good deeds, will determine his justification. If Torrance is reading Ignatius correctly that love is a moral quality that leads to salvation, then he is right to draw the conclusion Ignatius has misunderstood the New Testament teaching on grace. But Torrance has not read Ignatius correctly in my estimation.

At the end of the section cited above, Torrance excessively overstates his case by asserting that these epistles show how little Ignatius understood New Testament grace. Since Torrance opens up the entire New Testament, and not just Paul, it is helpful to call on other New Testament authors to shed light on this matter. One thinks immediately of 1 John and the emphasis placed on love for others (2:9, 11; 3:14; 4:7; et al.).[128] The author of 1 John does not violate the broader New Testament teaching on grace when he claims that a believer will love. First John even makes a very similar claim that Ignatius would make: "whoever keeps his word, in him truly the love of God is perfected" (2:5). Exhortations to love and free grace are not mutually exclusive ideas.[129] When Ignatius demands love, he does not do so as a work of righteousness but as the fruit of faith, as he makes clear in *Eph.* 14: "No one professing faith sins, nor does anyone possessing love

---

127 Torrance, *Doctrine of Grace in the Apostolic Fathers*, 69–70.
128 The point here is not whether Ignatius knew of 1 John, but if his statements are congruent to those in 1 John, although a worthwhile study could be produced examining this question of dependence on 1 John.
129 In the passage Torrance cites in which Ignatius claims the Smyrnaeans are "rewarded by grace," Ignatius states, "Grace will reward him in every respect" (12.1). Schoedel interprets this use of grace in this way: "Grace, then is thought of here as divine favor providing assurance that kindness (especially in such a cause) meets with God's approval and reward" (Schoedel, *Ignatius*, 251). Grace is used here in the generic sense of approval and reward, not grace in a soteriological sense.

hate. The tree is known by its fruit; thus those who profess to be Christ's will be recognized by their actions." Failure to love reveals a lack of faith, for love is a mark that one has professed belief in Christ. He is using both Paul and John, where Paul emphasizes faith and John emphasizes love. Faith and love are the two sides of the same salvific coin. Love is not a work leading to moralism in Ignatius—rather, he exhorts believers to love as a true sign of godliness.

Torrance's main argument is that Ignatius abandoned a Pauline doctrine of grace. "Grace," says Torrance, "is therefore the principle of new life and power issuing from the death of Christ." He even asserts that "there is no doubt about the fact that this grace is thought of as coming wholly from God." The problem for Torrance is that "it is a grace that is infused and thus becomes associated with man's own φύσις."[130] By confining his study to the use of the word χάρις and its cognates, Torrance misses many facets of grace that are present in Ignatius's letters.[131] There are times when it is hard to deny that Ignatius has Paul in mind when he speaks of grace.[132] Corwin evaluated grace in Ignatius, partly in

---

130 Torrance, *Doctrine of Grace in the Apostolic Fathers*, 77.
131 Bower takes issue with Torrance on grace in Ignatius. He writes, "The question of a conflict between grace and works in Ignatius—largely a Western question, and a question raised recently in Ignatius studies by Thomas F. Torrance ... is false" (Bower, "ΕΠΙΤΥΓΧΑΝΩ," 11). Bower continues further on, "The question is a false one simply because Ignatius does not make distinctions between grace and works. 'Faith and love' have merit only as a unity; so, too, grace (i.e. divine action) and works (human response) are impossible to separate" (11). This is a faithful rendering of the interplay between grace and works in the Ignatian corpus.
132 Two glaring examples of a Pauline use of grace need to be examined, the first *Magn.* 8.1: "For if we continue to live in accordance with Judaism, we admit that we have not received grace" (Holmes, *Apostolic Fathers*, 209). Those who practice Judaism have not received grace because they continue to rely on Jewish practices and not on the Gospel. Torrance says of this passage, "At first one feels that Ignatius is quite Pauline here, recalling one of the Apostle's most forceful words on grace to the Galatians, but the next sentence warns us that he is using χάρις in an un-Pauline sense" (Torrance, *The Doctrine of Grace in the Apostolic Fathers*, 80–81). He cites Gal 2:21, 4:4, and Irenaeus *Adv Haer* 4.20.4, 4.33.9 in support of the possibility, and I would argue the strong possibility, that Ignatius is intentionally Pauline in this comment. The next sentence that Torrance thought was un-Pauline (*Magn.* 8.2) reads, "For the most godly prophets lived in accordance with Christ Jesus. This is why they were persecuted, *being inspired as they were by his grace* in order that those who are disobedient might be fully convinced that there is one God who revealed himself through Jesus Christ his Son, who is his Word that came forth in silence, who in every respect pleased the one who sent him" (Holmes, *Apostolic Fathers*, 209, emphasis added). Based on Ignatius's comment that the prophets were inspired by grace, Torrance cautions, "We approach here closely to a doctrine of *gratia infusa*. Evidently in the prophets of the Old Testament we have parallels to the Bishops in the Christian churches" (Torrance, *The Doctrine of Grace in the Apostolic Fathers*, 81). His connection to bishops is off point. He must have *Magn.* 6–7 in mind where the authority of the bishop is expounded. But to think that he is con-

response to Torrance, and she too thought it necessary to widen the scope of grace to incorporate conceptual links.[133] Of grace she writes, "Grace is thus essentially a soteriological word, for it means the divine help extended to men for their salvation."[134] Swartley gives a good summary of her work: "Corwin ... show[s] Ignatius's awareness of the divine salvific *priority*, in the doctrine of grace. She observes *Smyr.* 6,2, the grace which 'has come to us'; *Eph.* 11,1, present salvation contrasted with coming wrath; *Mag.* 8,1, man's utter lack apart from Christ; and similarly, *Phld.* 8,1; 11,1; *Rom.* 1,2; *Smyr.* 11,1. She takes Ignatius' use of the word *life* (of God and Christ) to be roughly equivalent to grace."[135] When these passages that do not contain "grace" are taken into account, Ignatius is seen to be in greater continuity with the Paul. Ignatius acknowledged that divine grace is necessary for new life and he attributed salvation to grace.

Torrance censures Ignatius because he is not as clear or as nuanced as Paul —that is, his language does not replicate Paul's. There is no debate that Ignatius is not as verbose about justification or even that justification occupied the same importance as it did in Paul, but their situations were different and the occasions of their writings were not the same. Robert Grant's words are important to remember: "What is significant here is that Ignatius does not restrict himself to Paul's words or to exact exegesis of what Paul said; he synthesizes New Testament teaching as he paraphrases."[136] He probably paraphrased Paul because

---

necting the grace given to the prophets in the Old Testament with the authority of bishops in the church is tenuous. Ignatius is overtly Pauline in this statement. Grace comes to those who believe apart from the law (Judaism). The prophets knew this and testified to this because they had already received grace and were living according to the Gospel (Corwin, *St. Ignatius and Christianity*, 164). The other example comes from *Smyr.* 6.2: "Now note well those who hold heretical opinions about the grace of Jesus Christ that came to us; note how contrary they are to the mind of God. They have no concern for love, none for the widow, none for the orphan, none for the hungry or thirsty." Those holding heretical opinions about grace display their heresy by a lack of care for the widow and orphan (cf. Js 1:27). To know the grace of Christ, for Ignatius, is to care for those who cannot care for themselves. God has imparted his gift through free grace and now believers are to do likewise.

133 Corwin, *St. Ignatius and Christianity in Antioch*, 164–71. She does, however, refer to Torrance's chapter on Ignatius as an "excellent essay" (164 n. 16).
134 Corwin, *St. Ignatius and Christianity in Antioch*, 164. She agrees with G. P. Wetter, who argued that "grace in Paul, as in Ignatius, [is] the definition of the saving act" (164 n.16). See G. P. Wetter, *Charis. Ein Beitrag zur Geschichte des ältesten Christentums* (Leipzig: Brandsetter, 1913), 78–87.
135 Swartley, "The Imitatio Christi in the Ignatian Letters," 90.
136 Grant, *After the New Testament*, 40.

he did not have the epistles on hand, which meant he had to abridge the apostle's writings.[137]

One final issue that touches on justification must be discussed and that is Ignatius's view of his impending death. Together Bultmann and Torrance, among others, sing the same note in regard to Ignatius and martyrdom, namely that martyrdom was a work that clinched his salvation. Bultmann says, "what is definitely un-Pauline is that Ignatius sees in martyrdom a kind of guarantee, that he does not simply accept it as ordained by the Lord, but, so to speak, makes it into a work that gives him security, and that he therefore prevails upon the Roman congregation to do nothing to hinder his martyr's death."[138] Misunderstandings of Ignatius's view of justification can often be traced back to misunderstandings of his view of martyrdom.

3.4 Martyrdom

Ignatius's journey ended in the sands of the Colosseum. There he would come face to face with the beasts that haunted his letters, and it was in the arena that his faith would undergo its greatest test. It is clear from his writings that his upcoming martyrdom somehow played into his salvation. However, it is absolutely essential to understand *how* martyrdom fit into Ignatius's view of salvation because many have a warped understanding of his martyrdom, some even suggesting that Ignatius was unstable.[139] He did, after all, say, "I am passionately in love with death" (*Rom.* 7) and, as Robert Louis Wilken has said, Ignatius had a

---

137 Again, see Grant, *After the New Testament*, 39, 42, 44. Also, Hill says that Ignatius would have had to rely on memory in his recall of the Scriptures ("Ignatius, 'the Gospel,' and the Gospels," 269).

138 Bultmann, "Ignatius and Paul," 277.

139 W. H. C. Frend claims Ignatius's letters reveal "a state of exaltation bordering mania" (Frend, *Martyrdom and Persecution in the Early Church* [Oxford: Basil Blackwell, 1965], 197). Brent calls Ignatius "disturbed" (Brent, *Ignatius of Antioch*, 19), and G. E. M. De Ste. Croix, in the most direct way, says Ignatius had a "pathological yearning for death," and that this displayed his "abnormal mentality" (De Ste. Croix, "Why were the Early Christians Persecuted?" *Past & Present* 26 [1963]: 23–24). By way of a modern example, Special Forces groups sing cadences that appear to glorify death. They sing not because they want to die; to the contrary, they sing because they do not want to shrink back out of fear of death in the heat of combat. Likewise, Ignatius's apparent glorification of death is to motivate himself to endure a persecution since it would be easy to surrender his faith in order to avoid being "ground by the teeth of the wild beasts" (καὶ δι' ὀδόντων θηρίων ἀλήθομαι).

"vivid and flamboyant imagination" as he contemplated his martyrdom.[140] But he was not unbalanced—he was determined. The temptation to over read his martyrdom as an act he saw as necessary to salvation, as though it were a work that earned his salvation, as Bultmann held, must be resisted.

Three things help keep perspective on Ignatius's view of his martyrdom and explain why he comes across as a man with an unhealthy obsession with death. First, Ignatius wanted to be faithful more than anything. As he was writing these letters, chained to soldiers and travelling to his death, martyrdom was a certainty —his condemnation was sealed. He had come to terms with his impending death, which is why he would even coax the lions to eat him if necessary. Should the lions fail in their mission, for whatever reason, then stories would circulate that Ignatius was a coward who disowned Christ when the threat of pain was applied. Anything short of death would destroy his ministry and bring reproach on Christ.

Second, Ignatius had received a word from the Spirit that he was to be killed for his faith.[141] Capitulation to his captors would be blasphemy against the Spirit who had revealed to him his fate in a vision. In *Rom.* 7.2 Ignatius wrote, "My passionate love has been crucified and there is no fire of material longing within me, but only water living and speaking in me, saying within me, 'Come to the Fa-

---

140 Robert Louis Wilken, *The First Thousand Years: A Global History of Christianity* (New Haven: Yale University Press, 2012), 29.
141 See Michael Haykin, "'Come to the Father': Ignatius of Antioch and His Calling to be a Martyr," *Themelios* 32 (2007): 26–39. Cf. William C. Weinrich, *Spirit and Martyrdom: A Study of the Work of the Holy Spirit in Contexts of Persecution and Martyrdom in the New Testament and Early Christian Literature* (Washington, DC: University Press of America, 1981). It is critical to remember that "Ignatius reflects upon *his own* coming martyrdom" (Weinrich, *Spirit and Martyrdom*, 115). He is never saying that martyrdom is every person's path to discipleship. One passage that has left this impression is *Magn.* 5: "unbelievers bear the stamp of this world, but the faithful in love bear the stamp of God the Father through Jesus Christ, whose life is not in us unless we voluntarily choose to die into his suffering." The world is divided into only two sets of people, unbelievers and the faithful, each bearing a stamp (χαρακτῆρα) that identifies into which group they belong. Unbelievers bear the stamp of this world, but the faithful the stamp of God. The condition that Ignatius gives for life is the voluntary acceptance of death. But he does not overstep the bounds of the New Testament. As Schoedel says, "The dualities connected with this imagery in Ignatius are well within the range of Pauline and Johannine thought—God and the 'world' (cf. 1 Cor 1:20–21; John 3:16), faith and unfaith (cf. 2 Cor 6:15; John 20:27). The acquisition of the imprint of God is described in Pauline terms (cf. Rom 6:5–11) as coming through participation in the death and resurrection of Christ" (Schoedel, *Ignatius*, 110). Even Jesus said that to live one must die (Mark 8:34–35).

ther.'"¹⁴² The water living in him (ὕδωρ ζῶν), a reference to the Holy Spirit (John 7:37–9), has beckoned him to his death with the words, "Come to the Father."

Finally, Ignatius's salvation is in some manner conditional on his martyrdom. Scholars are not wrong to think that Ignatius is linking his martyrdom to his own salvation. Given what has been said, a failure to follow through with martyrdom would have meant that he backed down out of fear, disobeyed the Spirit's call, and ultimately denied his Lord. He is echoing ideas he has read in the New Testament. Paul incessantly exhorts his readers to endure persecution to the point that when he wrote to his protégé Timothy, he said that "if we deny [Jesus], then [Jesus] will deny us" (2 Tim 2:12). This is also why conditional statements occur sporadically in Paul's writings (e.g., 1 Cor 15:2). Endurance to the end was essential. Likewise, Jesus says much the same thing in his letters to the churches of Asia Minor, some of which were the same churches Ignatius wrote. There he said not a few times, "To the one who conquers" an eschatological prize would be given (Rev 2:7, 11, 17, 26; 3:5, 12, 21). Ignatius must conquer his final test and endure his persecution, lest his faith be in vain.

Thus, Ignatius's view of his forthcoming martyrdom is not beyond the pale of Pauline soteriology. Ignatius neither negates justification by faith because he believes that he must die, nor is he wrong to assume that his martyrdom secures his salvation. He is justified by his belief in Jesus but the flames of martyrdom will test the genuineness of his faith. As Haykin notes: "A careful study, though, of Ignatius' thinking about his own death reveals a man who rightly knows that Christian believing demands passionate engagement of the entire person, even to the point of physical death."¹⁴³

3.5 Conclusion

It could be easy to overstate the case for justification in Ignatius. To claim that justification was at the fore of his thoughts, or even that justification is a main idea in his letters, would be to overargue. After all, of only two occurrences of δικαιόω in his letters, one is pertinent (*Phld.* 8.2). The purpose of this chapter has not been to claim that Ignatius championed the doctrine of justification

---

142 What Ignatius means by "my passionate love" (ὁ ἐμὸς ἔρως ἐσταύρωται) has been a subject of debate since Origen, who said that this phrase referred to Christ. Given the context this interpretation seems doubtful. Ignatius is declaring that his love for the world has been crucified and that he no longer takes delight in earthly possessions. Instead, he remains determined to leave this world through his martyrdom.
143 Haykin, "Come to the Father," 28.

by faith, but rather simply to show that he does speak of justification by faith. The presence of this doctrine in *Phld.* 8.2, along with its close connection to the Gospel message, is an example that Ignatius thought himself in line with Paul's teaching.

The opposite could also be true that the case for justification in Ignatius is all too often understated. Added to his use of δικαιόω in *Phld.* 8.2 are many other issues he spoke to that touch upon justification, most significantly his polemic against the Judaizers. There were some, especially in Philadelphia and Magnesia, who were encouraging the believers to live according to the "archives," or the Old Testament, which included Sabbath keeping and circumcision. Ignatius's response was telling in that he declared that those who live according to Judaism have not received grace. When one takes into account the ways in which Ignatius spoke of salvation, and not just for the appearance of the words grace and justification, then his letters bear a striking resemblance to Paul.

Ignatius was consumed with a burning desire to attain God, and for this reason, he willingly marched to his death. His concern for the churches along the way was for their unity lest they fall short of attaining God. Whether it was a defense of Christology or a plea for submission to the bishop, his ultimate concern was soteriological. He never did this in a way that undermined salvation by grace, but he did issue sincere warnings just as Paul had. Justification was a result of faith in the Gospel but this faith must be evident in love for Christ and others. Bruce Metzger summarizes Ignatius's letters well saying that they contain "such strong faith and overwhelming love of Christ as to make them one of the finest literary expressions of Christianity during the second century."[144]

---

[144] Bruce Metzger, *The Canon of the New Testament: Its Origin, Development, and Significance* (Oxford: Clarendon Press, 1987), 44.

4 "O Sweet Exchange!": *Epistle to Diognetus*

Among second-century writings, the *Epistle to Diognetus* has a remarkable clarity with regard to the doctrines of justification and the atonement. As such, it is the most obvious second-century writing that refutes T. F. Torrance's theory that the Apostolic Fathers abandoned a Pauline doctrine of grace. In a book that engages each of the Apostolic Fathers, Torrance rarely even mentions the *Epistle to Diognetus* and when he does, it is with the casual tip of the pen in a brief citation or footnote.[1] He does not devote a chapter to this important work nor does he explain its conspicuous omission. It is strange that a work that so openly conflicts with his thesis is not represented in his work.[2] Given that the *Epistle to Diognetus* is traditionally placed among the Apostolic Fathers, an oversight of this magnitude should have at least been explained.[3]

The author of *Diognetus* is consistent with the New Testament from his view of Christology[4] to his clear affirmation of substitutionary atonement.[5] Regarding

---

[1] According to his index, Torrance references the *Epistle to Diognetus* five times (*The Doctrine of Grace in the Apostolic Fathers* [Grand Rapids: Eerdmans, 1959], 147). Four of these five are in footnotes and contain only a chapter and verse citation. Two of these references come from chap. 11, a chap. that is not likely part of the original letter (see n. 39 below).

[2] In fairness to Torrance, he may not have included the *Epistle to Diognetus* in his book because he thought it belonged with the writings of the apologists in the latter half of the second century and not with the Apostolic Fathers. Regardless, he does not explain the reason for the omission. See below for the discussion on genre.

[3] A. Gallandi was the first to place *Diognetus* among the Apostolic Fathers when he published the epistle in 1765. He believed that Apollos, Paul's companion in Acts, wrote this letter (see Charles Hill, *From the Lost Teaching of Polycarp: Identifying Irenaeus' Apostolic Presbyter and the Author of* Ad Diognetum [Tübingen: Mohr Siebeck, 2006], 97 n. 1), and this based on the ascription ἀποστόλων μαθητής, which was misinterpreted. See J. B. Lightfoot and J. R. Harmer, eds. *The Apostolic Fathers: Revised Greek Texts with Introductions and English Translations* (Grand Rapids: Baker Book House, 1891), 489.

[4] See Joseph T. Lienhard, "The Christology of the Epistle to Diognetus," *VC* 24 (1970): 280–89. Although Jesus is never presented as the Χριστός, the language used of him is consistent with the Apostle Paul's (cp. Col 1:15–20 and *Diog.* 7.2). H. G. Meecham also believes the author presented a high Christology (Meecham, "Theology of the Epistle to Diognetus," *ExpT* 54 [1943]: 100–01). It is important to note that while both Lienhard and Meecham postulate that chapters 11–12 do not belong to *Diognetus*, Meecham analyzes the Christology of these chapters to further elucidate the author's doctrine on this matter (101), whereas Lienhard wants to "avoid the possibility of conflating two distinct Christologies" (280).

[5] Traces of Pauline influence can be found sprinkled all through the epistle. Charles Nielson observed quite some time ago that "Pauline influence appears not only very often but also at crucial points where the actual definition of Christianity is at stake" (Nielson, "The Epistle to Diognetus: Its Date and Relationship to Marcion," *ATR* 52 [1970]: 88). Michael Bird has recently

grace, there is perhaps no other document in the Patristic literature, certainly nothing in the ante-Nicene period, that renders a clearer exposition of justification by faith than this apologetic letter. More specifically, the author of *Diognetus* expounds a view of justification that is in harmony with the so-called "traditional" understanding of Paul's doctrine of justification, and his view of the atonement is likewise Pauline. Thus, this chapter argues that the *Epistle to Diognetus* presents a forensic view of justification that is rooted in grace and stems from substitutionary atonement.

Primarily this chapter will consist of an exegetical analysis of *Diognetus* 9, for it is in chapter nine that the author puts forth an exceptional case for justification. Various grammatical concerns will be addressed and a significant commentary will be given. Following this in-depth examination of the text, there will be an evaluation of the theological considerations raised, specifically substitutionary atonement and forensic justification. However, before getting into the text itself, a few preliminary remarks are in order regarding background issues.

4.1 Background

Almost all of the background materials of this work lie hidden behind a veil of mystery.[6] No consensus exists on any of the traditional background matters and this is probably for several reasons. First, the *Epistle to Diognetus* was unknown to the early church. The first time it makes an appearance in history is in a manuscript in the thirteenth or fourteenth century. The fathers appear to be entirely

---

conducted a brilliant study on how Paul was received in the *Epistle to Diognetus* (Bird, "The Reception of Paul in the *Epistle to Diognetus*," in *Paul and the Second Century*, ed. Michael Bird and Joseph Dodson, LNTS 412 [New York: T&T Clark, 2011], 70–90). He boldly claims, "If we have to identify the largest single literary influence on [the *Epistle to Diognetus*] then it would have to be the letters of Paul" (72). Bird classifies his findings under the rubrics of citation, allusion, and echoes (73). The only discernible citation he discovered was the use of 1 Cor 8:1 in *Diognetus* 12.5 (which is problematic when the question of *Diognetus's* integrity is posed). The number of allusions is plentiful and the number of echoes to be heard is greater still. The echoes of Paul that Bird identifies in regard to justification will be discussed in turn. Suffice it to say for now that since the author of *Diognetus* clearly knew of and used Paul, it is no stretch whatsoever to suggest that his views of justification and the atonement were also derived from the Apostle he admired.

6 Most scholars who work on *Diognetus* use similar language to explain the enigmatic origins of this correspondence. See, for instance, Michael Bird, "The Reception of Paul in the *Epistle to Diognetus*," 70. Remarks such as this vent the frustration that modern commentators share over *Diognetus* not yielding its most basic secrets.

ignorant of this text, even the exhaustive Eusebius who usually at least makes reference to most of his predecessors' writings. Because of its relatively short reception history when compared to the writings of the other fathers, it is difficult to situate in history. Second, the document itself makes no claim of authorship and only a vague reference to the recipient. Without knowing either who wrote this letter or for whom it was intended, it is difficult to date with certainty.

Genre

Determining the genre of this letter is important, for it may give a clue as to when it was written. If it was written as paraenetic letter to Diognetus, then it could rightly be classified among the Apostolic Fathers.[7] Almost all the writings of the Apostolic Fathers are epistolary in nature, that is, they are occasional documents usually written to a church, as in *1 Clement* and most of Ignatius' letters, or to another believer, such as the letter of Ignatius to Polycarp. Typically *Diognetus* is placed with the Apostolic Fathers because of its epistolary framework, thus giving the impression that it was written in the early decades of the second century.

But this is where the similarity comes to an end. Avery Dulles has dubbed *Diognetus* "the pearl of early Christian apologetics," and rightly so.[8] The tone throughout the work is protreptic and more consistent with the apologetic literature that dominated the latter half of the second century. Michael Bird has come closest to pinpointing the genre of *Diognetus* by calling it an "apologetic-protrep-

---

[7] Stanley Stowers has carefully differentiated between protreptic and paraenetic literature in the ancient world (Stowers, *Letter Writing in Greco-Roman Antiquity* [Philadelphia: Westminster Press, 1986], 92). Cf. Diana M. Swancutt, "Paraenesis in Light of Protrepsis," in *Early Christian Paraenesis in Context*, ed. James Starr and Troels Engberg-Pedersen (New York: Walter de Gruyter, 2004), 113.

[8] Avery Cardinal Dulles, *A History of Apologetics* (Eugene, OR: Wipf and Stock, 1999), 35. Many who take to studying the *Epistle of Diognetus* have marveled over the profundity of the letter. Christian C. J. Bunsen, for instance, says of *Diognetus*, "After Scripture, [it is] the finest monument we know of sound Christian feeling, noble courage, and manly eloquence" (Bunsen, *Christianity and Mankind*, [London: Longman, Brown, Green, and Longmans, 1854], 1:171). F. L. Cross renders a similar accolade, calling the epistle a "persuasive and attractive apology for the Christian code of life" (Cross, *The Early Christian Fathers* [London: G. Duckworth, 1960], 27). The notable exception is E. J. Goodspeed, who claims that *Diognetus* "lacks entirely the convincing and gripping quality of early Christian literature" (Goodspeed, *A History of Early Christian Literature* [Chicago: University of Chicago Press, 1966], 148). The majority of those who have studied *Diognetus*, however, hold this epistle in high esteem.

tic."[9] It is probable that this letter was written to an individual within the upper echelon of the Roman Empire with the intent to give a defense of Christianity and to proselytize. The sophistication of the arguments, the acuity of the rhetoric, and the loftiness of the doxologies combine to make this work a "spirited and stirring defense of the truth of the Christian worldview."[10] Thus, this letter would be better placed among the apologists rather than the Apostolic Fathers.[11]

Authorship

Identifying the author of the *Epistle to Diognetus* is like trying to solve an ancient crime for which there were no witnesses and scant evidence. The fathers bear no witness to the author of this treatise, and the internal evidence is of little help. Therefore, opinions over authorship are varied, ranging from Polycarp[12] in the early second century to Hippolytus in the early third century, and include most of the other known Christian authors in-between.[13] There are, however,

---

[9] Bird, "The Reception of Paul," 71. Cf. C. S. Wansink, "*Epistula ad Diognetum:* A School Exercise in the Use of Protreptic," *Church Divinity* (1986): 97–109. See also Bryan C. Hollon, "Is the *Epistle to Diognetus* an apology? A Rhetorical Analysis," *JCR* 28 (2005): 127–146.

[10] Michael A. G. Haykin, *Rediscovering the Church Fathers: Who They Were and How They Shaped the Church* (Wheaton, IL: Crossway, 2011), 49–50.

[11] Robert M. Grant wrote an excellent essay entitled, "The Chronology of the Greek Apologists" (*VC* 9 [1955]: 25–33) that used historical data buried within the various writings to date them. Curiously, Grant made no mention of the *Epistle to Diognetus*, which is a strange oversight especially because Grant places the *Epistle to Diognetus* with the apologists and not with the Apostolic Fathers where it is traditionally placed (Grant, *Greek Apologists of the Second Century* [Philadelphia: The Westminster Press, 1988], 178).

[12] See Hill, *From the Lost Teaching of Polycarp*, who devoted half of a monograph to Polycarp as the author of *Diognetus*. Hill seeks to excavate additional teachings from Polycarp, who, citing Helmut Koester, was "doubtlessly the most significant ecclesiastical leader of the first half of II CE" (*Introduction to the New Testament*, vol. 2, *History and Literature of Early Christianity* [New York: Walter de Gruyter, 1982], 308), by uncovering imbedded references in Irenaeus's *Adversus Haereses* and by arguing that *Ad Diognetum* is from Polycarp's pen. The former case, that Polycarp's teachings can be extracted from Irenaeus, he says "may be treated as a certainty"; while the latter, that Polycarp is the anonymous author of *Ad Diognetum*, rests "high in the realms of probability" (Hill, *From the Lost Teaching of Polycarp*, 3). While Hill is persuasive on the first account, he is less so on the second.

[13] The most fascinating suggestion was put forth by Bunsen who believes that Marcion wrote this document prior to his apostasy (*Christianity and Mankind*, 170 ff.). Marcion's authorship is attractive because it accounts for the reason that no other authors use this work and for there being very little textual evidence. The epistle would have been a scandalous document from which the fathers would have readily distanced themselves.

three primary forerunners in the debate who deserve attention: Pantaenus, Hippolytus, and Quadratus.

Pantaenus (c.180–210) presided over the catechetical school in Alexandria and was a mentor to Clement, who succeeded him as head of the school. Alexandria, legendary as the wellspring of Christian philosophy, seems to fit the philosophical bent that is evident throughout the work. J. B. Lightfoot went so far as to say, "Clearly [*Diognetus*] is Alexandrian, as its phraseology and its sentiments alike show."[14] Pantaenus becomes more attractive as the possible author if one accepts chapters 11–12 as a part of the original epistle, because in chapter 11 the author makes frequent reference to Christ as the λόγος, a motif that would come to predominate the Alexandrian school.[15] However, this view suffers greatly in that neither Clement nor Origen alluded to this letter.[16]

Hippolytus (c.170–236) is another popular suggestion put forward. A disciple of Irenaeus, Hippolytus was the last of the Western fathers to write in Greek. Throughout his life Hippolytus was involved in several fierce struggles over Trinitarian issues. One particular skirmish took place between himself and Calixtus. Hippolytus charged Calixtus as a Monarchian and Calixtus charged Hippolytus as a ditheist. Both claimed to be the true bishop of Rome which led to Hippolytus being labeled the first anti-bishop.

Like the other Christian writers of his day, Hippolytus was engaged in writing apologetic works as well. His major work, *Refutio omnium Haeresium*, is very similar to Irenaeus' *Adversus Haereses*, and includes an introductory chapter which was circulated separately. This chapter, entitled *Philosophoumena*, pro-

---

[14] J. B. Lightfoot and J. R. Harmer, eds., *Apostolic Fathers* (Whitefish, MT: Kessinger, 2003), 248. The remainder of Lightfoot's argument focuses on information that comes from chaps. 11–12. For instance, Pantaenus also treats creation and the Garden of Eden as spiritual accounts of the church. Moreover, he suggests that the phrase ἀποστόλων γενόμενος μαθητὴς γίνομαι διδάσκαλος ἐθνῶν in chap. 11 could not be more appropriately applied to another. The problem is that Lightfoot emphatically denies that these two chapters were originally part of the letter, saying, "The Epistle to Diognetus, however, does not reach beyond the tenth chapter, where it ends abruptly" (248). Thus Pantaenus may very well be the author of these chaps. that were later tacked on after chap. 10 and not be the author of the letter itself.

[15] J. J. Thierry, "The Logos as Teacher in Ad Diognetum XI, 1," *VC* 20 (1966): 146–49. The doctrine of the Logos in Alexandria actually owes its origin to Philo of Alexandria several centuries before (see David Winston, *Logos and Mystical Theology in Philo of Alexandria* [Cincinnati: Hebrew Union College Press, 1985]). However, it would become very prominent under Clement of Alexandria, Pantaenus' pupil. See M. J. Edwards, "Clement of Alexandria and His Doctrine of the Logos," *VC* 54 (2000): 159–77. It is important to note that speaking of Christ as the Logos is not exclusive to chap. 11. Thierry also points out that the author speaks of Christ in this way prior to chap. 11, as for example in 7.2 (147).

[16] Hill, *From the Lost Teaching of Polycarp*, 100.

vides the reader with an introduction to philosophy. After reading this work, R. H. Connolly observed significant parallels between it and the *Epistle to Diognetus*, especially when comparing *Diognetus* 7.1–5 and *Philosophoumena* 10.33. The similarities, Connolly argues, extend to both the content and the structure of the passages.[17] While Connolly presents a fairly convincing case, his dating of *Diognetus* extends to the early third century which is unlikely.[18] Also, his juxtaposition of these works concentrates on such a small cross-section of each volume that it is difficult for his argument to be sustained.

Quadratus is the most probable of all the contenders for authorship, though little is known about him. We do know that he was the first Christian apologist and that he presented his apology to Hadrian while the Emperor was visiting either Asia Minor (123/124 or 129) or Athens (125/126 or 129).[19] Though this treatise is no longer extant, we do have a brief snippet preserved for us in the annals of Eusebius' *Historia Ecclesiae*. Citing Quadratus, Eusebius writes,

> Our Savior's deeds were always there to see, for they were true: those who were cured or those who rose from the dead were seen not only when they were cured or raised but were constantly there to see, not only while the Savior was living among us, but also for some time after his departure. Some of them, in fact, survived right up to our own time.[20]

Originally proposed by Isaak A. Dorner,[21] the case for Quadratus' authorship of *Diognetus* gained momentum under Dom Andriessen. Andriessen postulates that this fragment from Quadratus fits the lacuna in the *Diognetus* text between 7.6–7.7. He opines that the material from Quadratus would "fit exceedingly well, of course not in such a manner that a continuous text would be obtained."[22] It

---

[17] R. H. Connolly, "The Date and Authorship of the Epistle to Diognetus," *JTS* 36 (1935): 348. Connolly knows that any outright claim to authorship is likely to be rejected, so he hedges his thesis with the following comment: "It will, I think, be found difficult to avoid the conclusion that the Epistle was written, if not by Hippolytus, a least by one who was, like Hippolytus, a student of Irenaeus" (347). See also, idem, "*Ad Diognetum* xi-xii," *JTS* 37 (1936): 2–15, where Connolly argues that Hippolytus was also the author of chaps. 11–12 of *Diognetus*.
[18] See below for a discussion on dating.
[19] Hubertus R. Drobner, *The Fathers of the Church: A Comprehensive Introduction*, trans. Siegfried S. Schatzmann (Peabody, MA: Hendrickson, 2007), 73.
[20] Eusebius, *The Church History*, 4.3, trans. Paul L. Maier (Grand Rapids: Kregel, 1999), 136.
[21] Isaak A. Dorner, *History of the Development of the Doctrine of the Person of Christ*, trans. William Alexander (Edinburgh: T&T Clark, 1868), 1:374.
[22] Dom P. Andriessen, "The Authorship of the Epistula Ad Diognetum," *VC* 1 (1947): 129.

is quite conceivable that this swath from Quadratus is a portion of the missing text in *Diognetus*, although it is far from certain.[23]

While the debate about authorship rests mostly upon conjecture, it is known that the letter was addressed to the obscure figure of Diognetus. The only serious candidate from history is the Diognetus that Marcus Aurelius mentions in the opening chapter of his *Meditations*.[24] Concerning the things Diognetus taught him, the Emperor writes, "Of Diognetus, not to be taken up with trifles; and not to give credence to the statements of miracle-mongers and wizards about incantations and the exorcizing of demons, and such-like marvels."[25] As an aside, one wonders if this statement could in some way be a warning against the miraculous claims that Christians made. He continues by thanking Diognetus for hunting advice as well as instilling in him a love of all things Greek, especially philosophy. This epitaph to his mentor fits exceptionally well with what is known of Hadrian, namely that he had an affinity for hunting and Greek culture.[26] Also striking is the fact that in all of his eulogies at the outset of his *Mediations*, he never mentions Hadrian. This is a glaring omission for an emperor who had such a profound impact on the young Marcus Aurelius. Andriessen made the astute observation that "whereever [sic] we should expect the name of this emperor, we find the name of Diognetus" and that Marcus Aurelius actually gives this title to Hadrian elsewhere.[27]

Just as with the other views, this theory has its problems. First, it is very convenient that the only portion which Eusebius quotes happens to fit the lacuna. The likelihood of this is doubtful. Second, no other sources from Quadratus exist with which to compare the style of his writing to that found in *Diognetus*. Finally, this theory must be based on the probability that Hadrian did in fact take

---

[23] Interestingly, Michael Holmes places the fragments of Quadratus with the *Epistle to Diognetus*, suggesting that Quadratus composed this work as well, an idea that he calls "intriguing" (688). See Michael W. Holmes, *The Apostolic Fathers*, 3rd ed. (Grand Rapids: Baker, 2007).

[24] Clayton N. Jefford proposes Claudius Diogenes, the procurator of Alexandria at the end of the second century, as the possible recipient (Clayton N. Jefford, Kenneth J. Harder, and Louis D. Amezaga, Jr., *Reading the Apostolic Fathers: An Introduction* [Peabody, MA: Hendrickson, 1996], 36). Bolstering this claim is the fact that Claudius Diogenes was referred to as "the most excellent Diognetus" (Grant, *Greek Apologists of the Second Century*, 179), and this places the letter in Alexandria, which accounts for the philosophical tenor. However, few follow Jefford in this speculation.

[25] Marcus Aurelius, *Meditations* 1.6, trans. C.R. Haines, LCL (London: William Heinemann, 1916), 5.

[26] See Anthony Everitt, *Hadrian and the Triumph of Rome* (New York: Random House, 2009), 22, 15 respectively.

[27] Andriessen, "The Authorship of the Epistula Ad Diognetum," 134.

the name Diognetus. At any rate, the author of *Diognetus* will remain behind his veil for now.

Date

Assigning a date to the *Epistle to Diognetus* depends on how one resolves the aforementioned difficulties. If, for instance, one is persuaded that Pantaenus wrote this remarkable work, then he would necessarily ascribe this work to the end of the second century. On the other hand, if one believes that it is Quadratus' voice coming through, then he would assume a date during the reign of Hadrian, and so on. Though nothing definitive can be said regarding the date, it is almost certain that this letter was written sometime during the second century. It seems to fit Christianity's plight in that turbulent century, addressing many of the same issues that the other apologists thought necessary to answer.[28]

One key that may unlock this conundrum comes from the frequent mention of persecution that can be traced throughout the treatise. In some places the descriptions of persecution are subtle and require shrewd listening. For instance, the author makes statements that Christians are "dishonored" (5.14), "insulted" (5.15), and "slandered" (5.14). There are other times, however, when the author speaks candidly about the persecution which Christians faced. Christians are "thrown to wild beasts" (7.7), "persecuted by all men" (5.11), "condemned" (5.12), and most poignantly, they "endure for the sake of righteousness the fire which is temporary" (10.8).

While the theme of persecution saturates the pages of this work, it is nevertheless inconclusive. Because persecution tells the story of Christianity for most of the second century, pinpointing a specific time of persecution is out of the question. From Trajan's response to Pliny the Younger,[29] to Marcus Aurelius' response of persecution on account of the Avidius Cassius revolt,[30] Christians

---

[28] The apologists of the second century, among whom *Diognetus* should be included, focused their writings against their two main antagonists—the Jews and the Romans. For second-century documents written in opposition to Judaism, see for example Melito of Sardis, *On Pascha and Fragments*, ed. S. G. Hall (Oxford: Clarendon, 1979), especially paragraphs 72–99, where Melito lambastes Jews for crucifying Christ; also see *The Epistle of Barnabas*. For a critique of pagans, see for example Theophilus of Antioch's *To Autolycus* (Michael Grant, *Theophilus of Antioch Ad Autolycum* [Oxford: Clarendon, 1970]).

[29] Pliny, *Letters*, 10.96, and Trajan's response in 10.97.

[30] Robert M. Grant, "Five Apologists and Marcus Aurelius," *VC* 42 (1988): 2.

found no respite from the onslaught of the Empire.³¹ It was not until the death of Marcus Aurelius in 180 CE that persecution finally came to a halt. This brief intermission lasted for a decade until Septimius Severus once again took up the mantle of killing Christians. Therefore, the little bit of light that this does shine on our problem suggests that it was written sometime in the middle to late second century.

Another possible clue of when this work was written may be found in 7.4 where the author states: "he sent him as a king sends his son who is a king" (ὡς βασιλεὺς πέμπων υἱὸν βασιλέα ἔπεμψεν). Lightfoot has made the reasonable assertion that this could refer to Antoninus Pius's adoption of Marcus Aurelius into the tribunal power (147 CE) or of Commodus' ascension into the co-regency (176 CE).³² Regardless, Lightfoot argues, "The simplicity in the mode of stating theological truths, and the absence of all reference to the manifold heresies of later times, both point to a somewhat early date."³³

Finally, in the vein of Lightfoot, Meecham assembles a series of arguments for an early date that is worth citing in its entirety:

> Some general considerations point to this relatively early date [of 150 AD]: the condemnation in common of paganism and Judaism; freedom in handling the N.T. writings; the lack of the tendency to identify the ideal of Christian excellence with the ascetic life, and the absence of traces of sacerdotalism; the relatively simple Christology less elaborate than that of Origen; the dominance of the doctrine of the Logos with no doctrine of the Holy Spi-

---

31 Candida Moss has challenged the notion of widespread persecution in the early church. According to her research, "Very few Christians died, and when they did, they were often executed for what we in the modern world would call political reasons. There is a difference between persecution and prosecution." (See *The Myth of Persecution: How Early Christians Invented a Story of Martyrdom* [New York: HarperOne, 2013], 14. This is the distilled version of her scholarly work *Ancient Christian Martyrdom: Diverse Practices, Theologies, and Traditions* [New Haven: Yale University Press, 2012].) Her work is a helpful correction to the popular image of Romans ushering tens of thousands of Christians to their deaths in the Colosseum. However, I do not think she appreciates the psychological impact persecution had on Christians in the first few centuries, especially since many of those martyred were in the upper ranks of the church. The sword of martyrdom may not have touched as many heads as was once thought, but it was the heads it did touch that sent shock waves through the church. Christians would have felt as though the Empire was unrelenting in its efforts to extinguish their faith. Also, I take issue with Moss's idea that Christians were prosecuted more than persecuted. In reality, they were prosecuted because they would not submit to Roman leadership who commanded them at times to sacrifice to the gods or to burn incense to the Emperor's *genius*. They would not submit because this would cause them to abandon their Christian beliefs, and thus they were prosecuted. Is this not a form of persecution? It would seem so.
32 Lightfoot, *Apostolic Fathers*, 248.
33 Lightfoot, *Apostolic Fathers*, 248.

rit; the problem why the Son had come late in time, which appears in Justin but finds little place in later apologists; the apparent unawareness of formulated heresies, apart from possible hints of the Gnostic emphasis; the traditional assignment of the Epistle to Justin and its place in the Codex with other writings ascribed to him.[34]

No concensus exists concerning the author of *Diognetus* but the argument for a date in the middle of the second century remains probable.

Much more could be said regarding the background materials but the discussion must move on toward the goal of understanding soteriology in *Diognetus*, lest this study fall into the trap that has captured many commentators on this epistle who confine their discussion to background issues and miss the theology that truly makes this the "noblest of early Christian writings."[35]

4.2 The Text: Summary, Translation, Commentary

The *Epistle to Diognetus* was preserved in a single manuscript from the thirteenth or fourteenth century.[36] Originally part of the *Codex Argentoratensis Graecus ix* manuscript, it was ascribed to Justin Martyr under the title τοῦ αὐτοῦ πρός Διόγνητον. The document was discovered accidentally in a fish market in the fifteenth century, and just a century later, the first edition was completed by Henricus Stephanus (1592).[37] Eventually it made its way to the public library in Strasbourg, where fire destroyed it on August 24, 1870, during the Franco-Prussian War.[38]

---

34 Henry G. Meecham, *The Epistle to Diognetus: The Greek Text with Introduction, Translation and Notes* (Manchester: Manchester University Press, 1949), 19.
35 J. B. Lightfoot, *St. Paul's Epistles to the Colossians and to Philemon* (London: Macmillan and Co., 1892), 154.
36 For modern critical editions of the text, see Meecham, *The Epistle to Diognetus*; H. I. Marrou, *A Diognète: Introduction, edition critique, traduction et commentaire*, 2nd ed., SC 33 (Paris: Cerf, 1997); Kirsopp Lake, *The Apostolic Fathers*, vol. 2, LCL (Cambridge, MA: Harvard University Press, 1976); Bart D. Ehrman, *The Apostolic Fathers*, vol. 2, LCL (Cambridge, MA: Harvard University Press, 2003); E. H. Blakeney, *The Epistle to Diognetus* (London: SPCK; New York: The Macmillan Co., 1943); J. J. Thierry, *The Epistle to Diognetus*, Textus Minores 33 (Leiden: E. J. Brill, 1964). The Greek text used throughout this chapter is from Holmes, *The Apostolic Fathers*—the translations are my own.
37 Drobner, *The Fathers of the Church*, 75.
38 Drobner, *The Fathers of the Church*, 75.

Summary

In the introduction to the epistle, the author seeks to answer three questions which Diognetus had raised concerning Christianity. First, what God do they believe in that makes them disregard the world and despise death, neither considering the Greek gods or Jewish superstitions? Second, what is the nature of their love for one another? Third, why has this new race or way of life come into world now and not before? The first ten chapters of the Epistle are dedicated to the author's response to these three questions.[39]

Beginning in chapter 2, the author wages a full intellectual assault against pagan idolatry. The foolishness of idolatry can be readily seen in that the idols made from more precious materials, like gold and silver, are guarded at night, whereas the idols made from more common materials go unprotected. If they were truly representations of the gods, then why do the gods not protect themselves? All of these gods were made by human hands and could have easily been fashioned into something else, an argument similar to that of Isaiah 44.

In chapters 3–4 the author shifts focus from pagan idolatry to Jewish superstition.[40] The Roman Empire had a longstanding relationship with Jews and made concessions for their right to worship Yahweh, but Diognetus understood that there were substantial differences between the Jews and the Christians. The author asserts that pagans offer sacrifices to gods who are unable to receive honor, while Jews think that they make effectual offerings to the one who is in need of nothing (3.5). In chapter 4 he examines the various laws which Jews adhere to (circumcision, Sabbath, new moons, qualms over meats), calling them "ridiculous" (καταγέλαστα). His point is that these outward signs could never convey inward realities. For example, pride about circumcision, which he calls mutilation of the flesh (μείωσιν τῆς σαρκός), is foolish because circumcision was never the basis of God's love of his people (4.4). Surprisingly, the author makes no reference to the Old Testament in his diatribe against the Jews, a "no-

---

39 Space will not permit a discussion on the integrity of the text. Scholarly consensus is that chaps. 11–12 were not originally a part of this work (see discussion scattered above, e.g., n. 4). These chaps. are more sermonic in nature and deviate from the apologetic tone the author used in the first ten chaps. In all likelihood, *Diognetus* was housed together with the sermon and were assumed to belong together. The dissonance of these documents makes it improbable that they form the same document, let alone that they were written by the same author.
40 Perhaps the author is mirroring Paul's argument in Romans. His attack on the Gentiles is followed by an attack on Jews, just as Paul uses strong invective against both these groups, in the same order, in Rom 1–2.

ticeable omission" given that "some Christian apologists made great play with Old Testament prophecies as predictions of the coming of Christ."[41]

Chapters 5–8 serve as a response to the second question and establish the foundation for the answer to the third question.[42] Diognetus's curiosity was piqued by the Christians' love for one another; after all, love was the most distinguishing mark of Christianity in the second century.[43] In order to answer the question of why Christians love one another, the author descends into a philosophical discussion about Christians being the soul of the world. He opens chapter 6 saying, "In a word, what the soul is to the body, this Christians are to the world" (6.1). The argument unfolds with a comparison of the Christians as the soul and the world as the flesh. "The soul loves the flesh that hates it and its members," he writes, "and Christians love those who hate them" (6.6). This fierce hatred of Christianity had the paradoxical effect of growing the faith (6.9; cf. 7.8), just as Tertullian would comment less than a century later of the irony of persecution: "the blood of the martyrs is the seed [of the church]" (*semen est sanguis Christianorum*).[44] Even daily persecution could not quench the conflagration set by Christianity; rather it fanned the flames into an uncontrollable blaze that spread throughout the Empire.

Chapters 7–8 give a positive response to who God is.[45] Instead of pointing out the absurdities in Greco-Roman religion and Judaism, the author finally tells Diognetus about the Christian God. This God, who is omnipotent (παντοκράτωρ) and invisible (ἀόρατος), established the truth among men through the "holy and incomprehensible word (τὸν λόγον τὸν ἅγιον καὶ ἀπερινόητον). In order to communicate this truth and "fix it firmly in their hearts" (ἐγκατεστήριξε ταῖς καρδίαις αὐτῶν), God sent the "designer and creator of the universe

---

[41] Meecham, "The Theology of the Epistle to Diognetus," 98.
[42] See Bruce Fawcett, "Similar yet Unique: Christians as Described in the *Letter to Diognetus*," *The Baptist Review of Theology* 6 (1996): 23–27. For Fawcett, chap. 5 is the "most interesting pericope" (23) in the letter because it is in chap. 5 that the author of *Diognetus* lists the ways in which Christians are similar and yet dissimilar to their Roman neighbors. Fawcett identifies four reasons the author gives for why Christian were different: "persecution, inverted responses to persecution, sexual practices, other-worldiness" (25).
[43] The satirist Lucian famously mocked Christians of the second century for their indiscriminate love in his "Passing of Peregrinus," *Lucian*, vol. 5, trans. A. M. Harmon, LCL (Cambridge, MA: Harvard, 1936), 13 ff.
[44] Tertullian, *Apology*, 50.
[45] Much of his argument thus far has focused on negative theology which was common in the early apologists, especially as a defense against the charge of atheism. See D. W. Palmer, "Atheism, Apologetic and Negative Theology in the Greek Apologists of the Second Century," *VC* 37 (1983): 252.

himself" (αὐτὸν τὸν τεχνίτην καὶ δημιουργὸν τῶν ὅλων), through whom all things were created (cf. Col 1.15–20). Though he never explicitly connects this to Christ, it is abundantly clear from the context that Jesus is the referent.

In chapter 8 he briefly slips back into a critique of pagan conceptions of this universe, whether it is made from fire, water, or some other element (8.2),[46] only to demonstrate the superiority of the Christians' God. For God is not only the "master and creator of the universe" (ὁ γὰρ δεσπότης καὶ δημιουργὸς τῶν ὅλων θεός), but he is also benevolent (φιλάνθρωπος) and patient (μακρόθυμος). He conceived a great and marvelous plan that he shared with his son alone. When Jesus came to earth his plan was revealed and his believers received everything at once (8.11). This leads to the passage at hand.

Translation

(1) Therefore, having already arranged all things in his own mind with his Child, he permitted[47] us, during[48] the previous time, to be carried away by undisciplined passions as we desired, being led off by pleasures and lusts, not at all taking delight[49] in our sins, but because of his forbearance, not because he approved of the former season of unrighteousness, but because he was creating the present season[50] of righteousness,[51] in order that

---

46 The author gives a blatant critique of classical philosophy here. The belief that the universe had one underlying natural cause dates to the Pre-Socratic philosophers. It was Thales who taught that the universe was fundamentally water, Heraclitus fire, and Anaximenes air. The author calls them "pretentious philosophers" (τῶν ἀξιοπίστων φιλοσόφων) who speak with "empty and nonsensical words" (τοὺς κενοὺ καὶ ληρώδεις ἐκείνων λόγους). This attack on philosophy comes unexpectedly because the recipient was almost certainly sympathetic to Greek philosophers, not to mention the fact that the author himself owes an obvious debt of gratitude to Greek philosophy as seen in his rhetoric.
47 ἐάω typically takes a complementary infinitive and accusative as it does here with φέρεσθαι and ἡμᾶς (BDAG, s.v. "ἐάω," 1).
48 It is necessary to translate μέχρι in a durative sense, "during," as opposed to "until" or "as far as," as it is often translated. Literally it could be rendered "as far as the previous time was concerned."
49 ἐφηδόμενος is an adverbial participle most likely functioning causally. It was not because he delighted in our sins that he endured, but it was *because* of his patience (ἀνεχόμενος—also adverbial/causal), as the author states in the following clause.
50 *Codex Argentoratensis Graecus ix* has νοῦν instead of νῦν. Quite clearly this is an easy mistake for a scribe to make. This reading would be: "but because he was creating the mind of righteousness." While this translation is conceivable, it is not as probable. The author is contrasting the former season of unrighteousness with the present season of righteousness (καιρός is elided from the latter clause but understood from the context), especially in light of the next clause that also contrasts the former times with the present.

we who in the former time had been convicted of our own works as unworthy of life might be considered worthy by the kindness[52] of God in the present time, and having revealed our inability to enter into the kingdom of God on our own,[53] we might be made able by the power of God. (2) But when our unrighteousness was fulfilled, and it was perfectly made known that its wages, namely punishment and death, were to be expected, then[54] the season came in which God determined finally[55] to reveal his kindness and power (O the surpassing kindness and love of God); he did not hate us neither did he reject nor bear a grudge against us, but he was patient and forbearing[56] and because of his mercy he took upon himself our sins,[57] he himself gave up his own son as a ransom on our behalf, the holy for the lawless, the innocent for the wicked, the righteous for the unrighteous, the incorruptible for the corruptible, the immortal for the mortal. (3) For what else was able to cover our sins except the righteousness of that one? (4) In whom was it possible for us, the lawless and ungodly to be justified except in the Son of God alone? (5) O the sweet exchange, O the inscrutable work (of God), O the unexpected benefits (of God), that the lawlessness of many might be hidden in one righteous man, while the righteousness of one might justify many lawless men. (6) Therefore, having demonstrated the powerlessness of our nature to obtain life in the previous time, and having shown the savior's power to save even the powerless in the present time, he willed that for both of these (reasons) we should believe in his goodness, and we should regard him as nurse, father, teacher, counselor, physician, mind, light, honor, glory, strength, and life, and not to be anxious[58] concerning clothing and food.[59]

Commentary

Christians generally faced three charges in the second century—atheism, incest, and cannibalism. They were thought to be cannibals because of a misunderstanding of the Lord's Supper. Pagans were not permitted into the service during the Lord's Supper, and only heard that those inside were feasting on the body of Christ. Incest was a charge hurled at Christians because they called one another

---

51 Once again the author is using adverbial participles causally (συνευδοκῶν, δημιουργῶν respectively).
52 Cf. Rom 2:4. Also, according to BDAG, this word has sense of uprightness in one's relations with others and can be translated as "uprightness."
53 The κατά is functioning with reference/respect.
54 δέ is here functioning as a transitional conjunction (see Daniel Wallace, *Greek Grammar beyond the Basics* [Grand Rapids: Zondervan, 1996], 674).
55 Adverbial use of λοιπόν.
56 See Herbert Smyth, *Greek Grammar*, rev. Gordon M. Messing (Cambridge, MA: Harvard University Press, 1984), §2166 for asyndeton in "rapid and lively descriptions."
57 Lampe offers "take upon oneself," "take responsibility for," and "stand as surety for" as possible glosses.
58 μεριμνᾶν is a complimentary infinitive going back to ἐβουλήθη.
59 This translation follows a formal equivalence methodology.

brother and sister. Thus, relationships might form between a man and a woman who called one another brother and sister and yet were unrelated, giving the impression these were incestuous relationships. While these were serious moral charges, the most severe, and the one punishable by death, was atheism.[60]

The label of atheism was assigned to Christians because of their rejection of the Greco-Roman pantheon. Christians had been the scapegoats of the Empire since Nero pinned the fire of 64 on them which ravaged nearly half of Rome.[61] Whenever something tragic happened to Rome, the Emperor would often assume that the gods were displeased because people were not as pious as they ought to be. Once more, Tertullian speaks of the fate of Christians who died at the whim of capricious governors and emperors: "If the Tiber floods its banks, if the Nile fails to flood the fields, if heaven holds back the rain, if the earth shakes or famine comes, or pestilence; at once the cry goes up: 'The Christians to the lions!'"[62] Their refusal to pay homage to these gods branded them atheists and it was thought that they brought bad fortune upon the Empire. And so it was that many Christians were thrust into the arena and their demise was accompanied by the rapturous applause of spectators.

The reason that the Romans were suspicious of Christianity was their deep-seated suspicion of any religion that was new. Rome could trace her lineage, and thus her religion, back to the eighth century (BCE).[63] How, then, could a religion with such longevity be ousted by a religion whose birth came only a century before? The logic was simple: if Christianity was new, then it could not be true. The

---

[60] Athenagoras wrote a tome to Marcus Aurelius and Commodus his coregent sometime between AD 176–180 in which he addressed these three charges (*Legatio pro Christianis*, ed. M. Marcovich [Berlin and New York: de Gruyter, 1990]). It is clear from this work that Athenagoras believed he had to defend Christians from the charge of atheism over incest and cannibalism, as seen from the chapters he devoted to each of these issues. He spends only two chapters on cannibalism and three on incest, but he sets aside twenty-eight chapters for the charge of atheism. Flavius Clemens and his wife, Flavia Domitilla, prominent members of Caesar's household, were sentenced to death for "atheism" (Seut. *Dom*. 15; Dio Cassius 67.14.2). For more on the charge of atheism in early Christianity, see William Schoedel, "Christian 'Atheism' and the Peace of the Roman Empire," *CH* 42 (1973): 309–19.
[61] Tacitus, *Annals*, 15.44. This has been challenged with enough fervency in recent years that many classicists find Tacitus's account doubtful. Still, something turned Nero's ferocity on the Christians so that he sent many of them to their deaths.
[62] Tertullian, *Apology*, 40.2.
[63] See Suetonius, *Suetonius in Two Volumes*, trans. J. C. Rolfe, LCL (London: William Heinemann, 1920) for the charge of novelty. Suetonius writes, almost in passing, that "Punishment was inflicted on the Christians, a class of men given to a new and mischievous superstition" (*Nero*, 16.2).

charges of atheism and novelty went hand in hand.⁶⁴ Christianity appeared new to the Romans and their belief in monotheism sounded like atheism to the Roman ear. This was the third question about which Diognetus queried.

The defense of Christianity against the charge of novelty takes up the entirety of chapter 9. It is in this chapter that the author gives the reason behind God's delay of his plan, thus proving that Christianity is not new, but ancient. He begins the chapter by harkening back to the end of chapter 8 (οὖν). For much of history God had kept his plan of redemption hidden (8.10) and it was only later made manifest through his son (8.11). However, the important thing for the author is that these plans had been "prepared from the beginning" (τὰ ἐξ ἀρχῆς ἡτοιμασμένα) thus eliminating any novelty to the Christian religion. It may be that the fullness of the plan had not come into fruition until the present, but God's plan was set from the foundation of the world, having been planned together with his child (πάντ οὖν ἤδη παρ ἑαυτῷ σὺν τῷ παιδὶ οἰκονομηκώς).

The plan was to permit all mankind to be carried away by undisciplined passions and to be led astray by pleasures and lusts (εἴασεν ἡμᾶς ὡς ἐβουλόμεθα ἀτάκτοις φοραῖς φέρεσθαι ἡδοναῖς καὶ ἐπιθυμίαις ἀπαγομένος; cf. Rom 5). All of this was in the previous time, however (μέχρι μὲν τοῦ πρόσθεν χρόνου), and it was not as though God delighted in sins during that time (οὐ πάντως ἐφηδόμενος τοῖ ἁμαρτήμασιν ἡμῶν), lest he give the impression that God is either evil or indifferent. Rather, it was because of God's forbearance (ἀνεχόμενος) that he allowed these things to take place—he never approved of unrighteousness in the former season (οὐδὲ τῷ τότε τῆς ἀδικίας καιρῷ συνευδοκῶν).

God allowed people to walk their passions because he was creating the present season of righteousness (τὸν νῦν τῆς δικαιοσύνης δημιουργῶν). Such teaching must have sounded strange to Diognetus that God would purposefully allow people to live in sin so that he could later bring about a time of righteousness, and yet that is precisely what the author is propounding (cf. Rom 3:25 ff.). The former time was meant to bring about the conviction of their own deeds (ἐλεγχθέντες ἐκ τῶν ἰδίων ἔργων) in order that people might recognize that they were

---

64 The author's departure from the standard answer to novelty is peculiar. The majority of his contemporaries responded by demonstrating the connection that Christianity has to Judaism that extends farther back in time than even the Jewish Patriachs—Christian lineage stems to the first man, Adam. (Irenaeus demonstrates this very thing through his doctrine of recapitulation [*Adv. Haer.*]. Melito and Justin also make significant strides in making connections to the Old Testament [*Peri Paschal* and *Dial. Trypho*, respectively].) However, the author has cut off his ability to make this very argument because he has lambasted the Jews and their practices. Haykin accurately deems this failure "the only major weakness of the letter" (*Rediscovering the Church Fathers*, 59).

unworthy of life (ἀνάξιοι ζωῆς).⁶⁵ Although they are unable to obtain life through their own merit, they are now considered worthy because of God's goodness (νῦν ὑπὸ τῆς χρηστότητος ἀξιωθῶμεν).

The reference to life (ζωή) here is eschatological, referring to eternal life. At the end of 9.1 the author speaks of one's inability to enter the kingdom of God on his or her own (καὶ τὸ καθ ἑαυτοὺς φανερώσαντες ἀδύνατον εἰσελθεῖν τὴν βασιλείαν τοῦ θεοῦ τῇ δυνάμει τοῦ θεοῦ δυνατοὶ γενηθῶμεν). Being considered worthy of life now, allows one to enter into the kingdom of God in the future. The author also makes it clear that this is a work of God alone. No one could enter the kingdom of God on his own merits; he is enabled only by the power of God (τῇ δυνάμει τοῦ θεοῦ δυνατοὶ γενηθῶμεν). This would have caught the attention of Diognetus who was unfamiliar with a religion built upon grace. To the pagan like Diognetus whose religion was built on appeasing the gods, a religion built upon grace would have seemed strange at the least, if not absurd. The entire religious system of the second-century was built on appeasing the gods through pious acts like sacrifice. Diognetus would have believed that he could earn the favor of the gods; the author, however, tells him that the true God rescues those who were once in sin through no effort of their own (cf. Eph 2:8–9).

In verse 2 the author again juxtaposes the former time (τοῦ πρόσθεν χρόνου/τῷ τότε καιρῷ) with the present time (τὸν νῦν χρόνον/καιρὸν),⁶⁶ a critical comparison for him thus far. In the former time unrighteousness was fulfilled and the punishment sinful actions was made perfectly clear (τελείως πεφανέρωτο ὅτι ὁ μισθὸς αὐτῆς κόλασις καὶ θάνατος προσεδοκᾶτο). The wages of the previous period of unrighteousness were punishment and death (κόλασις καὶ θάνατος; cf. Rom 6:23).

A shift occurs at this point in the text. No longer does the author look back to the earlier time, but his eyes now focus solely on the acts of God in the present. He says that "the season came in which God determined finally to reveal his kindness and power" (ἧλε δὲ ὁ καιρὸς ὃν θεὸς προέθετο λοιπὸν φανερῶσαι τὴν ἑαυτοῦ χρηστότητα καὶ δύναμιν). Throughout human history God has permitted people to wallow in the muck of sin but this was so that he could reveal his kindness and power in his Son. The very idea that God would send his Son as part of his eternal plan causes the author to break from his main thought with

---

⁶⁵ The dependent clause is introduced with a ἵνα, indicating purpose in this instance.
⁶⁶ The author switches back and forth between χρόνος and καιρός without any apparent change in meaning.

the exclamation "O the surpassing kindness and love of God" (ὤ τῆς ὑπερβαλλούσης φιλανθρωπίας καὶ ἀγάπης τοῦ θεοῦ).⁶⁷ It was not as though God was wicked in allowing man to continue in sin, as Diognetus may have been tempted to think. Instead, the author makes plain that "he did not hate us neither did he reject nor bear a grudge against us, but he was patient and forbearing and because of his mercy he took upon himself our sins" (οὐκ ἐμίσησεν ἡμᾶς οὐδὲ ἀπώσατο οὐδὲ ἐμνησικάκησεν ἀλλὰ ἐμακροθύμησεν ἠνέσχετο ἐλεῶν αὐτὸς τὰς ἡμετέρας ἁμαρτίας ἀνεδέξατο). God was merciful not to visit people with wrath prior to the coming of the Son.

The next few lines contain some of the clearest teachings on the atonement and justification in the ante-Nicene church. Continuing with his argument, the author expounds on the mercy of God by informing Diognetus that the Son actually took mankind's sin upon himself. Then, in language that can only be described as substitutionary, he writes: "he himself gave up his own son as a ransom on our behalf, the holy for the lawless, the innocent for the wicked, the righteous for the unrighteous, the incorruptible for the corruptible, the immortal for the mortal" (αὐτὸς τὸν ἴδιον υἱὸν ἀπέδοτο λύτρον ὑπὲρ ἡμῶν τὸν ἅγιον ὑπὲρ ἀνόμων τὸν ἄκακον ὑπὲρ τῶν κακῶν τὸν δίκαιον ὑπὲρ τῶν ἀδίκων τὸν ἄφθαρτον ὑπὲρ τῶν φθαρτῶν τὸν ἀθάνατον ὑπὲρ τῶν θνητῶν). Humanity is painted in the worst possible hues in this text in order to show the exceedingly righteous character of the Son. Where sinful humanity is weak and prone to decay, he is strong and incorruptible. Where humanity is full of impurity and wickedness, he is full of innocence and righteousness. The Son is everything sinful people are not and yet must become.

In verses 3–4 he interposes two rhetorical questions: "For what else was able to cover our sins except the righteousness of that one?" (τί γὰρ ἄλλο τὰς ἁμαρτίας ἡμῶν ἠδυνήθη καλύψαι ἢ ἐκείνου δικαιοσύνη). And, "In whom was it possible for us, the lawless and ungodly, to be justified except in the Son of God alone?" (ἐν τίνι δικαιωθῆναι δυνατὸν τοὺς ἀνόμους ἡμᾶς καὶ ἀσεβεῖς ἢ ἐν μόνῳ τῷ υἱῷ τοῦ θεοῦ). The questions are meant to be answered "nothing" and "no one" respectively. There was no hope apart from the sinless Son dying in the place of the sinful people. His righteousness was necessary to cover over sin, and in covering sin, he justified the lawless and the ungodly.⁶⁸

---

67 BDF classifies this use of the genitive under "genitive with verbs of emotion." In the interjection in 9.2 as well as the three interjections that follow in 9.5, they state that it is "the genitive of the cause with interjections" (§ 176).
68 Perhaps the author is thinking in Jewish terms here of atonement as a covering over (כפר) of sins. It may be that Rom 4:7 is in the background where the blessed person is the one whose sins are covered (ἐπικαλύπτω).

Once again the author interjects with an expression of praise using the majestic words of exchange and benefit: "O the sweet exchange, O the inscrutable work of God, O the unexpected benefits of God, that the lawlessness of many might be hidden in one righteous man, while the righteousness of one might justify many lawless men" (ὦ τῆς γλυκείας ἀνταλλαγῆς ὦ τῆς ἀνεξιχνιάστου δημιουργίας ὦ τῶν ἀπροσδοκήτων εὐεργεσιῶν ἵνα ἀνομία μὲν πολλῶν ἐν δικαίῳ ἑνὶ κρυβῇ δικαιοσύνη δὲ ἑνὸς πολλοὺς ἀνόμους δικαιώσῃ). The work of God wherein he placed the punishment that was due the many on the one righteous man while simultaneously giving his righteousness to those who did not deserve it, is the essence of the message Paul preached. God sent his innocent Son to stand in the stead of the guilty. The language used is that of substitution and imputation, two doctrines which will be discussed in greater detail in the following section.

In verse 6, the author reiterates that in the former time people were powerless to obtain life (ἐλέγξας οὖν ἐν μὲν τῷ πρόσθεν χρόνῳ τὸ ἀδύνατον τῆς ἡμετέρας φύσεως εἰς τὸ τυχεῖν ζωῆς). The purpose of the previous time was to reveal the Savior's power in the present to save those who were powerless (νῦν δὲ τὸν σωτῆρα δείξας δυνατὸν σῴζειν καὶ τὰ ἀδύνατα). Both the former time of powerlessness and the present time of salvation through the Son are meant to be the reasons for belief in the goodness of God. Although it may seem counterintuitive to believe that God is good when it appears as though he abandoned people to their sins, the author maintains that it is precisely the reason to believe in God's goodness (ἐξ ἀμφοτέρων ἐβουλήθη πιστεύειν ἡμᾶς τῇ χρηστότητι αὐτοῦ). Had God not patiently endured in the former time of disobedience, then there would be no efficacious salvation through the Son in the present. As a result of the goodness of God, we should regard him as "nurse, father, teacher, counselor, physician, mind, light, honor, glory, strength, and life, and not to be anxious concerning clothing and food" (αὐτὸν ἡγεῖσθαι τροφέα πατέρα διδάσκαλον σύμβουλον ἰατρόν νοῦν φῶς τιμήν δόξαν ἰσχὺν ζωήν περὶ ἐνδύσεως καὶ τροφῆς μὴ μεριμνᾶν). This string of descriptions each highlights a separate aspect of God's character. He is the nurse who tenderly nurtures his children (Isa 66:13); he is the Father who provides for his own (Ps 104:27–28); he is the physician who heals those physically and spiritually sick (Gen 20:17; Matt 9:11–13); he is the one who possesses an infinite mind (Ps 147:5); he is the brilliant light shinning since the beginning of time (Ps 36:9); he is the one to whom all glory is due (Isa 43:6–7); he is the God who boasts all strength (Isa 40:28); he is the progenitor of life now and life eternal (Deut 32:39). The final clause, "and not to be anxious concerning clothing and food" (περὶ ἐνδύσεως καὶ τροφῆς μὴ μεριμνᾶν), demonstrates the uncertainty of these basic necessities in the second century. The author informs Diognetus that Christians do not worry about these things because the God he just vividly described is capable of supplying all these needs (Cf. Matt 6:25; Phil 4:19).

4.3 Theological Considerations: Atonement and Justification

Until recently, not much work has been done on the theology in *Diognetus*.[69] Because of its obscure history, many commentators confine their discussion to issues of authorship and dating, thus missing the purpose of the letter altogether. As shown, the author was writing in response to three questions which Diognetus had raised regarding Christianity. The first two questions were handled with exceptional care in the first eight chapters, leaving the answer to the third question for the remaining two chapters. In order to answer why Christianity had come into existence at such a late period of human history, the author felt obliged to give a brief synopsis of salvation history. God was patient with humanity's sins in the former time so that he might be the one to save them in the present through the vicarious death of his Son. Naturally he needed to discuss Jesus' death to answer the question and he thought it necessary to explain how an individual can be justified. Two important doctrines that are highlighted in the *Epistle to Diognetus* are of particular interest today, namely justification and substitutionary atonement.

Atonement

For the author, the atonement is the answer for why God waited so long to intervene. God was overlooking people's sin because it was always his plan to redeem mankind through the work of his Son on the cross.[70] Interestingly, the author does not explicitly mention the cross or death a single time in chapter 9. Though

---

[69] The notable exceptions are the brief articles already mentioned: Lienhard, "Christology," and Meecham, "Theology." The recent studies will be examined in the discussion that follows.
[70] Cf. Rom 5. Michael Haykin suggests that the author is especially dependent on Paul when discussing the atonement. Haykin writes, "What is highlighted in this dialectic [on this act of substitution] are the twin soteriological themes of the Son's utter sinlessness and humanity's radical depravity, a dialectic that recalls the rich Pauline theology of salvation as found in passages like Romans 5:6–10" (Haykin, *Rediscovering the Church Fathers*, 60). See also Brandon Crowe, "Oh Sweet Exchange: The Soteriological Significance of the Incarnation in the *Epistle to Diognetus*," *ZNW* 102 (2011): 96–109, who says, "Given the Pauline resonances in Diogn. 9, the author's focus on the Son's righteousness may be an example of an early Christian interpretation of Rom. 5" (109).

it is definitely implied, the author uses other language to communicate the atonement, assuming that Diognetus already knew about Jesus' death on the Roman cross.

Regardless of one's view of the atonement in the New Testament, it would be difficult to deny that the author of *Diognetus* believed in substitutionary atonement.[71] Verse 2 unmistakably teaches that the Son was made a substitute who stood in the place of sinful humanity. Repeatedly the author uses the preposition ὑπέρ, which when governing the genitive case, means "in behalf of" or "for the sake of," and this preposition is frequently used in the New Testament with reference to substitutionary atonement.[72] The holy, guiltless, just, incorruptible,

---

[71] Meecham, for one, misses the significance of the atonement as substitution in *Diognetus* when he claims, "It is clear that in the main *Diognetus* conceives the Atonement from the point of view of 'moral influence'" (Meecham, "The Theology of the Epistle to Diognetus," 99). Meecham at least allows for other theories of the atonement in *Diognetus*, like ransom, satisfaction, and even "vicarious penal and substitutionary theories," but these are all subordinate to the moral influence theory (100). Although on 9.5 he writes, "[the author's] language ... trembles on the verge of the substitutionary principle" (100).

Yet, substitution was not forgotten, overlooked, or disbelieved by the fathers. One recent work that has delved into this important and controversial issue from an historical perspective can be found in John Aloisi, "'His Flesh for Our Flesh': The Doctrine of the Atonement in the Second Century," *DBSJ* 14 (2009): 23–44. Aloisi casts doubt on Aulén's thesis, a thesis that has held sway for well over a half century, that until Anslem, the church largely subscribed to a *Christus Victor* model of the atonement. Confining his study to the second century, Aloisi examines Clement of Rome, the *Epistle of Barnabas*, Polycarp, Justin Martyr, the *Epistle to Diognetus*, and Irenaeus to argue that "many of the second-century church fathers viewed the atonement of Christ as involving substitution for sinners and satisfaction for sins" (25). Aloisi is careful not to overstep and claim that substitution is the only, or even the primary, theory of the atonement.

[72] BDAG, s.v. "ὑπέρ." For the use of ὑπέρ in relation to substitutionary atonement see especially 2 Cor 5:14, Gal 3:13, and John 11:50. Wallace approaches the preposition carefully, saying that the "case for a substitutionary sense for ὑπέρ is faced with the difficulty that the preposition can bear several nuances that, on a lexical level, at least, are equally plausible in the theologically significant passages" (Wallace, *Greek Grammar*, 383). Ὑπέρ is not always used soteriologically, but it does seem that when substitution is in view, the New Testament overwhelmingly uses ὑπέρ and ἀντί. See Wallace, *Greek Grammar*, 383–89, for an extended discussion, as well as Rupert E. Davies, "Christ in our Place—The Contribution of Prepositions," *TynBul* 21 (1970): 71–91. Meecham seems inconsistent in his handling of these prepositions. In one breath he says, in relation to Mark 10:45, that "no exegetical importance can be attached to the change from Mark's ἀντί to ὑπέρ. The two prepositions are not infrequently interchanged" (Meecham, *Diognetus*, 129). Then in the next breath he says, "ὑπέρ seems occasionally to approximate to the idea of substitution" (129). He then calls upon the following texts to give warrant to this latter claim: "Cf. Plato, *Gorgias*, 515C: ἐγὼ ὑπὲρ σοῦ ἀποκρινοῦμαι, Xen., *Anab*. vii, 4,9: ἐθέλοις ἄν, ὦ Ἐπίσθενες, ὑπὲρ τούτου ἀποθανεῖν; Philemon 13 ('as your deputy', Moffatt), P. Oxy. II, 275 (AD 66): ἔγραψα ὑπὲρ

and immortal one died on behalf of (ὑπὲρ) the lawless, guilty, unjust, corruptible, and mortal ones. If that was not clear enough, the author speaks of the cross as a mechanism of exchange, exclaiming, "O sweet exchange" (ὢ τῆς γλυκείας ἀνταλλαγῆς). This doxological outburst sums up his view in a single word, "exchange," which lies at the heart of substitution.

Brandon Crowe discusses soteriology in *Diognetus* in his noteworthy article, "Oh Sweet Exchange: The Soteriological Significance of the Incarnation in the *Epistle to Diognetus*."[73] Crowe promotes the thesis that soteriology, situated in the incarnation of the Son, forms the basis of the author's argument in chapters 7–9 and "may well be the high point of the entire epistle."[74] Furthermore, he thinks that the "climactic proclamation" in 9.5, "O sweet exchange," could very well be "a summary of the epistle's soteriological perspective."[75]

Crowe acknowledges that the entire epistle climaxes in the word ἀνταλλαγή, but this word causes immediate difficulty. Few instances of ἀνταλλαγή exist before the second century.[76] Without any previous appearance of the word with which to compare it, and relative rare use of the word afterwards, lexicographers are left to decide based off cognates and contexts.[77] Here, the context unlocks the meaning with near certainty. Even if ἀνταλλαγή was a *hapax legomenon* in the ancient world, which it is not, its meaning would still be readily apparent from the surrounding discussion.

The string of doxological exclamations in the first half of 9.5, of which the first is "O the sweet exchange," is followed in the remainder of the verse with a play on the one and the many, again reminiscent of Romans 5.[78] What strikes

---

αὐτοῦ μὴ ἰδότος γράμματα" (129). Given the use of ὑπέρ in Paul as the typical preposition for substitution when referring to the atonement, it seems likely that the author is using it in a similar fashion, particularly when this evidence is adduced to the context that is rich in substitution metaphors.

73 Brandon Crowe, "Oh Sweet Exchange: The Soteriological Significance of the Incarnation in the *Epistle to Diognetus*," ZNW 102 (2011): 96–109.

74 Crowe, "Oh Sweet Exchange," 97. Meecham also claims that chaps. 7–9 form the heart of the epistle, giving *Diognetus* a soteriological thrust.

75 Crowe, "Oh Sweet Exchange," 97.

76 See Simplicius's *In Aristotelis categorias commentarium* 8.66.16; idem, *In Aristotelis physicorum libros commentaria* 10.1350.32; idem, *Commentarius in Epicteti enchiridion* 39.9; Diogenis Sinopensis *Ep.* 10.1.10.

77 The cognate ἀντάλλαγμα, found in Matt 16:26 and Mark 8:37, parallel passages, where Jesus asks what a man will give in exchange (ἀντάλλαγμα) for his soul.

78 *Pace*, Meecham, who says when evaluating the use of ἀνταλλαγή, "The context suggests that the 'exchange' is one of *state* rather than of *person*, of wickedness for justification, not the substitution of Christ for men" (*The Epistle to Diognetus*, 130, emphases original). However, the sub-

4.3 Theological Considerations: Atonement and Justification — 99

the writer with wonder and amazement is that "the sinfulness of many should be hidden in one righteous person, while the righteousness of one should justify many sinners." The "one," the Son, is righteous and the sinfulness of many is hidden in him, while simultaneously his righteousness is imputed to many and they are justified.[79] They receive his righteousness, he receives their sin. How else could this be described but by ἀνταλλαγή?[80]

Before leaving the topic of atonement, it is important to address the use of λύτρον. One could argue that the author is espousing a ransom view of the atonement because he begins this section by saying "he himself gave up his own Son as a ransom for us" (αὐτὸς τὸν ἴδιον υἱὸν ἀπέδοτο λύτρον ὑπὲρ ἡμῶν). The ransom theory of the atonement, prevalent among theologians in the early church, holds that the Devil had right over mankind because of sin and therefore Christ was sent to pay him ransom. Origen was the first major proponent of this view giving it its classic expression in his commentary on Matthew.[81] At the most basic level, any attempt to suggest that the author subscribed to this view is anachronistic. More than likely, the author is thinking of biblical passages such as Mark 10:45 where Jesus said that he came as a ransom. Furthermore, the author explains his conception of ransom with his catalog of substitutionary adjectives. As Crowe notes, "Pointing to the substitutionary idea is the phrase τὰς ἡμετέρας ἁμαρτίας ἀνεδέξατο, and the phrase in which λύτρον is found: αὐτὸς τὸν ἴδιον υἱὸν ἀπέδοτο λύτρον ἡμῶν."[82] Read in the larger context, ransom for this author must fit within his paradigm of substitution.

---

stantival adjectives indicate the personal aspect of the text. The focus remains on the one and the many.

79 More on imputation in the section that follows.

80 Crowe has an extended discussion on ἀνταλλαγή that is worth examining ("Oh Sweet Exchange," 106–07). On this word he concludes, "The 'exchange' in view should be viewed as the entirety of the work of the Son in the Incarnation, extending both to a positive accomplishment of righteousness, and serving as a sacrificial λύτρον in his death" ("Oh Sweet Exchange," 107). For Marrou, "exchange" signals an objective change in the relationship between God and man. He states, "ce mysterieux 'échange' entre la Justice du Fils de Dieu et le peche des hommes: plus qu'un effet purement subjectif de la justification, ce mot parait bien designer une transformation objective de la situation des hommes par rapport a Dieu" (Marrou, *A Diognète*, 200).

81 J. N. D. Kelly points out that Irenaeus broke from his view of recapitulation at times to describe the atonement in terms of ransom and substitution (*Early Christian Doctrines*, 5th ed. [London: Adam and Charles Black, 1977], 173–74). It is generally argued that the second-century fathers held to a *Christus Victor* theory of the atonement, especially since the publication of Gustaf Aulén's influential, *Christus Victor: An Historical Study of the Three Main Types of the Idea of the Atonement*, trans. A. G. Hebert (London: SPCK, 1937).

82 Crowe, "Oh Sweet Exchange," 104.

Justification

The *Epistle to Diognetus* is the *locus classicus* of justification by faith in the second century. Rooted in grace and mercy, justification equates to the forgiveness of sins and the imputation of Christ's righteousness. Again, he is responding here to the question of why God delayed in sending his Son (cf. Rom 3:25 ff.).[83] The delay allowed for humanity to have a season of unrighteousness that would prepare them for the season of righteousness that was to come. The first mention of righteousness comes in 9.1 where the author says that God permitted sin in the former season "because he was creating the present season of righteousness" (τόν νῦν τῆς δικαιοσύνης δημιουργῶν). The idea of creating a season of righteousness implies that something new was taking place. He gives the purpose in the next clause saying that the former time was meant to bring mankind under conviction so that now they might be "considered worthy" by the goodness of God. The worthiness does not come from individual merit as he makes plain in the following clause, saying that this new season "clearly demonstrated our inability to enter the kingdom of God on our own." It is God, according to the author, who considers an individual worthy to enter into the kingdom.

When speaking of justification it is essential to listen for non-traditional ways of mentioning it. Just because the δικ- word group is not used, does not mean that justification is not being addressed. In this case, the author speaks of being "considered worthy" (ἀξιόω) instead of the more Pauline sense of "declared righteous" (δικαιόω), but his meaning, as fleshed out in the remainder of the chapter, goes to the nerve center of Pauline thought. Meecham rightly translates ἀξιωθῶμεν as "be deemed worthy"[84] as opposed to Holmes whose translation "be made worthy"[85] misses the meaning of the word and the point that is made in the context. Being "made worthy" has a transformative sense to it, but this is not what the author has in mind. The word itself cannot even mean this; it can only mean to be "considered worthy."[86] The point is that people

---

[83] Even his emphasis on God's delay is Pauline. Cf. Gal 4:4–6; Rom 1–11.

[84] Meecham, *Diognetus*, 85. Meecham has the following note on this verb: "In verbs in -όω derived from adj. of *moral* meaning the factitive sense is modified = 'to regard as', rather than 'to make'" (128, emphasis original). This has significant ramifications on δικαιόω as well, for it too bears the οω ending. See also Elizabeth Tucker, "Greek Factitive Verbs in οω, αινω, and υνω," *Transactions of the Philological Society* 79 (1981): 15–34.

[85] Holmes, *Apostolic Fathers*, 709. Lightfoot also translates it along the same lines as Holmes: "we might now be made deserving" (Lightfoot, *Apostolic Fathers*, 508).

[86] BDAG, s.v. "ἀξιόω." LSJ, s.v. " ἀξιόω," "think, deem worthy." Lampe, s.v. ἀξιόω, in *Diogn.* 9.1, "deem worthy."

are unworthy on their own merits but that God considers them worthy on account of the substitutionary atonement of the Son (9.2).[87] If there was a sense in which individuals are being made worthy, then that would suggest works, an idea the author utterly rejects.

Hearing alternative ways of speaking of justification is important, but the author does not shy away from using the Pauline language of δικαιοσύνην and δικαιόω. Seven times throughout this chapter he uses some variation of the δικ- word group (5 nouns; 1 adjective; 1 infinitive). Much debate exists on exactly what this word group means, especially in its verbal form. The first two entries under δικαιόω in BDAG make reference to legal verdicts and there are no entries that contradict this meaning.

The majority of the occurrences of the δικ- word group in this pericope are in noun form and all but one of these instances refer to the Son's righteousness. The emphasis is on the Son's perfect righteousness as the grounds for justification (9.3), for if he had not lived a life free from sin, then he could not have imputed his righteousness to sinners. The idea of imputation comes especially from 9.5 where the author states that while the sinfulness of many was hidden in the one righteous person, the righteousness of the one justified many sinners. Sin was imputed to Christ via his substitutionary atonement and his righteousness was imputed to sinners for their justification (cf. 2 Cor 5:21).

Verses 3–5 fit together in a tightly woven argument. In verse 3 it is the righteousness of the Son that is imperative for the covering over of sins, though phrased in a rhetorical question. In verse 4 he asks yet another rhetorical question concerning how the lawless and ungodly could be justified except in the Son. Only the Son can justify and he justifies on the basis of his own righteous-

---

[87] Lienhard writes, "In the first age, man lacks righteousness, or is positively unrighteous; and he is powerless to change this situation ... . At the beginning of the second age, the Son does come, and by his power and righteousness renders man capable—or gives him the power—to become righteous" (Lienhard, "Christology," 285–86). Lienhard seems to take a transformative view in this statement, opening up the possibility that man is given the power to become righteous. Quoting this section from Lienhard, Crowe raises the same issue, namely, "more needs to be said regarding how man is *capable* or *has the power* to become righteous" (Crowe, "O Sweet Exchange," 104, emphasis original). Crowe goes on to answer this objection in his examination of the nature of exchange (ἀναταλλαγή). This approach is partially correct. That is, Crowe is correct to see a more definite solution in the exchange metaphor, asserting that there is no righteousness conjured up by the individual—it is entirely the lawful for the lawless. While this is true, the meaning of the word ἀξιόω itself demonstrates this as well. The question is not, as Lienhard seems to indicate, whether or not man now has the capability to become righteous. This is the wrong question based on a wrong translation. The question is how one becomes considered worthy, and the answer is discussed below.

ness. This righteousness is imputed to the sinner on the basis of the vicarious atonement wherein the sins were hidden (i.e., imputed) in the Son and his righteousness justifies the many.

Not only does this passage speak to Christ's righteousness and his imputation of this righteousness to sinners, but the author also argues that justification comes on the basis of faith alone. In 9.4 the author asks, "In whom was it possible for us, the lawless and ungodly to be justified *except in the Son of God alone?*" (emphasis added). For the author, justification comes through Christ alone and is on the basis of faith. This he makes certain in 8.6 saying, "And he revealed (himself) through faith, which is the only means by which one is permitted to see God" (ἐπέδειξε δὲ διὰ πίστεως ᾗ μόνῃ θεὸν ἰδεῖν συγκεχώρηται). Seeing God, in this case, is a metonymy used for eternal life. Therefore, faith alone is the only way an individual can obtain eternal life, and this faith must be in the Son of God alone.[88]

4.4 Conclusion

The case for forensic justification in the *Epistle to Diognetus* stands on solid ground.[89] The language of justification by faith alone is borrowed from the New Testament but it is presented in the author's own voice. The author is not attempting to lay out a defense of justification or give commentary on Romans or Galatians; he is merely answering a question that Diognetus raised and, in order to give a full response, he appealed to Paul's teaching of justification by faith alone. God's plan all along was to send his Son to die on behalf of transgressors so that he might impute to them the righteousness of Christ. Michael Bird sums up justification in *Diognetus* well: "[The *Epistle to Diognetus*] poetical-

---

88 On this verse, Bird says, "[The *Epistle to Diognetus*] echoes the Pauline pneumatic epistemology about the mode of attaining knowledge of God" ("The Reception of Paul in the *Epistle to Diognetus*," 85). But he goes on to agree more or less with Meecham, who said that the "place of 'faith' in the work of justification is doubtless present to his mind, though not explicitly stated" (*Epistle to Diognetus*, 130). For Bird, "The Pauline formulation of righteousness by faith (διά/ἐκ πιστεως) does not loom at all" ("The Reception of Paul in the *Epistle to Diognetus*, 87). Though he does highlight the centrality of faith throughout the epistle (8.6; 9.6; 10.1), he seems bothered that there is not an explicit claim that justification is by faith. The author places all the pieces of this puzzle down in front of the reader, even showing how they link together. There should be no consternation that he did not link them together since the picture itself is so obvious.
89 *Pace*, Meecham, "Theology," who says, "The Pauline term [δικαιοσύνη] is used, but with a less forensic sense" (100).

ly expands upon Paul's theme of the justification of the ungodly and presents an array of images to demonstrate the *forensic* and Christocentric nature of justification."[90]

The *Epistle to Diognetus* is the clearest evidence that the doctrine of grace neither disappeared nor diminished in the second century.[91] Chapter 9 of the *Epistle to Diognetus* resonates with the twin Pauline doctrines of substitutionary atonement and forensic justification, leading the author to declare, "O the sweet exchange, O the inscrutable work of God, O the unexpected benefits of God, that the lawlessness of many might be hidden in one righteous man, while the righteousness of one might justify many lawless men." Although the *Epistle to Diognetus* is the high point of Paul's doctrine of justification in the second century, it cannot be as Bird suggests that *Diognetus* "stands as a middle point between Paul and Protestantism," as though this is the only document that contains a Pauline doctrine of justification until Luther.[92] The chapters that flank this one disallow such a conclusion.

---

[90] Bird, "The Reception of Paul in the *Epistle to Diognetus*," 87. Emphasis added.
[91] Meecham, "Theology," 100, where he writes, "Redemption is solely the work of divine grace. In this again the author is thoroughly Pauline."
[92] Bird, "The Reception of Paul in the *Epistle to Diognetus*," 87. At another point he even calls the soteriology of chap. 9 "proto-Protestantism" (85).

5 "My Chains Were Cut Off": *Odes of Solomon*

Music has always been the fullest expression of faith. From Moses' song of liberation that was sung as the Israelites made their way out of Egypt to King David's lengthy book of musical compositions, up through modern hymnody, people have expressed their faith in song. This was no different for the early church.[1] By the second century Christians were in the practice of composing hymns, especially in light of the advent of Christ.

The *Odes of Solomon* survive as the earliest example of a hymnbook in the history of the church.[2] Nearly forgotten, the *Odes of Solomon* have had little attestation in church history and were not even discovered until 1909 when J. Rendel Harris found them while sifting through a pile of Syriac documents in his office.[3] When the *Odes* were finally published, scholars worked to determine their relationship to the New Testament, and John in particular, in light of this newly-found manuscript. They were also concerned about background issues like their connection to Gnosticism or the Essene community and the original language in which they were composed. However, the dust soon settled and the *Odes* have

---

[1] The Apostle Paul alludes to Christians singing psalms, hymns and spiritual songs in Col 3:16. There is also reason to believe that Phil 2:5–11 was not only an early Christological creed, but that it was actually a song as well. See Peter T. O'Brien, *The Epistle to the Philippians: A Commentary on the Greek Text*, NIGTC (Grand Rapids: Eerdmans, 1991), 186–202, in favor of this view. *Pace* Gordon D. Fee, who disagrees that this was a hymn (Fee, "Philippians 2:5–11: Hymn or Exalted Pauline Prose?" *BBR* 2 [1992]: 29–46). In addition, Pliny the Younger reported (c. 110 CE) in his famous letter to Trajan (10.96) that Christians "are accustomed to meet together on a set day before light and sing a song to Christ as to a god" (*quod essent soliti stato die ante lucem convenire, carmenque Christo quasi deo dicere*). See *Pliny: Letters and Panegyricus*, trans. Betty Radice, LCL, 59 (Cambridge, MA: Harvard University Press, 1975), 288. Since Pliny the Younger was governor of Bithynia, a province in Syria, it is possible that these Christians were singing the *Odes of Solomon*, but this is speculation of course. See Michael Lattke, *Odes of Solomon: A Commentary*, ed. Harold W. Attridge, trans. Marianne Ehrhardt, Hermeneia (Minneapolis: Fortress Press, 2009), 3–4, who put forth this possibility.

[2] There is debate as to whether or not the *Odes* should be called a hymnal since their precise use is unknown. The general consensus, however, is that the *Odes* were a hymnal used for worship in the church and this is the position taken in this chapter. See Gustav Diettrich, "Eine jüdisch-christliche Liedersammlung (aus dem apostolischen Zeitalter)," *Die Reformation: Deutsche evangelische Kirchenzeitung für die Gemeinde* 9 (1910): 306–10, 370–76, 513–18, 533–36.

[3] J. Rendel Harris, *The Odes and Psalms of Solomon* (Cambridge: University Press, 1909); idem, "An Early Christian Hymn-Book," *Contemporary Review* 95 (1909): 414–28. In the article Harris recounts his experience of finding this treasure trove amidst various other Syriac documents.

received only a smattering of attention since the early twentieth century.[4] Even when the *Odes* are discussed today, the focus is largely on the historical milieu surrounding the text and the theology remains virtually unstudied.

This chapter seeks to take initial steps towards rectifying this situation by the examination of soteriology in the *Odes of Solomon*, especially as it relates to justification. It will be argued that the author of the *Odes* held to a view of justification by faith and that his conception of justification was predominately forensic. Closely related to this view of justification is the doctrine of imputation, which is also present in the *Odes*. The Odist believed not only that he was saved by grace through faith, but that he received his righteousness from Christ.

Before delving into the *Odes* themselves, various background issues relating to the text must be discussed. These issues are significant, for if the *Odes* were written soon after the New Testament, then they provide profound insight into how the church understood the teachings of the apostles. However, it is needful to move beyond the investigations of such background issues, since there is a rich theology that informs the *Odes*. Several *Odes* lend themselves well to the investigation on justification and they will be commented on in turn. Specifically, this chapter will cover God's sovereignty in salvation, the individual as one bound in sin, and the imputation of Christ's righteousness.

5.1 Background

The *Odes of Solomon* present a unique challenge to the scholar who comes to study them because there is little consensus on the traditional background issues. In the few extant manuscripts available there is no author singled out, no provenance suggested, and no date specified. The difficulties deepen in view of the fact that there is almost no historical attestation of the *Odes*. Thus, the student of the *Odes* must examine the limited internal and external data that exists in order to arrive at likely solutions, always waiting for further evidence that might shed light on this elusive document.

---

[4] Discussion on the history of interpretation as it relates to authorship, dating, and provenance follows.

Manuscripts and Languages

There are only four manuscripts containing the *Odes of Solomon*, none of which are complete: two in Syriac, one in Greek, and another in Coptic.[5] In the Syriac manuscripts, Codex Nitriensis (N; ninth–tenth centuries) and Codex Harris (H; thirteenth–fifteenth centuries), are curtailed at both ends.[6] Lacking the introductory *Odes*, they begin at Ode 3 and the *Psalms of Solomon*, which make up the remaining eighteen chapters of the collection, are missing as well.[7] N starts in 17.7 and continues through 42 whereas H stretches back to the middle of *Ode* 3 and also ends in 42. However, H has many more lacunae than does N.

The Greek and Coptic manuscripts are considerably less impressive. The Greek manuscript, *P. Bodmer XI* (G; second–third centuries), is the earliest witness but it contains only *Ode* 11.[8] In the Coptic manuscript, Codex Askew (C; third century), the *Odes* are found preserved in the *Pistis Sophia* which appears to be the first commentary on the *Odes*. This document is a translation from the Greek.[9]

Regrettably, the manuscript evidence does not help determine the original language of the *Odes*. While the Greek codex is the earliest known copy of the *Odes*, it does not follow that they were written in Greek. An argument could equally be made that Syriac is the original language of the text because it has

---

[5] This section relies heavily on the work of Michael Lattke (Lattke, *Odes of Solomon*, 3–4). See also James H. Charlesworth, "Odes of Solomon (Late First to Early Second Century A.D.)," in *The Old Testament Pseudepigraphia*, ed. James H. Charlesworth (New York: Doubleday, 1985), 2:725–26 for another brief discussion of the manuscripts.

[6] Codex Harris also shows emendations in at least two places (17.11; 28.17). This reveals that there were other Syriac texts which have since been lost (Lattke, *Odes of Solomon*, 4). Charlesworth further observes that "the scribe who copied MS H frequently omitted a word or phrase," charging him with haplography and parablepsis (James H. Charlesworth, "Haplography and Philology: A Study of Ode of Solomon 16:8," *NTS* 25 [1979]: 223).

[7] The *Odes of Solomon* were originally known only by its title which was recorded in other sources. Thus, even when there were no extant copies of the *Odes* themselves, scholars still knew of their existence from the lists of canonical books which had been preserved. For instance, Nicephorus, ninth-century patriarch of Constantinople, placed the *Odes of Solomon* together with the *Psalms of Solomon* (Ψαλμοὶ καὶ ᾠδαὶ Σολομῶντος). See Lattke, *Odes of Solomon*, 1–2.

[8] The Greek manuscript was discovered after the Syriac texts. Its discovery prompted linguists to determine which language depended on the other. For instance, Willem Baars noticed a problem in the Syriac text of *Ode* 11 that he thought could only be solved with a Greek original (Baars, "A Note on Ode of Solomon XI 14," *VT* 12 [1962]: 196).

[9] Only *Odes* 1.1–5, 5.1–11, 6.8–18, 22.1–12, and 25.12 have survived in this text. However, it is significant that the Coptic reflects the Greek in some places as this could bolster the case for a Greek original (Lattke, *Odes of Solomon*, 3).

better attestation from the codices. Yet the manuscripts are just one piece of this multifaceted puzzle—nothing conclusive can be drawn from them. Scholars are generally split between a Greek[10] or Syriac[11] original, though some have opted for a Hebrew text.[12] Charlesworth has made the best argument for a Syriac original based upon word plays within the text that all but demand the Syriac language.[13]

Authorship and Influences

The debate over authorship is really a debate over the communities that may have influenced the author. There are a few who have ventured a guess as to the actual identity of the Odist. William Newbold, for instance, posited that Bardaisan, the mid second-century Gnostic teacher from Syria, seemed to fit the

---

10 Wilhelm Frankenberg, *Das Verständnis der Oden Salomos* (Gießen, Germany: Töpelmann, 1911). Frankenberg translated the *Odes* into Greek because he was certain that Greek was actually the original language. See also Lattke, *Odes of Solomon*, 10–11, for additional arguments.
11 J. Rendel Harris and Alphonse Mingana, *The Odes and Psalms of Solomon*, vol. 2 (Manchester: Manchester University Press, 1916–20), 165. Harris held to a Greek original at first but was later persuaded that Syriac was the original language of composition. Cf. Arthus Vööbus, "Neues Licht zur Frage der Originalsprache der Oden Salomos," *Le Muséon* 75 (1962): 275–90; John A. Emerton, "Some Problems of Text and Language in the Odes of Solomon," *JTS* n.s.18 (1967): 372–406; idem, "Notes on Some Passages in the Odes of Solomon," *JTS* n.s. 28 (1977): 507–19.
12 See Hubert Grimme, *Die Oden Salomos: Syrisch-Hebräisch-Deutsch* (Heidelberg: Carl Winters Universitätsbuchhandlung, 1911), who was so convinced that the *Odes* were composed in Hebrew that he translated the Syriac back into Hebrew before translating them into his native German. See also Jean Carmignac, "Recherches sur la langue originelle des Odes de Salomon," *RevQ* 4 (1963): 429–32, who argues "que les *Odes de Salomon* auraient bel et bien été composes en hébreu, tout comme les *Hymnes* de Qumrân" (432). Carmignac believed the Odist was influenced by the Essenes (see below).
13 James H. Charlesworth, "Paronomasia and Assonance in the Syriac Text of the Odes of Solomon," *Semitics* 1 (1970): 12–26. Although Charlesworth aligns himself with the Syriac camp, he nuances his position by claiming that the parent text was an Aramaic-Syriac hybrid (James H. Charlesworth, *The Earliest Christian Hymnbook* [Eugene, OR: Cascade Books, 2009], xxii). He does concede that the Syriac could be a translation from the Greek if the translator was exceptionally gifted. G. R. Driver, while agreeing that the *Odes* were composed in Syraic, alters Charlesworth's translation in a few places in order to bring out more strongly "the paronomasia to which the author of these Odes is so strongly addicted" (G.R. Driver, "Notes on Two Passages in the Odes of Solomon," *JTS* n.s. 25 [1974]: 437). That the original language was Syriac is all but certain.

mold of the Odist.[14] For the most part, researchers are content to unearth as much as they can about the author without assigning a specific person to the *Odes*.

An important issue that must be discussed when working through the prolegomena of the *Odes* is whether or not it reveals Gnostic influence. It is not surprising that German scholars in the early twentieth century favored a close connection between the *Odes* and Gnosticism in light of their penchant for labeling documents Gnostic prematurely.[15] However, this theory cannot be rejected simply because of the ideological perspectives underlying it. After all, there are several *Odes* that easily lend themselves to being Gnostic. The clearest example comes from *Ode* 19.1–4 which runs as follows:[16]

> A cup of milk was offered to me, and I drank it in the sweetness of the Lord's kindness. The Son is the cup, and the Father is He who was milked; and the Holy Spirit is She who milked Him
> Because His breasts were full, and it was undesirable that His milk should be ineffectually

---

14 William R. Newbold, "Bardaisan and the Odes of Solomon," *JBL* 30 (1911): 161–204. Eugene Merrill has rightly critiqued this view saying, "If Bardaisan is, indeed, the author, his theological stance shifted considerably from the position reflected in the Acts [of Thomas] and that manifested in most of his other writings including ... Liber Legum Regionum" (Eugene Merrill, "The Odes of Solomon and the Acts of Thomas: A Comparative Study," *JETS* 17 [1974]: 232). Judging from the works that are typically associated with Bardaisan, it can be safely assumed that the *Odes of Solomon* were not from his hand, despite the many conceptual links (Merrill, "The Odes of Solomon and the Acts of Thomas," 233).
15 Specifically in view here is the *religionsgeschichtliche Schule* which dominated the German landscape at the turn of the twentieth century. See Hermann Gunkel, "Die Oden Salomos," *ZNW* 11 (1910): 291–328, who is the first to draw a connection between Gnosticism and the *Odes*. Many followed Gunkel in this theory, including Willy Stölten, "Gnostische Parallelen zu den Oden Salomos," *ZNW* 13 (1912): 29–58, and H. Duensing, "Zur vierund-zwanzigsten der Oden Salomos," *ZNW* 12 (1911): 86–87. Several modern scholars have also suggested Gnostic influence behind the *Odes*, perhaps most notably Robert Grant who perceived a Valentinian bent in the Odist (Robert Grant, "Notes on Gnosis," *VC* 11 [1957]: 149–51).
16 Unless otherwise noted, the text used for the *Odes*, both the Syriac and the English translation, is taken from *The Odes of Solomon*, ed. and trans. by James H. Charlesworth (Chico, CA: Scholars Press, 1977). For other translations and editions, see Majella Franzmann, *The Odes of Solomon: An Analysis of the Poetical Structure and Form* (Göttingen: Vandenhoeck & Ruprecht, 1991); John H. Bernard, *The Odes of Solomon*, Texts and Studies 8.3 (Cambridge: Cambridge University Press, 1912); Walter Bauer, *Die Oden Salomos* (Berlin: Walter de Gruyter, 1933); Michael Lattke, *Oden Salomos: Ubersetze und Eingeleitet*, Fontes Christiani 19 (Frieburg, Germany: Herder, 1995); Éphrem Azar, *Les Odes de Salomon: Presentation et Traduction* (Paris: Les Editions du Cerf, 1996); Marie-Joseph Pierre, *Les Odes de Salomon*, Apocryphes 4 (Turnhout: Brépols, 1994).

released.
The Holy Spirit opened Her bosom, and mixed the milk of the two breasts of the Father.[17]

This esoteric and bizarre language has garnered attention amongst those who see a Gnostic leaning in the Odist. Henry Chadwick has carefully surveyed the *Odes* in order to determine if they are in fact Gnostic and he has rightly concluded that verses such as these in the *Odes* have "not prevented [the Odist] from presenting a reasonably intelligible picture of the redemption story, expressed, it is true, in vivid and sometimes grotesque images, but never passing into the kind of pretentious mumbo-jumbo we find in the gnostic systems attacked by Irenaeus and Hippolytus."[18] The picture of Christianity was never distorted to such a degree that the simplicity of the faith was obscured. There is too much in the *Odes of Solomon* that reflects later Christian orthodoxy to suggest that it had its roots in a nascent form of Gnosticism.[19]

One observation that has gained almost universal acceptance is that the *Odes* are a Christian production with a strong Jewish undercurrent.[20] More than likely, the author was raised as a Jew and later converted to Christianity. The *Odes* resemble the Psalms far too much to be the work of a recently-converted pagan. Since the discovery of the Dead Sea Scrolls in 1946, it has been further conjectured that the Odist was an Essene who was profoundly impacted by the

---

[17] Charlesworth, *Odes of Solomon*, 82. The description of the Holy Spirit in feminine language was ordinary in Syriac Christianity. Important to note is that the Holy Spirit was not spoken of in terms of feminine imagery simply because the word is feminine. In some cases, the Syriac word underlying "Spirit" is masculine, not feminine. See Susan Ashbrook Harvey, "Feminine Imagery for the Divine: The Holy Spirit, the Odes of Solomon, and Early Syriac Tradition," *St. Vladimir's Theological Seminary* 37 (1993): 117. For Harvey, the feminine gender is used "to capture the complexity of human experience of the divine" (Harvey, "Feminine Imagery for the Divine," 128). See also Han J. W. Drijvers, "The 19th Ode of Solomon: Its Interpretation and Place in Syrian Christianity," *JTS* n.s. 31 (1980): 337–55 for a helpful commentary. Drijvers does go astray, however, in seeing too much of a dependence on Tatian's *Diatessaron* in this Ode. This leads him to dating the *Odes* around 200 CE—a date which is surely too late (Hans J. W. Drijvers, "The 19th Ode of Solomon," 351; see next section).
[18] Henry Chadwick, "Some Reflections on the Character and Theology of the Odes of Solomon," in *Kyriakon: Festschrift Johannes Quasten*, ed. P. Granfield and J. A. Jungmann (Münster: Verlag Achendorff, 1970), 267.
[19] Also very helpful on refuting the charge of Gnosticism in the *Odes* is James H. Charlesworth, "The Odes of Solomon—Not Gnostic," *CBQ* 31 (1969): 357–69. He gives nine reasons why the *Odes* should not be considered Gnostic (366–68).
[20] Adolf von Harnack opined that the *Odes* were a Jewish document that Christians later emended (*Ein jüdisch-christliches Psalmbuch aus dem ersten Jahrhundert*, TU 35.4 [Leipzig: Hinrichs, 1910], 74 ff.).

Ḥodayot (1QH) and the *Community Rule* (1QS).²¹ However, trying to determine out of which strand of Judaism the Odist sprung is fruitless. Suffice it to say that the style, themes, and language are suggestive of a Jewish-Christian author.²²

Another potential influence on the Odist was the Apostle John. James Charlesworth cogently argues that the *Odes* share both verbal and conceptual connections with John's Gospel.²³ The verbal relationships focus on words like "love," "rest," "eternal life," "Spirit," "word," and "know" that pervade the *Odes*. In regard to the conceptual relationship, Charlesworth looks at two primary themes: word and living water. Not everyone agrees that the Odist used John, however.²⁴ Robert Grant denies a strict dependence but he does think that these two documents arose from individuals within the same spiritual community.²⁵ Though demonstrating the Odist's dependence on John is speculative, it is clear that there are many similarities between the two.

Apart from the aforementioned influences, one thing can be said with certainty—the *Odes* are decisively Christian. Despite the fact that Jesus is never mentioned by name, many of the *Odes* allude to him, although some references are more veiled than others. For instance, *Ode* 19.6 refers to the virgin birth: "The womb of the Virgin took (it), and she received conception and gave birth,"²⁶ and

---

21 Jean Carmignac argued for a connection between the *Odes* and the Dead Sea Scrolls ("Les Affinités qumraniennes de la onzième Ode de Salomon," *RevQ* 3 [1961]: 71–102). If the Odist had come out of Qumran, then this might explain the dualism found in the *Odes*. See James H. Charlesworth, "Qumran, John and the Odes of Solomon," in *John and Qumran*, ed. J. H. Charlesworth (London: Geoffrey Chapman, 1972), 117–35.

22 Charlesworth has created a table where he guesses the influence of each *Ode*, whether Christian or Jewish. This table is not helpful because it assumes that if an explicitly Christian theme is absent from the text, then the *Ode* is Jewish and not Christian. The *Odes* are undeniably Christian, although they still bear a Jewish tinge due to the author's background. There are no *Odes* in which he is reverting back to his former days in Judaism. Even the *Odes* which bear a striking resemblance to Jewish Psalms are still to be understood in their new Christian context (Charlesworth, *The Earliest Christian Hymnbook*, xviii-xix).

23 James H. Charlesworth and R. Alan Culpepper, "The Odes of Solomon and the Gospel of John," *CBQ* 35 (1973): 298–322.

24 Charlesworth does acknowledge that "almost all scholars who have published a detailed comparison of the Odes and John have concluded that it is highly improbable that the Odes depend upon John" (Charlesworth, "The Odes of Solomon and the Gospel of John," 318–9). He cites the following individuals who do not think there is a likely dependence: Harris and Mingana, *The Odes and Psalms of Solomon*, 2:120; Jean Daniélou, *Primitive Christian Symbols*, trans. D. Attwater (Baltimore: Helicon, 1964), 48; J. T. Sanders, *The New Testament Christological Hymns: Their Historical Religious Background*, SNTS 15 (Cambridge: University Press, 1971), 118. Yet Charlesworth's evidence is staggering and deserving of careful reflection.

25 Robert Grant, "The Origin of the Fourth Gospel," *JBL* 69 (1950): 321.

26 Charlesworth, *Odes of Solomon*, 82.

7.6 contains an acknowledgement of the incarnation: "Like my nature He became, that I might understand Him. And like my form, that I might not turn away from Him."[27] The Odist also sings of Jesus as the Son of God when he reflects that "because I love Him that is the Son, I shall become a Son" (3.7b).[28] In *Ode* 36.3 the Odist personifies Jesus saying, "because I was the Son of Man, I was named the Light, the Son of God."[29] The Odist also composed lyrics on Jesus' death: "I extended my hands and hallowed my Lord, for the expansion of my hands is His sign. And my extension is the upright cross" (27; cf. 42.1–2).[30] And Jesus says he suffered this punishment "that I might redeem my nation" (31:12). This is but a sampling of the many places throughout the *Odes* where Jesus is clearly envisaged, even if his name is absent from the text. The *Odes* are full of Christological statements that are void of Gnosticism or even Docetism.[31]

Dating and Provenance

Answering the question of provenance for any document in the early church is an exceptionally difficult task. The relative ease with which documents circulated around the Mediterranean during the *Pax Romana* makes it possible for the *Odes* to have been penned anywhere. There are some clues, however, that point east towards Syria.

The eastern origin of the *Odes* might account for the lack of witness in the ancient world. Had this songbook been written in Rome or Alexandria, the intellectual hubs of the early church, then it may have had more influence on posterity. Perhaps the most concrete piece of evidence linking the *Odes* to Syria is Ignatius's apparent knowledge of the *Odes*.[32] One interesting connection between the two is their realized eschatology (*Odes* 15.8; Ignatius, *Phil* 9.2).[33] Robert Grant also observed linguistic parallels such as *Ode* 7.24, "Ignorance has been dissipated because the knowledge of the Lord has arrived," and *Eph* 19.3, "Ignorance was

---

[27] Charlesworth, *Odes of Solomon*, 35.
[28] Charlesworth, *Odes of Solomon*, 19.
[29] Charlesworth, *Odes of Solomon*, 127.
[30] Charlesworth, *Odes of Solomon*, 106.
[31] Pierre Batiffol was the first to perceive a hint of Docetism in the *Odes* (Batiffol, "Les Odes de Salomon," *RB* 8 [1911]: 858).
[32] Lattke rightly warns that Ignatius's potential awareness of the *Odes* does not mandate a provenance of Syria—it merely opens up the possibility (Lattke, *Odes of Solomon*, 11).
[33] Brian Daley, "Eschatology," in *Encyclopedia of Early Christianity*, ed. Everett Ferguson et al., 2nd ed. (New York: Garland Publishers, 1999), 1:383.

dissipated, the ancient kingdom was destroyed, when God was manifested as man for the renewal of eternal life."[34] If Ignatius is betraying his awareness of the *Odes*, then it could signal a provenance in the east near Antioch, and more importantly, it can help solidify an early date.

It is certain that the *Odes* were written some time before the early fourth century because Lactantius, the only witness of the *Odes* in the fathers, quoted *Ode* 19 in his *Divine Institutes*.[35] However, based on the manuscript evidence, a much earlier date can be secured. As mentioned, the oldest manuscript (G), dates to the waning years of the second century or into the early years of the third century. Yet if a connection to Ignatius is warranted, then this date is pushed back all the way to the opening decade of the second century.[36] Given that Montanus and Valentinus, and even other Apostolic Fathers, such as *2 Clement* and the *Epistle of Barnabas*, may have known the *Odes*, Lattke suggests a date in the first quarter of the second century.[37] The collective evidence suggests that the *Odes of Solomon* is one of the most ancient documents in the history of the church.

5.2 The Text

The remainder of this chapter will focus on soteriology in the *Odes*. The *Odes* are predominantly a collection of hymns written out of a heart full of joy and thankfulness for salvation.[38] In this way, the Odist remains in close connection to the

---

[34] Robert Grant, "The Odes of Solomon and the Church of Antioch," *JBL* 63 (1944): 370–71. (Note: the translations of the *Odes* and Ignatius here come from Grant.) Grant also lists the connections between *Ode* 11.6 and *Rom.* 7.2 as well as *Ode* 38.8 and *Trall.* 6.2. He allows that these are not quite as strong as the one cited above, but the evidence, when taken together, is very compelling. The conclusion he reaches on the provenance of the *Odes* is specific: "The Odes of Solomon, composed in Syriac at Edessa, were known to the bi-lingual Ignatius either there or at Antioch" (377).
[35] Lactantius, *Divine Institutes*, 4.12.
[36] One should not follow Harris and Mingana who placed the *Odes* in the first century (Harris and Mingana, *Odes of Solomon*, 69). Not only is there a strong connection to the Gospel of John (written c. 90 CE), but it is also likely that the Odist knew of Rev 12 in *Ode* 22.5 (cf. Rev 5.3 and *Ode* 23.8–9) where he speaks of a dragon with seven heads. Again, positing a likely date of Revelation c. 90 CE, the conclusion must be that the *Odes* were not written in the first century.
[37] Lattke, *Odes of Solomon*, 7–10.
[38] Pace J. L. Wu and S. C. Pearson, "Hymns, Songs," in *DLNT*, ed. Ralph P. Martin and Peter H. Davids (Downers Grove, IL: InterVarsity Press, 1997), 525, who state, "A close examination of the entire document reveals its incomplete (if sometimes faulty) presentations of christology and other doctrinal beliefs (e.g. *the silence about sin and judgment*)" (emphasis added).

biblical Psalmists. Salvific language and metaphors pour from the Odist's pen whose constant refrain is praise for a God who graciously breaks the bonds of slavery on the basis of faith.[39] Salvation thus begins with a sovereign God who elects.

The God of Salvation

The Odist firmly believes that God is the main actor in the drama of salvation. Humanity, unable to obtain salvation on their own because of their bondage to sin and death, must depend on the grace of God.[40] The Odist was gripped by this truth and this led him to praise the God who was the right hand of his salvation.[41] On account of this, the majority of the references to divine sovereignty are directly related to God's role in election. It may seem somewhat surprising that election plays such a prominent role in the thinking of the Odist given the fact that many of the second-century authors emphasized free will in response to pagan fatalism, but it was the Odist's background in Judaism that gave him the necessary framework to believe that God elects whomever he chooses.

For the Odist, God's divine purpose in salvation began with the corruption of the present world: "Thou hast brought Thy world to corruption, that everything might be resolved and renewed."[42] And yet even prior to the formation of the world, God could say of the elect, "before they had existed, I recognized them; and imprinted a seal on their faces."[43] Later in the same *Ode* he writes, "I willed and fashioned mind and heart, and they are my own; and upon my right hand I have set my elect ones."[44] God elects and seals those whom he possessed from the beginning[45] and it is only the elect who receive grace and love.[46] It is God who opens hearts by his light[47] and who causes his knowledge to abound in men.[48] Because God is the creator of man and the author and instiga-

---

[39] As Lattke notes, "Among the most common theologico-soteriological terms are faith, fruit, grace, holiness, imperishability, joy, life, light, love, redemption, rest, salvation, strength, truth, understanding (*gnōsis*), and word" (Lattke, *Odes of Solomon*, 14).
[40] *Ode* 17.2–4; 25.1.
[41] *Ode* 25.2; 8.18; 14.4.
[42] *Ode* 22.11. Cf. Rom 8:20–21.
[43] *Ode* 8.13.
[44] *Ode* 8.13.
[45] *Ode* 41.9; 4.7.
[46] *Ode* 23.2–3.
[47] *Ode* 10.3.
[48] *Ode* 12.3.

tor of salvation, he rhetorically asks in regards to election, "Who can stand against my work?"[49] The obvious answer is that no one can thwart his purpose in election, a theme he shares with Paul in Romans 9–11.

Establishing the centrality of God's sovereignty in the *Odes* is critical in order to understand the Odist's view of justification. As it will be shown in the next section, the Odist saw humanity's condition as bleak, if not hopeless. God had to blaze the path to salvation himself because men and women could not come to the waters of salvation on their own apart from divine intervention.

5.3 Justification in the *Odes*

Although scholars acknowledge that soteriological themes pervade the *Odes*, the doctrine of justification is overlooked and even disregarded.[50] This is in spite of the frequent usage of the δικ– word group.[51] The verb ܙܕܩ, which corresponds to δικαιόω, is found a total of four times in the *Odes*,[52] while the noun ܙܕܝܩܘܬܐ, corresponding to δικαιοσύνη, appears seven times.[53] The disregard for the frequency

---

49 *Ode* 8.17.
50 Lattke has an excursus entitled "'Righteousness' and 'Justification' in the *Odes of Solomon*," where he examines the meaning of righteousness and justification in the *Odes* (Lattke, *Odes of Solomon*, 365–6). For the most part, he understands the Odist's usage of the verb in a similar vein of 1 Tim 3:16 where Jesus is said to be "vindicated in the Spirit" (ἐδικαιώθη ἐν πνεύματι). This view is found wanting in light of the contexts in *Ode* 17.2, 25.12, and 29.5. Only in *Ode* 31.5 does the verb "justified" mean vindicated in the sense of 1 Tim 3:16.
51 This chapter relies heavily on the labors of Michael Lattke. His research on the *Odes* is unsurpassed. In addition to the Hermeneia commentary already cited, see his four volume *Die Oden Salomos in ihrer Bedeutung für Neues Testament und Gnosis*, Orbis Biblicus et Orientalis 25 (Göttingen: Vandenhoeck & Ruprecht, 1979–1998). He serves as a robust interlocutor when a position contrary to his own is taken and a strong voice for agreement when there is concord. Even where this chapter disagrees with him, it does so only with profound respect.
52 *Ode* 29.5 uses the Pael whereas the other uses are in the Ethpa. ܐܙܕܕܩ and are equivalent to a passive form of δικαιόω (*Odes* 17.2; 25.12; 31.5). I am grateful for the help of Peter Gentry and John Meade with the Syriac of the *Odes*.
53 *Odes* 8.5, 19; 9.10; 20.4; 25.10; 36.6; 41.12. This noun is "never opposed as *righteousness based on faith* to *righteousness based on the law*" in the *Odes* (Lattke, *Odes of Solomon*, 365–6, emphasis original). While this is true, it does need clarification. The Odist never juxtaposes the law and faith, but several uses of "righteousness" assume perfection (the Odist cannot attain to). In *Ode* 25.10, the speaker declares he has been made "holy in Your righteousness," which acknowledges his need for another's righteousness. Righteousness is the appropriate offering for the Lord in *Ode* 20.4, but the righteousness spoken of here is not law, *per se*, but "purity of heart and lips."

5.3 Justification in the Odes

of justification language is made more surprising when one considers the contexts in which these words generally appear where the theme is freedom from bondage. The doctrine of forensic justification emerges in three particular *Odes*—17, 25, and 29.

Ode 17

1. Then I was crowned by my God,
   And my crown is living.
2. And I was justified by my Lord,
   For my salvation is incorruptible.[54]
3. I have been freed from vanities,
   And am not condemned.
4. My chains were cut off by His hands;
   I received the face and likeness of a new person,
   And I walked in Him and was saved.
5. And the thought of truth led me,
   And I went after it and wandered not.

(Christ speaks)[55]
6. And all who saw me were amazed,
   And I seemed to them like a stranger.
7. And He who knew and exalted me,
   Is the Most High in all His perfection.
8. And He glorified me by His kindness,
   And raised my understanding to the height of truth.
9. And from there He gave me the way of His steps,
   And I opened the doors which were closed.
10. And I shattered the bars of iron,
    For my own iron(s) had grown hot and melted before me.
11. And nothing appeared closed to me,
    Because I was the opening of everything.
12. And I went towards all my bondsmen in order to loose them;
    That I might not leave anyone bound or binding.
13. And I gave my knowledge generously,
    And my resurrection through my love.
14. And I sowed my fruits in hearts,
    And transformed them through myself.
15. Then they received my blessing and lived,
    And they were gathered to me and were saved;
16. Because they became my members,

---

54 Lattke, *Odes of Solomon*, 233 translates this "imperishable."
55 This parenthetical statement is included in Charlesworth's text at the beginning of v. 6.

And I was their Head.
17. Glory to Thee, our Head, O Lord Messiah.
Hallelujah.

A major complication in *Ode* 17 has to do with identifying the speaker. Lattke comments that "the main difficulty, which is that the 'I' of stanzas I–III (vv. 1–8a), who is to be distinguished from the author or performer of the Ode, speaks of his salvation by 'God' the 'Lord' and the 'Most High,' while the speaking 'I' of stanzas IV–V (8b–15) describes himself as the 'head' and speaks of his own already accomplished liberation and salvation of his 'members.' There is no indication of a change of grammatical subject."[56] Because there is no obvious change in speaker, Lattke wishes to see the Messiah as the "I" of the entire Ode.

Richard Reitzenstein's theory of an *Erlöster Erlöser* has gained traction with some who wish to see the Kyrios Christos of verse 16 as the subject of the entire *Ode*, but this interpretation is unlikely for several reasons.[57] To begin with, the ability to change subjects without a clear discourse marker is a prominent phenomenon in Semitic languages.[58] In the Old Testament this phenomenon occurs

---

[56] Lattke, *Odes of Solomon*, 234. Lattke's versification is slightly different than Charlesworth's, for Lattke collapses vv. 7–8 into one verse.

[57] Richard Reitzenstein, *Das mandäische Buch des Herrn der Größe und die Evangelienüberlieferung*, SHAW.PH (Heidelberg: Winter, 1919), 31–32. Because Reitzenstein's argument applies more to Manichaeism, Lattke warns against seeing a direct application of this term (Lattke, *Odes of Solomon*, 234). However, this does not prevent Lattke from using the phrase "redeemed Redeemer" when speaking of the "I" in *Ode* 17. Hermann Gunkel also sees Christ as the redeemed Redeemer saying, "der Erlöste (I. Teil) ist zum Erlöser geworden (II. Teil)" (Hermann Gunkel, "Die Oden Salomos," *ZNW* 11 [1910]: 307). Though it is argued in this chapter that *Ode* 17 does not speak of a redeemed Redeemer, a more problematic passage is *Ode* 8.21 where the Odist writes, "And you who are saved in Him who was saved." See Hans-Martin Schenke, *Der Gott 'Mensch' in der Gnosis: Ein religionsgeschichtlicher Beitrag zur Diskussion über die paulinische Anschauung von der Kirche als Leib Christi* (Göttingen: Vandenhoeck & Ruprecht, 1962), 30, who strongly argues against the idea of a redeemed Redeemer in 8.21, saying that if one sees Jesus as the redeemed Redeemer, "dann könnte man ja auch den Christus der Orthodoxie als 'erlösten Erlöser' bezeichnen!" It is possible that this reference to salvation has the resurrection in view. Not only does 8.21b emphasize that the believer is "kept in Him who lives," but this interpretation is also attractive because v. 22 says that "you shall be found incorrupted in all ages," which could refer to the promise of Ps 16:10 that the Holy One will not see corruption. The promise of salvation in this text is the hope of resurrection, a truth the Odist affirms concerning the Messiah and believers. In this way, it can be said the Messiah was "saved" without introducing an aberrant Christology.

[58] For the most recent work on this phenomenon see Oliver Glanz, "Who Is Speaking? Who is Addressed? A Critical Study into the Conditions of Exegetical Method and Its Consequences for

regularly in poetry and prophecy.⁵⁹ For example, in Jeremiah 11:14–17 scholars are at odds over who the subject is, since it seems to change without warning in v. 16.⁶⁰ Likewise, there are some clues in *Ode* 17 that point to a new speaker in verse 6 without a change in first person singular verbs. Verse 6b contains the first use of the third person plural pronoun, which becomes a common occurrence throughout the remainder of the *Ode*. This shift in pronouns indicates that the focus of the first five verses, namely individual liberation from bondage, switches in the last twelve verses to the exalted Messiah who is the agent of redemption. The lack of clarity in this subject change is purposeful and is meant to heighten the theme of union with Christ, which is particularly evident in vv. 14–16.

Second, the notion of a redeemed Redeemer crumbles if Jesus is the "Lord" of v. 2, since that would mean that Jesus justified Jesus, a nonsensical idea. Besides v. 2 the only other occurrence use of "Lord" (ܡܪܝܐ) in this *Ode* comes in v. 17 where Jesus is unmistakably the referent.⁶¹ While it is true that the word κύριος itself is used for YHWH in the LXX, so the Odist can, and often does, use ܡܪܝܐ/κύριος to speak of God, it would be confusing to the reader to use the same word in two ways without a clear indicator. Moreover, if "Lord" is used once for God (v. 1) and once for Jesus (v. 2) in this *Ode*, then it would be the only place in the *Odes* where the word "Lord" can refer to both persons in the same *Ode*.⁶²

---

the Interpretation of Participant Reference-Shifts in the Book of Jeremiah" (Ph.D. diss., Vrije University, 2010). Another thorough investigation of this discourse phenomenon can be found in Steven E. Runge, "A Discourse-Functional Description of Participant Reference in Biblical Hebrew Narrative" (D.Litt. diss., University of Stellenbosch, 2007).

59 Glanz, "Who is Speaking?" 257.

60 Oliver Glanz, "Who is Speaking—Who is Listening? How Information Technology Can Confirm the Integrity of the Text," in *Tradition and Innovation in Biblical Interpretation: Studies Presented to Professor Eep Talstra on the Occasion of his Sixty-Fifth Birthday*, ed. W. Th. van Peursen and J. W. Dyk (Leiden: Brill, 2011), 339–44.

61 Lattke supplies an impressive chart on 552–54 in which he tries to show the places where "Lord" refers to Christ/Messiah and where it refers to "God." Remarkably, he finds only a handful of times where "Lord" is to be understood as Christ/Messiah, and *Ode* 17.2 is not one of them. Lattke argues that God of 1a should be seen as parallel to Lord of 2a, thus equating the two. While this is not impossible, normal poetic parallelism would suggest that 1a and 1b are parallel and not 1a/2a and 1b/2b. Franzmann also recognizes the parallelism between 1a/1b and 2a/2b and not 1a/2a and 1b/2b (Franzmann, *Odes of Solomon*, 132).

62 This detail is according to Lattke's own investigation, which is seen in his chart on 552–4 (Lattke, *Odes of Solomon*). The only exception to this comes in *Ode* 29.6: "For I believed in the Lord's Messiah, and considered that He is the Lord." But in this verse it is abundantly clear that the first mention of Lord is the "Most High" whereas the second mention is the "Kyrios Christos." See the comments on this verse below under the investigation of *Ode* 29.

The resemblance of *Ode* 17.1–2 and *Ode* 1.1 is striking and might also shed light onto this problem. The *Odes* begin in this manner: "The Lord is on my head like a crown, and I shall never be without Him." After deliberating as to whether Christ or God is in view here, Lattke comes to no solid conclusion except to suggest that it is "more likely" that the Lord in 1.1 is the "Kyrios (Son, Messiah)."[63] However, he hedges on this point, saying that if "'Lord' represents κύριος, the 'normal title of God,' the 'I' could also be the redeemed Redeemer of *Ode* 17."[64] His only hesitation comes from wanting to see "Lord" in 17.2 as God. Finally, a Christ in need of redemption stands outside the picture of Jesus as portrayed in the rest of the *Odes*.[65]

Thus, Charlesworth's decision to introduce a change of speaker in verse 6 does not appear to be arbitrary as Lattke would suppose.[66] And Charlesworth is not alone in perceiving this change. On this *Ode* Harris states,

> That it is a Christian Psalm is evident: the Messiah or Christ is definitely referred to, and he is spoken of as being to believers in the relation of the head to the members. But we have again in this Psalm the *peculiar change of personality:* this time it comes so imperceptibly that we might be tempted to doubt the reality of the transition, if it were not for the abruptness of the return from it at the close of the Psalm.[67]

Instead of this *Ode* chronicling the journey of the redeemed Redeemer from captivity to freedom, this *Ode* is better understood as a song of praise for the Redeemer who shattered the bonds of imprisonment so that the believer can be united to the head.

The redeemed. The speaker begins the *Ode* with the statement that he was crowned with a living crown (ܚܠܠܐ ܣܒܐ).[68] The "living crown" motif signals that the focus of the *Ode* is salvation. In light of the following verses on justification, the "crown of life" is the eschatological prize that Jesus promises to the faithful

---

63 Lattke, *Odes of Solomon*, 30.
64 Lattke, *Odes of Solomon*, 30.
65 See Rudolf Abramowski, "Der Christus der Salomooden," *ZNW* 35 (1936): 44–69, for a thorough discussion on the Christology of the *Odes*.
66 Lattke, "To maintain that '[Jesus] Christ speaks' only from 6a on is as arbitrary as declaring *Ode* 17 to be 'full of the thought of the Redemption of the Baptized'" (Lattke, *Odes of Solomon*, 234). The latter reference to the redemption of the baptized is a response to Bernard, *Odes of Solomon*, 82.
67 Harris, *The Odes and Psalms of Solomon*, 114, emphasis added.
68 Underneath the Syriac is στέφανος which in this context is an "award or prize for exceptional service or conduct" (BDAG, s.v. "στέφανος").

in Revelation 2:10 (δώσω σοι τὸν στέφανον τῆς ζωῆς).⁶⁹ Lattke translates *Ode* 17.1b to read "[God] is my living crown." This translation brings out even more the theme of union, which is the key to understanding this *Ode*. God is both the giver of the crown and the crown itself.

In verse 2, the "I" states that he was justified by the Lord. As noted above, "Lord" is a reference to Jesus, so the speaker recognizes that his justification comes from the Kyrios Christos. The parallelism of 2a and 2b reveals that his justification *is* imperishable salvation.⁷⁰ That his salvation is imperishable (ἄφθαρτος)⁷¹ hearkens to 1 Peter 1:4 where the inheritance, which in this case is metaphorically symbolized by the crown, is kept safe in heaven. In the context of the first four verses, justification should be understood in a forensic sense.

The Ethpa. ܐܙܕܕܩ means "to be justified."⁷² Since words derive their meaning from their immediate context, it is critical to examine the general flow of this *Ode* in order to see if ܙܕܩ does in fact have a forensic sense to it in 17.2 or if it is being used more like ἐδικαιώθη ("to vindicate") in 1 Timothy 3:16. Simply because both 17.2 and 1 Timothy 3:16 use a passive form of the verb does not mean that their meaning is the same, as Lattke seems to suggest.⁷³ Lattke's shallow argument does not account for the strong language the Odist employs in *Ode* 17. Terms like bonds, chains, condemnation, and freedom surround the use of ܙܕܩ, which make it necessary, or at least very probable, to see a forensic use of the word in this text. Franzmann's translation is best in this context since she translates ܐܙܕܕܩ as "I was declared righteous."⁷⁴ Such a claim in the New Testament is never made of Jesus but Paul uses this terminology regularly for the believer. At the heart of the issue is the need for righteousness. For the sinner, condem-

---

69 Cf. 2 Tim 4:8, Js 1:12, 1 Pet 5:4. Walter Bauer also takes this as the "crown of life" (Bauer, *Die Oden Salomos*, 597). Bernard's attempt to read this as a "baptismal crown" should not be followed for there is nothing in this context which alludes to baptism (Bernard, *Odes of Solomon*, 82). Regarding the allusion to Revelation, it is certain that the Odist knew of this book since he makes reference to it in several places (e.g., *Ode* 23.8–9 relies on Rev 5:3).
70 Lattke's comment on this verse that "justification brought about a 'salvation' ... that cannot be shaken" is not strong enough (Lattke, *Odes of Solomon*, 236). Justification does not just bring about salvation for the Odist—it is synonymous with salvation in this verse.
71 Lattke's conjecture of the Greek behind the Syriac (Lattke, *Odes of Solomon*, 236).
72 Payne Smith. ܙܕܩ, Hebr. צדק. Smith is of little help on this matter because his work is in Latin. Thus, he gives the gloss *justus fuit* for ܙܕܩ which has the more transformative sense "make righteous" instead of the Greek word' δικαιόω which often means to "declare righteous." Sokoloff does provide "to justify" as a gloss (Sokoloff, s.v. ܙܕܩ).
73 Lattke, *Odes of Solomon*, 366.
74 Franzmann, *Odes of Solomon*, 131.

nation is his just reward, which is the precise connection the Odist makes in the next verse.

In verse 3 the forensic language intensifies as the "I" declares that he has been freed (ܐܬܐ; ἀπολύω) from vanities and this freedom is from condemnation.⁷⁵ Freedom from vanities encompasses much more than liberty from the "futility and decay of this world and age (cf. Rom 8:18–21)."⁷⁶ Vanities should be expanded to include sinful behavior as well. If this were not the case, then why does the "I" rejoice that he is not condemned in verse 3b? The Greek κατάκριτος or ἀκατάκριτος,⁷⁷ both of which carry a "basic forensic meaning,"⁷⁸ underlie "condemnation" (ܕܝܢܐ), adding weight to the argument that the speaker's justification means that he will not suffer condemnation for succumbing to the "vanities" of the world.

This notion of freedom from condemnation is palpably illustrated in v. 4 where the "I" is set free from his bonds.⁷⁹ The Odist sings of his liberation, saying, "My chains were cut off by His hands; I received the face and likeness of a new person, and I walked in Him and was saved."⁸⁰ The forensic nature of the passage is particularly noticeable in the incarceration images of this verse. The "I" visualized himself in custody under a sentence of condemnation, his only companions were his fellow prisoners.⁸¹ These chains were cut off "by Him," who, judging by the nearest antecedent, is to be understood as the Lord of v. 2. The result of his justification is the reception of a new nature. He received the "face and likeness of a new person," which resembles Paul's language in 2 Cor 5:17 that "if anyone is in Christ, he is a new creation; old things have passed away, behold new things have come" (ὥστε εἴ τις ἐν Χριστῷ, καινὴ κτίσις· τὰ ἀρχαῖα παρῆλθεν, ἰδοὺ γέγονεν καινά). Now justified, the "I" walks in Him,

---

75 *Ode* 17.3.
76 Lattke, *Odes of Solomon*, 237.
77 BDAG, "pert. to not undergoing a proper legal process, *uncondemned, without due process*." This word occurs twice in the New Testament, both in Acts (16:37, 22:25) and both pertaining to legal process (s.v., "ἀκατάκριτος").
78 Lattke, *Odes of Solomon*, 237.
79 There is no reason to succumb to August Vogl's pessimistic conclusion to 17.4: "eine brauchbare, begründete Erklärung dieser schwierigen Stelle läßt sich nicht finden" (Vogl, "Oden Salomos 17, 22, 24, 42: Übersetzung und Kommentar," ed. Brian McNeil, *OrChr* 62 [1978]: 61). Vogl's inability to find a solution stems from not seeing two different speakers in this text.
80 *Ode* 17.4.
81 *Ode* 17.12.

the Redeemer, and is saved.[82] The new nature subsequently provoked the Odist to follow the thought of truth and to not wander from it.[83] The path of truth set before him and the bonds of condemnation shattered behind him ensured that his feet would not stumble along the way.

The Redeemer. The Messiah assumes the role of speaker starting in verse 6. It is undisputed that the last few verses of the *Ode* envision the personified Messiah since he speaks of his resurrection and the ingathering of those who were transformed into members of his body, thus making it inconceivable that the "I" could refer to anyone but Jesus. Verse 6 is the likely place of this shift because of the introduction of the third person pronouns and because of the change of focus from personal redemption to the Redeemer. The change of speaker from the indeterminate "I" to Christ is not unique to this *Ode*. In at least two other places, Charlesworth recognizes a shift of this type.

In *Ode* 41 the speaker changes from the first person plurals "us" and "our" to the first person singulars "I" and "me" for three verses in the middle of the *Ode* (vv. 8–10) and then switches back again for the remainder of the *Ode*. *Ode* 28 has a similar phenomenon to *Ode* 17 in that the speaker uses the first person singular throughout, and yet Charlesworth detects a change of speaker in v. 9 there as well. What makes this even more remarkable is that the first words out of Christ's mouth as the speaker in each of these *Odes* are "and all who saw me were amazed" (17.6), "all those who see me will be amazed" (41.8), and "those who saw me were amazed" (28.9), as though the look of amazement was the signal that Christ has assumed the role of speaker.[84]

---

[82] Lattke says, "the 'being saved' of 4c is not a consequence of 'walking' in the new role but synonymous with it" (Lattke, *Odes of Solomon*, 237). Walking as a metaphor for salvation is commonplace in the *Odes*.

[83] *Ode* 17.5. A subjective genitive, the stress of the phrase "thought of truth" is on personified truth here and not on thought (Lattke, *Odes of Solomon*, 238). Franzmann capitalizes "Truth" in her translation to bring this idea out (Franzmann, *Odes of Solomon*, 131). It is possible, then, to see this personified truth as Jesus, who is the way, the *truth*, and the life (John 14:6, emphasis added).

[84] Another example is *Ode* 42 where the change of speaker is evident even though, once again, the speaker uses "I" the entire time. What makes *Ode* 42 a noteworthy case is the certainty with which the speaker changes even though there is no discourse marker cluing the reader in to this change. The Odist goes from speaking of Christ's crucifixion to Jesus himself speaking of the event, yet "I" is used in both sections.

Those who look upon the Redeemer are "amazed" at him who seemed to them like a "stranger" (ξένος).[85] The Redeemer appeared as a stranger in much the same way as the resurrected Jesus was hidden from the disciples (his fellow travelers on the Emmaus road) in Luke 24:16, who were also amazed when their blindness was lifted.[86] In verse 7 the Redeemer is exalted by the Most High on account of his salvific work and resurrection.[87] In addition to his exaltation, he was also glorified by the Most High's kindness and his understanding was raised to the height of truth.[88] There is no reason to see a Gnostic tinge in the elevation of understanding in 8b.[89] Rather, this could simply be a reference to the fact that the resurrected and exalted Messiah does not now lack any knowledge as he did during the time of his earthly ministry (Mark 13:35).

Verses 9–13 should be read together. The Most High gave "the way of His steps" as a gift so that the Messiah might walk in them. As a result, he was able to "open the doors which were closed." The reference to the closed doors has sparked debate amongst scholars over whether there is an allusion to Jesus' *descensus ad inferos* in verse 9. Hermann Gunkel was the first to argue the affirmative based on the strong similarity of these verses to 1 Peter 4:6 where Christ "had preached to the dead" (νεκροῖς εὐηγγελίσθη).[90] Although it

---

[85] It is tempting to follow Adolf von Harnack who sees v. 6 connected to 4b. For von Harnack, the speaker seems like a "stranger" because he has the appearance of a "new person" (*Ein jüdisch-christliches Psalmbuch*, 46). This is the strongest argument for the unity of the speaker throughout the *Ode*. However, the majority of the evidence presented here points away from this interpretation.

[86] Charlesworth goes astray in following Batiffol who labeled this statement Docetic (Charlesworth, *Odes of Solomon*, 76). Lattke, who makes the connection to Luke 24, is correct that this reference to the Greek loanword ξένος is "quite unconnected to any possible Docetism in the *Odes of Solomon*" (Lattke, *Odes of Solomon*, 239).

[87] Cf. Phil 2:6–11.

[88] *Ode* 17.8. The Son receiving glory from the Father is an important Johannine theme (cf. John 8:54; 12:28; 13:31; 17:1, 4). See Lattke, *Odes of Solomon*, 243 n. 133.

[89] Lattke stops short of calling this "heretical *Gnosis*," but he does venture to say that "by this metaphorical raising up to the 'height of truth' … , the 'understanding' of the redeemed one partakes of the '*gnōsis*' of the Lord and Most High in the *plērōma*" (Lattke, *Odes of Solomon*, 243).

[90] Gunkel, "Die Oden Salomos," 305–06. It is astonishing that he does not cite the stronger allusion from 1 Pet 3:19 where Peter claims that Jesus "went and proclaimed to the spirits in prison" (ἐν ᾧ καὶ τοῖς ἐν φυλακῇ πνεύμασιν πορευθεὶς ἐκήρυξεν), which could have been in the Odist's mind. Many have followed Gunkel on this, among whom are Daniel Plooij, "Der Descensus ad inferos in Aphrahat und den Oden Salomos," *ZNW* 14 (1913): 227–28, and Sebastian P. Brock, "The Gates/Bars of Sheol Revisited," in *Sayings of Jesus: Canonical and Non-Canonical. Essays in Honor of Tjitze Baarda*, NovTSup 89 (Leiden: Brill, 1997), 12. (See Lattke, *Odes of Solomon*, 244 n. 149 for a full list.) Many others have not been willing to follow Gunkel's theory that this passage speaks to Christ's descent. See, for example, Adolf von Harnack, *Ein jüdisch-chris-*

is not necessary to interpret verse 9 as Christ's descent into hell, it is a doctrine that the Odist seems to have held.[91] Given the soteriological context of *Ode* 17 as a whole, Charlesworth is correct to posit that this verse "may refer to those who are bound by sin on earth."[92] The Messiah comes to those living who are fettered to their sins and he breaks their chains, symbolizing their justification.

The relationship between verse 4 and verse 10 is complicated on the surface. Verse 4 was the triumphant moment for the condemned one when the Redeemer cut off his chains. Verse 10, on the other hand, employs a similar illustration, yet with a different meaning. In this case, the Redeemer also wore shackles and says, "And I shattered the bars of iron, for my own iron(s) had grown hot and melted before me." In verse 4, the chains are connected to the vanities of the world for which the prisoner deserved condemnation. However, this notion is entirely absent from the context in verse 10. What, then, were the shackles that bound the Redeemer?

The answer most assuredly lies in the Messianic prophecies of the Old Testament. In keeping with his rich Jewish heritage, the Odist draws his inspiration from Isaiah 45:2: "I will go before you, and I will level the mountains, I will smash the door of bronze and I will shatter the bars of iron" (Ἐγὼ ἔμπροσθέν σου πορεύσομαι καὶ ὄρη ὁμαλιῶ, θύρας χαλκᾶς συντρίψω καὶ μοχλοὺς σιδηροῦς συγκλάσω LXX).[93] This promise in Isaiah is spoken to Cyrus to give him comfort that no barrier will obstruct him so long as Yahweh goes before him. Commenting on this passage in Isaiah, Edward J. Young observes that this "is the language of redemption, although it does not refer to the actual redemption itself but only to the preparation for it. The stage must be set, and the proper conditions established for the Deliverer to appear."[94] This is related to the view of the Redeemer in *Ode* 17 in that Christ too had to prepare the way of salvation by breaking his bonds. Unlike the captive in verse 4, however, who needed another to break his

---

tliches Psalmbuch, 47, Jean Labourt and Pierre Batiffol, *Les Odes de Salomon: Une œuvre chrétienne des environs de l'an 100–120* (Paris: Gabalda, 1911), 73, and Harris, who concedes that this verse could but "need not be an allusion to the descent into Hades" (Harris, *Odes of Solomon*, 114).

91 *Ode* 42 is an undisputed example of Christ's descent into Sheol.
92 Charlesworth, *Odes of Solomon*, 76.
93 An echo of Ps 106:16 is also to be heard here: "For he smashed the gates of bronze, and shattered the bars of iron" (ὅτι συνέτριψεν πύλας χαλκᾶς καὶ μοχλοὺς συνέκλασεν LXX). See Lattke, *Odes of Solomon*, 245.
94 Edward J. Young, *The Book of Isaiah: The English Text, with Introduction, Exposition, and Notes* (Grand Rapids: Eerdmans, 1972), 3:196. Cf. John Oswalt, *Isaiah 40–66*, NICOT (Grand Rapids: Eerdmans, 1998), who comments, "It is God who will go before the conqueror and prepare the way for him" (201).

bonds, the Redeemer shattered his own bars of iron that had grown hot and melted away. Also in contrast to the redeemed of verse 4, the Redeemer's bonds were not sinful vanities, but rather his bondage to death, which served as his preparation for redemption.

Once he was free from his bonds, the Redeemer remarks "nothing appeared closed to me, because I was the opening of everything." Quite possibly the Odist is remembering Jesus' words in Revelation 3:7—"He who has the key of David, who opens and no one will close, and closes and no one opens" (ὁ ἔχων τὴν κλεῖν Δαυίδ, ὁ ἀνοίγων καὶ οὐδεὶς κλείσει καὶ κλείων καὶ οὐδεὶς ἀνοίγει).[95] The Messiah possesses the "keys over death and Hades" (τὰς κλεῖς τοῦ θανάτου καὶ τοῦ ᾅδου; Rev 1:18) because he conquered death and the grave through his cross and resurrection. As the victorious key holder, the Redeemer went to those who were bound in order to destroy their chains. This is the picture the Odist paints in the introductory verses—the Redeemer coming to the incarcerated one and severing his shackles. His desire is that not one be left bound and even to transform those guilty of binding (17.12).

The final verses (vv. 13–17) are essential for understanding *Ode* 17. The theme of the *Ode*, namely salvation through the union of the believer with the Messiah, ties together the otherwise confusing parts of the *Ode*, such as the difficulty of identifying the speaker. The reason why the speaker seamlessly changes is because whatever is true of the redeemed is true of the Redeemer. These twin themes of forensic justification and union with Christ make the Odist's dependence on Paul likely. Not only does the Odist demonstrate a Pauline use of justification in verses 1–4, but he also holds to a Pauline view of union with Christ in verses 13–17. The union motif is evident in that he uses one of Paul's favorite metaphors for the church as the body of Christ, where Christ is the head and believers are the members (*Ode* 17.16). This will become clear in the following discussion.

To those he came to rescue, the Messiah gave his knowledge generously (v. 13). This verse resembles verse 8 where the Redeemer's understanding was raised to the height of truth. The emphasis now is on the distribution of his knowledge to those he came to save. This should not be taken to mean, however, that knowledge is tantamount to salvation. The knowledge given is the knowledge of the resurrection, since this stands parallel to verse 13b. It is the knowledge of the Messiah that the Redeemer uses to shatter the bonds of sin.

---

[95] In addition to the passage in Rev 3, Charlesworth also sees a connection to John 10:7–10 (Charlesworth, *Odes of Solomon*, 76). Lattke makes the connection to John 10:9 as well (Lattke, *Odes of Solomon*, 246).

The translation of the verse 13b is quite contested.⁹⁶ Charlesworth translates the verse to read, "And my resurrection through my love."⁹⁷ Lattke, quibbling over Charlesworth's translation of ܒܥܘܬܐ into resurrection, labels this translation "convoluted"⁹⁸ and prefers to render the second half of the bicolon, "and my *consolation* through my love."⁹⁹ While Charlesworth's translation does involve several steps, it is convincing in this context and it should not be dismissed without careful reflection. Charlesworth's argument is that ܒܥܘܬܐ "literally means 'my prayer'" and that "in Judaism prayer for the dead usually presupposed belief in the resurrection (2 Macc 12:44 f., cf. 1 Cor 15:29)."¹⁰⁰ He traces the evolution of the Aramaic בעותא from "petition" to "consolation" and finally into the Christianized meaning of "resurrection."¹⁰¹ Furthermore, he conjectures that "if one could push aside the veil of history, *et hoc genus omne*, that separates us from the earliest Palestinian Christians, and ask them what was their consolation, or what was their salvation, the answer would probably be the same, viz. the resurrection of the Messiah."¹⁰² Resurrection fits well with the sown fruits in verse 14 and the opening of things which were closed, such as death and the grave. The result of the Messiah's resurrection is the unloosing of those bound.¹⁰³

Of greater significance is that the resurrection is given to the one who is united to the Redeemer through his justification.¹⁰⁴ For Paul, union with Christ occurs when believers identify with Jesus' resurrection through baptism. His point in Romans 6:1–5 is that believers are no longer under the power of sin because they have been united to Christ. Particularly, in verse 5 Paul writes, "For if we have been united with him in a death like his, we shall certainly be united with him in a resurrection like his" (εἰ γὰρ σύμφυτοι γεγόναμεν τῷ ὁμοιώματι τοῦ θανάτου αὐτοῦ, ἀλλὰ καὶ τῆς ἀναστάσεως ἐσόμεθα). On this pericope Thomas Schreiner notes, "Union with Christ in his death and burial and his resurrec-

---

96 In resignation, Harris and Mingana concluded on this verse, "The sense is very doubtful" (Harris and Mingana, *Odes of Solomon*, 2:291).
97 Charlesworth, *Odes of Solomon*, 75.
98 Lattke, *Odes of Solomon*, 248.
99 Lattke, *Odes of Solomon*, 233, emphasis added. Lattke argues that the consolation of the "I" and the gift of *gnōsis* "are the two sides of one soteriological coin" (248).
100 Charlesworth, *Odes of Solomon*, 77.
101 See James H. Charlesworth, "בעותא in Earliest Christianity," in *The Use of the Old Testament in the New and Other Essays: Studies in Honor of William Franklin Stinespring*, ed. James M. Efrid (Durham, NC: Duke University Press, 1972), 274–75.
102 Charlesworth, "בעותא in Earliest Christianity," 275.
103 Charlesworth, "בעותא in Earliest Christianity," 278.
104 The verb "gave" (ܝܗܒ) is elided from 13b but assumed from 13a.

tion becomes a reality for believers through baptism."[105] As the believer is plunged below the waters to show his death to sin, so he rises from his watery grave to show his union with Christ's resurrection.[106]

In addition to the gift of resurrection, the Redeemer also sows his fruits in the hearts of believers. What is envisaged by "fruits" is not clear. Perhaps the Odist is recalling Paul's "fruits of the Spirit," which yield a perennial crop in the believer's life (see Gal 5:22–23). What is certain is that these fruits lead to a transformation in the redeemed (v. 14b). The Redeemer "transformed them through [himself]," leading one to suspect that there is an organic union between the Redeemer and the one he has redeemed.[107] Lattke acknowledges the presence of Paul's doctrine of union with Christ in this verse, saying, "This would bring a reminiscence of the formulaic ἐν κυρίῳ and/or ἐν Χριστῷ of the New Testament,"[108] since the believer is transformed through the Messiah.

N. T. Wright has persuasively argued that union with Christ was central to Paul's theology based on the many variations of these prepositional phrases in his letters.[109] At the heart of union is the concept that what is true of the head is also true of the members. Having been reared in a Jewish community, the idea of union to a monarch would have come as naturally to the Odist as it did for Paul. As Wright observes, "It is endemic in the understanding of kingship, in many societies and certainly in ancient Israel, that the king and the people are bound together in such a way that what is true of the one is true in principle of the other."[110] For support of the doctrine of union in the Old Testament, Wright looks to 2 Samuel 19:40–20:1 and its parallel passage, 1 Kings 12:16. In these texts the Israelites boast of their inextricable connection with their monarch, King David. Even in the world in which the Odist found himself, the principle of union would have been abundantly clear as the Emperor of Rome stood as the *princeps civitatis* and *pontifex maximus* over his people.

---

[105] Thomas Schreiner, *Romans*, BECNT (Grand Rapids: Baker Academic, 1998), 306. Many commentators recognize the doctrine of union with Christ in Rom 6. Among them are Douglas Moo, *Romans*, NICNT (Grand Rapids: Eerdmans, 1996), 360, Robert Jewett, *Romans*, Hermeneia (Minneapolis: Fortress Press, 2007), 400, and John Murray, *Romans*, NICNT (Grand Rapids: Eerdmans, 1968), 214.
[106] J. H. Bernard argues unconvincingly that the *Odes* are a collection of baptismal songs (Bernard, *Odes of Solomon*).
[107] Jewett speaks of an organic connection (Jewett, *Romans*, 400). See below.
[108] Lattke, *Odes of Solomon*, 249.
[109] N. T. Wright, *The Climax of the Covenant* (Minneapolis: Fortress Press, 1993), 44–45. Wright lists all the places where Χριστός, Κύριος, and Ἰησοῦς, or any combination of these names/titles, appear in conjunction with ἐν, εἰς, διά, and σύν.
[110] Wright, *Climax of the Covenant*, 46.

Of course the Odist's most obvious source of inspiration for the doctrine of union with Christ, as noted above, was Paul. The Odist's belief in union is made explicit in *Ode* 3.7 where he declares, "I have been united (to Him), because the lover has found the Beloved, because I love Him that is the Son, I shall become a son."[111] Sonship means union with the Messiah for the Odist. ܐܚܠܛ, "to mix" (cf. *Ode* 19.4),[112] is similar to σύμφυτος, a *hapax legomenon* in the New Testament, which Paul uses in Romans 6:5 to speak of union. Σύμφυτος derives from συμφύω and carries the biological connotation, "make to grow together, unite (a wound)."[113] The Odist's unequivocal use of "union" bolsters the case that he not only believed in union with Christ, but that he derived his belief from Paul in Romans 6.

Any doubt that union with Christ is pictured in *Ode* 17 is dispelled when reading the final three verses. The personified Christ states that those whom he gathered to himself were saved and transformed into members of his body. As it is with the physical body, so too whatever is true of the head is true of the body and vice versa. For the Odist, and for Paul, there is one body and one head. This metaphor, typically used for Christ and the Church (1 Cor 12:12–13; Eph 4:4–16), is adopted by the Odist to bring together the disparate parts of this *Ode*. The redeemed and the Redeemer are both freed from their own respective chains so that they might become part of one body.

---

111 Charlesworth, *Odes of Solomon*, 19. This theme seems too advanced for Charlesworth because he suggests that this may be "an interpolation by a later more dogmatic Christian" (20). David E. Aune, on the other hand, sees several references to a "soteriological union with Christ" (Aune, *The Cultic Setting of Realized Eschatology in Early Christianity* [Leiden: Brill, 1972], 192). In addition to *Ode* 3.7–9, he also sees this union in 8.22–23, in what he calls a "Liebesvereinigung," a term he gets from Philipp Vielhauer (*Aufsätze zum Neuen Testament* [München: Chr. Kaiser Verlag, 1965], 226), though Aune cautions that "Vielhauer tends to overemphasize the Gnostic character of *anapusis*-speculation in early Christianity" (Aune, *The Cultic Setting of Realized Eschatology*, 189).

112 Payne Smith, s.v. "ܐܚܠܛ," states that this word can be used theologically "to join Godhead and manhood." Also, Smith says this word is used *de corpora Christi nostris corporibus immixto* (2:2059). (Cf. Sokoloff, s.v. "ܐܚܠܛ." Sokoloff notes that the word is used in the Peshitta of Heb 4:2 meaning "united together with faith.") While believer's mixing with Christ became a common motif in Syriac Christianity, Lattke believes it is anachronistic to assume that it occurs this early (Lattke, *Odes of Solomon*, 274), even though the evidence in the *Odes of Solomon* appears to tilt away from Lattke and in favor of a mixture, or union, with Christ.

113 James D. G. Dunn, *Romans*, WBC (Dallas: Word Books, 1988), 316. BDAG, s.v. "σύμφυτος," "identified with." Jewett allows a wider variety of uses "including horticultural references to grafting or growing together, biological references to knitting together the edges of a wound or the ends of broken bones, and social references to citizens clustering around their leader or sharing a particular ethos" (Jewett, *Romans*, 400).

The *Ode* concludes with the doxological statement "Glory to Thee, our Head, O Lord Messiah. Hallelujah." The speaker reverts back to the redeemed one who ascribes glory to the Lord Messiah, Jesus, who is once more called the head of the body. The exclamation of praise is fitting in light of the undeserved gifts he has received from the Messiah who condescended to enter into his own prison, that of death and the grave, to rescue those who are bound. New life, knowledge, resurrection, and union with Christ are all benefits of his incorruptible salvation that comes through justification.

Ode 17 is a soteriological hymn that begins in the bowels of sinful imprisonment and rises to the height of resurrection hope. The sinner, justified by the Lord, becomes a new person on account of his union to the Head. Pauline themes of forensic justification and union with Christ underpin the Odist's understanding of salvation and serve as the foundation for his song.

Ode 25

1. I was rescued from my chains,
   And I fled unto Thee, O my God.
2. Because Thou art the right hand of salvation,
   And my Helper.
3. Thou hast retrained those who rise up against me,
   And no more were they seen.
4. Because Thy face was with me,
   Which saved me by Thy grace.
5. But I was despised and rejected in the eyes of many,
   And I was in their eyes like lead.
6. And I acquired strength from Thee,
   And help.
7. A lamp Thou didst set for me both on my right and on my left,
   So that there might not be in me anything that is not light.
8. And I was covered with the covering of Thy Spirit,
   And I removed from me my garments of skin.
9. Because Thy right hand exalted me,
   And caused sickness to pass from me.
10. And I became mighty in Thy truth,
    And holy in Thy righteousness.
11. And all my adversaries were afraid of me,
    And I became the Lord's by the name of the Lord.
12. And I was justified by His kindness,
    And His rest is for ever and ever.

    Hallelujah.

Should the case for forensic justification in the *Odes of Solomon* rest on *Ode* 17 alone, some may wonder whether the first four verses of that *Ode* are representative of the Odist's theology. Yet the resemblance of *Ode* 25 to *Ode* 17 is remarkable. Once more the "I" starts out locked away in sin and, just as in *Ode* 17, the Redeemer brings salvation through justification. In addition to the many similarities with *Ode* 17, there are added phrases and ideas in this *Ode* that enhance his connection to a Pauline view of salvation.[114] In this *Ode*, for instance, forensic justification is combined with imputation and salvation by grace. Central to this *Ode* is the fact that salvation from sin comes via justification by grace in which the believer receives an imputation of righteousness through the Spirit.[115]

Before the soteriology of this *Ode* can be delineated, the reader is first met with the same initial problem that was faced in *Ode* 17—the identification of the speaker. The unspecified "I" distinguishes himself from both "God" (v. 1) and the "Lord" (v. 11), even though there are places where the speaker could potentially be Christ. The speaker is despised and rejected, pursued by adversaries, and there is an allusion to lamps placed on either side of him that could refer to Zechariah's vision of a lampstand or, more awkwardly, to the transfiguration, which is how Lattke takes it.[116] These themes raise the potential that this *Ode* is *ex ore Christi* but they do not necessitate it. The language of salvation by grace (v. 4) and justification by kindness (v. 12) make it all but certain that the speaker is a person offering up a hymn of praise to God for his salvation.[117] Moreover, it will be argued from verse 8 in particular that the "I" is speaking of salvation from sin as evidenced by his removal of fleshly garments, which represent

---

114 The connection to Paul is strong enough, as it will be shown, to outright reject Friedrich Spitta's assertion that "die 25. und 26. Ode enthalten keinen christlichen Gedanken" (Spitta, "Zum Verständnis der Oden Salomos," *ZNW* 11 [1910]: 282).

115 Richard Reitzenstein said this *Ode* is a "Darstellung der Erlösung" (Reitzenstein, *Das iranische Erlösungsmysterium: Religionsgeschichtliche Untersuchungen* [Bonn: Marcus & Weber, 1921], 91. Even Lattke titles this *Ode*, "A Redeemed One Speaks of Being Saved" (Lattke, *Odes of Solomon*, 356).

116 Lattke, *Odes of Solomon*, 361–2.

117 Abramowski called this *Ode* a "reines Dankgebet" (Abramowski, "Der Christus der Salomooden," 52) and Carsten Colpe a "Danklied" ("Heidnische, jüdische und christliche Überlieferung in den Schriften aus Nag Hammadi X," *JAC* [1982]: 77). Harris sums up the *Ode* in this way: "The writer, whether Christian or Jew, has been brought out of spiritual bondage into liberty: he has had to face contempt and scorn, but the Lord has filled him with brightness and covered him with beauty, and given him health of mind and body: his enemies have turned back, and his portion is with the justified saints of the Most High" (Harris, *Odes and Psalms of Solomon*, 126). He does concede, though, that "it is possible that this Psalm may be meant to express the experience of the Messiah" (Harris, *Odes and Psalms of Solomon*, 126). He affirms the former over the latter.

sin, so Jesus cannot be envisaged as the speaker without introducing a wayward Christology.

Unlike *Ode* 17 that commenced with the salvific metaphor of a "living crown" before the writer recalled his woeful condition, *Ode* 25 begins straightaway with his "rescue from chains." The fact that these bonds kept him fettered to sin is apparent from the context of salvation. Once his hands were free from the chains, he was able to flee to his God. Not until the clasps of the chains were loosened was the speaker able to approach God, yet he recognizes that salvation has come to him by the hand of God, saying, "Because Thou art the right hand of salvation."

The synecdoche of "right hand" as God's power for salvation is prevalent in the Old Testament. It was God's right hand that brought Israel up out of bondage in Egypt (Ex 15:6, 12), ushered them into the Promised Land (Ps 44:1–3), and secured for them salvation (Ps 98:1). With his mighty right hand God also judges the enemy (Hab 2:16) and delivers the believer from his adversary (Ps 17:7)—a constant refrain in *Ode* 25.[118] The Odist is most directly dependent on Psalm 117 (LXX) where the Psalmist asserts both that "the Lord is my help" (v. 6: κύριος ἐμοὶ βοηθός) and that "the right hand of the Lord exalts me, the right hand of the Lord performs miracles" (v. 16: δεξιὰ κυρίου ὕψωσέν με, δεξιὰ κυρίου ἐποίησεν δύναμιν).[119] Surely the right hand of Israel's God is the primary background for the Odist's thought in this verse.

Yet, one might wonder if the Odist is making a veiled reference to Christ, who is exalted to the right hand of God (Eph 1:19–21; Acts 2:33–34 [cf. Ps 110:1]; Heb 1:3) and who is the agent of salvation. Be this as it may, God is depicted by the Odist as the liberator and the refuge to whom the speaker flees. The Lord is the "helper" (ܡܥܕܪܢܐ: *Ode* 25.2) who brings freedom to those in prison. A similar statement is made in Ode 21.2: "Because He cast off my bonds from me, and my Helper lifted me up according to His compassion and salvation," where God is lauded as the Helper who casts off bonds. Again, the metaphor holds that salvation is liberation from bonds, which, given the context of *Ode* 21, must represent human sinfulness, for the next verse says, "I put off darkness, and put on light" (*Ode* 21.3), immediately conjuring up the Johannine motif of light and darkness.[120]

---

[118] Leland Ryken, James Wilhoit and Tremper Longman III, eds., "Right, Right Hand," *DBI* (Downers Grove, IL: InterVarsity Press, 1998), 727–28.

[119] BDAG, s.v. "ποιέω" 2b, gives the idiom for ποιέω plus δυνάμεις as "do, perform miracles."

[120] Andreas Köstenberger believes that the light/darkness concept in John's prologue comes from Gen 1:3–4 and that in the Qumran literature, which could extend some influence to the Odist, the light/darkness "contrast is set within the framework of an eschatological dualism"

Not only did God stoop to rescue the imprisoned one, but he then restrained those who rose up against the newly freed "I" (*Ode* 25.3). Here the *Ode* takes a similar shape to that of the Psalms. David's lyrics frequently recollect the days when he was fleeing from his enemies, be it Saul or Absalom, and he was forced into hiding. It was in those moments that David would call out to his God for deliverance.[121] The Odist returns to this theme in verse 5 where he is rejected by men and in verse 11 where he overcomes his adversaries. For the Odist, the freedom wrought by God brings safety from enemies as a part of redemption.

Verse 4 grounds the Odist's assertion that God subdued his enemies—it was "because [His] face was with [me]." The "face" of God, another synecdoche, refers to the entire person of God.[122] Using "face" as the figure of speech relays the personal connection the Odist feels with his God, and it is an important way to communicate God's favor. Like the Psalmist who urges his reader to "seek [God's] face continually" (Ps 105:4; בַּקְּשׁוּ פָנָיו תָּמִיד), and who pleads with God "do not hide your face from me" (Ps 27:9; אַל־תַּסְתֵּר פָּנֶיךָ מִמֶּנִּי), so too the Odist looks to God's face for protection and salvation. When God's face shines down on the speaker, he knows that his enemies are subdued, and more significantly, he receives salvation by the grace revealed at the appearing of his face. It is God's face, his favor, which the Odist says, "saved me by Thy grace."[123]

Excursus: Saved by grace. A brief excursus is in order at this juncture to investigate the concept of grace in the *Odes*, since the Odist appeals to grace as the basis of his salvation. On *Ode* 25.4b Lattke puts forth the possibility that "the juxtaposition of χάρις/ܛܝܒܘܬܐ and σῴζω/ܦܪܩ may derive from Eph 2:5, 8 (χάριτί ἐστε σεσωσμένοι, 'by grace you have been saved')."[124] Though Lattke offers this point tentatively, it could be said with utmost confidence that grace is *a*, if not *the*, leitmotif of the *Odes*. The Odist's remarks about grace are in agreement with the way that Paul speaks of grace, so that drawing a connection to Paul's

---

(*John*, BECNT [Grand Rapids: Baker Academic, 2004],13). Moreover, the light/darkness theme carries important moral overtones, as it does in the *Odes*. While commenting on John 3:19–21 Köstenberger states, "'Light' and 'darkness' have clear moral connotations," which in the case of John 3 regard the "world's rejection of Jesus ... which is the result of the fall" (131).
121 The word "enemy" occurs over 100 times in the Psalms.
122 *Pace* Lattke who argues, "The underlying neuter πρόσωπον does not here mean 'person' but 'face' or 'countenance' as the bearer of God's presence" (Lattke, *Odes of Solomon*, 359).
123 Charlesworth, *Odes of Solomon*, 101.
124 Lattke, *Odes of Solomon*, 359.

use of grace in the *Odes* does not stretch one's credulity. A quick survey of grace in the *Odes* will bring this point to bear.

The word grace (ܛܝܒܘܬܐ / χάρις) is found no less than twenty times in the *Odes*,[125] not counting the places where grace is assumed, as for example in *Ode* 4.13: "For that which You gave, You gave freely."[126] The connection of grace is made explicit in *Ode* 5.3, "Freely did I receive Your grace," which is the very meaning of grace. "Grace is for the elect ones" (23.2)[127] and it is grace that is the necessary prerequisite for entrance into eternal life (31.7). Again, "Grace has been revealed for your salvation. Believe and live and be saved" (34.6).[128] This short verse from *Ode* 34 is bursting at the seams with salvific language, so much so that Lattke regards this verse as "the crowning soteriological statement."[129] Salvation is possible only after grace has paved the way—all that is left is for the individual to grab hold of this grace through belief. Grace, combined with belief, results in salvation for the Odist. Of course, there is the ethical component in *Ode* 34.6 as well that requires the individual to "live," presumably meaning that a holy lifestyle is also essential. However, the Odist is misread if one supposes that a moral life supplants the basis of grace for salvation in his thought.

Calling his reader to holiness of life neither negates nor overshadows grace. On the contrary, it is only through grace that the Odist can accomplish the ethical demands of his Lord. He exhorts his reader, "Walk in the knowledge of the Lord, and you will know the grace of the Lord generously" (23.4).[130] To walk in the knowledge of the Lord implies obedience to the Lord's teachings and, consequently, a life that reflects this knowledge. Yet, to know the Lord is to experience the grace that he "generously" lavishes on those who know him. Elsewhere he writes, "We live in the Lord by His grace, and life we receive by His Messiah" (41.3).[131] In *Ode* 34.6 he says, "Believe and live and be saved" and also in *Ode* 41.3 he says, "We live in the Lord by His grace." While both verses encourage the reader to "live," the latter gives a helpful commentary on the former. The ability to live the moral life, that is, to "live in the Lord," is possible only when grace

---

[125] *Odes* 4.6; 5.3; 7.5, 10, 22; 9.5; 11.1; 15.8; 20.7, 9; 23.2, 4; 24.13; 25.4; 29.2; 29.5; 31.7; 33.1; 34.6; 37.4; 41.3.
[126] See, for example, *Ode* 33.1 where grace is personified, presumably by Christ.
[127] Charlesworth, *Odes of Solomon*, 94.
[128] Charlesworth, *Odes of Solomon*, 123.
[129] Lattke, *Odes of Solomon*, 461.
[130] Charlesworth, *Odes of Solomon*, 94.
[131] Charlesworth, *Odes of Solomon*, 140.

has become a reality in the life of the believer. He receives life by the Messiah and he lives in "His abundant grace" (7.10).

Since T. F. Torrance's thesis that a Pauline view of grace was lost in the time of the Apostolic Fathers looms large in this work, it should be noted that his thesis cannot be extended to include the *Odes of Solomon*. In fairness to Torrance, the author of the *Odes* is Jewish and therefore probably not imbued with the same degree of Hellenism that the Gentile authors were. The Odist was deeply influenced by his Jewish background, particularly the Psalms, which are saturated with the doctrine of God's grace.[132] However, the larger issue is how the fathers of the second-century understood and propagated a Pauline view of justification by faith. Thus far it has been demonstrated that the Odist's view of grace, the peg upon which justification hangs, is in harmony with that of the Apostle. If any reservations still linger, the most potent connection to Paul comes out in *Ode* 29.5: "And He justified me by His grace," which will be discussed in the comments on that *Ode* which follows.

Returning now to *Ode* 25, verse 5 revisits the theme of persecution for now the "I" claims to have been "despised and rejected in the eyes of many" (ܐܬܬܫܝܛܬ ܘܐܣܬܠܝܬ ܒܥܝܢܝ ܣܓܝܐܐ).[133] The background for this verse is not difficult to discern. This language is taken directly from Isa 53:3, "He was despised and rejected by men" (נִבְזֶה וַחֲדַל אִישִׁים), which is used by Christ himself to understand his messianic ministry (cf. Mark 8:31; 9:12; Luke 9:22; 17:25). This buttresses the case that this is indeed *ex ore Christi* since the "I" speaks in the first person as if he were Christ.[134] However, this can once more be attributed to the Odist's understanding of his union with his Messiah. Just as Christ was despised and rejected by men, so too the Odist must endure the same type of suffering. Many Psalms function in this way. The trials that David underwent were appropriated to Christ by the New Testament writers.[135] In similar fashion, the Odist can, and often does, record tumultuous events in his life using biblical imagery that was

---

[132] More than the sheer frequency of חנן and חֵן in the Old Testament is the role that grace played in the relationship between Yahweh and Israel, particularly in regards to soteriology, whether explicit or implicit.
[133] Charlesworth, *Odes of Solomon*, 102.
[134] Harris and Mingana, *Odes of Solomon*, 2:347–48. They put forth the possibility that this *Ode* could come from the mouth of Christ, but think that it is "not, however, easy to see how to refer this Ode generally to the mouth of Christ" (348).
[135] Jesus himself acknowledged that he had come to fulfill what was spoken of in the Psalms (Luke 24:44). Many of these fulfillments were demonstrated in Hebrews—Ps 45:6–7 in Heb 1:8–9; Ps 2:7 in Heb 1:5; Ps 97:7 in Heb 1:6. Other examples would include—Ps 22:1 in Matt 27:46; Ps 22:8 in Matt 27:43; Ps 22:16 in John 20:25.

intended for Christ. After all, it was Jesus who said that a disciple is not greater than his master and that his disciples should expect to suffer similar persecutions (Matt 10:24). When trials come, Jesus' disciples, among whom the Odist numbers himself, find solace in interpreting their hardship through a Christological lens.

The second half of the bicolon (5b) is a bit more curious. He writes, "And I was in their eyes like lead." There is no scholarly consensus on exactly what is meant by "lead" (ܐܒܪܐ). Charlesworth admits that if this word were pointed differently, then if could mean "feather," but that the Coptic translation for this word (ⲧⲁϩⲧ) is most definitely "lead."[136] Harris and Mingana wish to emend ܐܒܪܐ to ܐܒܝܕܐ, which means "a lost, damned [person]."[137] Lattke offers the best explanation by reading 5b in parallel with 5a and suggesting that "lead" is a "valueless ... metal."[138] The rejection incurred by the "I" made him feel as though he were like lead, a valueless material that could be easily tossed aside.

Despite the severity of the persecution, the Odist derives his strength from the God who is his help. This could be seen as an *inclusio* that began in the first two verses. The *Ode* commences with praise to God as his deliverer and helper, who rescues him from the trappings of his enemies. Strength provided him endurance to stand up under the maltreatment thrust upon him by his foes.

Verse 7 reads, "A lamp Thou didst set for me both on my right and on my left, so that there might not be in me anything that is not light."[139] Though the meaning is not clear on the surface, Franzmann still wishes to see this verse as the "central focus of the Ode, describing a watershed action by God which moves the 'I' out of the situation of oppression."[140] Certainly the verse is surrounded by salvific themes and metaphors, and the Odist does shift his focus from oppression in the first half of the *Ode* to the results of his salvation. Yet, to call this the watershed action, it must be determined what is meant by the lamps. Several options are plausible.

Lattke attempts to trace the Odist's inspiration for this verse to the transfiguration by suggesting that the lamps represent Moses and Elijah who appeared in glory on either side of Jesus. He thinks that perhaps the mention of clothing in the next verse in this *Ode* supports this view, since the account of the transfiguration also highlights the garments worn by Jesus, "garments [that] became glistening, intensely white" (τὰ ἱμάτια αὐτοῦ ἐγένετο στίλβοντα λευκὰ λίαν; Mark

---

136 Charlesworth, *Odes of Solomon*, 102.
137 Harris and Mingana, *Odes of Solomon*, 2:347.
138 Lattke, *Odes of Solomon*, 360.
139 Charlesworth, *Odes of Solomon*, 102.
140 Franzmann, *Odes of Solomon*, 194.

9:3). This connection is unconvincing, however, because the bright garments worn by Jesus in the Synoptic Gospels represent his purity and divinity, whereas the Odist has something altogether different in mind when he speaks of garments of skin. The only relation is the word ἱμάτιον. It would seem that the point of departure between the transfiguration scene and the passage from *Ode* 25, namely the bright garments of glory versus the garment of skin, is the key to understanding this passage.

Lattke does mention the most promising solution in passing, writing, "there is merely a denial that it is dark (cf. such 'light'/'darkness' passages as, e. g. 15:2; 21:3; 42:16)."[141] Unearthing the influence behind this verse is unfruitful due to the lack of evidence. It seems best to say that salvation encircled the Odist as light and caused any remaining darkness to scatter—this light chased away "anything that [was] not light" in him (25.7b). Verse 7b starts with a negative result clause (ܕܠܐ; "so that ... not") indicating the outcome of the lamps placed on his right and left.[142] Light in this verse is not *either* spatial *or* a substitute for good and evil, it is both. The light metaphorically surrounds the Odist on his left and right as salvation *and* the light metaphorically keeps the Odist from evil. The lamps were placed on either side so that darkness, representing any residual evil left in his life, would vanish.

Verse 8 corroborates the idea that the light in verse 7 is a metaphor for salvation and that darkness refers to sin. The Odist writes, "And I was covered with the covering of Thy Spirit, and I removed from me my garments of skin."[143] This verse is pregnant with soteriological symbolism. First of all, in v. 8a the Odist

---

141 Lattke, *Odes of Solomon*, 361.
142 Verse 7b contains a significant textual variant. As Charlesworth notes, "H has a Waw conjunctive but the Dālath of N is better Syriac" (Charlesworth, *Odes of Solomon*, 102). Both Charlesworth and Lattke follow N, Charlesworth believing it to be "better Syriac," though Lattke thinks that neither are better Syriac *per se* (Lattke, *Odes of Solomon*, 361).
143 Charlesworth, *Odes of Solomon*, 102. This verse is not the only significant mention of "putting on" and "putting off" in the *Odes*. In *Ode* 21 the Odist says, "And I put off darkness and put on light." The relevance of this verse for *Ode* 25 is obvious. The author has just spoken of light and implicitly of darkness, and then in the next verse he says that he was covered in the Spirit instead of garments of skin. Worthy of note are several passages from 1 Baruch where a similar use of clothing metaphor is employed. 1 Bar. 4:20 states, "I have put off the clothing of peace, and put upon me the sackcloth of my prayer: I will cry unto the Everlasting in my days." Peace is put on and taken off as an article of clothing, just as the sackcloth of prayer is. In 1 Bar 5:1–2 a similar exhortation is found: "Put off, O Jerusalem, the garment of mourning and affliction, and put on the comeliness of the glory that cometh from God for ever. Cast about thee a double garment of the righteousness which cometh from God; and set a diadem on thine head of the glory of the Everlasting." Metaphorical language of clothing abounds in these verses as the reader is encouraged to add or remove virtues as if they were garments.

claims to have been covered by the Spirit as a result of the light that shined all around him. This is contrasted in v. 8b with the garments of skin that were removed on account of his salvation. He traded off his old self, which was wrapped in fleshly garments, for his new self, which is covered by the Spirit, much like Paul's declaration in 2 Cor 5:17, that "if anyone is in Christ, he is a new creation; old things have passed away, behold, new things have come" (ὥστε εἴ τις ἐν Χριστῷ, καινὴ κτίσις· τὰ ἀρχαῖα παρῆλθεν, ἰδοὺ γέγονεν καινά).

The imagery of covering over is common in the Bible and often symbolizes imputation, as it does here.[144] The "garments of skin" harkens back to Gen 3:21 where the "Lord God made for Adam and for his wife *garments of skins* and clothed them" (וַיַּעַשׂ יְהוָה אֱלֹהִים לְאָדָם וּלְאִשְׁתּוֹ כָּתְנוֹת עוֹר וַיַּלְבִּשֵׁם:).[145] These garments were fashioned by God in order to cover Adam and Eve's transgression. The animal was slaughtered as atonement for sin, and then Adam and Eve were clothed with the animal's skin, representing that their sin was covered.[146] But the garments, while representing atonement, first and foremost acknowledge Adam and Eve's sin, since such a drastic measure would not have been necessary had they not violated God's command. The garments of skin are not only an older picture of insufficient atonement and imputation (i.e., the covering of animal garments), but it is probable that he has in mind a flesh/spirit dichotomy,

---

144 The doctrine of imputation has a long and controversial history, particularly in the past century. Tracing the entire history is beyond the scope of this chapter and this book. See Brian J. Vickers, *Jesus' Blood and Righteousness: Paul's Theology of Imputation* (Wheaton, IL: Crossway, 2006), 23–70, for a summation on the history of and argument for the doctrine of imputation.

145 ESV, emphasis added. The use of clothing metaphor was prevalent in Syriac Christianity, even more so than in Greek and Latin writers (see Sebastian Brock, "Clothing metaphors as a means of theological expression in Syriac tradition," in *Studies in Syriac Christianity: History, Literature and Theology* [Brookfield, VT: Variorum, 1992], 11). Brock identifies four scenes of salvation history that progress in terms of clothing. Of utmost importance to the drama of salvation history is the clothing metaphor of "putting on" and "putting off," which is primarily seen in Adam and Christ. Brock writes, "The first Adam loses the robe of glory at the Fall; the second Adam puts on the body of the first Adam in order to restore the robe of glory to mankind in baptism; the Christian puts on 'the new man' (Eph 4.24) or 'Christ' (Rom 13:14, Gal 3:27) at baptism, at the same time putting on the 'robe of glory.' In these three closely linked stages of salvation history there is a certain merging of identity between the first and the second Adam: the Fall brought a loss of the first Adam's true identity; God then puts on Adam/Man in order that Adam/Man may put on God, in other words, may attain, not just his pre-Fall status, but the status of divinity which was the intention of his creation" (16).

146 Cf. Zech 3:1–5. An angel tells Joshua to take off his filthy clothes (בְּגָדִים צוֹאִים), and after Joshua obeys this command, he is told "See, I have taken away your sin, and I will put rich garments on you." Sinful, fleshly garments were exchanged for a clean turban representing new righteousness.

much like the one that Paul makes in Galatians 5:16, "But I say, walk by the spirit and you will not gratify fleshly desires" (Λέγω δέ, πνεύματι περιπατεῖτε καὶ ἐπιθυμίαν σαρκὸς οὐ μὴ τελέσητε).

Bauer has rightly noticed that for the Odist, "Der Zustand von Gen. 3, 21 wird rückgängig gemacht."[147] Skins are no longer efficacious, as the Spirit is needed. Harris remarks that this verse makes a "curious contact with Judaism,"[148] saying, "Now it is not difficult to recognise the traces of the clothing of the Old Adam and the clothing of the original Man, who is also the New Adam, in the New Testament. We have, for example, the instruction to put off the Old Man, and to put on the New Man, or to put on (it is the language of clothing) the Lord Jesus Christ."[149] The old man is taken off with the removal of the garments of skin and the new man is put on with the covering of the Spirit.

---

[147] Bauer, *Die Oden Salomos*, 607. Von Harnack goes far beyond the evidence when he said, "'Die Kleider von Fell' sind der Leib, an dessen Stelle ein neuer geistiger Leib getreten ist" (von Harnack, *Ein jüdisch-christliches Psalmbuch*, 58).

[148] Harris, *Odes of Solomon*, 67. Harris detects a potential play on words. According to him, Gen 3:21 has a long history of interpretive difficulty within Judaism. In a manuscript belonging to Rabbi Meir of the Midrash Rabboth the reading was כתנות אור instead of כתנות עור (68). This homophonic change in the silent guttural alters the meaning from 'garments of skin' to 'garments of light.' There is no other manuscript evidence for such a departure, but it does seem in line with the Philonic Platonism that characterized a substantial strand of Judaism in that day. But one need not look to Philo and a Hellenized version of Judaism. Syriac tradition emphasized the "robe of glory/light" that Adam and Eve wore prior to the fall. Zohar 1.36b, a work found in the Middle Ages with little know about its origins, states, "Before the Fall they were dressed in garments of light, but after their trespass in garments of skin." In a similar vein Solomon of Bosra, writing in the thirteenth century, says, "Adam and Eve were stripped of the fair glory and the glorious light of purity with which they had been clothed" (Brock, "Clothing metaphors," 14). It would seem for those in Syriac Christianity that Adam and Eve were originally clothed in light but these garments of light were lost in the fall and they were instead clothed with garments of skin.

[149] Harris, *Odes of Solomon*, 69. Cf. Rom 13:14 where Paul instructs his reader to "clothe yourselves with the Lord Jesus Christ, and make no provision for the flesh, to gratify its desires." Ἐνδύω carries the imagery of clothing in this verse, just as it does two verses earlier where Paul admonishes, "therefore, let us take off the works of darkness and let us put on the armor of light." "Take off" (ἀποτίθημι) and "put on" (ἐνδύω) are clothing metaphors that function as shorthand for salvation. Paul, like the Odist, makes a strong connection between salvation and light. To clothe oneself with Christ is also to clothe oneself with the armor of light. Both of these must be "put on" or better the individual must be "clothed" with them instead of unrighteousness.

Jung Hoon Kim has devoted an entire monograph to the clothing metaphor in Paul, *The Significance of Clothing Imagery in the Pauline Corpus*, JSNTSup (NewYork: T&T Clark International, 2004). Within the Pauline epistles, Kim identifies the three ways that Paul encourages believers to be clothed—with Christ, with the new man, and with the resurrected body (5). Most sig-

Elsewhere the Odist employs the phrases put on/take off in similar ways. For instance, in *Ode* 33.12 he writes of putting on Christ: "And they who have put me on shall not be falsely accused, but they shall possess incorruption in the new world."[150] Then again in *Ode* 15.8 he says, "I put on incorruption through His name, and took off corruption by His grace."[151] Since the word for corruption (ܚܒܠܐ) could also mean "immortality,"[152] it is best to interpret this verse in terms of salvation. He was able to put on immortality, the eschatological rest that he speaks of in *Ode* 25.12b, through the name of the Lord. If immortality was put on through trust in the Lord's name (*Ode* 15.10c), then the former life of mortality and corruptibility was taken off "by His grace." It is grace that he pinpoints as the conduit of salvation. The connection of grace and salvation in the eschaton is made explicit in *Ode* 20.7, "But put on the grace of the Lord generously, and come into His Paradise, And make for thyself a crown from His tree."[153] The one who comes to the Lord's paradise is he who puts on the grace that the Lord gives so generously.

In verse 9 the Odist recognizes the source of his strength, saying, "Because Thy right hand exalted me, and caused sickness to pass from me."[154] Lest one question whether the Odist has a synergistic view of salvation because he says in verse 8b, "*I removed* from me my garments of skin," it is of utmost importance that he begins verse 9 with the causal "because" (ܡܛܠ ܕ). He was able to remove the fleshly garments *because* he was exalted by God's right hand. The omnipotent right hand of God surfaces again as it had in verse 2, simply reiterating that God alone is powerful to save. If verses 8–9 are read together, as they should be, then it is clear that the sickness in verse 9b must be more than a minor infirmity. The garments of skins are antithetical to the covering of the Spirit, and he had a salvific experience in which he shed the skins for the Spirit. Due to this experience, he was exalted and sickness passed from him. The sickness referred to corresponds to those former times when he was still shrouded in his skins. The Spirit brought light and new life. Most importantly, the Spirit brought righteousness.

---

nificantly, he argues that "the clothing-with-a-person metaphor describes the believer's inward change in union with Christ" (6). Union is the way Paul anchors his metaphor in theological reality.
150 Charlesworth, *Odes of Solomon*, 120.
151 Charlesworth, *Odes of Solomon*, 68.
152 Charlesworth, *Odes of Solomon*, 68.
153 Charlesworth, *Odes of Solomon*, 86.
154 Charlesworth, *Odes of Solomon*, 102. Emphasis added.

Verse 10 contains a highly significant reference to alien righteousness where the Odist professes that his strength comes from the truth he has received from the Lord. Not only does he say, "I became mighty in Thy truth," but then he notably adds, "and holy in Thy righteousness."[155] The main verb is elided in the second half of the bicolon but assumed from the parallel clause in verse 10a.[156] Thus, verse 10b should read, "I became holy in Thy righteousness." There is no element of transformative righteousness to be found here. The Odist declares that he has been made holy and not in his own righteousness. The key to this verse is that he is made holy in "Thy righteousness," presumably in Christ's righteousness.

There is no leap in presuming that Christ is envisioned by "your" in the pronominal suffix (ܟܐܢܘܬܟ). In the very next verse the Odist says, "I became the Lord's by the name of the Lord."[157] That is to say, he belongs to Jesus by the name of Jesus. The Odist recognizes that any righteousness he possesses has come from another quarter—he is considered holy on the basis of the righteousness that he received from Christ. Righteousness (δικαιοσύνη)[158] is in contrast with the garments of skin and sickness, which both passed away from him. On account of the righteousness he received from the Lord, the Odist was able to cast aside his former life marked by sin. Again, one discovers the doctrine of imputed righteousness in this verse, especially when coupled with the imputation seen in verse 8 where the old self is displaced when it is covered by the Spirit. There the Spirit is imputed; here righteousness is imputed. These are two sides of the same proverbial coin. For the Odist, imputation of the Spirit necessarily means the imputation of righteousness.

Due to his recently found strength and righteousness, his enemies became afraid. The adversaries who had despised and rejected him were now cowering from him. A radical transformation had taken place for the speaker, so much so that he was free from harm. The second part of verse 11 strikes the reader as odd at first. "And I became the Lord's by the name of the Lord." Who is meant by "the Lord" in both instances? Even here the overarching question of who has been speaking throughout the *Ode* resurfaces. Judging from the data already presented, namely that 'garments of skins' and 'sickness' could not be

---

155 Charlesworth, *Odes of Solomon*, 102.
156 Franzmann translates 25.10, "And I was strong by your truth, and holy by your righteousness" (Franzmann, *Odes of Solomon*, 190). Interpreting the verb like this avoids the notion of transformative righteousness.
157 Charlesworth, *Odes of Solomon*, 102. See discussion below.
158 Lattke, *Odes of Solomon*, 365. He is right to assert that δικαιοσύνη would lie underneath the Syriac.

used to refer to Christ,[159] then it must be concluded that the "I" is stating that he "became a Christian by the name of Christ."[160]

The word justified (ܐܙܕܕܩܬ) appears only in the final verse of the *Ode*.[161] The Odist states, "And I was justified by His kindness, and His rest is for ever and ever."[162] Lattke wishes to interpret the use of justified in *Ode* 25.12 as "victory" because "the adversaries are mentioned in 25.11a," though he concedes, "the correctness of this interpretation depends largely on the answer to the question who is actually being 'justified' here."[163] By this Lattke means that if Christ is the one justified, then "victory" seems to be the best interpretation. However, his hedging on this interpretation points to the fact that if Christ is not the one justified, then the word "justified" could have more of a Pauline ring to it. Having ruled out Christ as the one justified, one naturally concludes that justification does not necessarily mean "victory" and that another solution may be more plausible.

The statement that he was justified comes as the soteriological climax of the *Ode*, which ends in eschatological rest—"And his rest is for ever and ever."[164] His

---

[159] This argument hangs on the aforementioned argument that the Odist did not possess an aberrant Christology.

[160] Lattke, *Odes of Solomon*, 367. Lattke does not land on this issue. He simply puts forth that this is what the "I" is essentially saying if "Lord" means Christ. "But," he writes, "if the speaker is the Κύριος Χριστός himself, the repeated term κύριος must refer to 'God'/ 'the Lord' of 1b" (367). A third possibility may even be adduced according to Lattke. This would see one mention of κύριος as the Κύριος Χριστός and the other as the Most High. The option taken above best fits the overall trajectory of the *Ode*.

[161] Franzmann again translates ܐܙܕܕܩܬ, "I was declared righteous" (Franzmann, *Odes of Solomon*, 190).

[162] Charlesworth, *Odes of Solomon*, 102.

[163] Lattke, *Odes of Solomon*, 366.

[164] Charlesworth, *Odes of Solomon*, 102. Rest is an important theme in the Bible and in the *Odes*. Critical for the Odist is Ps 95:11 as it is used in Heb 4:3. Rest was equated to eschatological hope that one would enter upon death, yet which could also be experienced in the present (Matt 11:28). David Aune states, "In the Odes of Solomon, the attainment of eschatological 'rest' is regarded as an eschatological reality fully realized in present experience" (Aune, *The Cultic Setting of Realized Eschatology*, 190). In this *Ode*, the speaker celebrates his salvation by acknowledging that he will one day enter into a rest that is eternal. Rest occurs eighteen times in the *Odes* many of which, if space permitted, would be shown to have an eschatological bent.

There is no reason to follow Lattke when he says, "'Rest,' and 'to rest' are technical, more or less abstract terms of the Gnostic understanding of salvation" (Lattke, *Odes of Solomon*, 38). Certainly, Gnostics did use the idea of rest in their conception of salvation, as Lattke has amply demonstrated in his citations of secondary literature (38), but the Odist could equally be using a biblical framework for rest. Likewise, Franzmann claims that "the similarities between Gnostic writings and the Odes, it is clear that there are strong indications that the Odes were influenced by this syncretistic system of thought" (Majella Franzmann, "The Odes of Solomon,

justification not only led to rest, but, working backwards through the *Ode*, he received many other benefits, only one of which is victory from his adversaries. All the other benefits deal with the spiritual side of salvation. Even at the outset of his commentary on this *Ode*, Lattke writes, "It is a personal testimony of salvation, which, at the end of the Syriac text, merges into a theological statement of eternity in the 'rest' of the totally other-worldly 'Lord.'"[165] This *Ode* of "personal testimony" forms around an *inclusio* of justification, which opens in chains and closes in victory—the victory of freedom from sinful flesh and spiritual sickness, the victory of justification.

The theme of his song is clear throughout this *Ode*—God is the architect and initiator of salvation. God's right hand is strong and sure, restraining enemies and rescuing from shackles, but his right hand also exalts the Odist on account of his grace and kindness. The Odist is saved by grace (v. 4), covered with the Spirit (v. 8), exalted (v. 9), made holy in His righteousness (v.10), and justified

---

Man of Rest," *OCP* 51 [1985]: 418). The glaring omission from Franzmann's article is the missing citations from Hebrews. While recognizing the places where ἀναπαύω and ἀνάπαυσις are found in the New Testament, she interestingly elides καταπαύω and κατάπαυσις, which the author of Hebrews uses, apparently supposing that the latter Greek words do not underlie ܢܚ, though it is guesswork to hypothesize which Greek words would be used to translate the Odist's Syriac. Lattke even admits, "there is no way ... to discover whether the Greek version used only a verb or whether it had a combination of a noun like ἀνάπαυσις or κατάπαυσις with verb meaning 'to find' or 'to enter into' (26:10a, 12a; 28:3a; 30:2b, 7; 35:6b)" (Lattke, *Odes of Solomon*, 38). Piecing together a Greek version with certainty is impossible. Likely, the Odist has in mind the rest spoken of through the author of Hebrews as he understood it from the Psalmist.

But even the biblical perspective on rest has not been immune to charges of Gnosticism, particularly in Hebrews. The most prominent advocate of this was Ernst Käsemann, who argued that "rest" had its roots in Alexandrian Gnosticism not in the Old Testament. The author of Hebrews cites the Old Testament only to "anchor in Scripture a speculation already in existence" (Ernst Käsemann, *The Wandering People of God: An Investigation of the Letter to the Hebrews*, trans. Roy A. Harrisville and Irving L. Sandberg [Minneapolis: Augsburg, 1984], 74–75). See also Gerd Theissen, *Untersuchungen zum Hebräerbrief* (Gütersloh: Mohn, 1969). Others have come to understand "rest" in Hebrews within Jewish apocalyptic expectations. See Otfried Hofius, *Katapausis: Die Vorstellung vom Endzeitlichen Ruheort im Hebräerbrief* (Tübingen: Mohr, 1970), and George Wesley Buchanan, *To the Hebrews*, AB (Garden City, NY: Doubleday, 1972). Cf. Judith Hoch Wray, *Rest as a Theological Metaphor in the Epistle to the Hebrews and the Gospel of Truth: Early Christian Homiletics of Rest* (Atlanta: Scholars Press, 1998). See in particular Harold W. Attridge, "'Let Us Strive to Enter that Rest': the Logic of Hebrews 4:1–11," *HTR* 73 (1980): 279–88, who, though not "definitely [solving] the questions of Hebrews' eschatology," has tried to understand both sides and offers helpful ways of coming to a solution.

165 Lattke, *Odes of Solomon*, 357.

by kindness (v.12). The Odist derives his soteriology from Paul, via his Jewish roots, and sets these themes to his own chorus.

The case for forensic justification in *Ode* 25 rests more on the context of the entire *Ode* than on the appearance of the word ܟܐܢܘܬܐ in v. 12. Imprisoned in sin (or sickness, v. 9), the Odist is set free by God who alone is powerful to break the bonds that incarcerated him. Part of his salvation is the removal of sinful clothes, the "garments of skin," with the replacement clothing of the Spirit. Then he received an alien righteousness, a righteousness given to him by God himself, and in this righteousness, he is positively holy. After all, he became the Lord's by the name of the Lord. When all is said and done, the Odist receives the eschatological rest promised to those who are justified.

Ode 29

1. The Lord is my hope,
   I shall not be confused in Him.
2. For according to His praise He made me,
   And according to His grace even so He gave to me.
3. And according to His mercies He exalted me,
   And according to His great honour He lifted me up.
4. And He caused me to ascend from the depths of Sheol,
   And from the mouth of death He drew me.
5. And I humbled my enemies,
   And He justified me by His grace.
6. For I believed in the Lord's Messiah,
   And considered that He is the Lord.
7. And He revealed to me His sign,
   And He led me by His light.
8. And He gave me the scepter of His power,
   That I might subdue the devices of the Gentiles,
   And humble the power of the mighty.
9. To make war by His Word,
   And to take victory by His power.
10. And the Lord overthrew my enemy by His Word,
    And he became like the dust which a breeze carries off.
11. And I gave praise to the Most High,
    Because He has magnified His servant and the son of His maidservant.

Hallelujah.

The final *Ode* under consideration is *Ode* 29. Unless one purports a shift in speaker from the Messiah to the redeemed in verse 5, which is unlikely in this particular *Ode* as there is nothing that must come from the mouth of Christ, then the

"I" should be taken throughout as an individual who is extolling God for his salvation.¹⁶⁶ As Harris recognized, the person who "wrote this Psalm ... was a follower of the Christ and had recognised Him to be the Lord."¹⁶⁷ The *Ode* is rich in soteriological images and metaphors, coming closer to the "traditional" view of Pauline salvation than any other *Ode*. The Odist is full of hope and praise on account of God's mercy and deliverance. Even in this *Ode* there is a less than veiled reference to the cross (v. 7), which serves as the basis for the Odist's belief in the Messiah (v. 6). From *Ode* 29 also comes the clearest declaration of justification in the *Odes*, "And he justified me by His grace." Taken together, these powerful expressions of salvation led Lattke to title this *Ode*, "Address of a Redeemed Believer in Christ."¹⁶⁸

The *Ode* commences positively with an affirmation of hope. It begins, "The Lord is my hope," and this hope gives the Odist confidence to say, "I shall not be ashamed in him."¹⁶⁹ The connection between hope and freedom from shame occurs regularly in the Old Testament, and even appears in the New Testament, though the Odist is likely drawing this idea from the Psalter.¹⁷⁰ Shame (ܒܗܬܐ) in this context has less to do with his standing before his enemies and more to do with the confidence that his footing will be firm in the eschatological judgment.¹⁷¹

The Odist turns his attention to the grounding of his hope over the next four lines of his song (vv. 2–3), each beginning with the prepositional phrase "according to" (ܐܝܟ). The first cause of his hope is that he has been recreated in God. He declares, "For according to His praise He made me, and according to

---

166 Lattke concurs that in *Ode* 29, even in the more difficult vv. 8–10, "any idea that Christ is the speaker can be excluded" (Lattke, *Odes of Solomon*, 403). Harris and Mingana seemed confused on this *Ode*, saying, "The discrimination of the parts of the Ode in which Christ speaks is difficult" (Harris and Mingana, *Odes of Solomon*, 2:365), and they even conclude that this *Ode* cannot have Christ as the speaker in the final part because the "word" in vv. 9–10 is the "Logos," thus making it impossible for Christ to be the subject (2:365). It's almost as if they are trying to find a place for Christ to be the subject, a step they do not need to take. It is difficult for them to find Christ as the speaker because Christ is not the speaker. So too, C. Brunston's contention "C'est encore le Christ glorifié qui parle" must be rejected (Brunston, *Les plus anciens cantiques chrétiens* [Paris: Librairie Fischbacher, 1912], 71).
167 Harris, *Odes of Solomon*, 130.
168 Lattke, *Odes of Solomon*, 402.
169 Charlesworth translates v. 1b, "I shall not be confused in Him." He acknowledges in a footnote that this line could also be translated, "I shall not be ashamed of Him."
170 See Ps 24:20b and especially Ps 30:2a LXX: Ἐπὶ σοί, κύριε, ἤλπισα, μὴ καταισχυνθείην εἰς τὸν αἰῶνα.
171 The wording of "hope" and "shame" is similar to that of Paul's in Phil 1:20. See O'Brien, *Philippians*, 114.

His grace even so He gave to me."[172] On verse 2a Lattke writes, "Here, as in 15:7b and 36:5a ['he made me'] is used of eschatological re-creation and renewal (cf. 36:5b)."[173] As a new man (cf. 2 Cor 5:17), the Odist can rest assured that he will not be ashamed. Despite the recreation motif he sees in v. 2a, Lattke refuses to understand "grace" in a "Pauline and deutero-Pauline" fashion.[174] He believes that "grace" is general here and used to "emphasize the extent of God's grace (cf. 2 Thess 2:12)," but that "God did not bestow 'grace' itself on the speaking 'I.'"[175] This reading is problematic. First, the Odist concludes that his new person, his re-creation, is the result of grace. He is attributing his individual rebirth to the grace of God. Second, the flow of the entire *Ode* is one of personal salvation in God, which the Odist frequently ascribes to grace.[176] The speaking "I" is the redeemed subject of the *Ode* and every salvific blessing he receives, he receives by grace.

The Odist continues his praise of God in verse 3, this time exalting God for his mercy (ܪ̈ܚܡܘܗܝ) and honor (ܐܝܩܪܗ). Once more the reader hears echoes of the Psalter reverberating through the *Ode*. Mercy is repeatedly accompanied by חֶסֶד in the Psalms,[177] and conveys that God's covenantal faithfulness. His חֶסֶד is an act of mercy. Grace and mercy combine early in this *Ode* to convey as strongly as possible that salvation is a gracious act of God.

In addition to being exalted by mercy, the Odist is also lifted up in accordance with God's majesty.[178] The meaning of this last clause (v. 3b) is not obvious on the face, but it touches the heart of the Odist's theology that was discussed at the outset of this chapter, namely the centrality of God's sovereignty in salvation. The majesty of God is at stake in the exaltation of a sinner, for only God has the ability to lift such a one up out of his miserable state. The Odist rhetorically asks

---

172 Charlesworth, *Odes of Solomon*, 112.
173 Lattke, *Odes of Solomon*, 404.
174 Lattke, *Odes of Solomon*, 404.
175 Lattke, *Odes of Solomon*, 404. His stated reason for this view of grace in v. 2 is that he sees the object of the gift as the "sceptre of His power" given in v. 8. Granted, the scepter of power is part of the gifts bestowed on the speaking "I," but that which was given to him should also include mercy, ascension from death, rescue from enemies, and justification (which is explicitly a gift of grace). It would seem that the totality of the gifts rendered to the speaker is bound up in the grace of God.
176 See excursus above on grace.
177 See, for example, Pss 25:6; 40:11; 103:4.
178 Lattke's translation of (ܐܝܩܪܗ ܪܒܘܬ) as "majesty" (Lattke, *Odes of Solomon*, 402) is superior to Charlesworth's blander translation of "great honor" (Charlesworth, *Odes of Solomon*, 112).

in *Ode* 26.8, "Who can train himself for life, so that he himself may be saved?"[179] Of course, the answer the Odist expects is an emphatic "no one." God alone has the power to lift up the unworthy individual and he does this to exhibit his majesty, or to say it another way, to put his glory on display. The rejoicing in *Ode* 29.1–3 reminds one of Ephesians 2:4–7 where Paul argues that God's mercy makes alive those who were dead in trespasses "so that in the coming ages he might show the immeasurable riches of his grace in kindness toward us in Christ." What is the display of his "immeasurable riches of grace in kindness" if not the display of his divine majesty that rescues sinners from divine wrath?

So distraught was the Odist that he felt himself on the precipice of Sheol, waiting to be swallowed up by death. It was in that moment of internal angst that God "caused [him] to ascend from the depths of Sheol," as he was drawn "from the mouth of death."[180] Death, in this instance, is not a literal cessation of life; rather, it is a continuation of the soteriological themes presented in verses 1–3, with liberation from death pointing to his salvation in the eschaton.[181] Elsewhere the Odist, speaking *ex ore Christi*, affirmed his belief that "death has been destroyed before my face, and Sheol has been vanquished by my word" (*Ode* 15.9).[182] In that case, the Redeemer has obliterated death and hell in accord with the promise from 1 Corinthians 15:26 that death, the final enemy, was destroyed through his death and resurrection.[183]

---

179 Charlesworth, *Odes of Solomon*, 105.
180 Charlesworth, *Odes of Solomon*, 112. ܐܣܩ, in the Aphel, is causative like the Hebrew Hiphil (Theodor Nöldeke, *Compendious Syriac Grammar*, trans. James A. Crichton [Eugene, OR: Wipf and Stock Publishers, 2003], 105), thus enforcing that God makes the speaking "I" ascend out of the pit. It is not his own doing, because it is not in his ability—God causes him to rise up.
181 As Wilhelm Frankenberg rightly observes, "Hölle und Tod sind wie schon in den Psalmen nichts anderes als rhetorische Ausdrücke der religiösen Sprache" (Frankenberg, *Das Verständnis der Oden Salomos*, 57).
182 Charlesworth, *Odes of Solomon*, 68.
183 While Lattke finds "no trace of a *descensus ad inferos*," in v. 4 (Lattke, *Odes of Solomon*, 405), it would not be difficult to see how others would draw the conclusion that Christ is the speaker who recalls his ascension from hell, as has William K. L. Clarke ("The First Epistle of St Peter and the Odes of Solomon," *JTS* 15 [1913]: 47–52). Clarke, who "assumes" Bernard's theory that the *Odes* are baptismal hymns (48), sees a "close association of baptism with the *Descensus ad Inferos*" (51). The Odist does hold to the doctrine of Christ's *descensus ad inferos* as is clearly seen in *Odes* 15.9 and 42.11. This point was argued above, and is summarized here. David often felt like he was on the brink of Sheol and he would cry out to God for deliverance, and the Odist is mimicking his plea (Pss 16:10; 18:5; 30:3; 49:15). Given the next few verses that envisage the "Lord's Messiah" as separate from the subject, there is no reason to suspect that the reference to Sheol is connected to the similar journey that he believed the Messiah made. This is the Odist's own existential plight.

The Odist's enemies were humbled (v. 5), not because he achieved a great victory over them, but on the contrary, victory was accomplished on his behalf. Verses 8–10, to be discussed below, confirm that the authority he was given to humble his enemies came directly from God.[184] Like the Psalter, the Odist composes many lyrics of triumph over his foes in order to demonstrate the surpassing power of his God over those who would stand against him.

If there is one statement in the *Odes* that strikes a Pauline chord, it is *Ode* 29.5b: "and He justified me by His grace" (ܘܙܕܩܢܝ ܒܛܝܒܘܬܗ).[185] So strong is the Pauline conception of justification here that Friedrich Spitta conjectured:

> Die Schilderung paßt, wenn man, was doch das Nächstliegende ist, das Subjekt in v. 7–9 nicht von Gott, sondern von Christus versteht, nur auf einen Apostel Christi, ja Zug für Zug auf Paulus: das Zeichen, daß Christus der Herr sei, ist das Wunder bei Damaskus; das Wandeln in seinem Licht klingt an die Heilung seiner Blindheit an.[186]

According to Spitta, the Odist is recapitulating Paul's conversion when he had an encounter with the Messiah on the Damascus road. To be sure, the Pauline similarity is undeniable, as justification is tied to grace and belief and nothing more. Yet, there is no reason to follow Spitta in his suggestion that the Odist is recounting Paul's conversion.[187] This song of salvation is the Odist's own existential experience and encapsulates his conviction that justification is by grace on the basis of belief.

On this important clause in *Ode* 29.5b Lattke makes the following remark:

> The connection with the term 'grace,' on the one hand, and the declaration of faith that follows, on the other, makes it necessary to pay more attention to the Pauline concept of

---

184 The plural "enemies" makes one wonder if death and Sheol, mentioned in the previous verse, are the enemies the Odist has in mind. Following Frankenberg, it is best to look to vv. 8–10, where the enemies are mentioned again (Frankenberg, *Das Verständnis der Oden Salomos*, 57). Lattke censures Frankenberg who surely goes too far when he suggests that the enemies are "Dämonen" (Lattke, *Odes of Solomon*, 406).
185 Charlesworth, *Odes of Solomon*, 112. Franzmann once more translates the verb ܙܕܩ with the forensic meaning "declare righteous" (Franzmann, *Odes of Solomon*, 218).
186 Spitta, "Zum Verständnis der Oden Salomos," 284.
187 Kittel gives a helpful critique against Spitta, calling Spitta's argument "sachlichen Unwahrscheinlichkeit" (Gerhard Kittel, *Die Oden Salomos—überarbeitet oder einheitlich? Beiträge zur Wissenschaft vom Alten Testament* 16 [Leipzig: Hinrichs, 1914], 112), but he does not account Pauline language that lead Spitta to his conclusion in the first place.

soteriological 'justification' by divine χάρις (Rom 3:24; cf. Gal 2:21) and human πίστις (Rom 3:22, 26, 28, 30; Gal 2:16).[188]

All the essential ingredients that Paul uses to explain justification are present and nothing is added, such as works or obedience. Grace and belief in the Messiah serve as the basis for soteriological justification. The question could be raised, however, as to whether or not the justification spoken of here, which is most definitely cloaked in Pauline terminology, is forensic.

Based on the preceding verses (vv. 1–4), there is good reason to believe that the Odist had in mind forensic justification when drafting this line.[189] As noted in verse 4, the speaking "I" stood on the threshold of death and Sheol. Yet, he ascended from the depths of Sheol, and was pulled back from the very mouth of death itself. Furthermore, he was exalted and lifted up by the grace of God (v. 2).[190] Justification in verse 5 is the foundation of the blessings he received when he "believed in the Lord's Messiah" (v. 6).[191]

Verse 6 contains the exegetically significant ܡܛܠ. Starting again in verse 5 the Odist writes: "And He justified me by His grace. *For* I believed in the Lord's Messiah."[192] He was justified "for," or "because," he believed (ܗܝܡܢ) in the Messiah.[193] "For" grounds the previous clause; that is, the "for" is causal, giving the reader the reason for his justification—namely belief. He parallels this thought in the second half of the bicolon: "And considered that He is the Lord."[194] To "consider" (ܐܬܪܥܝ ܠ) that the Messiah is Lord is much the same as the "confession" that he is such. Once more, the influence comes from Paul and his declaration in Romans 10:9–10 that if one confesses that "Jesus is

---

188 Lattke, *Odes of Solomon*, 406. Bauer surely goes astray on this verse when he suggests that "*Rechtfertigen* im Sinne von *zum Siege führen* wie 1. Tim. 3,16" (Bauer, "Die Oden Salomos," 610). Although space did not allow him to elaborate on this decision, one assumes he would support his position with the abundance of victory language in *Ode* 29. However, he does not account for the all the language surrounding "justified" particularly v. 6, which seems to envisage personal salvation founded on belief.
189 This use of justification is especially true if Lattke is correct to see an *inclusio* with "Lord" in v. 1 and v. 6 (Lattke, *Odes of Solomon*, 405). If so, then these verses hang together as a unit, and this unit is thoroughly soteriological. Franzmann divides the stanzas differently, thus revealing that she does not see this *inclusio* (Franzmann, *Odes of Solomon*, 217–19).
190 See the excursus above on "grace."
191 Charlesworth, *Odes of Solomon*, 112.
192 Charlesworth, *Odes of Solomon*, 112, emphasis added.
193 This verse excludes the possibility that the *Ode* is rendered *ex ore Christi*, for the speaker professes his belief in the "Lord's Messiah." Bound up in this phrase is a reference to God ("Lord") and Jesus ("Messiah"). The Odist believes in (ܒ) the Lord's Messiah, who is Jesus.
194 Charlesworth, *Odes of Solomon*, 112.

Lord," he will be saved, "for with the heart *one believes for righteousness*, and with the mouth one confesses and is saved" (καρδίᾳ γὰρ πιστεύεται εἰς δικαιοσύνη, στόματι δὲ ὁμολογεῖται εἰς σωτηρίαν).[195]

"Belief" (ܗܝܡܢ) has the same meaning as faith,[196] which coincides with the Greek πιστεύω,[197] and occurs just under twenty times, leading Lattke to downplay the importance of "belief" in the *Odes* from both a quantitative and qualitative standpoint.[198] But this is a mistake. Just as the case is being made that justification plays an important role in the Odist's theology, despite the relative infrequency of the word, it could also be said that belief is an equally vital doctrine. Because the genre is poetry, the reader should not expect a systematic treatment of any doctrine, but should approach the text with a fine-tuned ear to draw out the significance of a word or phrase as it used throughout the songbook.

In the case of *Ode* 29.6, belief is inextricably bound to justification. The Odist is justified by his faith. Franzmann translates verses 5b–6a in this way: "and he declared me righteous by his grace. For I had faith in the Messiah of the Lord."[199] This is not the only place where the Odist speaks of his faith in the Messiah. *Ode* 16.4 has the Odist explaining the purpose behind his writing the *Odes*. Just as the ploughman works the plough-share and the helmsman steers the ship, so also his work is the singing of psalms of praise to the Lord (16.1). As part of his chorus to God, he declares, "For my love is the Lord; Hence I will sing unto Him" (16.3). Then in verse 4 he is strengthened by God's praises and then he states, "And I have faith in him."[200] *Ode* 29.6 and *Ode* 16.4 give two clear examples of faith in God—the former for justification, and the latter for strength.

---

195 The ESV translates Rom 10:10: "For with the heart one believes and is justified, and with the mouth one confesses and is saved." Moo translates the prepositional phrase εἰς δικαιοσύνην "for righteousness" (Moo, *Romans*, 644). Schreiner takes a semantically similar approach to εἰς δικαιοσύνην, translating it as a result clause and rendering it "resulting in righteousness" (Schreiner, *Romans*, 551). He notes, "Believing 'results' in righteousness" (Schreiner, *Romans*, 560). The difference between purpose and result is negligible in this case—either works to advance the argument.
196 Payne Smith defines this word as "to believe, have faith or confidence in, to be faithful, trusted" (s.v. ܗܝܡܢ).
197 Lattke, *Odes of Solomon*, 476. Cf. Bultmann who said that the word used most often for belief in the Old Testament, אמן, is "almost without exception expressed by πιστεύειν in the LXX" (Bultmann, "πιστεύω," *TDNT* 6:197).
198 Lattke, *Odes of Solomon*, 475–76.
199 Franzmann, *Odes of Solomon*, 218.
200 Charlesworth, *Odes of Solomon*, 71. Lattke takes the prepositional phrase ܒܗ in the sense of "by him" and not "in him," though he does not expand on what he means by this (Lattke, *Odes*

The Odist continues in *Ode* 29 to speak of the Lord in whom he believes. In verse 7 he states, "And He revealed to me His sign."[201] Identifying the referents of the third person singular pronouns determines the way the remainder of the *Ode* is read. Important to note is that both God and Jesus are mentioned together in verse 6 when the Odist speaks of the "Lord's Messiah." It would seem that from this point on the Odist has both God ("Lord") and Christ ("Messiah") in mind, so that the first mention of "he" is referring to God while the second use of the pronoun is Christ.[202] Consequently, verse 7 could then be read, "And God revealed to me Jesus' sign, and God led me by Jesus' light," and so on.

Throughout the *Odes* there is frequent reference to the Lord's sign, and in most cases the "sign" is explicitly connected to the cross.[203] For instance, *Ode* 27 reads:

1. I extended my hands
   And hallowed my Lord
2. For the expansion of my hands
   Is His sign.
3. And my extension
   Is the upright cross.
   Hallelujah.[204]

In this *Ode*, there is no doubt that the sign in verse 2 is the upright cross of verse 3, with the sign of the cross being graphically portrayed as the extension of the hands. *Ode* 42 begins likewise: "I extended my hands and approached my Lord,

---

of Solomon, 476). The ܒ preposition can mean "in" or "by" (Payne Smith, s.v. "ܒ") but typically it means "in" when used with the verb ܗܝܡܢ (Payne Smith, 1:232–33).
201 Charlesworth, *Odes of Solomon*, 112.
202 Lattke takes an entirely different, yet unconvincing, view. He starts off on the right foot acknowledging that "Word" used later in vv. 9–10 is actually in reference to the Logos. Since "Word" is to be taken as the Logos, then he reasons that all the third person pronouns of v. 7 ff must refer to God, because "Word" is modified with the pronoun "His." "His sign" of v. 7, then, cannot refer to the sign of Jesus, that is, the cross. Lattke, following R. H. Connolly ("Greek the Original Language of the Odes of Solomon," *JTS* 14 [1912]: 303–05), concludes, "So the 'sign' of 29:7a is finally the 'way' leading to *gnōsis*, which is 'shown' and revealed, in this case, not by the Kyrios Christos (24:1, 13) but by the Most High Lord" (Lattke, *Odes of Solomon*, 408). His insertion of *gnōsis* is buttressed by the second half of v. 7 that says, "And He led me by His light." See discussion below for the position taken herein. Regardless of how the pronouns are taken, this does not alter in any way the soteriology of the *Ode*.
203 There are two notable exceptions to the "sign" as the cross—*Odes* 23.12 and 39.7. In both cases the "sign" spoken of is vague, unlike the "sign" in *Ode* 29.7, which, when directly connected to the Messiah, must be taken as the cross.
204 Charlesworth, *Odes of Solomon*, 106.

for the expansion of my hands is His sign. And my extension is the common cross, that was lifted up on the way of the Righteous One" (vv. 1–2).[205] The vocabulary is strikingly similar. The sign is the expansion of the hands in the outstretched position of the cross. Having just expressed his belief in the Messiah, it seems natural to take the "sign" of *Ode* 29.7a as the cross of Christ, which is the instrument by which salvation came.[206]

The second half of the bicolon in *Ode* 29.7 reads: "And He led me by His light." Those who see Gnostic influence in the *Odes* look to expressions like this one.[207] Even though Gnostics were fond of using light as a metaphor for salvation,[208] the Odist could just as easily be writing with the Gospel of John in mind,[209] or even have an eye to Paul who described salvation as living in the light instead of the darkness (Eph 5:8). There is little warrant, then, to suggest that the mention of light is intrinsically Gnostic. The Odist is led by the light of the Messiah who often referred to himself as the light (John 8:12).

Verses 8–9 form a small chiasm.[210] The Odist is given the "sceptre of His power," so that he can "subdue the devices of the Gentiles, and humble the power of the mighty."[211] This Messianic scepter (Gen 49:10) harkens back to Psalm 110, a Psalm that envisions a Messiah who will subjugate his enemies under foot. He will rule over his enemies with his mighty scepter (Ps 110:2) and serve as a priest after the order of Melchizedek (Ps 110:4). The Odist sees this promise fulfilled with the advent of the Messiah. His Jewish heritage comes shinning through at this point with his "pejorative attitude towards Gentiles,"[212] who are to be subdued.[213] Furthermore, in verse 9 the Odist wages war

---

205 Charlesworth, *Odes of Solomon*, 145.
206 See von Harnack, *Ein jüdisch-christliches Psalmbuch*, 62, and Bauer, "Die Oden Salomos," 610.
207 Lattke reads this verse together with 7.13–14: "For towards knowledge He has set His way, He has widened it and lengthened it and brought it to complete perfection. And has set over it the traces of His light, and it proceeded from the beginning until the end" (Lattke, *Odes of Solomon*, 36).
208 Hans Jonas, a foremost Gnostic scholar of the preceding generation, observed, "The antithesis of light and darkness is so constant a feature ... . Its symbolism meets us everywhere in gnostic literature" (Jonas, *The Gnostic Religion*, 2nd ed. [Boston: Beacon Press, 1963], 57). See also the recent work by Barbara Aland, *Was ist Gnosis?* (Tübingen: Mohr Siebeck, 2009), 261.
209 "Light" is found more than twenty times in the Gospel of John. See especially the introduction to this chapter where both Gnosticism and Johannine influence are discussed in relation to the *Odes*.
210 See Lattke, *Odes of Solomon*, 410, and Franzmann, *Odes of Solomon*, 220.
211 Charlesworth, *Odes of Solomon*, 112.
212 Charlesworth, *Odes of Solomon*, 113. Both Charlesworth (*Odes of Solomon*, 112) and Franzmann (*Odes of Solomon*, 218) take ܥܡܡ as an emphatic plural which can mean "Gentiles" (Payne

"by His Word," which is the Logos. Harris and Mingana, also recognizing that the Odist is "under the influence of the 110th Psalm" in verse 7 and following, affirm "that the Word in our Ode is to have a capital letter."[214] The war he speaks of may be a "possible allusion to the wars in Revelation," where the Odist fights alongside the Word with the assurance of victory.[215] The brief chiasm ends as it began with a reference to power (ܚܝܠܬܢܘܬܐ in v. 8; ܚܝܠܗ in v. 9).

All along it is God's power that aids the speaking "I" with the assistance of the Word, the Messiah. Twice in two verses he uses the prepositional phrase ܒܡܠܬܗ, using the ܒ preposition to designate instrumentality. For, he writes, "the Lord overthrew my enemy *by His Word*" (v. 10).[216] As in verse 5a, the Odist makes mention of his enemy who stands against the purpose of the Lord.[217] Yet, he is confident that his enemy will become "like the dust which a breeze carries off,"[218] because the power of the Lord, specifically His Word, will go forth and subdue him.

The *Ode* draws to a close with the doxological exclamation, "And I gave praise to the Most High, because He has magnified His servant and the son of His maidservant. Hallelujah."[219] Scholars are at odds over how to translate the elusive pronouns of verse 11. Do these third person singular pronouns refer to the Messiah or is the author the referent? There is a general consensus that Psalm 116:16 serves as the background for the Odist, but this does not resolve the issue, for one could argue that either the Psalmist is speaking or that this verse is Messianic.[220] The inability to distinguish between the speaker and the Messiah is purposeful and can be explained once again under the rubric of

---

Smith, s.v. "ܥܡ"), just as ἔθνος in the plural can mean "Gentiles" (BDAG, "ἔθνος"). Lattke disagrees, preferring to translate ܥܡ as "nations" (Lattke, *Odes of Solomon*, 411).
213 Not too much should be read into his attitude about Gentiles, however. In Ode 10.5 the Odist, speaking *ex ore Christi*, says, "And the Gentiles who had been dispersed were gathered together, but I was not defiled by my love (for them), because they had praised me in high places" (Charlesworth, *Odes of Solomon*, 48). There is pictured here an ingathering of the Gentiles who "walked according to [the Messiah's] life and were saved, and they became [His] people for ever and ever" (*Ode* 10.6; Charlesworth, *Odes of Solomon*, 48).
214 Harris and Mingana, *Odes of Solomon*, 2:365.
215 Lattke, *Odes of Solomon*, 411. Lattke cites Rev 11:7; 12:17; 13:7; and 19:19 in favor of his view.
216 Charlesworth, *Odes of Solomon*, 112. Emphasis added.
217 It is worthy to note that v. 5 has the plural "enemies" whereas v. 10 speaks of the singular "enemy," though H has the plural "enemies" in v. 10, perhaps to keep consonance with v. 5.
218 Charlesworth, *Odes of Solomon*, 112.
219 Charlesworth, *Odes of Solomon*, 112. Franzmann calls this verse an "indirect doxology" (Franzmann, *Odes of Solomon*, 221).
220 Cf. Ps 86:16 for the phrase "son of your maidservant."

union.²²¹ Just as Harris and Mingana observed that the use of Psalm 110 in verse 8 of this *Ode* "could be used to express the experience of a believer in Christ as well as of Christ Himself," so too can the indecipherability of the pronouns intentionally heighten the theme of union that is prevalent in the *Odes*.²²² The best solution, then, is to say that the pronouns could refer to both or either of them without much of a shift in meaning.

Ode 29 contains the clearest example of justification by faith in the *Odes of Solomon*. The Odist is justified by grace on the sole basis of his belief in the Messiah, and his justification is forensic because he is pulled back from the abyss of death and Sheol. The Lord is the lead actor in the drama of the *Ode*, securing for the believer justification by faith, hope from despair, and victory over adversaries. This *Ode* is yet another example of the profuse soteriology that the Odist, who is undoubtedly a believer in Jesus as the Messiah, gleaned not only from his Jewish heritage, but also from New Testament authors, especially Paul.

5.4 Conclusion

The *Odes of Solomon* offers a unique glimpse into the early church. More than a collection of hymns, the *Odes* peel back the veil that typically drapes over the so-called average Christian in the second century who would otherwise remain hidden from sight. Most treatises from this time address a particular apologetic issue or doctrinal crisis, and thus may not be concerned with presenting the specific characterizations of the faith that animated the lives of the individual adherents to Christianity. The *Odes* afford the chance to listen in to the songs that were sung when the church gathered together for corporate worship, at least in the East. Some might argue that drawing doctrinal conclusions from a collection of songs violates the genre. To the contrary, it is precisely to the songs that one must look in order to discover what the majority of Christians believed, for it is by songs that doctrines are so easily disseminated.²²³

---

221 So indistinguishable is the believer from the Redeemer at points that Frants Buhl thinks that Christ and the speaking "I" converge in this *Ode* (Buhl, "Salomos Oder," *Teologisk tidsskrift for den danske folkekirke*, 3. Raekke, 2 [1911]: 114). Kittel discusses Buhl's position (Kittel, *Die Oden Salomos*, 112).
222 Harris and Mingana, *Odes of Solomon*, 2:365.
223 Martin Luther understood this point and it is reported that he once said, "Let others write the catechisms and the theology, but let me write the hymns!"

What Christians sang from the *Odes* was as doctrinally rich as it was lyrically beautiful. Together they sang of Christ's divinity (29.6), his death on the cross (27), and his resurrection from the grave (42.6).[224] This chapter had shown that they also sang in accord with Pauline soteriology. Though the word justification occurs only a small handful of times, nevertheless the Odist did compose songs that included a robust doctrine of justification by faith. In *Ode* 29.5–6 justification is given by grace on the basis of belief. The very fact that in *Ode* 17 and *Ode* 25 justification is linked to freedom from bondage in chains reveals that the Odist believed that justification is forensic. There is a legal component involved for him, for he conceives of justification by grace that breaks these bonds, bonds which held him captive to sin, and frees his soul to flee to God (25.1). In addition to forensic justification, the Odist appropriated other important Pauline motifs such as imputation of righteousness and union with Christ. These doctrines, which are usually associated with the Reformation, were not just present in the second century, they were sung.

---

224 On *Ode* 42.6 Charlesworth plainly comments, "The verse refers to the resurrection of Jesus Christ" (Charlesworth, *Odes of Solomon*, 147). Lattke seems to be in agreement (Lattke, *Odes of Solomon*, 588). *Pace*, von Harnack, *Ein jüdisch-christliches Psalmbuch*, 72.

6 "Δικαιοπραξιας Εργον": *Dialogue with Trypho*

Dressed in a long, flowing philosopher's robe and equipped with a philosopher's mind, Justin Martyr introduced a new way of thinking into the burgeoning Christian faith.[1] Born in Flavia Neapolis, Samaria, he embarked on a philosophical journey through his early life that brought him under the tutelage of the Stoics, the Peripatetics, the Pythagoreans, and finally the Platonists. Then, while walking to his favorite spot by the sea (*Dial.* 3.1), desiring to contemplate philosophy in solitude, he encountered an old man who converted him to Christianity.[2] Years later he would recall his conversion with these words:

> But my spirit was immediately set on fire, and an affection for the prophets, and for those who are friends of Christ, took hold of me; while pondering on his words, I discovered that his was the only sure and useful philosophy. Thus it is that I am now a philosopher.[3]

Justin never doffed his philosopher's garb.[4] Eusebius chronicled of Justin, "In the guise of a philosopher he preached the divine word, and contended for the faith

---

[1] Aside from a few autobiographical remarks Justin makes, not much is known of his life. There are several works that piece together the little we do know as well as give helpful commentary on the surrounding world to fill in what is lacking. For overviews on his life and thought, see Leslie W. Barnard, *Justin Martyr: His Life and Thought* (Cambridge: Cambridge University Press, 1967), and Eric F. Osborn, *Justin Martyr*, Beiträge zur Historischen Theologie 47 (Tübingen: Mohr Siebeck, 1973).

[2] Andrew Hofer makes the intriguing but unconvincing argument that the old man symbolizes Christ. He maintains that Justin used the Emmaus account in Luke 24 as the model for his conversion. There is no need, however, to suppose that Justin is allegorizing his conversion story. This thesis might be more convincing to those who see the entire *Dialogue* as a spurious encounter, which is not the position taken here. See Andrew Hofer, "The Old Man as Christ in Justin's *Dialogue with Trypho*," *VC* 57 (2003): 1–21. See also Oskar Skarsaune, "The Conversion of Justin Martyr," *ST* 30 (1976): 53–73. Skarsaune rejects the commonly held idea that Justin brought a philosophy that was saturated in Hellenism to Christianity. Skarsaune is, in fact, taken aback by how un-greek Justin's philosophy was and how determined he was to use Jewish prophecy.

[3] *Dial.* 8.1–2. Translations are mine unless otherwise indicated. The translation of the *Dialogue* used throughout this chapter comes from Michael Slusser, ed., *St. Justin Martyr: Dialogue with Trypho*, trans. Thomas B. Falls, rev. ed. Thomas P. Halton, Selections from the Fathers 3 (Washington, DC: The Catholic University of America Press, 2003), 15.

[4] Studies on Justin as philosopher abound. See Robert Joly, *Christianisme et Philosophie: Études sur Justin et les Apologistes grecs du deuxième siècle* (Brussels: Éditions de l'Université Libre de Bruxelles, 1973); Ragnar Holte, "Logos Spermaticos: Christianity and Ancient Philosophy according to St.-Justin's Apologies," *ST* 12 (1958): 109–68; N. Hydahl, *Philosophie und Christentum: Eine Interpretation der Einleitung zum Dialog Justins*, ATDan 9 (Copenhagen: Munksgaard, 1966); and

in his writings."⁵ Christianity to him was a system that could withstand the most rigorous philosophical argument and it alone was true. From the moment of his conversion Justin was fascinated by the Hebrew prophets and those who actually knew Christ. It is also evident from the copious amount of Scripture in his writings that he had read deeply in the Old and New Testaments.

Justin wrote two apologies on behalf of Christians to Emperor Antoninus Pius in an effort to legitimize the Christian faith.⁶ These apologies fell on deaf ears and it was not long before Rome took up the sword against the Christians once more. Justin was no exception to the onslaught, and he was likely beheaded under the Prefect Junius Rusticus during the tumultuous reign (at least as far as the Christians were concerned) of Marcus Aurelius.⁷ His death has forever earned him his surname Martyr.

The other work for which Justin is famous, and the work under examination in this chapter, is the *Dialogue with Trypho*. Justin provides a window into Christian and Jewish relations in the second century through the record of a two-day dialogue between Justin the Christian and Trypho the Jew. Ironically, the same Justin who infused Greek philosophy into Christianity is also the same Justin who aptly demonstrated that Christianity's true roots lie in Judaism. Justin had a surprising command of the Old Testament for a Gentile who was not raised with a consistent intake of the Hebrew Scriptures.⁸ The *Dialogue* is a mutual attempt at proselytizing; Trypho the Jew tried to persuade Justin to follow the Mosaic law, while Justin tried to persuade Trypho that Christianity is the fulfillment of the Old Testament.

This chapter demonstrates that Justin opposed Trypho's legalistic conception of Judaism with a doctrine of justification by faith. In chapter eight of the *Dialogue* Trypho makes a remarkable statement that Justin must obey all of the Mo-

---

J. C. M. van Winden, *An Early Christian Philosopher: Justin Martyr's Dialogue with Trypho, Chapters One to Nine*, PP 1 (Leiden: Brill, 1971).
5 Eusebius, *The Church History*, 4.11.8, trans. Paul L. Maier (Grand Rapids: Kregel, 1999), 143.
6 Debate continues as to whether Justin wrote one or two apologies. Denis Minns and Paul Parvis argue that the *Second Apology* was actually edited material taken from an original version of the *First Apology* (See Denis Minns and Paul Parvis, eds., *Justin, Philosopher and Martyr: Apologies* [Oxford: Oxford University Press, 2009], 21–31, for a good, up-to-date discussion).
7 Persecution had dwindled while Hadrian and Antoninus Pius ruled. However, persecution did break out sporadically under Marcus Aurelius. Marcus Aurelius might be remembered as an able Emperor to those studying Roman history, but for the Christians he was responsible for substantial persecution. The account of Justin's death comes from *The Martyrdom of Justin*.
8 Far and away the best study on Justin's knowledge and use of the Old Testament is Oskar Skarsaunne's magisterial work *Proof from Prophecy—A Study in Justin Martyr's Proof-Text Tradition: Text-Type, Provenance, Theological Profile* (Leiden: Brill, 1987).

saic law if he is to be saved. Justin rejects this idea multiple times throughout their discussion and argues instead for salvation by faith apart from works. Justin uses Abraham as an example of justification apart from circumcision, just as Paul did, in order to dissuade Trypho about the merits of the Mosaic law. Of great significance is Justin's use of ἔργον δικαιοσύνης and δικαιοπραξίας ἔργον which evokes Paul's use of ἔργα νόμου in Romans and Galatians. Justin invents his own terminology to make Pauline arguments against salvation through the law.

Important questions of the text are necessarily discussed in what follows. These issues range from the existence and identity of Trypho to the dating of the *Dialogue*. Following these introductory matters is a thorough exegesis of chapters 8, 23, 92, and 137. These chapters, infrequently brought into the discussion of justification, reveal a view of justification very similar to that of Paul in the New Testament. The first matter of importance is the issue of Justin's knowledge of Paul and/or his writings.

6.1 Justin and Paul

A fair question to ask at the outset of this chapter is whether or not Justin even knew of Paul, a question over which scholars radically disagree.[9] Since the position taken in this chapter is that Justin used Pauline arguments, then it would seem necessary first to prove that Justin was even aware of Paul's epistles, even though it could be every bit as telling if Justin did not know of Paul's letters and yet made an identical argument. The broader thesis of this book, that justification by faith was present amongst the earliest church fathers, could carry more weight if Justin did not read Paul. It could show that Paul's argument concerning justification was so standard that second-century authors like Justin used Paul without realizing it. However, it is probable that Justin did know of Paul's writings.

Justin, though, never mentions Paul by name. To make matters more difficult, Justin never explicitly cites any of Paul's writings. Andreas Lindemann offers four possibilities of Justin's relationship to Paul, especially as it pertains to the *Dialogue*:

1. Justin habe die Paulus-Tradition anscheinend gar nicht gekannt.

---

[9] This section relies on Paul Foster's recent chapter "Justin and Paul," in *Paul and the Second Century*, ed. Michael Bird and Joseph Dodson (London: T&T Clark, 2012), 108–25. Foster's scholarship is well done even though his conclusions are opposed here.

2. Justin habe Paulus durchaus gekannt, diese Kenntnis aber bewußt verschwiegen, weil Paulus der Kronzeuge des (von Justin bekämpften) Marcion gewesen sei.
3. Justin erwähne Paulus aus Rücksicht auf seine judenschristlichen Gesprächspartner nicht.
4. Justin sei, ganz im Gegensatz zum ersten Eindruck, geradezu ein Verfechter paulinischer Theologie.[10]

Of the possibilities Lindemann gives, the fourth option is most attractive, namely that Justin is actually an "advocate," or "champion" (*Verfechter*), of Pauline theology.[11]

How is it that Justin can be considered an advocate of Paul's theology if there is no overt mention of the man or his writings? Such a claim seems to overextend the evidence. Yet there is ample reason to suspect that Justin not only knew of Paul and his letters, but that he was absorbed with Paul's arguments.[12] For whatever reason, Justin decided not to speak of Paul or to quote him.[13] One possible theory, which is promising for Justin's use of Paul, is the newer concept of secondary orality. According to this theory, those in a literate culture are more reliant on thoughts and expressions, and not on verbatim repetition of words. The literate Justin, then, could imbibe Pauline arguments and reproduce them without demonstrating a direct dependence on Paul.[14] At the very least Justin had either read Paul or he was influenced by Christians who had studied

---

[10] Andreas Lindemann, *Paulus im ältesten Christentum: Das Bild des Apostels und die Rezeption der paulinischen Theologie in der frühchristlichen Literatur bis Marcion*, BHT 58 (Tübingen: Mohr Siebeck, 1979), 353.

[11] Foster is right to reject the second option because it reflects modern sensitivities and to reject the third option because it introduces a concern that Justin would not have had ("Justin and Paul," 110). Foster opts for the first option that Justin did not know of Paul. He remarks, "When it comes to Paul, and to the use of his writings, there is a strange, almost deathly, silence" (123). He is skeptical of the claims made by a vast number of scholars who find allusions to Paul's thoughts and epistles.

[12] Theodore Stylianopoulos makes the fascinating connection between Justin and Paul in regards to the metaphor of old and new leaven. Though Justin does not name Paul, he does use Paul's antithesis of the old and new leaven from 1 Cor 5. No writer before Justin uses this and nearly every writer after Justin explicitly ties this illustration to Paul (Stylianopoulos, *Justin Martyr and the Mosaic Law*, SBLDS 20 [Missoula, MT: Scholars Press, 1975], 96).

[13] The solution could be as simple as the fact that Justin wanted to do battle against Trypho on his own ground—the Old Testament. He wanted to prove to Trypho using the Old Testament alone that Jesus was the promised messiah. Had he overtly introduced New Testament scripture into the discussion, he might have lost Trypho's attention. Instead, he cryptically used New Testament approaches, mainly Pauline arguments, to persuade Trypho of his point of view.

[14] See the pioneering work of Walter J. Ong, *Orality and Literacy: The Technologizing of the Word*, 3rd ed. (New York: Routledge, 2012).

Paul's letters, since the path of Justin's argument in the *Dialogue* takes a determinedly Pauline trajectory.

What matters particularly for this chapter is that many scholars, some of whom are even experts on Justin, think the Apologist appealed to Romans and Galatians in particular, Paul's most potent tractates on justification apart from works of the law. For example, Oskar Skarsaune, the preeminent Justin scholar, claims, "There is no reason to doubt that Justin made extensive use of Paul's letters, especially Romans and Galatians."[15] Lindemann likewise concludes, "Justin hat paulinische Briefe, jedenfalls Röm, 1 Kor, und Gal, gekannt und bei der Abfassung des Dial zu Rate gezogen."[16] The key is that Justin used Paul's style of argument more than his words.[17]

The argument that Justin knew of Paul and yet did not cite him is in many ways more compelling than a direct quotation or a mere mention of the name. A quotation could have an ambiguous interpretation or be simple proof texting, and a reference to Paul's name could reveal little more than that Justin had heard of Paul, which is hard to believe was not the case, especially since Justin had made his way to Rome. What Justin does is far more impressive and important—he uses Paul's argument of justification apart from the law. That Justin knew Paul will be made clearer as the chapter unfolds, but there is another pressing question in order to understand Justin's argument—who was Trypho?

---

[15] Oskar Skarsaune, "Justin and His Bible," in *Justin Martyr and His Worlds*, ed. Sarah Parvis and Paul Foster (Minneapolis: Fortress, 2007), 74. For Skarsaune, "the reason [Justin] preferred these two letters is obvious: it was here more than anywhere else he found Paul engaged in extensive and detailed interpretation of scriptural texts." Skarsaune observes the way that Paul argued from the Old Testament and sees Justin doing something similar. To be sure, Skarsaune is correct to make this statement. In a careful and detailed manner, Skarsaunne observes that "of a sum total of 49 explicit and implicit OT quotations in Romans, Justin has parallels to 14 (29%)" (Skarsaune, *Proof from Prophecy*, 93). But the argument advanced here is that Justin was doing more than quoting from the Old Testament like Paul did—Justin was also picking up on Paul's polemic against the Jews that comes out in Romans and Galatians. Skarsaune concludes on Justin and Paul: "within the *corpus Paulinum*, Justin seems to have made special use of Romans and Galatians—and almost only in the *Dialogue*" (Skarsaune, *Proof from Prophecy*, 100).

[16] Andreas Lindemann, *Paulus im ältesten Christentum*, 366. Cf. Rodney A. Werline, "The Transformation of Pauline Arguments in Justin Martyr's Dialogue with Trypho," *HTR* 92 (1999): 79–93, for an argument that Justin used Pauline arguments, even though he never explicitly quotes the Apostle. Specifically, Werline finds traces of Rom 2–4 and 9–11 in the *Dial.*

[17] See David Rokéah's important work, *Justin Martyr and the Jews*, Jewish and Christian Perspective Series 5 (Leiden: Brill, 2002), especially pp. 43–85, where he discusses "Paul and Justin on the Law (Torah) of Moses," "Paul and Justin on Abraham and the Status of the Gentiles," and "More on the Attitudes of Paul and Jesus to the Torah and the Gentiles."

6.2 Rhetorical Device or Genuine Interlocutor?

The *Dialogue* is one of the most important documents on Jewish-Christian relations in the early church. It records a two day conversation held in Ephesus between Justin and a well-known Jew named Trypho, which commenced when Trypho drew Justin into a discussion upon seeing Justin's philosopher's robe.[18] The *Dialogue* quickly turned to a debate about the Old Testament and Justin exposited prophetic passages for the duration of the *Dialogue* with the hope of proselytizing Trypho.[19]

With the exception of the short letter *Epistle of Barnabas*,[20] the *Dialogue* is the first thorough treatment of Old Testament texts and how the Old Testament applies in light of the new covenant. Because of its widely recognized importance there is plentiful research, but the most important background issues enjoy little scholarly consensus. Traversing the *Dialogue* without first settling some of these issues is difficult because the arguments made in this chapter depend to some degree on the reliability of the portrait of Judaism that is presented. The two most pressing concerns are the historical reliability of the account and the identity of Trypho. In actuality these issues are bound together and must be handled as a single problem. Those who argue that this account is not factual also make the claim that Justin invented the character of Trypho. One the other hand, those who hear a ring of truth in the *Dialogue* typically accept Trypho as a genuine interlocutor.

Many have doubted the historicity of the *Dialogue*. Some point to the genre of dialogue as the basis of discrediting the account while others question the *Dialogue* on the grounds that it reads more like a monologue than a dialogue. The former suggest that it was never meant to be taken literally as though Justin

---

[18] Eusebius records that the *Dial.* took place in Ephesus and that Trypho was a well-known Jew (*Ecclesiastial History* 4.18.6). While most scholars accept the location, many reject the notion that Trypho was a famous Jew claiming that Eusebius "created a suitably impressive opponent for Justin by building on Trypho's description of himself as a Hebrew" in order to add clout to the *Dial.* (Judith Lieu, *Image and Reality: the Jews in World of the Christians in the Second Century* [Edinburgh: T&T Clark, 1996], 110). Since Eusebius' account is the only source by which to go, it is difficult to reject his claim about Trypho outright. Those who disagree with Eusebius do so because they assume that Justin was caricaturing Judaism through his Christian lens in order to show the superiority of Christianity.
[19] *Dial.* 8.2 and 142.
[20] See Michael Holmes, *The Apostolic Fathers: Greek Texts and English Translations*, 3rd ed. (Grand Rapids: Baker Academic, 2007). Holmes summarizes the *Epistle of Barnabas* with the following question: "How ought Christians to interpret the Jewish scriptures, and what is the nature of the relationship between Christianity and Judaism?" (370).

had an actual two-day conversation with a Jew and his companions. It was merely a rhetorical device used in the hands of a philosopher who was seeking converts, much like the Socratic Dialogues.[21] This view is difficult to maintain because Justin fails in his efforts to convert Trypho at the end. If Justin fabricated the *Dialogue*, then it is shocking that he was unable to convince his imaginary opponent.

The latter view contends that the *Dialogue* is too lopsided to reflect a realistic conversation. Not only did Justin dominate the conversation but, as some claim, Trypho did not accurately reflect Judaism. Jon Nilson captured this position well when he said,

> As for the figure of Trypho in the *Dialogue*, it is hard to see him as anything more than a straw man. He, as well as his companions, are such poor spokesmen for Judaism that using them to present the Jewish position could hardly be expected to win a neutral, much less a sympathetic, hearing among an intended Jewish audience. Trypho never even throws Justin off stride. Justin dominates the *Dialogue* to the point where it would not be inappropriate to name it the *Monologue* with Trypho.[22]

It is common for those not accepting the validity of the *Dialogue* to charge Justin with building a "straw man."[23] Granted, the portions of the *Dialogue* given to Trypho are limited but this cannot be a sufficient reason to reject the authenticity of the *Dialogue*. Trypho comes across as much more than a fictitious foil for Justin's arguments.[24] Nilson's statement also fails because it does not adequately account for the varying forms of Judaism that existed in the second century. How can he say that Trypho and his companions are "poor spokesmen for Judaism"? Is he referring here to Palestinian Judaism or Diaspora Judaism? Moreover, was Trypho a representative of the maturing Rabbinic Judaism? In the second century, there was no singular "spokesman for Judaism" or even a standard "Jewish position" of which to speak. Judaism was much too diverse to make the claim he has made. There is too much in the *Dialogue* which sounds authentic to dismiss it entirely.

---

[21] Sara Denning-Bolle, "Christian Dialogue as Apologetic: the Case of Justin Martyr seen in Historical Context," *Bulletin of the John Rylands University Library of Manchester* 69 (1987): 492–510.
[22] Jon Nilson, "To Whom is Justin's *Dialogue* addressed?" *Theological Studies* 38 (1977): 540–41.
[23] E. R. Goodenough also makes the argument that Trypho is a "straw man" (*The Theology of Justin Martyr: An Investigation into the Conceptions of the Earliest Christian Literature and its Hellenistic and Judaistic Influences* [Jena: Verlag Frommansche Buchhandlung, 1923], 90–93).
[24] Lieu, *Image and Reality*, 113.

6.2 Rhetorical Device or Genuine Interlocutor? — 161

It is best to understand the *Dialogue* as an actual event that took place *c.* 133–135 CE between Justin and a real Jew named Trypho.[25] In chapter one of the *Dialogue* Trypho says that he escaped from the war, a reference to the Bar Kokhba rebellion that scattered many Jews who were left in Palestine after Titus decimated the Temple in 70 CE. However, Justin did not record the encounter until around 160 CE which allowed for more freedom in his recall.[26] On this point Jaroslav Pelikan is instructive: "Justin's work represented the literary form of an actual interview, but … it was composed many years after the fact and reflected the author's hindsight on the debate."[27] In some ways, Adolf von Harnack was correct to call the *Dialogue* the "monologue of the victor" (*der Monolog des Siegers*) since Justin could polish the conversation using his own editorial license.[28] Though, as has been said, it is not necessarily appropriate to call it a monologue, this comment does corroborate the idea that Justin painted the dialogue in a better light when he wrote it years later. This does not mean, though, that Justin misrepresented Trypho or that Trypho was not given the opportunity to interject with his counterpoints.[29]

Justin, trained in the art of philosophy, would not have purposefully made an unsustainable argument that was based on a faulty view of his opponent.

---

[25] Recently there has been a resurgence in the belief that Trypho was a true interlocutor. See especially, Barnard, *Justin Martyr*, 7–12.

[26] Though the specific date of the *Dial.* is unknown, various clues help narrow down the range of possibilities. First of all, the *Dialogue* refers to the *I Apology* which is typically dated between 150–155 CE (*Dial.* 120.5) (see Leslie W. Barnard, *St. Justin Martyr the First and Second Apologies* [New York: Paulist Press, 1997], 11). Also, since Justin was martyred around 165 CE, the *Dial.* had to have been written somewhere in this ten to fifteen year span.

[27] Jaroslav Pelikan, *The Christian Tradition: A History of the Development of Doctrine*, vol. 1, *The Emergence of the Catholic Tradition (100–600)* (Chicago: University of Chicago Press, 1971), 15.

[28] Adolf von Harnack, *Judentum und Judenchristentum in Justins Dialog mit Trypho*, TU 39 (Leipzig: Hinrichs, 1913), 92. Although Harnack may have questioned the veracity of the *Dial.* in its final form, he nonetheless believed that the *Dial.* occurred.

[29] Timothy Horner wrote the interesting monograph *Listening to Trypho: Justin Martyr's Dialogue Reconsidered*, Contributions to Biblical Exegesis and Theology 28 (Leuvan: Peeters, 2001), wherein he examined all the places that Trypho's speaks. His thesis is that Trypho is a "voice which defies fiction" and, therefore, was a voice which deserves a hearing (12). He also makes it clear that Trypho is consistent throughout and interjects with concerns that were consistent with the Judaism of that day. Trypho does take the opportunity from time to time to stop Justin, especially when he thinks that Justin has not seriously considered his point of view. In *Dial.* 27, for instance, Trypho accuses Justin of proof-texting and not addressing the texts that he thinks supports his argument. Trypho believed that Christians felt the liberty to jettison the portions of the Old Testament which they found obsolete, and this without reason. Justin's response will be taken up later in the chapter.

If in his recounting of the initial dialogue Justin misrepresented Judaism beyond the point of recognition, then his work would have quickly faded away and been forgotten. Demetrios Trakatellis made this point well saying, "It could be safely assumed, though, that there must be at least a nucleus of historical fact in Justin's presentation. Otherwise the readers of the *Dialogue*, no matter who they were, would have discarded the document out of hand as unacceptable fiction."[30] Since part of Justin's readership included Jews, it makes the most sense that Justin interacted with the most prominent arguments that they raised in the early years of the second century.[31] Nevertheless, what matters most is Justin's own perception of Judaism, especially as it relates to salvation.[32] The issue

---

[30] Demetrios Trakatellis, "Justin Martyr's Trypho," *HTR* 79 (1986): 297.

[31] The debate over audience is extensive. There are four positions generally taken with respect to Justin's audience. First, that Justin was writing to a pagan audience. Helping this view is a reference to Marcus Pompeius to whom the Dialogue appears to be addressed (*Dial.* 141). Among those supporting this view is J. Nilson, "To Whom is Justin's *Dialogue with Trypho* addressed?", 539. Second, some argue for a gentile Christian audience. See C. H. Cosgrove, "Justin Martyr and the Emerging Christian Canon," *VC* 36 (1982): 211. The third view, which is the traditional view, is that Justin was writing for a Jewish audience seeking converts. The final view, which seems best, sees a mixed audience of Jews and Christians. Those holding this position include Craig D. Allert, *Revelation, Truth, Canon and Interpretation: Studies in Justin Martyr's Dialogue with Trypho*, Supplements to Vigiliae Christianae 64 (Leiden: Brill, 2002), 61, and Theodore Stylianopoulos, *Justin Martyr and the Mosaic Law*, 10–20. Another mark of authenticity that deserves attention is the cordialness with which the discussion transpired. The *Dial.* is the only document in the early church where Jews and Christians had an amicable conversation (See Stephen Wilson, "Dialogue and Dispute," in *Related Strangers: Jews and Christians, 70–170 CE* [Minneapolis: Fortress Press, 1995], 258). Typically Christians addressed Jews only with a polemical tone and vice versa, each portraying the other group with unkind and unsympathetic characterizations. The fissure between these groups widened at an accelerated rate which means that the *Dial.* must have taken place before the animosity was too severe, even though there are multiple places in the *Dial.* where Justin referred to a curse which Jews would invoke on Christians during their prayers. Daniel Boyarin argues that Justin Martyr used these curses as an unfounded polemic against the Jews. In other words, both groups were in the process of discovering their boundaries of orthodoxy and it was unfair for Justin to use this material in such a way (Daniel Boyarin, "Justin Martyr Invents Judaism," *CH* 70 [2001]: 427–61).

[32] Many do believe that Justin was correct in his portrayal of second-century Judaism. Though Harold Remus does not think that the *Dialogue* was a historical event, he nonetheless thinks that it accurately represents the Jewish teachings of Justin's times (Harold Remus, "Justin Martyr's Argument with Judaism," in *Separation and Polemic*, ed. Stephen G. Wilson, vol. 2 of *Anti-Judaism in Early Christianity*, Studies in Christianity and Judaism 2.2 [Waterloo, Ontario: Wilfrid Laurier University, 1986], 72). Graham Stanton, cautioning against E. P. Sanders's overstated case of an univocal Judaism that was not legalistic, argues, "Although Trypho is sometimes no more than a puppet who feeds Justin lines which can then be readily refuted, in numerous passages it can be shown that Trypho does indeed set out Jewish views which are well-attested elsewhere"

here is not primarily the rectitude of Justin's portrayal of Judaism, but rather how he understood Jewish theology and how he articulated his own view of justification in response.

6.3 Structure of the *Dialogue*

According to Leslie Barnard, the *Dialogue* can be broken down into three main sections. Chapters 11–31 deal with "the Mosaic law which Trypho represents as universally binding." Then, chapters 32–110 focus on "the nature and significance of Jesus Christ who, Justin declares, is the fulfillment of the Old Testament prophetic witness." Finally, chapters 111–142 are concerned "with the conversion of the Gentiles—God will receive, as the prophets declared, all of any race who seek him."[33] But actually, the *Dialogue* does not allow for such a neat and clear-cut structure. There is a general flow in the *Dialogue* along the course that Barnard plots, but there is too much tangential material to draw the hard and fast divisions he makes.

Skarsaunne gives vent to the frustration of trying to discern Justin's structure in the *Dialogue:* "A feature that has struck most commentators reading Justin's exegetical expositions is his remarkably bad organization of the material. One often searches in vain for a coherent line of argument, because Justin allows himself to follow all kinds of digressions, and sometimes seems to follow rather far-fetched associations."[34] Despite this frustration, Skarsaune ventures his own tripartite outline that is very similar to Barnard's: the new law and the new covenant (11–47), the proof that Jesus is the Messiah (48–107), and the new law and the new people (108–141).[35]

(Graham Stanton, "The Law of Moses and the Law of Christ," in *Paul and the Mosaic Law*, ed. James D. G. Dunn, WUNT 89 [Tübingen: Mohr Siebeck, 1996], 105–06). Justin is at least representing the attitude of some within second-century Judaism.
33 Barnard, *Justin Martyr*, 21–22.
34 Skarsaune, *Proof from Prophecy*, 135.
35 Skarsaune, *Proof from Prophecy*, 165–227. Tellingly, Skarsaune discusses the first part and then the third part. Only after this does he discuss the second as if the structure is less clear to him. Stylianopoulos, *Justin Martyr and the Mosaic Law*, divides the book in three sections as well (after the Prologue, 1–9): chaps. 10–30 deal with the Mosaic law, chaps. 31–118 deal with Christology, and chaps. 119–142 deal with true Israel. This outline also fails to recognize the frequency with which Justin backtracks and repeats lines of thought throughout the entirety of the *Dial.*

The problem is that modern commentators are trying to place an artificial structure on the text where Justin may not have intended one.[36] Any attempt to make a firm outline according to chapter divisions is futile. The best way forward is to define Justin's overarching argument and then specify which chapters correspond to his major concerns.

Broadly speaking, everything in the *Dialogue* moves to one goal—the conversion of Trypho and his companions. To achieve this end, Justin employs two lines of arguments: first, the Mosaic law cannot save, and second, Jesus Christ is the promised Messiah.[37] If he can show the insufficiency of Judaism on its own terms, and simultaneously prove that Jesus fulfills Old Testament prophecy, then he is sure he can win over Trypho. This is why there is no clear structure. Justin regularly weaves in and out of this twofold plot, retracing previously traveled ground, repeating large sections of Scripture, and reiterating the same argument over and over to make his point. The remainder of this chapter focuses on the first part of Justin's argument—observing that the Mosaic law cannot bring salvation.

6.4 Exegesis of Selected Passages

Four passages stand out for their remarkable clarity with regard to Justin's position on the law as it relates to justification. In these passages it is not so much his positive statements on justification that remind the reader of Paul, but his pointed treatment of the law's inability to justify that makes it sound as though Paul himself could be the author. The first of these passages comes from *Dialogue* 8 which is the catalyst for the entire dialogue, for it is in chapter 8 that Trypho tells Justin that he must keep the law in its entirety if he is to obtain mercy (i.e., salvation) from God. On at least three occasions Justin refers Trypho back to chapter 8 of the *Dialogue* to remind Trypho of his remarks at the outset about the centrality of the law for salvation. This opening comment of Trypho's stays fresh on Justin's mind throughout their conversation.

---

[36] A century ago Karl Hubík tried to base Justin's structure in ancient rhetorical style, but few have followed him. See Karl Hubík, Die Apologien des hl. Justinus: Des Philosophen und Märtyrers. Literarhistorische untersuchungen, Theologische Studien der Leo Gesellschaft 19 (Vienna: Mayer & Co., 1912). Perhaps the lack of structure corroborates the historical validity of the *Dial.* in that it moves along the contours of a natural dialogue, moving in whatever direction the conversation leads.

[37] Even the ingathering of the Gentiles, a division that both Bernard and Skarsaune have, serves to show that salvation has come in Christ apart from the law.

Justin's response to Trypho's explanation of how one can obtain mercy from God (*Dial.* 8) in chapters 23 and 92 is of utmost importance. These two chapters will be handled together because the argument that is made is identical. But the repetition should not lessen the force of the argument. By duplicating his answer to Trypho's initial comments in chapter 8 for those who were absent on the first day of the dialogue, Justin highlights the significance of his main point. Repeating this portion of his argument is not rhetorical flare; his answer in chapter 8 is the centerpiece of the entire dialogue. Can a person be justified by the Mosaic law or does justification come from belief in a crucified messiah? He emphasizes for his partially new audience that salvation comes through Christ and not the law.

Finally, chapter 137 is studied briefly. Just before the *Dialogue* concludes, Justin returns to aspects of the Mosaic law as if to clarify one last time that the law cannot save. Circumcision, he reminds his Jewish friends, was not given as a "work of righteousness" but as a sign. And then he exhorts them to disobey the "Pharisaic teachers" who were compelling them to find salvation in obedience to the law. In the treatment of the law in the *Dialogue*, one cannot help but hear loud echoes of Paul reverberating through Justin's arguments. Acceptance of and obedience to the law was tantamount to salvation in Trypho's reckoning, whereas the law was simply a precursor and pointer to Christ according the Justin. This drives the entire *Dialogue* as Justin seeks to prove how the coming of the Messiah rendered the law null and void.

Dialogue 8

The conversation really takes flight after chapter 8, for it is in this chapter that Trypho puts forth his conception of salvation, which in turn leads to Justin's verbose response, that is, the rest of the *Dialogue*. After Justin recounts his conversion and the reason he has remained a philosopher (the passage recited in the introduction to this chapter from *Dial.* 8.1), it is Trypho's turn to share with Justin how he might be saved.

> At these words, my dearest [Pompey], Trypho's friends began to laugh, and he himself replied, smiling, 'I commend all your other statements, and I admire your burning desire to know divine things, but it would be better for you to concentrate on the philosophy of Plato or some other philosopher, and in this way cultivate constancy, continency, and moderation, rather than be ensnared by false teachings, and become a partisan of worthless men. For, while you adhered to your former school of philosophy and lived a blameless life, there was hope of a better destiny for you, but, when you have turned away from God and have placed your hope in man, what chance of salvation do you have? *If you*

> will listen to me (indeed I already think of you as a friend), first be circumcised, then observe the precepts concerning the Sabbath, the feasts, and God's new moons; in brief, fulfill the whole written law, and then, probably, you will experience the mercy of God. But if the Messiah has been born and exists anywhere, he is not known, nor is he conscious of his own existence, nor has he any power until Elijah comes to anoint him and to make him manifest to all. But you [Christians] have believed this foolish rumor, and you have invented for yourselves a Christ for whom you blindly give up your lives.[38]

In the first half of chapter 8, not only did Justin recount his conversion, but he also tipped his hand and told Trypho that his purpose in their dialogue was to convert him saying, "Thus, if you have any regard for your own welfare and for the salvation of your soul, and if you believe in God, you may have the chance, since I know you are no stranger to this matter, of attaining a knowledge of the Christ of God, and, after becoming a Christian, of enjoying a happy life."[39] From the outset he affirms that salvation concerns belief in God and the Christ. Though this is fleshed out in greater detail as the *Dialogue* progresses, he is clear that salvation entails belief only, in contradistinction to Trypho who argues for adherence to the law.

The section (*Dial*. 8.3) opens with Justin's closing remarks about his own conversion: "When I had said these things, my beloved, those with Trypho laughed out loud, and he was smiling a little" (Ταῦτά μου, φίλτατε,[40] εἰπόντος οἱ μετὰ τοῦ Τρύφωνος ἀνεγέλασαν, αὐτὸς δὲ ὑπομειδιάσας).[41] This statement comes just after Justin implored those men to seek salvation in the "Christ of God" and it was met with boisterous laughter (ἀναγελάω) and pejorative smiles (ὑπομειδιάω). Certainly this reaction would have grieved Justin who, in a show of vulnerability, had laid out his new-found faith and this could account for some

---

38 *Dial*. 8.3. Falls, *Dialogue with Trypho*, 15. Emphasis added.

39 *Dial*. 8.2. Falls, *Dialogue with Trypho*, 15.

40 The word φίλτατε appears only one other place in the *Dialogue* (141.1) where Justin calls Marcus Pompeius (Μάρκε Πομπήϊε) φίλτατε, corroborating the argument that the *Dialogue* is addressed to this figure. The Latin version actually includes Marcus Pompeius in 8.3, probably indicating a scribe who saw this connection and wished to remove the ambiguity. However, for reasons covered above, it is best to understand the *Dial*. as written to a broad audience (see n. 31 of this chapter). Even though it may have been written to this individual does not mean that Justin did not intend a wider audience.

41 The critical edition used is Justin Martyr, *Dialogus cum Tryphone*, ed. Miroslav Marcovich (Berlin: Walter de Gruyter, 1997). Graham Stanton believes that "Trypho's companions are portrayed as being more cynical about Justin's Christian claims than Trypho himself" throughout the *Dial* (Graham Stanton, "'God-Fearers': Neglected Evidence in Justin Martyr's *Dialogue with Trypho*," in *Ancient History in a Modern University*, vol. 2 of *Early Christianity, Late Antiquity and Beyond*, ed. T. W. Hillard et al. [Grand Rapids: Eerdmans, 1998], 45–46).

of the sarcastic remarks that Justin made throughout the remainder of the *Dialogue*.

The conversation then turned to Trypho who was given the chance to outline his objections to Justin. After the laughter had subsided Trypho stated, "'But these things of which you [have spoken] I accept' he said, 'and admire your eagerness concerning divine things'" (Τὰ μὲν ἄλλα σου, φησίν, ἀποδέχομαι καὶ ἄγαμαι τῆς περὶ τὸ θεῖον ὁρμῆς). It is difficult to discern if Trypho offered these words in a friendly manner or if he was simply patronizing Justin. Those things (τὰ) which Trypho accepts are probably Justin's critique of philosophy in chapter 6 and his eagerness to use the prophets in chapter 7, certainly not the part about the Christ. Justin, who extensively quoted from the prophets, never had to make an apology for his use of the LXX since both of them understood it as an authoritative source.[42]

Trypho then exhorted Justin to return to philosophy. He established a contrast here between the erudite teachings of philosophers and the rudimentary teachings of the apostles. He supposed, "it were better for you still to pursue Plato's philosophy or the philosophy of another, practicing patient endurance, and self-control, and prudence" (ἄμεινον δὲ ἦν φιλοσοφεῖν ἔτι σε τὴν Πλάτωνος ἢ ἄλλου του φιλοσοφίαν, ἀσκοῦντα καρτερίαν καὶ ἐγκράτειαν καὶ σωφροσύνην). Trypho believed that Justin would only find intellectual fulfillment in the ancient art of philosophy and not in the nascent religion of Christianity. The virtues which he listed, namely endurance (καρτερίαν), self-control (ἐγκράτειαν) and prudence (σωφροσύνην), were all common themes amongst the early Greek philosophers.[43]

The second half of the contrast came in his following statement: "rather than to be deceived by false words, and to follow men who are not worthy" (ἢ λόγοις ἐξαπατηθῆναι ψευδέσι καὶ ἀνθρώποις ἀκολουθῆσαι οὐδενὸς ἀξίοις). The "men who are not worthy" is a reference to the apostles. The notion of an intellectual Greek philosopher following peasant fishermen would not only have been absurd, but embarrassing. Greeks had a long tradition of academic excellence which pervaded the entire Mediterranean basin, even after the Romans had subjugated them.[44] Thus, abandoning his prestigious pedigree for the religion of barbarians was strange indeed. It is surprising, though, that Trypho, a "Hebrew of the circumcision,"[45] would have made such a comment. Trypho

---

[42] See J. Smit Sibinga, *The Old Testament Text of Justin Martyr* (Leiden: Brill, 1963). Cf. Styliaopoulos, *Justin Martyr and the Mosaic Law*, 102.
[43] See for example, Aristotle, *Nicomachean Ethics* 2.2.
[44] Ferguson, *Backgrounds of Early Christianity*, 21–22.
[45] *Dial.* 1.3.

not only identified himself as a Jew but he also demonstrated a deep knowledge of the Old Testament throughout the book.⁴⁶ This lends support to those who call into question Trypho as an accurate representative of Judaism, but it cannot stand alone as a reason to reject Trypho's authenticity because the rest of the *Dialogue* reflects his strong Jewish tendencies.

Trypho continued with a strand of conditional statements in order to explain to Justin that philosophy triumphs over the foolishness of Christianity, but even philosophy falls short in its ability to merit salvation. In fact, there is no salvation for the one who forsakes God to place his faith in philosophy. He said, "For hope of a better destiny is being left for you if you remain in that course of philosophy and live blamelessly; but what salvation still awaits you if you abandon God and hope in man?" (μένοντι γάρ σοι ἐν ἐκείνῳ τῷ τῆς φιλοσοφίας τρόπῳ καὶ ζῶντι⁴⁷ ἀμέμπτως ἐλπὶς ὑπελείπετο ἀμείνονος μοίρας· καταλιπόντι δὲ τὸν θεὸν καὶ εἰς ἄνθρωπον ἐλπίσαντι ποία ἔτι περιλείπεται σωτηρία;). He begins with the apodosis for the various protases which follow. Justin could have a good destiny if he returned to philosophy and lived according to the wholesome virtues taught by the great thinkers, but salvation would still escape him. Trypho solved this problem for Justin in the next few lines, which are the crux of the passage.

Trypho advised Justin that he would obtain mercy from God if he was willing to pause and listen (εἰ οὖν καὶ ἐμοῦ θέλεις ἀκοῦσαι). The basis for Trypho's taking the time to share with Justin was their new-found friendship (φίλον γάρ σε ἤδη νενόμικα). The friendliness of the *Dialogue* is particularly apparent in several places in this chapter. It began with Justin's concern for Trypho and his companion's conversion (8.2) and then Trypho took his turn in trying to convert Justin.

What follows is the most revealing statement about second-century Judaism in the *Dialogue*. Trypho listed the things which Justin must do if he was to receive mercy from God: "First be circumcised, then observe the Sabbath, as it has been customary, and the feasts and the new moons of God" (πρῶτον μὲν περιτεμοῦ, εἶτα φύλαξον, ὡς νενόμισται, τὸ σάββατον καὶ τὰς ἑορτὰς καὶ τὰς νουμηνίας τοῦ θεοῦ). For Trypho (or Justin), these three or four guidelines were essential in the Jewish mindset for earning God's favor. Apart from these works a Jew could have no confidence in his standing before God, much less a Gentile. If circumcision, Sabbath keeping, and celebrations of feasts did not provide a clear enough pic-

---

46 The argument could be made that Trypho was telling Justin that it is better to be a philosopher than a Christian and does not have anything negative about Judaism in mind. It seems unlikely, however, because he calls his fellow Jews unworthy men. The reader gets the impression that Trypho views himself as superior to these Jewish men because of his knowledge of philosophy.

47 Both μένοντι and ζῶντι are adverbial participles functioning as conditionals.

ture of the works one must do, then Trypho included the blanket statement, "in a word do all things which have been written in the Law" (καὶ ἁπλῶς τὰ ἐν τῷ νόμῳ γεγραμμένα πάντα ποίει). Trypho summarized his understanding of justification, without using this word of course, by saying one must do (ποίει) *everything* which is written in the law if he wishes to obtain God's mercy. Philosophy, according to Trypho, may be a more suitable path than Christianity, but ultimate truth is found in obedience to the God of the Old Testament. This alone will secure salvation for Justin and any other who seeks God's favor.

The τότε which introduces the next clause is exegetically significant. If aspects of the law such as circumcision and Sabbath keeping were merely ways to remain within the covenant, then why did Trypho indicate that one can only obtain mercy from God *after* doing these things? When he completed the aforementioned list of works he remarked, "and *then* perhaps you will receive mercy from God."[48] The τότε is a temporal marker signaling that the latter will not become a reality until the former is complete. In other words, those specified works of the law are necessary for a person to obtain mercy from God. Only after the works have been completed is the individual awarded God's favor.

Other scholars have picked up on Trypho's legalistic tone in chapter 8. Most notably, Graham Stanton has written an important essay on Paul's use of the law in Galatians and has seen a significant parallel to Justin's argument in the *Dialogue*. He wades into the debate on the New Perspective on Paul by juxtaposing Paul and Justin's argument and asking, "Is it likely that two Christian thinkers who both wrestled with the question of the law should have operated independently with a mistaken view of Jewish opinion on such a crucial point?"[49] Justin and Paul arrive at a remarkably similar position on the law. At the center of chapter 8 is the question of "getting in" the covenant, not the boundary markers of those who are already in the covenant. For Justin to proselytize, he must set his heart to obeying the law in its entirety. Stanton concludes on *Dialogue* 8.4,

---

48 Literally, "and then perhaps there will be mercy for you from God." Emphasis added.
49 Stanton, "The Law of Moses and the Law of Christ," 105. Stanton is confident that "Justin did not know Galatians, and used Romans only to a very limited extent" (103), and he also points out, "I am not claiming that a line can be traced back from Justin to Paul" (107). Though there seems to be too much agreement between Paul and Justin for Justin to not know of Galatians, it does not matter. The point Stanton makes here is critical—Justin, not writing too long after Paul, has a similar assessment of Judaism, a view of Judaism that has come under scrutiny in recent years. However, if it can be shown that Justin also thought that a portion of the Jews had a legalistic conception of salvation, and it is not just Paul who holds this view, then perhaps the Judaism of this time period needs more review.

In short, I am inclined to think that Galatians and the *Dialogue* suggest that for at least some strands of Jewish opinion, 'getting in' was on the basis of keeping the law of Moses. I do not think it at all unlikely that many Jews in the first and second centuries would have accepted that entry into the people of God was on the basis of acceptance of God's gracious covenant with his people *and at the same time* have maintained that carrying out the law was a *sine qua non* for past, present and future acceptance by God.[50]

Second-century Judaism, not nearly as homogenous as was once thought, could certainly contain many different understandings of salvation and the place of the law. But Paul and Justin were both confronted with Jews who thought salvation could be obtained through the law, a view that they harmoniously opposed.

Up to this point Trypho had not made a direct assault on Christianity. He may have made off-handed comments about the superiority of philosophy and the inferiority of the apostles, but he mainly wanted to argue positively for his understanding of justification. However, in the remainder of the passage he took aim at the central claim of Christianity over and against Judaism—the advent of the Messiah. Trypho went on the offensive saying, "But Christ, if even he has been born and exists somewhere, is unknown, and neither yet knows himself nor does he have any power, until Elijah comes and anoints him and makes him manifest to all" (Χριστὸς δέ, εἰ καὶ γεγένηται καὶ ἔστι που, ἄγνωστός ἐστι καὶ οὐδὲ αὐτός πω ἑαυτὸν ἐπίσταται οὐδὲ ἔχει δύναμίν τινα, μέχρις ἂν ἐλθὼν Ἠλίας χρίσῃ αὐτὸν καὶ φανερὸν πᾶσι ποιήσῃ). Trypho was correct to say that Elijah had to precede Christ. This accounts for the statement that if Christ has been born and exists, he is unaware of it. By this Trypho meant that if the Christ has entered the world, then he has not made his appearance known because Elijah had not yet come. Justin answers this objection later in the *Dialogue* (chaps. 48–54) by informing Trypho that Elijah had in fact appeared and that he did anoint the Christ. Justin followed the New Testament authors in understanding John the Baptist as Elijah and baptism as the anointing of Christ.

Trypho's conclusion about Christianity is clear and direct: "And you, having accepted a groundless report, invent some Christ for yourselves and for his sake are perishing inconsiderately" (ὑμεῖς δέ, ματαίαν ἀκοὴν παραδεξάμενοι, Χριστὸν ἑαυτοῖς τινα ἀναπλάσσετε καὶ αὐτοῦ χάριντα νῦν ἀσκόπως ἀπόλλυσθε). According to Trypho, Christians have ignorantly believed an unfounded account of the messiah and have invented an elaborate gospel to manufacture the details of Jesus' life. Even more appalling than their gullibility was the fact that they were dying for this pseudo-messiah.

---

50 Stanton, "The Law of Moses and the Law of Christ," 106.

The outline of the *Dialogue* comes from these succinct comments of Trypho. Throughout the remainder of this work Justin addresses the two concerns Trypho raised, namely the efficacy of the Mosaic law and the coming of the messiah. At the minimum, chapter 8 demonstrates the legalistic nature of second-century Judaism, whether real or perceived.[51] More than a few scholars have argued that Justin is accurately portraying Palestinian Judaism of his day, to the point that E. R. Goodenough said, "Throughout the Dialogue Justin shows the most unexpected acquaintance with the details of Palestinian Judaistic teaching."[52] Trypho highlights the boundary markers as necessary works of salvation, which will become clear in the following sections since Justin calls these "works of righteousness."

Dialogue 10

Before exegeting the remaining passages, it is needful first to show that Christians' failure to keep the law was the primary issue at hand. In chapter 10, Justin asks Trypho, "Is there any accusation you have against us other than this, that we do not observe the Law, nor circumcise the flesh as your forefathers did, nor observe the Sabbath as you do?"[53] To this Trypho answers,

> But this is what we are most puzzled about, that you who claim to be pious and believe yourselves to be different from the others do not segregate yourselves from them, nor do you observe a manner of life different from that of the Gentiles, for you do not keep the feasts or Sabbaths, nor do you practice the rite of circumcision. You place your hope in a crucified man, and still expect to receive favors from God when you disregard his commandments.[54]

---

[51] Both sides contended over boundary markers. In a summary statement, Graham Stanton observed, "Justin's *Dialogue* indicates that in the middle of the second century both Judaism and Christianity were concerned to maintain tight boundaries" (Stanton, "'God-Fearers': Neglected Evidence in Justin Martyr's *Dialogue with Trypho*," 49).
[52] Goodenough, *The Theology of Justin Martyr*, 95. Cf. Shotwell who claims that instead of thinking of Justin first as a philosopher, "it is necessary to consider Justin as an interpreter influenced greatly by Palestinian Judaism" (Shotwell, *Biblical Exegesis of Justin Martyr*, 116). Of course one needs to consider the dates of these publications. Much work has been done on Judaism during this time that casts doubt on these older positions.
[53] *Dial.* 10.1; Falls, *Dialogue with Trypho*, 18. In the next part of this question Justin also asks if Christians are despised because of the rumors that had circulated about them that they are cannibals and engage in illicit sexual relationships. For Trypho, the problem is that Christians do not keep the law.
[54] *Dial.* 10.3; Falls, *Dialogue with Trypho*, 18.

Justin was correct to perceive that the main issue for Trypho is that Christians do not keep the law. Trypho cannot comprehend how Christians believe that God favors them and yet they do not obey his simplest commands. Christians profess to be pious apart from the law, but piety only comes through obedience to what God has revealed. They place their hopes on a crucified man (ἐπ' ἄνθρωπον σταυρωθέντα τὰς ἐλπίδας ποιούμενοι), Jesus, as though that were enough to save them. He seems to understand accurately the Christian position of justification by faith apart from works in what he says here. Christians rely on this man and do not practice works of the law, an idea that obviously flabbergasts Trypho. Trypho then challenges Justin, "If, therefore, you can defend yourself on these things, and make it manifest in what way you hope for anything whatsoever, even though you do not observe the law, this we would very gladly hear from you" (Εἰ οὖν ἔχεις πρὸς ταῦτα ἀπολογήσασθαι, καὶ ἐπιδεῖξαι ᾧτινι τρόπῳ ἐλπίζετε ὁτιοῦν, κἂν μὴ φυλάσσοντες τὸν νόμον, τοῦτό σου ἡδέως ἀκούσαιμεν μάλιστα). Trypho calls for an ἀπολογία from the great Apologist, and Justin delivers with over a hundred chapters of defense.[55]

Dialogue 23 and 92

While Justin spends an exorbitant amount of space answering Trypho's objection, two chapters in particular are crucial for understanding Justin's overall argument. In these chapters Justin makes an argument so close to that made by Paul in Romans and Galatians that it is almost inconceivable that he is not borrowing from the Apostle. Justin believed his case to Trypho in chapter 23 was so important that he felt compelled "on account of those who came today," that is, the second day of the dialogue, "to repeat nearly all the same thing" (*Dial.* 92.5; διὰ δὲ τοὺς σήμερον ἐλθόντας καὶ τὰ αὐτὰ σχεδὸν πάντα βούλομαι ἀναλαμβάνειν). He does not choose to repeat all his material, so the repetition in chapter 92 should not pass by unnoticed.

---

[55] Even the chapters devoted to proving that Jesus is the Messiah are a response to Trypho's inquiry about Christians and the law. Christians no longer follow the law because the Messiah has come. Shotwell, who shows little sensitivity for Jesus' and Paul's positive comments on the Law, says, "Jesus criticized the Law, but Paul carried his criticism to rejection" (Shotwell, *Biblical Exegesis of Justin Martyr*, 51). Paul carried this attitude because he had a Christocentric interpretation of the Old Testament, including the law, and Justin picks up on this Pauline theme (Shotwell, *Biblical Exegesis of Justin Martyr*, 50 – 1).

Justin's plan of attack was to prove that salvation came before circumcision and the laws concerning the Sabbath; therefore, these works cannot be necessary in order to earn God's mercy. Circumcision in a sense functions as shorthand for the entire ritual law. As Jeffrey Siker notes, "The most important contexts in which Abraham appears revolve around discussions about circumcision,"[56] because, as he goes on to say, "Justin repeatedly links ritual law with circumcision, so that we may see circumcision as the focal point of the dispute. If circumcision falls, the rest of the ritual law goes with it."[57] And Justin wants to see the entire ritual law topple. In chapter 23 Justin argues,

> For if circumcision was not required before the time of Abraham, and if there was no need of Sabbaths, festivals, and sacrifices before Moses, they are not needed now, when, in accordance with the will of God, Jesus Christ, his Son, has been born of the Virgin Mary, a descendant of Abraham.[58]

Those before Abraham were not circumcised and those before Moses did not keep the Sabbath, yet no one doubts that salvation was possible before them. And now that Christ has come, there is no more need of these practices. Though the argument is very similar in chapter 92, it is worth citing from there as well because of a few significant additions:

> For, if anyone were to ask you why, when Enoch, and Noah with his children, and any others like them, were pleasing to God without being circumcised or without observing the Sabbath, God required by new leaders and another law, after the lapse of so many generations, that those who lived between the times of Abraham and Moses should be justified by circumcision, and that those who lived after Moses be justified by both circumcision and the other precepts, that is, the Sabbaths, sacrifices, burnt offerings, and oblations, [God would be unjustly criticized] unless you point out, as I have already said, that God in his foreknowledge was aware that your people would deserve to be expelled from Jerusalem and never be allowed to enter there.[59]

How is it, Justin wants to know, that many people in the Old Testament were "justified" before God apart from circumcision and the Sabbath? If these works are essential to gain God's favor, as Trypho argued in chapter 8, then how could so many people be spoken of as righteous in the Old Testament without ever having been circumcised or kept a Sabbath? Evidently, there were many

---

[56] Jeffrey S. Siker, *Disinheriting the Jews: Abraham in Early Christian Controversy* (Louisville: Westminster/John Knox, 1991), 164–65.
[57] Siker, *Disinheriting the Jews*, 166.
[58] *Dial.* 23.3; Falls, *Dialogue with Trypho*, 37–8.
[59] *Dial.* 92.2; Falls, *Dialogue with Trypho*, 142.

who were justified in their uncircumcision just as there were many justified who were circumcised. It cannot stand to reason, then, that it was the circumcision that justified the latter group since the former group was also justified in their uncircumcision. Circumcision, the cherished rite of the Jews, was a sign of God's covenant with Abraham, but many were born and died long before the sign of circumcision was given.[60]

All of chapter 19 is taken up with this very point. Justin speaks of Adam, Abel, Enoch, Lot, Noah, and Melchizedek who were justified before God but were never circumcised. Likewise, the Sabbath was given as a sign because of the hardness of Israel's heart (*Dial.* 18), never as a work of righteousness. None of the patriarchs observed the Sabbath, for the Sabbath laws were not instituted until Moses. Were these people outside of God's mercy before this? Most certainly not, says Justin, whose point is evident—neither circumcision nor the Sabbath, nor any other work of the Law, can be practiced to gain God's mercy because many were justified before these laws were enacted.

In both chapters 23 and 92 Justin looks to Abraham for proof that justification existed apart from circumcision on the basis of faith, an argument he most likely took from Paul. Justin writes in 23.4,

> Indeed, *while Abraham himself was still uncircumcised, he was justified and blessed by God because of his faith in him,* as the Scripture tells us. Furthermore, the Scriptures and the facts of the case force us to admit that Abraham received circumcision for a sign, not for justification itself.[61]

And again in 92.3–4,

> Abraham, indeed, was considered just, not by reason of his circumcision, but because of his faith. For, before his circumcision it was said of him, *Abraham believed God, and it was reputed to him unto justice.* We also, therefore, because of our belief in God through Christ, even though we are uncircumcised in the flesh, have the salutary circumcision, namely, that of the heart, and we thereby hope to be just and pleasing to God, since we have already obtained this testimony from him through the words of the prophets.[62]

In keeping with his fondness of quoting the Old Testament and not the New, Justin cites Genesis 15:6 for his text. The LXX of Genesis 15:6 reads, "καὶ ἐπίστευσεν Αβραμ τῷ θεῷ, καὶ ἐλογίσθη αὐτῷ εἰς δικαιοσύνην," an almost direct citation in 92.3, whereas in 23.4 he appears to paraphrase the idea. Still, the climax of Jus-

---

[60] See Allert, *Revelation, Truth, Canon and Interpretation,* 226–27.
[61] Falls, *Dialogue with Trypho,* 38, emphasis original.
[62] Falls, *Dialogue with Trypho,* 143, emphasis original.

tin's argument is that Abraham, and those who came before him, were justified by their faith.[63] Justin, like Paul, appealed to Genesis 15 as his prooftext.[64]

Paul also uses Abraham as his illustration for justification apart from circumcision in Romans 4 and Galatians 3 where he too quotes Genesis 15.[65] Abraham was justified by faith before the sign of circumcision was given to him and his descendents. Paul quotes Genesis 15:6 in Galatians 3:5–9, where he says,

ὁ οὖν ἐπιχορηγῶν ὑμῖν τὸ πνεῦμα καὶ ἐνεργῶν δυνάμεις ἐν ὑμῖν, ἐξ ἔργων νόμου ἢ ἐξ ἀκοῆς πίστεως; καθὼς Ἀβραὰμ ἐπίστευσεν τῷ θεῷ, καὶ ἐλογίσθη αὐτῷ εἰς δικαιοσύνην· Γινώσκετε ἄρα ὅτι οἱ ἐκ πίστεως, οὗτοι υἱοί εἰσιν Ἀβραάμ. προϊδοῦσα δὲ ἡ γραφὴ ὅτι ἐκ πίστεως δικαιοῖ τὰ ἔθνη ὁ θεός, προευηγγελίσατο τῷ Ἀβραὰμ ὅτι Ἐνευλογηθήσονται ἐν σοὶ πάντα τὰ ἔθνη· ὥστε οἱ ἐκ πίστεως εὐλογοῦνται σὺν τῷ πιστῷ Ἀβραάμ.

Paul rhetorically asks the Galatians whether they received the Spirit by "works of the Law" (ἐξ ἔργων νόμου) or by "hearing with faith" (ἐξ ἀκοῆς πίστεως). The faith that justified Abraham is the same faith that now justifies Gentiles, among whom Justin is numbered. Justin makes this abundantly clear in *Dialogue* 92.4 when he says "and we, therefore, in the uncircumcision of our flesh, believing God through Christ ... hope to appear righteous before and well-pleasing to God." Believing in God through Christ is the sole condition that will give Justin and other Christians a righteous standing before God; circumcision avails nothing, which is why he continued uncircumcised.[66]

---

63 See Siker, *Disinheriting the Jews*, 163–84. Siker argues that "Justin uses Abraham to render the Jews orphaned, without legitimate claim to Abraham as their father in any meaningful way." Abraham is critical for Justin's argument, and, as Siker observes, Justin "appeals to Abraham over one hundred times (103 to be exact)" (163).

64 Siker, *Disinheriting the Jews*, 166. Siker gives this caveat: "Although Justin's use of Abraham ... closely parallels much of what we find in Paul (Romans 4; Galatians 3), Justin could never affirm Paul's assertion in Romans 3:1–2" (168). For Paul, circumcision was given as a blessing to the Jews; for Justin, circumcision is a curse (168). Paul's heart for the Jews as fellow kinsmen was not shared by Justin, a Gentile.

65 As Stylianopoulos notes, "While Justin never refers to Paul, nor does he explicitly quote him, his interpretation of Abraham as an example of justification through faith, not through circumcision, is nevertheless strikingly Pauline and cannot be explained solely on the basis of Genesis 15 ff" (*Justin Martyr and the Mosaic Law*, 116). He goes on to say, "It is thoroughly possible that at least the ultimate reference to Justin's use of the Genesis text is Paul. The indications, however, which definitely link Justin with the Apostle have to do with the content of Justin's argument about Abraham. This argument seems to presuppose in particular Romans 4 more than Genesis 15 ff" (117). Justin's conceptual link to Abraham has more in common with Paul than the mere quotation of the same Old Testament text.

66 If Justin's use of Gal 3 is not abundantly obvious from this text, then it may help to see another place in the *Dial.* where Justin must have a knowledge of this epistle. In *Dial.* 95 Justin

The connection to Romans 4 is even more apparent. The purpose of Romans 4, as Thomas Schreiner puts it, is that "Paul wants to demonstrate that Abraham, the fountainhead of the Jewish people, was justified by faith and that it was always God's intention to bless the Gentiles through Abraham."[67] Genesis 15:6 is the key text in Paul's sustained argument that justification comes by faith and not through keeping the law. Even Abraham, who was circumcised, was justified prior to his circumcision. As Paul maintained that Abraham "σημεῖον ἔλαβεν περιτομῆς σφραγῖδα τῆς δικαιοσύνης τῆς πίστεως τῆς ἐν τῇ ἀκροβυστίᾳ, εἰς τὸ εἶναι αὐτὸν πατέρα πάτων τῶν πιστευόντων δι' ἀκροβυστίας, εἰς τὸ λογισθῆναι [καὶ] αὐτοῖς [τὴν] διακιοσύνην" (Rom 4:11). Justin appropriates Paul's argument in the same twofold way. Like Abraham, Justin and many Gentile believers were uncircumcised but their hope is that they will be justified by faith just as Abraham was before his circumcision. It is also Justin's purpose to prove that salvation has come to the Gentiles and that they too look to Abraham as their spiritual father.[68] Justin and Paul share remarkable similarity in their arguments. Werline goes so far as to suggest, "Several of Justin's arguments directly rely on Paul's thinking. For example, Justin probably has Galatians 3 before him as he composes *Dialogue* 95–96."[69]

Justin even admits to using the apostles in drafting his doctrine of justification, particularly in his appeal to Abraham. Of Abraham, he writes, "For, just as he believed the voice of God, and was thereby justified, so have we likewise believed the voice of God (which was spoken again to us by the prophets and the apostles of Christ), and have renounced all worldly things even to death."[70] At issue in this text is the call to renounce the things of this world, but Justin points to Abraham's justification by faith and explicitly connects this to what he learned from Christ's apostles. Abraham forsook the pleasures of the world

---

takes up the issue of Jesus' crucifixion on a tree, which is a curse in the Old Testament. Stylianopoulos compares Deut 27:26 (LXX) with Gal 3:10 and *Dial.* 95.1 as well as Deut 21:23 (LXX) with Gal 3:13 and *Dial.* 96.1 and twice calls the parallel "strikingly Pauline" (Stylianopoulos, *Justin Martyr and the Mosaic Law*, 103–05). *Pace* Sibinga who thinks that the difference in the quotations renders a Pauline connection less viable (Sibinga, *The Old Testament Text of Justin Martyr*, 98–99). Justin modifies the words in order to suit his own argument that is slightly different than Paul's (Stylianopoulos, *Justin Martyr and the Mosaic Law*, 106).

67 Thomas Schreiner, *Romans*, BECNT (Grand Rapids: Baker Academic, 1998), 209.
68 Werline, "The Transformation of Pauline Arguments," 84.
69 Werline, "Transformation of Pauline Arguments," 80.
70 *Dial.* 119.6. Falls, *Dialogue with Trypho*, 179. The Greek text brings out the notion of imputation (ἐλογίσθη αὐτῷ εἰς δικαιοσύνη), where Falls' translation does not.

when he decided to believe the promises of God, just as Justin had. Following God and trusting in his promises equates to righteousness.[71]

A major question remains—is there any place, then, for circumcision? At one point Trypho asks Justin, "But if someone ... after he recognizes that this man is Christ, and has believed in and trusted[72] Him, wishes, namely, to observe these things, will he be saved?" (*Dial.* 47). Trypho wants to know if circumcision and Sabbath keeping entirely preclude the possibility of salvation. Suppose, he says, that a person believes in Christ, can he still be circumcised and keep the Sabbath if he wishes? Justin's main concern is that this person would not try to persuade others to follow this course. And then he says, "This you also did at the beginning of the discourse, when you declared that I would not be saved unless I observed these things." Justin recalls chapter 8 where Trypho told him that he must do all the things in the law if he wishes to be saved. This, Justin says, a person should not do.[73] But it is possible that one could

---

[71] It is not uncommon for scholars to argue that Justin has personal righteousness in mind. Even Stanton sees a divergence in Justin from Paul. He writes, "In a quite un-Pauline way Justin urges Trypho to follow his example and pay attention to the words of Christ" (Stanton, "The Law of Moses and the Law of Christ," 105). At a fundamental level, this is no different than Paul who said, "Follow my example as I follow the example of Christ" (1 Cor 11:1; cf. Skarsaunne who shows parallels from the *Dial.* to 1 Cor, though concluding, "there is no certain borowing [sic] from 1 Cor in Justin" [*Proof from Prophecy*, 99]. Regardless of whether or not he borrowed from 1 Cor, it is not un-Pauline to speak of imitation, rather it is thoroughly Pauline). What Justin had in mind by righteousness must also be determined. The biblical passages cited above make Stanton's point difficult to sustain. There are, however, other passages which lean in this direction, for instance *Dial.* 95.3: "If you would say this while you repent for your wicked actions, and acknowledge Jesus to be the Christ, and observe his precepts, then, as I said before, you will receive remission of your sins" (Falls, *Dialogue with Trypho*, 146–7). The argument could be made that Justin has introduced works into salvation by the inclusion of following Christ's precepts. In fact, this statement could be seen as tantamount to Trypho telling Justin that one must observe all the law in order to be saved, but this is a hasty conclusion. The early fathers do not seem to possess a category that comes later in church history of ordering when works play into salvation. But Justin does not say anything that would conflict with Paul on this. Earlier in the *Dial.*, in fact, he does give a better ordering: "There is no other way [to be saved] than this, that you come to know our Christ, be baptized with the baptism which cleanses you of sin (as Isaiah testified) and thus live a life free of sin" (*Dial.* 44:4; Falls, *Dialogue with Trypho*, 67). The sole condition here when he addresses how to become a Christian is to come to Christ and be baptized. Only after this is a person exhorted to live a life free from sin. The condition of works postdates salvation by faith.
[72] LSJ, s.v. "πείθω" (B.II) on πείθεσθαί τινι as "believe, trust in ..." as opposed to "be persuaded" or "obey" in this context.
[73] Stanton puts it well: "Neither Paul nor Justin will tolerate Jewish Christians who stress continuity and who are not in full fellowship with Gentile Christians, nor will either tolerate Jewish

keep portions of the law and still be saved, so long as he has believed that Jesus is the messiah and does not try to persuade others to keep the law. He reasons thus:

> But if some, due to their instability of will, desire to observe as many of the Mosaic precepts as possible—precepts which we think were instituted because of your hardness of heart—while at the same time they place their hope in Christ, and if they desire to perform the eternal and natural acts of justice and piety, yet wish to live with us Christians and believers, as I already stated, not persuading them to be circumcised like themselves, or to observe the Sabbath, or to perform any other similar acts, then it is my opinion that we Christians should receive them and associate with them in every way as kinsmen and brethren. But if any of your people, Trypho, profess their belief in Christ, and at the same time force the Gentiles who believe in Christ to observe the Law instituted through Moses, or refuse to share with them this same common life, I certainly will also not approve of them. But I think that those Gentiles who have been induced to follow the practices of the Jewish Law, and at the same time profess their faith in the Christ of God, will probably be saved.[74]

Many important ideas surface in this quotation. First, Justin does not forbid salvation to those who keep portions of the law in addition to their faith in Christ, even though he does not prefer it.[75] Second, obedience to the law is weak-mindedness and should not be thought to add anything to salvation. Third, "hope in Christ" is the salvific cry, or the *sine qua non*, of Christians. Fourth, those who have professed Christ but have returned to the law for the hope of their salvation will not be saved unless they repent of this travesty before death.

Justin does not entirely wish to jettison the idea of circumcision, only physical circumcision. Justin pleads with Trypho to "be circumcised rather in your

---

Christians who persuade Gentile Christians to keep the law" (Stanton, "The Law of Moses and the Law of Christ," 102).

74 *Dial.* 47.3 – 4; Falls, *Dialogue with Trypho*, 71–72.

75 *Pace* Werline who thinks that Justin has such a supercessionism that he would not hold any place for those who hold to portions of the law. According to Werline, Justin borrowed Paul's ideas and exegetical arguments ("Transformation of Pauline Arguments," 92), but he "ignores the original contexts of Paul's letters and reads them through his own sociohistorical setting and theological agenda" (93). His sociological setting referring to the Bar Kochba rebellion and laws against Jews that Hadrian had enacted. Regarding Gal 3, Paul does not use Abraham as a way to say that Christians are accepted but Jews are not. Rather, "both Jews and Gentiles inherit the promise made to Abraham. Justin, however, has employed Paul's argument but has transformed it by coupling it with his ideas of the new covenant, new people, and understanding of the Hebrew prophets as witnesses to Jewish unfaithfulness and rejection" (Werline, "Transformation of Pauline Arguments," 86). This seems to be an unfair reading of Justin. Justin recognizes that in Christ there is ultimate fulfillment of the promises to Abraham which are realized in the new covenant community, the new Israel. These ideas are germane to Paul's thoughts as well.

heart, as the above-quoted words of God demand" (*Dial.* 15.7).⁷⁶ Believers in Christ are those τῆς ἀληθινῆς περιτομῆς (*Dial.* 41.4) who are circumcised of the heart (*Dial.* 92.4).⁷⁷ Of course Justin appears to be dependent on Paul here as well, for Paul urges the Jews to see that circumcision is a matter of the heart and not of the flesh (Rom 2:29). After Justin adequately demonstrated that neither circumcision nor Sabbaths can earn salvation, Trypho perceptively asks, "Do I understand you to say ... that none of us Jews will inherit anything on the holy mountain of God?" (*Dial.* 25.6).⁷⁸ He recognizes that Justin has dismantled his concept of salvation, and that should he not receive circumcision of the heart, then he will not enjoy the holy mountain of God, a circumlocution for heaven. For Justin, one receives circumcision of the heart through repentance and belief in the Christ. In *Dialogue* 24 Justin informs Trypho that "the blood of circumcision is now abolished, and we now trust in the blood of salvation. Now another covenant, another law has gone forth from Zion, Jesus Christ."⁷⁹ Earlier Justin contended, "that bath of salvation which [Isaiah] mentioned and which was for the repentant, who are no longer made pure by the blood of goats and sheep, or by the ashes of a heifer, or by the offerings of fine flour, but by faith through the blood and the death of Christ, who suffered death for this precise purpose" (*Dial.* 13.1).⁸⁰ With more than an echo of Hebrews, Justin makes plain that the rituals and ceremonies of the law, be it circumcision, Sabbath keeping, or sacrifices, all fall short in their ability to save in light of the "new covenant"(διαθήκην καινὴν) (*Dial.* 11).⁸¹ The blood of Christ washes away the

---

76 Falls, *Dialogue with Trypho*, 27.
77 P. J. Donahue wrestles with Justin's sustained polemic against circumcision. On one hand, Justin desperately wants to show that circumcision avails nothing, while simultaneously not going the route of Marcion who completely cast off the Old Testament. The solution for Justin, Donahue argues, is to locate circumcision in God's immutability. God did give circumcision to the Jewish people and he continues to require circumcision, only now the circumcision is of the heart. See P. J. Donahue, "Jewish-Christian Controversy in the Second Century: A Study in the 'Dialogue' of Justin Martyr" (Ph.D. diss., Yale University, 1973), 150–74.
78 Falls, *Dialogue with Trypho*, 40.
79 Falls, *Dialogue with Trypho*, 38.
80 Falls, *Dialogue with Trypho*, 22. Following the citation given above, Justin launches into a very long citation from Isa 52–54. A Christological interpretation of Isa 53 figures prominently in the *Dial.* For Justin, Isa 53 served more than just as a proof-text for Jesus as the Messiah, it also had a liturgical and catechetical function. See D. Jeffrey Bingham, "Justin and Isaiah 53," *VC* 53 (2000): 261.
81 Stylianopoulos believes that Justin used Hebrews, especially in his interpretation of Melchizedek in Hebrews 7, though we cannot be certain (*Justin Martyr and the Mosaic Law*, 115–16). See also Skarsaunne, *Proof from Prophecy*, 107–08, for Justin's use of Hebrews.

sin of the repentant believer as the individual is transformed through the only circumcision that ever mattered—the circumcision of the heart.

Dialogue 137

In keeping with the topic of circumcision, which permeates the *Dial.* from beginning to end, there is an important passage in chapter 137. Justin, in a last ditch effort to convert Trypho, entreats his Jewish counterparts, saying,

> For it would be wonderful if you in obedience to the Scriptures would be circumcised from the hardness of your heart, not with the circumcision which you have according to your deep-rooted idea, for the Scriptures convince us that such a circumcision was given as a sign and not as a work of righteousness. Act in accord with us, therefore, and do not insult the Son of God; ignore your Pharisaic teachers and do not scorn the king of Israel (as the chiefs of your synagogues instruct you to do after prayers).[82]

As if he had not hammered on this anvil long enough, Justin strikes once more to see if he might ignite a spark in his listeners' hearts. He wants them to realize that he has argued almost exclusively from the Scriptures to show what the original intention of circumcision was.

Two things stand out in this passage—circumcision as a "work of righteousness" and the remark about the Pharisaic teachers. Justin speaks of Pharisaic teachers in a derogatory way, as though the title Pharisee carried with it a connotation of legalism. He issues a firm warning not to follow the Pharisees who were ridiculing the Son of God and encouraging the Jews to place their hope in their circumcision.

The second remarkable comment in this passage is Justin's calling circumcision a δικαιοπραξίας ἔργον. Amazingly, δικαιοπραξίας ἔργον along with ἔργον δικαιοσύνης have gone without notice by commentators on Justin, and yet these phrases summarize his view of the law and add weight to his connection to Paul, though perhaps indirectly. In chapter 137 circumcision is considered a δικαιοπραξίας ἔργον and in chapters 23 circumcision is labeled an ἔργον δικαιοσύνης, phrases that appear to be synonymous in Justin. Δικαιοπραξίας ἔργον is a neologism meaning "doing a righteous work," though the appendage of ἔργον seems superfluous.[83] The word itself means to "do righteousness" so it is unclear

---

[82] *Dial.* 137.1–2; Falls, *Dialogue with Trypho*, 206.
[83] Δικαιοπραξίας also occurs in *Dial.* 46.7 where it is unaccompanied by ἔργον. Besides the *Dial.*, Lampe has no other entries for this word.

why he would add ἔργον, unless perhaps, it is used to conjure up Paul's memorable, but controversial, phrase ἔργα νόμου. Justin understands Jews to practice deeds like circumcision and Sabbath keeping as ways to earn righteousness. When in the throes of the most passionate parts of his argument, Justin forcefully claims that Trypho must stop believing that circumcision can make one righteous. Justin's point is that circumcision was never intended to be a work or righteousness but rather was given because of hardheartedness. The similarity to Paul is noticeable but the slight modification of terms (i.e., δικαιοπραξίας ἔργον instead of ἔργα νόμου) strengthens the argument because Justin's own voice is heard.

Circumcision, Justin argues, was always meant to be a sign and nothing more. If circumcision could bring righteousness, then why can only men receive it? Are women not able to be righteous, if circumcision is performed as an act of righteousness? (*Dial.* 23.5). The fact that women cannot receive circumcision proves (δείκνυσιν) that circumcision is a σημεῖον and not an ἔργον δικαιοσύνης. This argument is original to Justin and sufficiently proves, he thinks, that circumcision cannot be a work of righteousness.[84]

6.5 Conclusion

Justin Martyr gave the first full-fledged account of how Jesus fulfilled Old Testament prophecy. Though his exegesis is occasionally presented in colorful allegory, most of his interpretations remain the standard responses today of how Jesus was foretold long before his coming. He not only quoted the prophets at length, but he also borrowed arguments he had learned from the apostles, especially Paul. The substance of the *Dialogue* comes as a direct response to Trypho's legalistic claim that if Justin wants to obtain salvation, then he must be circumcised, keep the Sabbath, and do all the things written in the law (*Dial.* 8). Justin, trying to convert Trypho, vehemently argues that the law cannot save and that Jesus is the one to whom the Old Testament points.

As part of his argument, Justin uses Genesis 15:6 to prove to Trypho that justification anteceded circumcision. If Abraham was justified before his circumcision, then it was not his circumcision that saved him—it was faith that justified Abraham. His point is that Christians are likewise justified on the basis of belief in the Lord's Messiah. Justin perceived that Trypho was clinging to these practices as "works of righteousness" as his basis of salvific hope and so Justin deals

---

[84] Lieu calls this a "surprising and novel appeal to female experience" (*Image and Reality*, 120).

with the impotence of the law at length. Throughout, Justin employs an argument very similar to Paul's use of Abraham in Galatians 3 and Romans 4.

While others have observed legalism in the *Dialogue*, and some of those have even rightly made the connection to Paul, few have taken the positive step of acknowledging that Justin held a view similar to the so-called "traditional" Pauline view of justification. Trypho placed his hope in his circumcision and other aspects of the law but Justin placed his hope in the Christ. At the center of their debate was one question—how can a person receive God's mercy? Herein lies the great difference between the two of them and they both spent two days trying to win the other person to their persuasion. Alas, neither was successful and so they parted company.

7 Conclusion

How did the second-century fathers understand justification? Through the paraenetic letter of *1 Clement*, the valedictory words of Ignatius of Antioch, the apologetic response to Diognetus, the Odist's hymnal, and Justin's two-day dialogue with Trypho, the answer emerges—a doctrine of justification by faith was preserved and propagated in the second century, despite the near ubiquitous claim that those in the second century made a decisive turn to works righteousness. Concerning the Apostolic Fathers in particular (but a comment that could easily extend to the rest of the second-century authors), Michael Holmes perceptively observes that they "have often been criticized, for example, for 'falling away' from the purity or high level of the apostolic faith and teaching, or for institutionalizing or otherwise restricting the freedom of the gospel. Such comments, however, generally reveal more about the perspective of the person making them than they do about those being criticized."[1]

Holmes strikes at the heart of the issue. The historical research conducted on this epoch has reflected the theological sensitivities of the historians who have come to study it, more than it has been an honest assessment of the sources. Those in the Tübingen School believed Paul was captive to the Gnostics, and T. F. Torrance thought the Apostolic Fathers forsook Paul's doctrine of grace, and thereby justification by faith. Justification was more often than not an ancillary concern for those trying to understand the reception of Paul. They were much more concerned about the figure of Paul and his letters, but nevertheless, there were occasions when they appealed to the Apostle for his doctrine on justification.

Of course the response could return that this study is also guilty of reading these documents through a particular lens. To be sure, no one is entirely immune from his or her own historical situation, as Hans-Georg Gadamer has insightfully shown.[2] However, the goal has been to let the text speak for itself and then show how that reading fits within the larger context of the work. It would be a mistake and an overstatement to argue that there was consensus on justification in the second century, much less on Pauline theology as a whole. Thus, the portrait of justification in the fathers cannot be painted with the broad stroke of one brush. There was no more complete agreement among the fathers in the second century then there has been in any other century since. Yet for the sources exam-

---

[1] Michael Holmes, *The Apostolic Fathers*, 3rd ed. (Grand Rapids: Baker Academic, 2007), 4.
[2] Hans-Georg Gadamer, *Truth and Method*, trans. J. Weinsheimer and D. G. Marshall, 2nd ed. (London: Continuum, 2004), 267–382.

ined in this study, there is remarkable continuity, which will come as a surprise to many who had written off justification by faith in the fathers.

To begin with, it was necessary to demonstrate that Paul had gained a prominent place in second-century Christianity. By the dawn of the second century, Christian writers could appeal to the Apostle Paul as an authority on doctrinal issues. Not, perhaps, in the sense that Paul's words carried the sole basis of orthodoxy, but they did believe that using Paul's epistles and his arguments would advance their cause.[3] As a figure, Paul served as an example of Christian morality and faithfulness, having suffered martyrdom for his stalwart commitment to Christ. As a writer, Paul's letters were collected, read, and elevated to a position of Scriptural authority. And, as it has been shown, Paul served as a doctrinal sounding board, giving the church a basic theological vocabulary with which they could express their faith.[4] Paul had many heirs in the next century, even though he is rarely mentioned, and in the majority of the sources examined here (*Epistle to Diognetus*, *Odes of Solomon*, and *Dialogue with Trypho*), he is not even named. Regardless, as the evidence has demonstrated, Paul exercised a deep influence over those who followed him.

The study commenced with a look at justification in *1 Clement*. Clement wrote a paranaetic letter to the dysfunctional Corinthian church that was on the precipice of ruin. Factions were threatening to overtake the church and it was Clement's purpose to encourage them to submit to their elders. In order to convey this message to the rebellious individuals in the congregation, Clement flooded his letter with moral exhortations, beseeching the Corinthians to follow the exemplary behavior of the saints who had preceded them. He even states that one is justified not by words but by works (*1 Clem.* 30.3). Because of this, Clement is often labeled as an advocate for works righteousness and the first of the fathers to deny Paul's view of justification by faith, which was Torrance's contention. But, Clement says with equal passion that everyone who has ever been justified is justified in the same way—through faith (*1 Clem.* 32.4). To discard Clement as hopelessly confused or ignorantly contradictory is to misread him.

---

[3] See Andreas Lindemann, "Paul in the Writings of the Apostolic Fathers," in *Paul and the Legacies of Paul*, ed. William S. Babcock (Dallas: Southern Methodist University Press, 1990), 28–29. For an example of how other apostles, such as Peter, were seen as authorities, see Markus Bockmuehl, *The Remembered Peter: in Ancient Reception and Modern Debate*, WUNT 262 (Tübingen: Mohr Siebeck, 2010).

[4] Daniel Marguerat gives three taxonomic poles around which the reception of Paul should be gauged—documentary, biographical, and doctrinal. See Daniel Marguerat, "Paul après Paul: une histoire de reception," *NTS* 54 (2008): 317–37.

There are two ways to solve the apparent discrepancy that do not accuse Clement of inconsistency. First, it could be argued that Clement is unconsciously bridging the gap between Paul and James, as Lightfoot had done. Lightfoot maintained that Clement was faithfully holding onto Paul's doctrine of justification by faith and James's doctrine of justification by works, and that he held these in tandem with justification by faith logically preceding justification by works. To say this another way, Paul looks at the frontside of justification as a matter of how one is saved, whereas James, unsatisfied with empty professions of faith, desired to see spiritual fruit. Clement informs the believers that they are justified through faith (like Paul) but that this faith must result in works (like James), the precise connection he makes in the opening verses of chapter 33.

The other solution is to see Clement as consistent with Paul himself without introducing James into the fray. The key here is Romans 5–6 where Paul lays out the indicative of salvation and then follows it up with imperatives. Clement makes a similar argument, informing them that they are justified by faith (indicative) but that they then must seek to do good works (imperative). Clement knew of Paul (*1 Clem* 5.5) and used him for his doctrine of justification by faith.

Chapter 3 explored the seven authentic letters of Ignatius of Antioch. Only one pertinent reference to justification occurs in these letters (*Phld* 8.2), but there are a host of other themes that have a direct bearing on his view of justification. For starters, Ignatius is an important player in the so-called "parting of the ways" between Judaism and Christianity. Ignatius's invective against Judaizers reflects his disdain towards Christians who continue to follow Jewish customs. In particular, Ignatius thinks that circumcision and Sabbath-keeping are absurd and out of place for those who have come to faith in Jesus. The law cannot benefit anyone. Ignatius is also fond of using the phrase "faith and love" (occurring sixteen times) which typifies his soteriology. Faith in and love for Christ and others is the path to salvation, which he sees as intertwined with the Gospel itself. For Ignatius, the Gospel is not as much a written document as it is the narrative of Jesus' death and resurrection. He derives this concept from Paul and he even connects it to justification in *Phld* 8.2, where he writes, "But for me, the 'archives' are Jesus Christ, the unalterable archives are his cross and death and his resurrection and the faith that comes through him; by these things I want, through your prayers, to be justified."[5] Finally, there has been a lot of confusion surrounding Ignatius's lust for martyrdom. He is gritty in detail as he describes getting torn to shreds by the beasts that await him in Rome (*Rom.* 5). Martyrdom needs to be better understood in Ignatius. It is not as though the act of martyr-

---

5 Holmes, *The Apostolic Fathers*, 243.

dom will save him; rather, his obedience unto death will prove his justification valid.

The *Epistle to Diognetus* (chap. 4), the enigma of the second century (in that very little is known about the provenance of the letter), contains the clearest reference to justification by faith in the second century. In answering the third question posed by Diognetus, namely, why Christianity has sprung into existence now and not at a former time, the author explains why God passed over sins in his forebearance, awaiting the time that he would send his Son as a ransom (*Diog.* 9.2). Those guilty of sin could only be justified by the righteousness of the Son (*Diog.* 9.2–4), an unmistakable reference to forensic justification. These twin ideas of substitution and justification led the author to exclaim: "O the sweet exchange, O the incomprehensible work of God, O the unexpected blessings, that the sinfulness of many should be hidden in one righteous person, while the righteousness of one should justify many sinners!"[6] Sinners are justified through faith in the substitutionary exchange, the righteous for the unrighteous. Although Paul is not explicitly cited, there is little doubt that the author of *Diognetus* has leaned heavily upon the Apostle for his view of justification.

The *Odes of Solomon*, the subject of chapter 5, is an untapped treasure trove of the second century. Representing the east, the *Odes* is the earliest known hymnal in the church and was in all likelihood composed by a Jewish convert to Christianity in the first half of the century. Songs have an important role in the dissemination of doctrine, giving the historian a special peek into the "average believer." What did the laymen believe about the doctrine of justification? We get an idea from listening in on the songs that were sung as they gathered together for worship.

Three *Odes* are especially insightful on justification. In *Odes* 17 and 25, the Odist laments the fact that he bore the chains of sin. He languishes in prison behind iron bars in anticipation of the one who can rescue his soul. This redeemer comes into the prison cell and breaks the chains as soon as the prisoner believes. Justification is forensic in the *Odes*, for it is always accompanied by juridical and punitive language. His hope comes across most clearly in *Ode* 29.5 where he writes, "He justified me by His grace." The lyrics immediately remind one of the Psalmist, who also likes to contrast his own trials with the salvation he receives from God, and of Paul who cast the sinners plight in bleak terms in the context of justification. Other noteworthy Pauline themes are present in these *Odes* as well. For instance, the Odist is familiar with imputation. He removed from himself the garments of skin, which represented sin, and replaced them

---

[6] Holmes, *The Apostolic Fathers*, 711.

with the Spirit (*Ode* 25.8). Even more, he acknowledges he has become holy in Christ's righteousness (*Ode* 25.10). Grace, a predominant theme of the *Odes*, is intertwined with faith, justification, and imputation to reveal a strong connection to Paul's doctrine of justification by faith.

The final work examined was Justin Martyr's *Dialogue with Trypho*. Trypho launched this two-day conversation after seeing Justin cloathed in his philosopher's garb. The statement that sparked the debate came from Trypho, who said, "If you will listen to me ... first be circumcised, then observe the precepts concerning the Sabbath, the feasts, and God's new moons; in brief, fulfill the whole written law, and then, probably, you will experience the mercy of God" (*Dial.* 8). It is the last phrase in particular, that one must fulfill the entire law to experience mercy from God, which catalyzed the dialogue. Justin used this declaration as fodder for the remainder of the discussion, returning to it often as he juxtaposed his view of salvation, justification by faith, with Trypho's understanding of salvation, justification through works of the law.

Several times Justin uses Paul's argument that Abraham is an example of a person who was justified by faith apart from circumcision or obedience to any other law. This argument was so critical to Justin that he felt obliged to repeat it in full for those on the second day who were absent the first time around (*Dial.* 23, 92). He employs this argument in much the same way that Paul does in Galatians 3 and Romans 4. The law avails nothing; it is only faith that counts. People were justified by faith in God before either the law or the command of circumcision was given. The law is no longer needed in Justin's reckoning, but for Trypho, it is the lifeblood of allegiance to God, and thus indispensable.

Much has been made of the absence of Paul in Justin. While Paul is never named, and allusions to his writings are debatable, it is difficult to sustain that Justin did not at least utilize Pauline arguments. Abraham is the typological example of justification by faith apart from works of the law and Justin even tells Trypho to eschew his Pharisaic teachers who press obedience to the law on him (*Dial.* 137). Add to this the neologism δικαιοπραξίας ἔργον, reminiscent of Paul's ἔργα νόμου, and Justin's connection to Paul grows stronger.

At the outset of this book it was stated that the thesis advanced, that justification by faith was present in the second century, is not novel. The primary contribution of this work is that for the first time these various strands of research have been pulled together to show one strong cord of continuity on the doctrine of justification between Paul in the first century and his heirs over the next hundred years after his death. Undoubtedly, some will quibble over the presence of justification in one or another of these works, but the collective evidence more than tips the scales in favor of a view of justification by faith in the second century. One hundred years after Paul's death, his keystone doctrine of justification was interpreted as justification by faith apart from works.

In keeping with the quotation from Holmes at the beginning of this chapter, it must be stressed that simply because a doctrine is not at the fore of a writer's mind, does not mean that it is altogether lacking. It is unfair to ask the second-century fathers to give a full-orbed understanding of justification. Soteriology was certainly important to them, since salvation is at the center of the message they received and passed on, but the scant writings they left behind have a different focal point, one of survival from internal and external threats. Thus, the purpose of this book has been to detect these rare snippets of justification when an author does use the word or the theme, in order to show that there was continuity between Paul's teaching on justification by faith in the first century and the reception of this doctrine by Paul's immediate successors in the second century. Thomas Oden may have spoken prematurely in *The Justification Reader* when he said, "So one modest objective will be accomplished. It will no longer be possible hereafter to say that the Fathers had no developed notion or doctrine of justification by grace through faith," but now the evidence has come in and the conclusion holds—one hundred years after Paul's death, justification by faith was alive and well.[7]

---

7 Thomas Oden, *The Justification Reader* (Grand Rapids: Eerdmans, 2002), 50.

Bibliography

General Works

Books

Alsted, Johann Heinrich. *Theologica scholastic didacta*. Hanover, 1618.
Aono, Tashio. *Die Entwicklung des paulinischen Gerichtsgedankens dei den Apostolischen Vätern*. Europäische Hochschulschriften Theologie 137. Las Vegas: Lang, 1979.
Babcock, William, ed. *Paul and the Legacies of Paul*. Dallas: Southern Methodist University, 1990.
Backus, Irena, ed. *The Reception of the Church Fathers in the West: From the Carolingians to the Maurists*. 2 vols. Leiden: Brill, 1997.
Barr, James. *The Semantics of Biblical Language*. Oxford: Oxford University Press, 1961.
Campbell, Douglas. *The Deliverance of God: An Apocalytpic Rereading of Justification in Paul*. Grand Rapids: Eerdmans, 2009.
Bird, Michael, and Joseph Dodson, eds. *Paul and the Second Century*. Library of New Testament Studies 412. New York: T&T Clark, 2011.
Carson, D. A., Peter O'Brien, and Mark Seifrid, eds. *Justification and Variegated Nomism: The Complexities of Second Temple Judaism*. Wissenshaftliche Untersuchungen zum Neuen Testament. 2 vols. Grand Rapids: Baker Academic, 2001.
Cooper, Jordan. *The Righteousness of One: An Evaluation of Early Patristic Soteriology in Light of the New Perspective on Paul*. Eugene, OR: Wipf and Stock, 2013.
Dassman, Ernst. *Der Stachel im Fleisch: Paulus in der frühchristlichen Literatur bis Irenäus*. Münster: Aschendorff, 1979.
Davies, W. D. *Paul and Rabbinic Judaism: Some Rabbinic Elements in Pauline Theology*. 4th ed. Philadelphia: Fortress, 1980.
Drobner, Hubertus. *The Fathers of the Church: A Comprehensive Introduction*. Translated by Siegfried S. Schatzmann. Peabody, MA: Hendrickson, 2007.
Ehrman, Bart D. *The Apostolic Fathers*. Loeb Classical Library. 2 vols. Cambridge, MA: Harvard University Press, 2003.
Eusebius. *The Church History*. Translated by Paul Maier. Grand Rapids: Kregel, 1999.
Faber, George Stanley. *The Primitive Doctrine of Justification*. 2nd ed. London: Seeley and Burnside, 1839.
Gaca, Kathy L., and L. L. Welborn, eds. *Early Patristic Readings of Romans*. New York: T&T Clark, 2005.
Gadamer, Hans-Georg. *Truth and Method*. Translated by J. Weinsheimer and D. G. Marshall. 2nd ed. London: Continuum, 2004.
Grant, Robert, ed. *The Apostolic Fathers: A New Translation and Commentary*. 6 vols. New York: Thomas Nelson & Sons, 1965.
Gregory, Andrew, and Christopher Tuckett, eds. *Trajectories through the New Testament and the Apostolic Fathers*. Oxford: Oxford University Press, 2005.
Harnack, Adolf von. *Marcion: The Gospel of the Alien God*. Translated by John E. Steely and Lyle D. Bierma. Durham, NC: Labyrinth Press, 1990.

Harnack, Adolf von. *History of Dogma*. Translated by Neil Buchanan. Vol. 1. Boston: Little, Brown, and Co., 1902.

Holmes, Michael. *The Apostolic Fathers*. 3rd ed. Grand Rapids: Baker, 2007.

Ferguson, Everett. *Backgrounds of Early Christianity*. 3rd ed. Grand Rapids: Eerdmans, 2003.

Jeffers, James S. *The Greco-Roman World of the New Testament Era: Exploring the Background of Early Christianity*. Downers Grove, IL: InterVarsity, 1999.

Klauck, Hans-Josef, and Brian McNeil. *The Religious Context of Early Christianity: A Guide to Graeco-Roman Religions*. London: T&T Clark, 2000.

Knopf, Rudolf. *Die apostolischen Väter*. Tübingen: Mohr, 1920.

Knox, J. *Marcion and the New Testament: An Essay in Early Christian History*. Chicago: University of Chicago Press, 1942.

Lieu, Judith. *Image and Reality: The Jews in the World of the Christians in the Second Century*. Edinburgh: T&T Clark, 1996.

Lightfoot, J. B. *The Apostolic Fathers*. Edited by J. R. Harmer. London: Macmillan and Co., 1891. Reprint, Grand Rapids: Baker Book House, 1987.

Lightfoot, J. B., ed. and trans. *The Apostolic Fathers: Clement, Ignatius, and Polycarp*. 2 parts in 5 vols. 2nd ed. London: Macmillan and Co., 1889–90. Reprint, Grand Rapids: Baker Book House, 1981.

Lindemann, Andreas. *Paulus im ältesten Christentum: Das Bild des Apostels und die Rezeption der paulinischen Theologie in der frühchristlichen Literatur bis Marcion*. Beiträge zur Historischen Theologie 58. Tübingen: Mohr, 1979.

McGrath, Alistair. *Iustitia Dei: A History of the Christian Doctrine of Justification*. 3rd ed. Cambridge: Cambridge University Press, 2005.

Oberman, Heiko. *Forerunners of the Reformation: The Shape of Late Medieval Thought*. Cambridge: James Clarke & Co., 1966.

Oden, Thomas. *The Justification Reader*. Grand Rapids: Wm. B. Eerdmans, 2002.

Parvo, Richard I. *The Making of Paul: Constructions of the Apostle in Early Christianity*. Minneapolis: Fortress Press, 2010.

Pelikan, Jaroslav. *The Christian Tradition: A History of the Development of Doctrine*. Vol. 1, *The Emergence of the Catholic Tradition (100–600)*. Chicago: University of Chicago Press, 1971.

Pelikan, Jaroslav. *Development of Christian Doctrine: Some Historical Prolegomena*. New Haven, CT: Yale University, 1969.

Ritschl, Albrecht. *The Christian Doctrine of Justification and Reconciliation: The Positive Development of the Doctrine*. Translated and edited by H. R. Mackintosh and A. B. Macaulay. 2nd ed. Edinburgh: T&T Clark, 1902.

Roetzel, Calvin J. *Paul: the Man and the Myth*. Minneapolis: Fortress Press, 1999.

Sanders, E. P. *Paul and Palestinian Judaism: A Comparison of Patterns of Religion*. Philadelphia: Fortress, 1977.

Scheck, Thomas. *Origen and the History of Justification: The Legacy of Origen's Commentary on Romans*. Notre Dame, IN: University of Notre Dame Press, 2008.

Schreiner, Thomas. *Romans*. Baker Exegetical Commentary on the New Testament. Grand Rapids: Baker Academic, 1998.

Schweitzer, Albert. *The Mysticism of Paul the Apostle*. Translate by W. Montgomery. Baltimore, MD: John Hopkins University Press, 1998.

Schweitzer, Albert. *Die Mystik des Apostels Paulus*. Tübingen: J. C. B. Mohr, 1930.

Seifrid, Mark. *Justification by Faith*. Leiden: Brill, 1992.

Silva, Moisés. *Biblical Words & Their Meanings*. Grand Rapids: Zondervan, 1983.
Smyth, Herbert. *Greek Grammar.* Revised by Gordon M. Messing. Cambridge, MA: Harvard University Press, 1984.
Torrance, Thomas F. *The Doctrine of Grace in the Apostolic Fathers*. Grand Rapids: Eerdmans, 1959.
Trobisch, David. *Die Enstehung der Paulusbriefsammlung: Studien zu den Anfängen christlicher Publizistik.* Novum Testamentum et Orbis Antiquus 10. Göttingen: Vandenhoeck & Ruprecht, 1989.
Trobisch, David. *The First Edition of the New Testament.* New York: Oxford University Press, 2000.
Trobisch, David. *Paul's Letter Collection: Tracing the Origins*. Minneapolis: Fortress Press, 1994.
Wallace, Daniel. *Greek Grammar beyond the Basics*. Grand Rapids: Zondervan, 1996.
Waters, Guy Prentiss. *Justification and the New Perspectives on Paul: A Review and Response*. Phillipsburg, NJ: P&R Publishing, 2004.
Westerholm, Stephen. *Perspectives Old and New on Paul: The "Lutheran" Paul and His Critics*. Grand Rapids: Eerdmans, 2004.
White, Benjamin L. *Remembering Paul: Ancient and Modern Contests over the Image of the Apostle*. New York: Oxfor University Press, 2014.
Wilken, Robert L. *The First Thousand Years: A Global History of Christianity.* New Haven, CT: Yale University Press, 2012.
Wright, N. T. *Paul in Fresh Perspective.* Philadelphia: Fortress Press, 2009.
Wright, N. T. *What Saint Paul Really Said: Was Paul of Tarsus the Read Founder of Christianity?* Grand Rapids: Eerdmans, 1997.
Wright, N. T. *Paul and the Faithfulness of God*, 2 vols. Minneapolis: Fortress, 2013.

Articles

Arnold, Brian J. Reivew of *The Righteousness of One: An Evaluation of Early Patristic Soteriology in Light of the New Perspective on Paul*, by Jordan Cooper, *Themelios* 39.1 (2014): 125–27.
Barrett, C. K. "Pauline Controversies in the Post-Pauline Period." *New Testament Studies* 20 (1974): 229–45.
Barrett, C. K. "Pauline Controversies in the Post Pauline Period." In *On Paul: Essays on His Life, Work, and Influence*, 155–77. New York: T&T Clark, 2003.
Blackwell, Ben. "Paul and Irenaeus." In *Paul and the Second Century*, ed. Michael Bird and Joseph Dodson, 190–206. Library of New Testament Studies 412. New York: T&T Clark, 2011.
Campbell, Douglas. "An Apocalyptic Rereading of 'Justification' in Paul: Or, an Overview of the Argument of Douglas Campbell's *The Deliverance of God*—by Douglass Campbell." *Expository Times* (2012): 382–93.
Dunn, James D. G. "The New Perspective on Paul." *Bulletin of the John Rylands Library* 65 (1983): 95–122.
Dunn, James D. G. "The New Perspective on Paul." In *Jesus, Paul and the Law: Studies in Mark and Galatians*, 183–214. London: SPCK, 1990.

Eddy, Paul Rhodes, James K. Beilby, and Steven E. Enderlein. "Justification in Historical Perspective." In *Justification Five Views*, ed. James K. Beilby and Paul Rhodes Eddy, 13–52. Downers Grove, IL: IVP Academic, 2011.

Eno, Robert. "Some Patristic Views on the Relationship of Faith and Works in Justification." *Recherches augustiniennes* 19 (1984): 3–27.

Holdcraft, I. T. "The Parable of the Pounds and Origen's Doctrine of Grace." *Journal of Theological Studes*, n.s. 24 (1973): 503–04.

Lindemann, Andreas. "Paul in the Writings of the Apostolic Fathers." In *Paul and the Legacies of Paul*, ed. William Babcock, 25–45. Dallas: Southern Methodist University Press, 1990.

Lindemann, Andreas. "Paul's Influence on 'Clement' and Ignatius." In *Trajectories through the New Testament*, ed. Andrew Gregory and Christopher Tuckett, 9–24. Oxford: Oxford University Press, 2005.

Marguerat, Daniel. "Paul après Paul: une histoire de reception." *New Testament Studies* 54 (2008): 317–37.

Needham, Nick. "Justification in the Early Church Fathers." In *Justification in Perspective: Historical Developments and Contemporary Challenges*, ed. Bruce L. McCormack, 25–54. Grand Rapids: Baker Academic, 2006.

Osborn, Eric. "Origen and Justification: The Good is One." *Australian Biblical Review* 24 (1976): 18–29.

Osborn, Eric. Review of *Paulus im ältesten Christentum: Das Bild des Apostels und die Rezeption der paulinischen Theologie in der frühchristlichen Literatur bis Marcion*, by Andreas Lindemann, *Australian Biblical Review* 28 (1980): 58–60.

Pasquier, Anne. "The Valentinian Exegesis." In *Handbook of Patristic Exegesis*, by Charles Kannengiesser, 1:454–70. Leiden: Brill, 2004.

Porter, Stanley. "Paul and the Pauline Letter Collection." In *Paul and the Second Century*, ed. Michael Bird and Joseph Dodson, 19–36. Library of New Testament Studies 412. New York: T&T Clark, 2011.

Rensberger, David. Review of *Paulus im ältesten Christentum: Das Bild des Apostels und die Rezeption der paulinischen Theologie in der frühchristlichen Literatur bis Marcion*, by Andreas Lindemann. *Journal of Biblical Literature* 101 (1982): 289.

Rensberger, David. "The Second Century Paul." In *The Writings of St. Paul*, ed. Wayne A. Meeks and John T. Fitzgerald, 341–51. 2nd ed. New York: Norton, 2007.

Roetzel, Calvin. "Paul in the Second Century." In *The Cambridge Companion to St. Paul*, ed. James D. G. Dunn, 227–41. Cambridge Companions to Religion. Cambridge: Cambridge University Press, 2003.

Stendahl, Krister. "The Apostle Paul and the Introspective Conscience of the West." *Harvard Theological Review* 56 (1963): 199–215.

Wesley, John. "The Doctrine of Salvation, Faith and Good Works, Extracted from the Homilies of the Church of England." In *John Wesley*, ed. Albert C. Outler, 123–33. New York: Oxford University Press, 1964.

Williams, D. H. "Justification by Faith: A Patristic Doctrine." *Journal of Ecclesiastical History* 57 (2006): 649–67.

Williams, Rowan. "Justification." In *Encyclopedia of Christian Theology*, ed. Jean-Yves Lacoste. 3 vols. New York: Routledge, 2005.

Wright, David. "Justification in Augustine." In *Justification in Perspective: Historical Developments and Contemporary Challenges*, ed. Bruce L. McCormack, 55–72. Grand Rapids: Baker Academic, 2006.

Dissertations

Penny, Donald N. "The Pseudo-Pauline Letters of the First Two Centuries." Ph.D. diss., Emory, 1980.
Rensberger, David. "As the Apostle Teaches: The Development of the Use of Paul's Letters in Second-Century Christianity." Ph.D. diss., Yale University, 1981.
Scarborough, Jason M. "The Making of an Apostle: Second and Third Century Interpretations of the Writings of Paul." Ph.D. diss., Union Theological Seminary, 2007.
Warren, David H. "The Text of the Apostle in the Second Century: A Contribution to the History of Reception." Th.D. diss., Harvard University, 2001.
White, Benjamin Lee. "*Imago Pauli*: Memory, Tradition, and Discourses on the 'Real' Paul in the Second Century." Ph.D. diss., University of North Carolina, 2011.

1 Clement

Books

Allison, Dale C., Jr. *A Critical and Exegetical Commentary on the Epistle of James*. ICC. New York: Bloomsbury, 2013.
Bakke, Odd Magne. *Concord and Peace*. Wissenshaftliche Untersuchungen zum Neuen Testament. Tübingen: Mohr Siebeck, 2001.
Bowe, Barbara Ellen. *A Church in Crisis: Ecclesiology and Paraenesis in Clement of Rome*. Harvard Dissertations in Religion 23. Minneapolis: Fortress Press, 1988.
Breytenbach, Cilliers, and Leslie L. Welborn. *Encounters with Hellenism: Studies on the First Letter of Clement*. Arbeiten zur Geschichte des Antiken Judentums und des Urchristentums 53. Leiden: Brill, 2004.
Clarke, W. K. Lowther. *The First Epistle of Clement to the Corinthians*. London: Society for Promoting Christian Knowledge, 1937.
Davids, Peter. *The Epistle of James*. New International Greek Testament Commentary. Grand Rapids: Eerdmans, 1982.
Good, Deirde J. *Reconstructing the Tradition of Sophia in Gnostic Literature*. Atlanta: Scholars Press, 1987.
Hagner, Donald. *The Use of the Old and New Testaments in Clement of Rome*. Supplements to Novum Testamentum 34. Leiden: Brill, 1973.
Harnack, Adolf von. *Einführung in die alte Kirchengeschichte: Das Schreiben der römischen Kirche an die korinthische aus der Zeit Domitians (1. Clemensbrief)*. Leipzig: Hinrichs, 1929.
Irenaeus. *Against Heresies*. Translated by A. Roberts and W.H. Rambaut. In *The Apostolic Fathers with Justin Martyr and Irenaeus*, 315–567. American ed. Ante-Nicene Fathers.

Vol. 1. Buffalo: Christian Literature, 1885. Reprint, Peabody, MA: Hendrickson Publishers, 2004.

Jaubert, A. *Épître aux Corinthiens*. Rev. ed. Sources Chrétiennes 167. Paris: Cerf, 2000.

Jeffers, James S. *Conflict at Rome: Social Order and Hierarchy in Early Christianity*. Minneapolis: Fortress, 1991.

Jefford, Clayton. *The Apostolic Fathers and the New Testament*. Peabody, MA: Hendrickson, 2006.

Lindemann, Andreas. *Die Clemensbriefe*. Handbuch zum Neuen Testament 17. Tübingen: Mohr Siebeck, 1992.

Luedemann, G. *Opposition to Paul in Jewish Christianity*. Minneapolis: Fortress, 1989.

Moo, Douglas. *The Letter of James*. Grand Rapids: Eerdmans, 2000.

Schneider, G. *Epistola ad Corinthios*. Fontes Christiani 15. New York: Herder, 1994.

van Unnik, W. C. *Studies over de zogenaamde eerste brief van Clemens*. Vol. 1 of *Het litteraire genre*. Mededelingen der Koninklijke Nederlandse Akademie van Wetenschappen, Afd. Letterkunde 33.4. Amsterdam: N. V. Noord-Hollandsche Uitgevers Maatschappij, 1970.

Weiss, Johannes, and Rudolf Knopf. *The History of Primitive Christianity*. Edited by Frederick C. Grant. 2 vols. New York: Wilson-Erickson, 1937.

Articles

Barnard, Leslie. "Clement of Rome and the Persecution of Domitian." *New Testament Studies* 10 (1964): 251–60.

Barnard, Leslie. "St. Clement of Rome and the persecution of Domitian." In *Studies in the Apostolic Fathers and their Background*, ed. Leslie Barnar. New York: Schocken, 1966.

Dennison, William D. "Indicative and Imperative: The Basic Structure of Pauline Ethics." *Calvin Theological Journal* 14 (1979): 55–78.

Fisher, Edmund. "Let us Look upon the Blood-of-Christ (1 Clement 7:4)." *Vigiliae christianae* 34 (1980): 218–36.

Jaeger, W. "Early Christianity and the Greek Paideia: 1 Clement." In *Encounters with Hellenism: Studies on the First Letter of Clement*, ed. Cilliers Breytenbach and Leslie L. Welborn, 104–14. Arbeiten zur Geschichte des Antiken Judentums und des Urchristentums 53. Leiden: Brill, 2004.

Newman, Carey C. "Righteousness." In *Dictionary of the Later New Testament*, ed. Ralph P. Martin and Peter H. Davids. Downers Grove, IL: InterVarsity Press, 1997.

Nielsen, Charles. "Clement of Rome and Moralism." *Church History* 31 (1962): 131–50.

Parsons, Michael. "Being Precedes Act: Indicative and Imperative in Paul's Writing." *Evangelical Quarterly* 88 (1988): 99–127.

Räisänen, Heikki. "'Righteousness by Works': An Early Catholic Doctrine? Thoughts on 1 Clement." In *Jesus, Paul, and Torah: Collected Essays*, trans. David E. Orton, 203–24. Journal for the Study of the New Testament Supplement Series 43. Sheffield: Sheffield Academic Press, 1992.

van Unnik, W. C. "Studies on the So-called First Epistle of Clement: The Literary Genre." In *Encounters with Hellenism: Studies on the First Letter of Clement*, ed. Cilliers

Breytenbach and Leslie L. Welborn, trans. L. L. Welborn, 115–81. Arbeiten zur Geschichte des Antiken Judentums und des Urchristentums 53. Leiden: Brill, 2004.
Welborn, L. L. "On the Date of First Clement." *Biblical Research* 29 (1984): 35–54.
Welborn, L. L. "The Preface to 1 Clement: the Rhetorical Situation and the Traditional Date." In *Encounters with Hellenism: Studies on the First Letter of Clement*, ed. Cilliers Breytenbach and Leslie L. Welborn, 197–216. Arbeiten zur Geschichte des Antiken Judentums und des Urchristentums 53. Leiden: Brill, 2004.
Wilhelm-Hooijberg, A. E. "A Different View of Clemens Romanus." *Heythrop Journal* 16 (1975): 266–88.

Theses

Newman, Carey C. "Righteousness/Justification Language in 1 Clement: A Linguistic and Theological Enquiry." M.Th. thesis, University of Aberdeen, 1985.

Ignatius of Antioch

Books

Lettres. Edited by P. T. Camelot. 4th ed. Sources chrétiennes 10. Paris: Cerf, 1969.
Barnard, Leslie W. *Studies in the Apostolic Fathers and their Background*. New Haven: Yale University, 1966.
Bauckham, Richard. *The Jewish World Around the New Testament*. Tübingen: Mohr Siebeck, 2008.
Bauer, Walter. *Die Apostolischen Väter*. Handbuch zum Neuen Testament 18. Tübingen: Mohr, 1920.
Becker, Adam H., and Annette Yoshiko Reed, eds. *The Ways that Never Parted: Jews and Christians in Late Antiquity and the Early Middle Ages*. Tübingen: Mohr Siebeck, 2003.
Brent, Allen. *Ignatius of Antioch: A Martyr Bishop and the Origin of the Episcopacy*. New York: T&T Clark, 2007.
Brown, Charles Thomas. *The Gospel and Ignatius of Antioch*. Studies in Biblical Literature 12. New York: Peter Lang, 2000.
Brown, Raymond E., and John P. Meier. *Antioch and Rome: New Testament Cradles of Catholic Christianity*. New York: Paulist Press, 1983.
Corwin, Virginia. *St. Ignatius and Christianity in Antioch*. New Haven: Yale University Press, 1960.
Cureton, William. *The Ancient Syriac Version of the Epistles of Saint Ignatius*. London: Rivington, 1845.
Cureton, William. *Vindiciae Ignatianae*. London: Rivington, 1846.
Dunn, James D. G. *The Partings of the Ways: Between Christianity and Judaism and the Significance for the Character of Christianity*. London: SCM Press, 1991.
Dunn, James D. G., ed. *Parting of the Ways with Jews and Christians: The Parting of the Ways A.D. 70–135*. Tübingen: Mohr Siebeck, 1992.

Ehrman, Bart. *The Apostolic Fathers*. Vol. 1, *I Clement. II Clement. Ignatius. Polycarp. Didache*. Loeb Classical Library 24. Cambridge, MA: Harvard University Press, 2003.

Frend, W. H. C. *Martyrdom and Persecution in the Early Church*. Oxford: Basil Blackwell, 1965.

Grant, Robert. *After the New Testament*. Philadelphia: Fortress, 1967.

Hurtado, Larry. *Lord Jesus Christ: Devotion to Jesus in Earliest Christianity*. Grand Rapids: Wm. B. Eerdmans, 2003.

Isacson, Mikael. *To Each Their Own Letter: Structure, Themes, and Rhetorical Strategies in the Letters of Ignatius of Antioch*. Coniectanea Biblica New Testament Series 42. Stockholm: Almqvist & Wiksell International, 2004.

Joly, Robert. *Le dossier d'Ignace d'Antioche*. Université Libre de Bruxelles, Faculté de Philosophie et Lettres 69. Brussels: Éditions de l'Université, 1979.

Koester, Helmut Koester. *Introduction to the New Testament: Volume Two: History and Literature of Early Christianity*. Philadelphia: Fortress, 1984.

Lechner, Thomas. *Ignatius Adversus Valentinianos? Chronologische und theologiegeschichtliche Studien zu den Briefen des Ignatius von Antiochien*. Supplements to Vigiliae Christianae 47. Leiden: Brill, 1999.

Liebeschuetz, J. H. W. G. *Antioch: City and Imperial Administration in the Later Roman Empire*. Oxford: Clarendon, 1972.

Lütgert, Wilhelm. *Amt und Geist im Kampf: Studien zur Geschichte des Urchristentums*. Beiträge zur Förderung christlicher Theologie. Gütersloh, Germany: Bertelsmann, 1911.

Massaux, Édouard. *The Influence of the Gospel of Saint Matthew on Christian Literature before Saint Irenaeus*. Vol. 1, *The First Ecclesiastical Writers*. Translated by N. J. Belval and S. Hecht. New Gospel Studies 5.1. Macon, GA: Mercer University Press, 1990.

Maurer, C. *Ignatius von Antiochien und das Johannesevangelium*. Zürich: Zwingli Verlag, 1949.

Meinhold, P. *Studien zu Ignatius von Antiochen*. Veröffentlichung des Instituts für Europäische Geschichte 97. Wiesbaden, Germany: Franz Steiner, 1979.

Metzger, Bruce. *The Canon of the New Testament: Its Origin, Development, and Significance*. Oxford: Clarendon Press, 1987.

Moss, Candida. *Ancient Christian Martrydom: Diverse Practices, Theologies, and Traditions*. New Haven: Yale University Press, 2012.

Moss, Candida. *The Myth of Persecution: How Early Christians Invented a Story of Martyrdom*. New York: HarperOne, 2013.

Parkes, James W. *The Conflict of the Church and the Synagogue: A Study in the Origins of Antisemitism*. London: Soncino, 1934.

Rius-Camps, Joseph. *The Four Authentic Letters of Ignatius, The Martyr*. Orientalia Christiana Analecta 213. Rome: Pontificium Institutum Orientalium Studiorum, 1980.

Robinson, Thomas. *Ignatius of Antioch and the Parting of the Ways: Early Jewish-Christian Relations*. Peabody, MA: Hendrickson Publishers, 2009.

Schoedel, William. *A Commentary on the Letters of Ignatius of Antioch*. Hermeneia. Philadelphia: Fortress, 1985.

Trevett, Christine. *A Study of Ignatius of Antioch in Syria and Asia*. Studies in the Bible and Early Christianity 29. Lewiston, NY: Edwin Mellen, 1992.

Weijenborg, Reinoud. *Les lettres d'Ignace d'Antioche*. Leiden: Brill, 1969.

Weinrich, William C. *Spirit and Martyrdom: A Study of the Work of the Holy Spirit in Contexts of Persecution and Martyrdom in the New Testament and Early Christian Literature.* Washington, DC: University Press of America, 1981.
Wetter, G. P. *Charis: Ein Beitrag zur Geschichte des ältesten Christentums.* Leipzig: Brandsetter, 1913.
Wilken, Robert L. *John Chrysostom and the Jews: Rhetoric and Reality in the Late Fourth Century.* Berkeley: University of California Press, 1983.
Zahn, Theodor. *Ignatii et Polycarpi epistulae martyria fragmenta.* Leipzig: Hinrichs, 1876.
Zahn, Theodor. *Ignatius von Antiochien.* Gotha, Germany: F. A. Perthes, 1873.

Articles

Barrett, C. K. "Jews and Judaizers in the Epistles of Ignatius." In *Jews, Greeks and Christians: Religious Cultures in Late Antiquity—Essays in Honor of William David Davies*, 220–44. Leiden: Brill, 1976.
Baur, F. C. "Die Christuspartei in der Korinthischen Gemeinde, der Gegensatz des petrinischen und Christentums in der ältesten Kirche, der Apostel Petrus in Rom." *Tübinger Zeitschrift für Theologie* 4 (1831): 61–206.
Bower, Richard. "The Meaning of ΕΠΙΤΥΓΧΑΝΩ in the Epistles of St. Ignatius of Antioch." *Vigiliae christianae* 28 (1974): 1–14.
Bultmann, Rudolf. "Ignatius and Paul." In *Existence and Faith: shorter writings of Rudolf Bultmann*, ed. Schubert M. Ogden, 267–77. New York: Meridian Books, 1960.
Bultmann, Rudolf. "Ignatius und Paulus." In *Studia Paulina, in honorem Johannes de Zwaan septuagenerii*, ed. J. N. Sevenster and W. C. van Unnik, 37–51. Haarlem, Netherlands: De Erven F. Bohn N.V., 1953.
Cohen, Shaye J. D. "Judaism without Circumcision and 'Judaism' without 'Circumcision' in Ignatius." *Harvard Theological Review* 95 (2002): 395–415.
Cohen, Shaye J. D. "Judaism without Circumcision and 'Judaism' without 'Circumcision' in Ignatius." In *The Significance of Yavneh and Other Essays in Jewish Hellenism*, 453–75. Texts and Studies in Ancient Judaism 136. Tübingen: Mohr Siebeck, 2010.
De Ste. Croix, G. E. M. "Why were the Early Christians Persecuted?" *Past & Present* 26 (1963): 6–38.
Dietze, P. "Die Briefe des Ignatius und das Johannesevangelium." *Theologische Studien und Kritiken* 78 (1905): 563–603.
Donahue, P. J. "Jewish Christianity in the Letters of Ignatius of Antioch." *Vigiliae christianae* 32 (1978): 81–93.
Goulder, Michael. "Ignatius' 'Docetists.'" *Vigiliae christianae* 53 (1999): 16–30.
Haykin, Michael. "'Come to the Father': Ignatius of Antioch and His Calling to be a Martyr." *Themelios* 32 (2007): 26–39.
Hill, Charles. "Ignatius, 'the Gospel,' and the Gospels." In *Trajectories through the New Testament and the Apostolic Fathers*, ed. Andrew F. Gregory and Christopher M. Tuckett, 267–85. Oxford: Oxford University Press, 2005.
Lilienfeld, Fairy von. "Zur syrischen Kurzrezension der Ignatianen: Von Paulus zur Spiritualität des Mönchtums der Wüste." *Studia Patristica VII*, Texte und Untersuchungen 92. Berlin: Akademie-Verlag, 1966.

Lieu, Judith. "'The Parting of the Ways': Theological Construct or Historical Reality?" *Journal for the Study of the New Testament* 56 (1994): 101–19.

Maier, Harry O. "The Politics and Rhetoric of Discord and Concord in Paul and Ignatius." In *Trajectories through the New Testament and the Apostolic Fathers*, ed. Andrew Gregory and Christopher Tuckett, 307–24. New York: Oxford University Press, 2005.

Munier, Charles. "Où en est la question d'Ignace d'Antioche?" *Aufstieg und Niedergang Der Römischen Welt II* 27 (1993): 404–13.

Myllykoski, Matti. "Wild Beasts and Rabid Dogs: The Riddle of the Heretics in the Letters of Ignatius." In *The Formation of the Early Church*, ed. Jostein Ådna, 341–77. Wissenshaftliche Untersuchungen zum Neuen Testament 183. Tübingen: Mohr Siebeck, 2005.

Petersen, Anders Klostergaard. "At the End of the Road—Reflections on a Popular Scholarly Metaphor." In *The Formation of the Early Church*, ed. Jostein Ådna, 45–72. Wissenshaftliche Untersuchungen zum Neuen Testament 183. Tübingen: Mohr Siebeck, 2005.

Preiss, Theodore. "La mystique de l'imitation du Christ et de l'unité chez Ignace d'Antioche." *Revue d'histoire et de philosophie religieuses* 18 (1938): 197–241.

Reis, David M. "Following in Paul's Footsteps: *Mimēsis* and Power in Ignatius of Antioch." In *Trajectories through the New Testament and the Apostolic Fathers*, ed. Andrew Gregory and Christopher Tuckett, 287–306. New York: Oxford University Press, 2005.

Schoedel, William. "Are the Letters of Ignatius of Antioch Authentic?" *Religious Studies Review* 6 (1980): 196–201.

Schoedel, William. "Judaism without Circumcision and 'Judaism' without 'Circumcision' in Ignatius." In *The Significance of Yavneh and Other Essays in Jewish Hellenism*, 453–75. Texts and Studies in Ancient Judaism 136. Tübingen: Mohr Siebeck, 2010.

Schoedel, William. "Ignatius and the Archives." *Harvard Theological Review* 71 (1978): 97–106.

Schreiner, Thomas. "'Works of Law' in Paul." *Novum Testamentum* 3 (1991): 217–45.

Sibinga, J. Smit. "Ignatius and Matthew." *Novum Testamentum* 8 (1966): 262–83.

Smith, Carl. "Ministry, Martyrdom, and Other Mysteries: Pauline Influence on Ignatius of Antioch." In *Paul in the Second Century*, ed. Michael Bird and Joseph Dodson, 37–56. Library of New Testament Studies 412. New York: T&T Clark, 2011.

Swartley, Willard. "The Imitatio Christi in the Ignatian Letters." *Vigiliae christianae* 27 (1973): 81–103.

Trevett, Christine. "Approaching Matthew from the Second Century: The Under-Used Ignatian Correspondence." *Journal for the Study of the New Testament* 20 (1984): 59–67.

Trevett, Christine. "Prophecy and Anti-Episcopal Activity: a Third Error combated by Ignatius." *Journal of Ecclesiastical History* 34 (1983): 1–13.

Epistle to Diognetus

Books

Athenagoras. *Legatio pro Christianis*. Edited by M. Marcovich. Berlin and New York: Walter de Gruyter, 1990.

Aulén, Gustaf. *Christus Victor: An Historical Study of the Three Main Types of the Idea of the Atonement.* Translated by A. G. Hebert. London: SPCK, 1937.
Blakeney, *The Epistle to Diognetus.* London: SPCK; New York: The Macmillan Co., 1943.
Bunsen, Christian C. J. *Christianity and Mankind.* Vol. 1. London: Longman, Brown, Green, and Longmans, 1854.
Chalke, Steve. *The Lost Message of Jesus.* Grand Rapids: Zondervan, 2003.
Cross, F. L. *The Early Christian Fathers.* London: G. Duckworth, 1960.
Dorner, Isaak A. *History of the Development of the Doctrine of the Person of Christ.* Translated by William Alexander. Vol. 1. Edinburgh: T&T Clark, 1868.
Drobner, Hubertus R. *The Fathers of the Church: A Comprehensive Introduction.* Translated by Siegfried S. Schatzmann. Peabody, MA: Hendrickson, 2007.
Dulles, Cardinal Avery. *A History of Apologetics.* Eugene, OR: Wipf and Stock, 1999.
Ehrman, Bart D. *The Apostolic Fathers.* Vol. 2. Loeb Classical Library. Cambridge, MA: Harvard University Press, 2003.
Everitt, Anthony. *Hadrian and the Triumph of Rome.* New York: Random House, 2009.
Goodspeed, E. J. *A History of Early Christian Literature.* Chicago: University of Chicago Press, 1966.
Grant, Robert M. *Greek Apologists of the Second Century.* Philadelphia: The Westminster Press, 1988.
Haykin, Michael A. G. *Rediscovering the Church Fathers: Who They were and How They Shaped the Church.* Wheaton, IL: Crossway, 2011.
Hill, Charles. *From the Lost Teaching of Polycarp: Identifying Irenaeus' Apostolic Presbyterand the Author of* Ad Diognetum. Tübingen: Mohr Siebeck, 2006.
Jeffery, Steve, Micahel Ovey, and Andrew Sach. *Pierced for Our Transgressions: Rediscovering the Glory of Penal Substitution.* Wheaton: Crossway, 2007.
Jefford, Clayton N., Kenneth J. Harder, and Louis D. Amezaga, Jr. *Reading the Apostolic Fathers: An Introduction.* Peabody, MA: Hendrickson, 1996.
Kelly, J. N. D. *Early Christian Doctrines.* 5th ed. London: Adam and Charles Black, 1977.
Koester, Helmut. *Introduction to the New Testament.* Vol. 2 of *History and Literature of Early Christianity.* New York: Walter de Gruyter, 1982.
Lake, Kirsopp. *The Apostolic Fathers.* Vol. 2. Loeb Classical Library. Cambridge, MA: Harvard University Press, 1976.
Lightfoot, J. B., and J. R. Harmer, eds. *The Apostolic Fathers: Revised Greek Texts with Introductions and English Translation.* Grand Rapids: Baker Book House, 1891.
Lightfoot, J. B. *St. Paul's Epistles to the Colossians and to Philemon.* London: MacMillan and Co., 1892.
Marrou, H. I. *A Diognéte: Introduction, edition critique, traduction et commentaire.* 2nd ed. Sources chrétiennes 33. Paris: Cerf, 1997.
Meecham, Henry G. *The Epistle to Diognetus: The Greek Text with Introduction, Translation and Notes.* Manchester: Manchester University Press, 1949.
Sanday, William. *Christologies: Ancient and Modern.* Reprint, Whitefish, MT: Kessinger, 2010.
Stowers, Stanley. *Letter Writing in Greco-Roman Antiquity.* Philadelphia: Westminster Press, 1986.
Suetonius. *Suetonius in Two Volumes.* Translated by J. C. Rolfe. Loeb Classical Library. London: William Heinemann, 1920.
Thierry, J. J. *The Epistle to Diognetus.* Textus Minores 33. Leiden: Brill, 1964.

Winston, David. *Logos and Mystical Theology in Philo of Alexandria*. Cincinnati: Hebrew Union College Press, 1985.

Articles

Aloisi, John. "'His Flesh for Our flesh': The Doctrine of the Atonement in the Second Century." *Detroit Baptist Seminary Journal* 14 (2009): 23–44.

Andriessen, Dom P. "The Authorship of the Epistula Ad Diognetum." *Vigiliae christianae* 1 (1947): 129–36.

Bird, Michael. "The Reception of Paul in the *Epistle to Diognetus*." In *Paul and the Second Century*, ed. Michael Bird and Joseph Dodson, 70–90. Library of New Testament Studies 412. New York: T&T Clark, 2011.

Connolly, R. H. "*Ad Diognetum* xi-xii." *Journal of Theological Studies* 37 (1936): 2–15.

Connolly, R. H. "The Date and Authorship of the Epistle to Diognetus," *Journal of Theological Studies* 36 (1935): 347–53.

Crowe, Brandon. "O Sweet Exchange! The Soteriological Significance of the Incarnation in the Epistle to Diognetus." *Zeitschrift für die Neutestamentliche Wissenschaft und Kunde der Älteren Kirche* 102 (2011): 96–109.

Davies, Rupert E. "Christ in our Place—The Contribution of Prepositions," *Tyndale Bulletin* 21 (1970): 71–91.

Edwards, M. J. "Clement of Alexandria and His Doctrine of the Logos." *Vigiliae christianae* 54 (2000): 159–77.

Fawcett, Bruce. "Similar yet Unique: Christians as Described in the *Letter to Diognetus*." *The Baptist Review of Theology* 6 (1996): 23–27.

Grant, Robert M. "The Chronology of the Greek Apologists." *Vigiliae christianae* 9 (1955): 25–33.

Grant, Robert M. "Five Apologists and Marcus Aurelius," *Vigiliae christianae* 42 (1988): 1–17.

Hollon, Bryan C. "Is the *Epistle to Diognetus* an apology? A Rhetorical Analysis." *Journal of Communication and Religion* 28 (2005): 127–146.

Lienhard, Joseph T. "The Christology of the Epistle to Diognetus." *Vigiliae christianae* 24 (1970): 280–89.

Meecham, H. G. "Theology of the Epistle to Diognetus." *Expository Times* 54 (1943): 97–101.

Nielson, Charles. "The Epistle to Diognetus: Its Date and Relationship to Marcion." *Anglican Theological Review* 52 (1970): 77–91.

Palmer, D. W. "Atheism, Apologetic and Negative Theology in the Greek Apologists of the Second Century." *Vigiliae christianae* 37 (1983): 234–59.

Schoedel, William. "Christian 'Atheism' and the Peace of the Roman Empire." *Church History* 42 (1973): 309–19.

Swancutt, Diana M. "Paraenesis in Light of Protrepsis." In *Early Christian Paraenesis in Context*, ed. James Starr and Troels Engberg-Pedersen, 113–54. New York: Walter de Gruyter, 2004.

Thierry, J. J. "The Logos as Teacher in Ad Diognetum XI, 1." *Vigiliae christianae* 20 (1966): 146–49.

Wansink, C.S. "*Epistula ad Diognetum*: A School Exercise in the Use of Protreptic." *Church Divinity* (1986): 97–109.

Odes of Solomon

Books

Aland, Barbara. *Was ist Gnosis?* Tübingen: Mohr Siebeck, 2009.
Aune, David E. *The Cultic Setting of Realized Eschatology in Early Christianity.* Leiden: Brill, 1972.
Azar, Éphrem. *Les Odes de Salomon: Presentation et Traduction.* Paris: Les Editions du Cerf, 1996.
Bauer, Walter. *Die Oden Salomos.* Berlin: Walter de Gruyter, 1933.
Bernard, John H. *The Odes of Solomon.* Texts and Studies 8.3. Cambridge: Cambridge University Press, 1912.
Brock, Sebastian P. "The Gates/Bars of Sheol Revisited." In *Sayings of Jesus: Canonical and Non-Canonical. Essays in Honor of Tjitze Baarda. Novum Testamentum*, Supplements 89. Leiden: Brill, 1997.
Brunston, C. *Les plus anciens cantiques chrétiens.* Paris: Librairie Fischbacher, 1912.
Buchanan, George Wesley. *To the Hebrews.* Anchor Bible Commenary. Garden City, NY: Doubleday, 1972.
Charlesworth, James H. *The Earliest Christian Hymnbook.* Eugene, OR: Cascade Books, 2009.
Charlesworth, James H. *The Odes of Solomon.* Chico, CA: Scholars Press, 1977.
Daniélou, Jean. *Primitive Christian Symbols.* Translated by D. Attwater. Baltimore: Helicon, 1964.
Dunn, James D. G. *Romans.* Word Biblical Commentary. Dallas: Word Books, 1988.
Frankenberg, Wilhelm. *Das Verständnis der Oden Salomos.* Gießen, Germany: Töpelmann, 1911.
Franzmann, Majella. *The Odes of Solomon: An Analysis of the Poetical Structure and Form.* Göttingen: Vandenhoeck & Ruprecht, 1991.
Grimme, Hubert. *Die Oden Salomos: Syrisch-Hebräisch-Deutsch.* Heidelberg: Carl Winters Universitätsbuchhandlung, 1911.
Harnack, Adolf von. *Ein jüdisch-christliches Psalmbuch aus dem ersten Jahrhundert.* Texte und Untersuchungen 35.4. Leipzig: Hinrichs, 1910.
Harris, J. Rendel. *The Odes and Psalms of Solomon.* Cambridge: University Press, 1909.
Harris, J. Rendel and Alphonse Mingana. *The Odes and Psalms of Solomon.* 2 vols. Manchester: Manchester University Press, 1916–1920.
Hofius, Otfried. *Katapausis: Die Vorstellung vom Endzeitlichen Ruheort im Hebräerbrief.* Tübingen: Mohr, 1970.
Jewett, Robert. *Romans.* Hermeneia. Minneapolis: Fortress Press, 2007.
Jonas, Hans. *The Gnostic Religion.* 2nd ed. Boston: Beacon Press, 1963.
Käsemann, Ernst. *The Wandering People of God: An Investigation of the Letter to the Hebrews.* Translated by Roy A. Harrisville and Irving L. Sandberg. Minneapolis: Augsburg, 1984.
Kim, Jung Hoon. *The Significance of Clothing Imagery in the Pauline Corpus.* Journal for the Study of the New Testament Supplement Series. NewYork: T&T Clark International, 2004.
Kittel, Gerhard. *Die Oden Salomos—überarbeitet oder einheitlich?* Beiträge zur Wissenschaft vom Alten Testament 16. Leipzig: Hinrichs, 1914.

Köstenberger, Andreas. *John*. Baker Exegetical Commentary on the New Testament. Grand Rapids: Baker Academic, 2004.
Lattke, Michael. *Oden Salomos: Übersetze und Eingeleitet*. Fontes Christiani 19. Frieburg, Germany: Herder, 1995.
Lattke, Michael. *Die Oden Salomos in Ihrer Bedeutung für Neues Testament und Gnosis*. 4 vols. Göttingen: Vandenhoeck & Ruprecht, 1979–1998.
Lattke, Michael. *Odes of Solomon*. Edited by Harold W. Attridge. Translated by Marianne Ehrhardt. Hermeneia. Minneapolis: Fortress Press, 2009.
Labourt, Jean, and Pierre Batiffol. *Les Odes de Salomon: Une œuvre chrétienne des environs de l'an 100–120*. Paris: Gabalda, 1911.
Moo, Douglas. *Romans*. New International Commentary on the New Testament. Grand Rapids: Eerdmans, 1996.
Murray, John. *Romans*. New International Commentary on the New Testament. Grand Rapids: Eerdmans, 1968.
Nöldeke, Theodor. *Compendious Syriac Grammar*. Translated by James A. Crichton. Eugene, OR: Wipf and Stock Publishers, 2003.
O'Brien, Peter T. *The Epistle to the Philippians: A Commentary on the Greek Text*. New International Greek Testament Commentary. Grand Rapids: Eerdmans, 1991.
Oswalt, John. *Isaiah 40–66*. New International Commentary on the Old Testament. Grand Rapids: Eerdmans, 1998.
Pierre, Marie-Joseph. *Les Odes de Salomon*. Apocryphes 4. Turnhout, Belgium: Brépols, 1994.
Reitzenstein, Richard. *Das iranische Erlösungsmysterium: Religionsgeschichtliche Untersuchungen*. Bonn: Marcus & Weber, 1921.
Reitzenstein, Richard. *Das mandäische Buch des Herrn der Größe und die Evangelienüberlieferung*. Sitzungsberichte der Heidelberger Akademie der Wissenschaften: Philosophischhistorische Klasse. Heidelberg: Winter, 1919.
Sanders, J. T. *The New Testament Christological Hymns: Their Historical Religious Background*. Society for New Testament Studies 15. Cambridge: Cambridge University Press, 1971.
Schenke, Hans-Martin. *Der Gott 'Mensch' in der Gnosis: Ein religionsgeschichtlicher Beitrag zur Diskussion über die paulinische Anschauung von der Kirche als Leib Christi*. Göttingen: Vandenhoeck & Ruprecht, 1962.
Schreiner, Thomas. *Romans*. Baker Exegetical Commentary on the New Testament. Grand Rapids: Baker Academic, 1998.
Theissen, Gerd. *Untersuchungen zum Hebräerbrief*. Gütersloh: Mohn, 1969.
Vickers, Brian J. *Jesus' Blood and Righteousness: Paul's Theology of Imputation*. Wheaton, IL: Crossway, 2006.
Vielhauer, Philipp. *Aufsätze zum Neuen Testament*. München: Chr. Kaiser Verlag, 1965.
Wray, Judith Hoch. *Rest as a Theological Metaphor in the Epistle to the Hebrews and the Gospel of Truth: Early Christian Homiletics of Rest*. Atlanta: Scholars Press, 1998.
Wright, N. T. *The Climax of the Covenant*. Minneapolis: Fortress Press, 1993.
Young, E. J. *The Book of Isaiah: The English Text, with Introduction, Exposition, and Notes*. 3 vols. Grand Rapids: Eerdmans, 1972.

Articles

Abramowski, Rudolf. "Der Christus der Salomooden." *Zeitschrift für die neutestamentliche Wissenshaft* 35 (1936): 44–69.

Attridge, Harold W. "'Let Us Strive to Enter that Rest': The Logic of Hebrews 4:1–11" *Harvard Theological Review* 73 (1980): 279–88.

Baars, Willem. "A Note on Ode of Solomon XI 14." *Vetus Testamentum* 12 (1962): 196–215.

Batiffol, Pierre. "Les Odes de Salomon." *Revue biblique* 8 (1911): 5–59.

Brock, Sebastian. "Clothing metaphors as a means of theological expression in Syriac tradition." In *Studies in Syriac Christianity: History, Literature and Theology*, 11–38. Brookfield, VT: Variorum, 1992.

Carmignac, Jean. "Les Affinités qumraniennes de la onzième Ode de Salomon." *Revue de Qumran* 3 (1961): 71–102.

Carmignac, Jean. "Recherches sur la langue originelle des Odes de Salomon." *Revue de Qumran* 4 (1963): 429–32.

Chadwick, Henry. "Some Reflections on the Character and Theology of the Odes of Solomon." In *Kyriakon: Festschrift Johannes Quasten*, ed. P. Granfield and J. A. Jungman, 265–70. Münster: Verlag Achendorff, 1970.

Charlesworth, James H., and R. Alan Culpepper. "The Odes of Solomon and the Gospel of John." *Catholic Biblical Quarterly* 35 (1973): 298–322.

Charlesworth, James H. "Haplography and Philology: A Study of Ode of Solomon 16:8." *New Testament Studies* 25 (1979): 221–27.

Charlesworth, James H. "Odes of Solomon (Late First to Early Second Century A.D.)." In *The Old Testament Pseudepigrapha*, ed. James H. Charlesworth. Vol. 2. 725–71. New York: Doubleday, 1985.

Charlesworth, James H. "The Odes of Solomon—Not Gnostic." *Catholic Biblical Quarterly* 31 (1969): 357–69.

Charlesworth, James H. "Paronomasia and Assonance in the Syraic text of the Odes of Solomon." *Semitics* 1 (1970): 12–26.

Charlesworth, James H. "Qumran, John and the Odes of Solomon." In *John and Qumran*, ed. James H. Charlesworth, 117–35. London: Geoffrey Chapman, 1972.

Charlesworth, James H. "בעמוא in Earliest Christianity." In *The Use of the Old Testament in the New and Other Essays: Studies in Honor of William Franklin Stinespring*, ed. James M. Efrid, 271–79. Durham, NC: Duke University Press, 1972.

Clarke, William K. L. "The First Epistle of St Peter and the Odes of Solomon." *Journal of Theological Studies* 15 (1913): 47–52.

Colpe, Carsten. "Heidnische, jüdische und christliche Überlieferung in den Schriften aus Nag Hammadi X." *Jahrbuch für Antike und Christentum* (1982): 65–101.

Connolly, R. H. "Greek the Original Language of the Odes of Solomon." *Journal of Theological Studies* 14 (1912): 530–38.

Daley, Brian. "Eschatology." In *Encyclopedia of Early Christianity*. Edited by Everett Ferguson, et al. 2nd ed. New York: Garland Publishers, 1999.

Diettrich, Gustav. "Eine jüdisch-christliche Liedersammlung (aus dem apostolischen Zeitalter)." *Die Reformation: Deutsche evangelische Kirchenzeitung für die Gemeinde* 9 (1910): 306–10, 370–76, 513–18, 533–36.

Drijver, Han J. W. "The 19th Ode of Solomon: Its Interpretation and Place in Syrian Christianity." *Journal of Theological Studies*, n.s. 31 (1980): 337–55.

Driver, G. R. "Notes on Two Passages in the Odes of Solomon." *Journal of Theological Studies*, n.s. 25 (1974): 434–37.
Duensing, H. "Zur vierund-zwanzigsten der Oden Salomos." *Zeitschrift für die neutestamentliche Wissenschaft* 12 (1911): 86–87.
Emerton, John A. "Notes on Some Passages in the Odes of Solomon." *Journal of Theological Studies*, n.s. 28 (1977): 507–19.
Emerton, John A. "Some Problems of Text and Language in the Odes of Solomon." *Journal of Theological Studies*, n.s. 18 (1967): 372–406.
Fee, Gordon D. "Philippians 2:5–11: Hymn or Exalted Pauline Prose?" *Bulletin for Biblical Research* 2 (1992): 29–46.
Franzmann, Majella. "The Odes of Solomon, Man of Rest." *Orientalia Christiana Periodica* 51 (1985): 408–21.
Glanz, Oliver. "Who is Speaking—Who is Listening? How Information Technology Can Confirm the Integrity of the Text." In *Tradition and Innovation in Biblical Interpretation: Studies Presented to Professor Eep Talstra on the Occasion of his Sixty-Fifth Birthday*, ed. W. Th. van Peursen and J. W. Dyk, 337–60. Leiden: Brill, 2011.
Grant, Robert. "Notes on Gnosis." *Vigiliae christianae* 11 (1957): 149–51.
Grant, Robert. "The Odes of Solomon and the Church of Antioch." *Journal of Biblical Literature* 63 (1944): 370–71.
Grant, Robert. "The Origin of the Fourth Gospel." *Journal of Biblical Literature* 69 (1950): 305–22.
Gunkel, Hermann. "Die Oden Salomos." *Zeitschrift für die neutestamentliche Wissenschaft* 11 (1910): 291–328.
Harris, J. Rendel. "An Early Christian Hymn-Book." *Contemporary Review* 95 (1909): 414–28.
Harvey, Susan Ashbrook. "Feminine Imagery for the Divine: The Holy Spirit, the Odes of Solomon, and Early Syriac Tradition." *St. Vladimir's Theological Seminary* 37 (1993): 111–39.
Merrill, Eugene. "The Odes of Solomon and the Acts of Thomas: A Comparative Study." *Journal of the Evangelical Theological Society* 17 (1974): 231–34.
Newbold, William R. "Bardaisan and the Odes of Solomon." *Journal of Biblical Literature* 30 (1911): 161–204.
Plooij, Daniel. "Der Descensus ad inferos in Aphrahat und den Oden Salomos." *Zeitschrift für die neutestamentliche Wissenschaft* 14 (1913): 222–31.
Ryken, Leland, James Wilhoit, and Tremper Longman III, eds. "Right, Right Hand." *Dictionary of Biblical Imagery*. Downers Grove, IL: InterVarsity Press, 1998.
Spitta, Friedrich. "Zum Verständnis der Oden Salomos." *Zeitschrift für die neutestamentliche Wissenschaft* 11 (1910): 193–203, 259–290.
Stölten, Willy. "Gnostische Parallelen zu den Oden Salomos." *Zeitschrift für die neutestamentliche Wissenschaft* 13 (1912): 29–58.
Vogl, August. "Oden Salomos 17, 22, 24, 42: Übersetzung und Kommentar." Edited by Brian McNeil. *Oriens Christianus* 62 (1978): 60–76.
Vööbus, Arthur. "Neues Licht zur Frage der Originalsprache der Oden Salomos." *Le Muséon* 75 (1962): 275–90.
Wu, J. L., and S. C. Pearson. "Hymns, Songs." In *Dictionary of the Later New Testament & Its Developments*. Edited by Ralph P. Martin and Peter H. Davids. Downers Grove, IL: InterVarsity Press, 1997.

Dissertations

Glanz, Oliver. "Who Is Speaking? Who is Addressed? A Critical Study into the Conditions of Exegetical Method and Its Consequences for the Interpretation of Participant Reference-Shifts in the Book of Jeremiah." Ph.D. diss., Vrije University, 2010.
Runge, Steven E. "A Discourse-Functional Description of Participant Reference in Biblical Hebrew Narrative." D.Litt. diss., University of Stellenbosch, 2007.

Dialogue with Trypho

Books

Allert, Craig D. *Revelation, Truth, Canon and Interpretation: Studies in Justin Martyr's Dialogue with Trypho.* Supplements to Vigiliae Christianae 64. Leiden: Brill, 2002.
Barnard, Leslie W. *Justin Martyr: His Life and Thought.* Cambridge: Cambridge University Press, 1967.
Barnard, Leslie W. *St. Justin Martyr the First and Second Apologies.* New York: Paulist Press, 1997.
Goodenough, E. R. *The Theology of Justin Martyr: An Investigation into the Conceptions of the Earliest Christian Literature and its Hellenistic and Judaistic Influences.* Jena: Verlag Frommansche Buchhandlung, 1923.
Horner, Timothy. *Listening to Trypho: Justin Martyr's Dialogue Reconsidered.* Contributions to Biblical Exegesis and Theology 28. Leuvan: Peeters, 2001.
Hubík, Karl. *Die Apologien des hl. Justinus: Des Philosophen und Märtyrers. Literarhistorische untersuchungen.* Theologische Studien der Leo Gesellschaft 19. Vienna: Mayer & Co., 1912.
Hydahl, N. *Philosophie und Christentum: Eine Interpretation der Einleitung zum Dialog Justins.* Acta theological danica 9. Copenhagen: Munksgaard, 1966.
Joly, Robert. *Christianisme et Philosophie: Études sur Justin et les Apologistes grecs du deuxième siècle.* Brussels: Éditions de l'Université Libre de Bruxelles, 1973.
Justin Martyr. *Dialogus cum Tryphone.* Edited by Miroslav Marcovich. Berlin: Walter de Gruyter, 1997.
Minns, Denis, and Paul Parvis, eds. *Justin, Philosopher and Martyr: Apologies.* Oxford: Oxford University Press, 2009.
Ong, Walter J. *Orality and Literacy: The Technologizing of the Word.* 3rd ed. New York: Routledge, 2012.
Osborn, Eric F. *Justin Martyr.* Beiträge zur Historischen Theologie 47. Tübingen: Mohr Siebeck, 1973.
Rokéah, David. *Justin Martyr and the Jews.* Jewish and Christian Perspective Series 5. Leiden: Brill, 2002.
Sibinga, J. Smit. *The Old Testament Text of Justin Martyr.* Leiden: Brill, 1963.
Siker, Jeffrey S. *Disinheriting the Jews: Abraham in Early Christian Controversy.* Louisville: Westminster/John Knox, 1991.
Skarsaunne, Oskar. *Proof from Prophecy—A Study in Justin Martyr's Proof-Text Tradition: Text-Type, Provenance, Theological Profile.* Leiden: Brill, 1987.

Slusser, Michael, ed. *St. Justin Martyr: Dialogue with Trypho.* Translated by Thomas B. Falls. Rev. ed. Thomas P. Halton. Selections from the Fathers 3. Washington, D.C.: The Catholic University of America Press, 2003.

van Winden, J. C. M. *An Early Christian Philosopher: Justin Martyr's Dialogue with Trypho, Chapters One to Nine.* Philosophia patrum, Leiden 1. Leiden: Brill, 1971.

Articles

Bingham, D. Jeffrey. "Justin and Isaiah 53." *Vigiliae christianae* 53 (2000): 248–61.

Boyarin, Daniel. "Justin Martyr Invents Judaism." *Church History* 70 (2001): 427–61.

Cosgrove, C. H. "Justin Martyr and the Emerging Christian Canon." *Vigiliae christianae* 36 (1982): 209–32.

Denning-Bolle, Sara. "Christian Dialogue as Apologetic: the Case of Justin Martyr Seen in Historical Context." *Bulletin of the John Rylands University Library of Manchester* 69 (1987): 492–510.

Foster, Paul. "Justin and Paul." In *Paul and the Second Century*, ed. Michael Bird and Joseph Dodson, 108–25. Library of New Testament Studies 412. London: T&T Clark, 2012.

Hofer, Andrew. "The Old Man as Christ in Justin's *Dialogue with Trypho.*" *Vigiliae christianae* 57 (2003): 1–21.

Holte, Ragnar. "Logos Spermaticos: Christianity and Ancient Philosophy according to St.-Justin's Apologies." *Studia Theologica* 12 (1958): 109–68.

Nilson, Jon. "To Whom is Justin's *Dialogue* addressed?" *Theological Studies* 38 (1977): 538–46.

Remus, Harold. "Justin Martyr's Argument with Judaism." In *Anti-Judaism in Early Christianity*, ed. Stephen G. Wilson, vol. 2 of *Separation and Polemic*, 59–80. Studies in Christianity and Judaism 2.2. Waterloo, Ontario: Wilfrid Laurier University, 1986.

Skarsaune, Oskar. "The Conversion of Justin Martyr." *Studia Theologica* 30 (1976): 53–73.

Skarsaune, Oskar. "Justin and His Bible." In *Justin Martyr and His Worlds*, ed. Sarah Parvis and Paul Foster, 53–76. Minneapolis: Fortress, 2007.

Stanton, Graham. "'God-Fearers': Neglected Evidence in Justin Martyr's *Dialogue with Trypho.*" In *Ancient History in a Modern University*, vol. 2 of *Early Christianity, Late Antiquity and Beyond*, ed. T. W. Hillard, 43–52. Grand Rapids: Eerdmans, 1998.

Stanton, Graham. "The Law of Moses and the Law of Christ." In *Paul and the Mosaic Law*, ed. James D. G. Dunn, 99–116. Wissenshaftliche Untersuchungen zum Neuen Testament 89. Tübingen: Mohr Siebeck, 1996.

Trakatellis, Demetrios. "Justin Martyr's Trypho." *Harvard Theological Review* 79 (1986): 289–97.

Werline, Rodney A. "The Transformation of Pauline Arguments in Justin Martyr's *Dialogue with Trypho.*" *Harvard Theological Review* 92 (1999): 79–93.

Wilson, Stephen. "Dialogue and Dispute." In *Related Strangers: Jews and Christians, 70–170 CE*, 258–84. Minneapolis: Fortress Press, 1995.

Dissertations

Donahue, P. J. "Jewish-Christian Controversy in the Second Century: A Study in the 'Dialogue' of Justin Martyr." Ph.D. diss., Yale, 1973.

Index of Authors

Abramowski, R.   118n, 129n
Aland, B.   150n
Allert, C. D.   162n, 174n
Allison, D.   31n
Aloisi, J.   97n
Alsted, J. H.   1n
Andriessen, D. P.   82, 82n, 83, 83n
Attridge, H. W.   141n
Aono, T.   12n
Aulén, G.   97n, 99n
Aune, D. E.   127n, 140n
Azar, É.   108n

Baars, W.   106n
Babcock, W.   11, 11n
Bakke, O. M.   23n
Barnard, L. W.   20, 21n, 154n, 161n, 163, 163n
Barr, J.   5, 5n
Barrett, C. K.   44, 44n, 53n
Batiffol, P.   111n, 122n, 123n
Bauckham, R.   43n
Bauer, W.   6, 6n, 45n, 108n, 119n, 137, 137n, 147n
Baur, F. C.   6, 6n, 42n
Barnard, L. W.   45n
Barret, C. K.   7n, 45n
Becker, A. H.   49n, 50n
Beilby, J. K.   13n
Bernard, J. H.   108n,118n, 119n, 126n, 163n
Bingham, D. J.   179n
Bird, M.   11, 11n, 77n, 78n, 79, 80n, 102, 103n
Blackwell, B.   15n
Blakeney, E. H.   86n
Bockmuehl, M.   184n
Bowe, B. E.   22, 23n
Bower, R.   55n, 65n, 71n
Boyarin, D.   162n
Brent, A.   38n, 40n, 41n, 73n
Brock, S. P.   122n, 136n, 137n
Brown, C. T.   54n, 58, 58n, 59, 59n, 60, 60n, 62

Brown, M.   57n
Brown, R.   42, 42n, 43n, 56n, 57n
Brunston, C.   143n
Buchanan, G. W.   141n
Buhl, F.   152n
Bultmann, R.   67, 67n, 68, 68n, 73, 73n, 74, 148n
Bunsen, C. C. J.   79n, 80n

Calvin, J.   1n
Campbell, D.   2n
Carmignac, J.   107n, 110n
Carson, D. A.   2n
Chadwick, H.   109, 109n
Charlesworth, J. H.   106n, 107, 107n, 108n, 109n, 110, 110n, 111n, 115n, 118, 121, 122n, 123, 123n, 124n, 125, 125n, 127n, 131n, 132n, 133n, 134, 134n, 135n, 138n, 139n, 140n, 143n, 144n, 145n, 146n, 147n, 148n, 149n, 150n, 151n, 153n
Chrysostom, J.   49n
Clarke, W. K. L   30n, 145n
Cohen, S. J. D.   51, 51n
Colpe, C.   129n
Connolly, R. H.   82, 82n, 149n
Conzelmann, H.   6, 6n
Cooper, J.   4n
Corwin, V.   48n, 58n, 66n, 71, 72n
Cosgrove, C. H.   162n
Cross, F. L.   79n
Crowe, B.   96n, 98, 98n, 99, 99n, 101n
Culpepper, R. A.   110n
Cureton, W.   39n

Daley, B.   111n
Daniélou, J.   110n
Dassman, E.   6n, 10
Davids, P.   31n
Davies, W. B.   1n
Davies, R. E.   97n
Denning-Bolle, S   160n
Dennison, W. D.   32n
De Ste. Croix G. E. M.   73n

Index of Authors — 209

Diettrich, G. 014n
Dietze, P. 58n
Dodson, J. 11, 11n
Donahue, P. J. 45n, 53n, 54n, 179n
Dorner, I. A. 82, 82n
Drijvers, H. J .W. 109n
Driver, G. R. 107n
Drobner, H. 22n, 82n, 86n
Dulles, A. C. 79n
Dunn, J. D. G. 1n, 42n, 43n, 48, 48n, 49, 49n, 50n, 127n

Eddy, P. R. 13n
Edwards, M. J. 81n
Ehrman, B. D. 20n, 46n, 86n
Emerton, J. A 107n
Enderlein, S. E. 13n
Eno, R. 14n, 32, 32n
Everitt, A. 83n

Falls, T. B. 166n, 171n, 173n, 174n, 176n, 177n, 178n, 179n, 180n
Fawcett, B. 88n
Fee, G. D. 104n
Ferguson, E. 27n, 167n
Fisher, E. 23n
Foster, P. 156n, 157n
Frankenberg, W. 106n, 145n, 146n
Franzmann, M. 108n, 117n, 119, 119n, 121n, 134, 134n, 139n, 140n, 141n, 146n, 147n, 148, 148n, 150n, 151n
Frend, W. H. C. 73n

Gaca, K. L. 16n
Gadamer, H. 183, 183n
Gallandi, A. 77n
Gentry, P. 114n
Glanz, O. 116n, 117n
Grant, R. 56n, 58n, 61n, 63n, 108n, 111, 112n
Gregory, A. F. 11n
Godspeed, E. J. 6, 79n
Good, D. J. 27n
Goodenough, E. R. 160n, 171, 171n
Goulder, M. 47n
Grant, R. M. 72, 72n, 73n, 80n, 83n, 84n, 110n

Grimme, H. 107n
Gunkel, H. 108n, 116n, 122, 122n

Hagner, D. 24n
Harmer, J. R. 77n, 81n
Harnack, A. von 7, 7n, 25n, 109n, 122n, 137n, 150n, 153n, 161, 161n
Harris, J. R. 104, 104n, 107n, 110n, 112n, 118n, 123n, 125n, 129n, 133n, 134, 134n, 127, 137n, 143, 143n, 151, 151n, 152, 152n
Harvey, A. 109n
Haykin, M. 74n, 75, 75n, 80n, 92n, 96n
Hill, C. 57, 57n, 73n, 77n, 80n, 81n
Hofer, A. 154n
Hofius, O. 141n
Holdcraft, I. T. 15n
Holmes, M. W. 20n, 21, 21n, 22n, 28n, 37, 37n, 40n, 41n, 46n, 48, 49n, 54n, 56n, 59n, 60n, 61n, 62n, 63n, 66n, 69n, 71n, 83n, 86n, 100, 100n, 159n, 183, 183n, 186n, 188
Hollon, B. C. 80n
Holte, R. 154n
Horner, T. 161n
Hubík, K. 164n
Hurtado, L. 47n
Hydahl, N. 154n

Isacson, M. 39n, 41n

Jaubert, A. 20n
Jeffers, J. S. 20n, 27, 27n
Jefford, C. N. 19n, 83n
Jewett, R. 126n, 127n
Joly, R. 38n, 41n, 154n
Jonas, H. 150n

Käsemann, E. 141n
Kelly, J. N. D. 99n
Kim, J. H. 137n
Kittel, G. 146n, 152n
Klauck, H. 27n
Knopf, R. 30n, 33n
Knox, J. 8n
Koester, H. 58n, 60n, 80n
Köstenberger, A. 130n, 131n

Labourt, J.   123n
Lake, K.   86n
Lattke, M.   104n, 106n, 107n, 108n, 111n, 112, 112n, 113n, 114n, 115n, 116n, 117n, 118, 118n, 119, 119n, 120n, 121n, 122n, 124n, 125, 125n, 126, 126n, 127n, 129, 129n, 131, 131n, 132, 132n, 134, 134n, 135, 135n, 139n, 140, 140n, 141, 141n, 143, 143n, 144, 144n, 145n, 146, 146n, 147n, 148, 148n, 149n, 150n, 151n, 153n
Lechner, T.   40n
Liebeschuetz, J. H.W. G.   42n
Lienhard, J. T.   77n, 96n, 101n
Lieu, J.   44n, 49n, 53, 53n, 54, 54n, 61n, 159n, 160n, 181n
Lightfoot, J. B.   22, 22n, 30, 30n, 38n, 39, 39n, 40, 40n, 41, 41n, 45n, 77n, 81, 81n, 85, 85n, 86n, 100n, 185
von Lilienfeld, F.   39n
Lindemann, A   6n, 7, 7n, 8, 9n, 11n, 24n, 25, 25n, 32n, 33, 36n, 156, 156n, 158, 158n, 184n
Longman III, T.   130n
Luedemann, G.   31n
Lütgert, W.   46n

Maier, H. O.   11n, 36n
Marguerat, D.   184n
Marrou, H. I.   86n, 99n
Massaux, É.   58n
Maurer, C.   58n
McGrath, A.   1n, 3, 4n
McNeil, B.   27n
Meade, J.   114n
Meecham H. G.   77n, 85, 86n, 88n, 96n, 97n, 98n, 100, 100n, 102n, 103n
Meier, J.   42, 42n, 43n, 56n, 57n
Meinhold, P.   45n
Merrill, E.   108n
Metzger, B.   76
Mingana, A.   106n, 110n, 112n, 125n, 133n, 134, 134n, 143n, 151, 151n, 152, 152n
Minns, D.   155n
Moo, D.   31n, 126n, 148n
Moss, C.   85n
Munier, C.   45n

Murray, J.   126n
Myllykoski, M.   45n, 50, 50n

Needham, N.   4n, 5n, 14, 14n, 15, 15n
Newbold, W.   107, 108n
Newman, C.   27n, 28n, 32n, 33, 33n
Nielsen, C.   30, 30n, 77n
Nilson, J.   160, 160n, 162n
Nöldeke, T.   145n

Oberman, H.   3n
O'Brien, P. T.   2n, 104n, 143n
Oden, T.   13, 14, 14n, 188, 188n
Ong, W. J.   157n
Osborn, E. F.   8, 8n, 9n, 15, 15n, 16, 16n, 154n
Oswalt, J.   123n

Palmer, D. W.   88n
Parkes, J. W.   49n
Parsons, M.   32n
Parvis, P.   155n
Parvo, R.   29n
Pasquier, A.   8n
Pearson, S. C.   112n
Pelikan, J.   13, 13n, 161, 161n
Penny, D. N.   6, 6n, 9
Petersen, A. K.   49n
Pierre, M.   108n
Plooij, D.   122n
Preiss, T.   36n

Räisänen, H.   24n, 27n, 30n, 32, 32n, 33, 33n, 34, 34n
Reed, A. Y.   49n, 50n
Reis, D. M.   11n, 36n
Reitzenstein, R.   116, 116n, 129n
Remus, H.   162n
Rensberger, D. K.   6n, 7n, 8n, 9, 9n
Ritschl, A.   7n
Rius-Camps, J.   41n
Robinson, T.   41, 41n, 42n, 43, 43n, 49n, 50, 50n
Roetzel, C.   8n
Rok.ah, D.   158n
Runge, S. E.   117n
Ryken, L.   130n

Sanders, E.P.   1n, 162n
Sanders, J. T.   110n
Scarborough, J.   8n
Scheck, T.   16, 16n
Schenke, H.   116n
Schneider, G.   20n
Schoedel, W.   39n, 40n, 41n, 47n, 52n, 54n, 56n, 57n, 58, 58n, 61, 61n, 62n, 65n, 66n, 70n, 74n, 91n
Schulz, S.   31n
Schreiner, T.   125, 126n, 148n, 176, 176n
Schweitzer, A   1n
Seifrid, M.   2n, 5n
Shotwell, ?   171n, 172n
Sibinga, J. S.   58n, 167n, 176n
Siker, J. S.   173, 173n, 175n
Silva, M.   5n
Skarsaune, O.   154n, 155n, 158, 158n, 163, 163n, 164n, 177n
Slusser, M.   154n
Smith, C.   36n, 52n, 53, 53n
Smyth, H.   28n, 90n
Spitta, F.   129n, 146, 146n
Stanton, G.   162n, 166n, 169, 169, 170n, 171n, 177n
Stendahl, K.   3n
Stölten, W.   108n
Stowers, S.   79n
Stylianopoulos, T.   157n, 162n, 163n, 167n, 175n, 176n, 179n
Swancutt, D. M.   79n
Swartley, W. M.   36n, 65n, 72, 72n

Theissen, G.   141n
Thierry, J. J.   81n, 86n
Torrance, T. F.   3n, 12, 12n, 29, 29n, 30, 30n, 47, 47n, 57n, 59n, 67n, 68, 68n, 69, 69n, 70, 70n, 71, 71n, 72, 72n, 73, 77, 77n, 133, 133n, 183, 184

Trakatellis, D.   162, 162n
Trevett, C.   37n, 45n, 58n, 60, 61n, 68, 68n
Tucker, E.   100n
Tuckett, C. M.   11n

van Unnik, W. C.   22n

Vickers, B. J.   136n
Vööbus, A.   107n
Vogl, A   120n

Wallace, D.   64n, 90n, 97n
Wansink, C. S.   80
Warren, D.   9n
Waters, G. P.   2n
Weijenborg, R.   41n
Weinrich, W. C.   74n
Weiss, J.   30, 30n
Welborn, L. L.   16n, 21, 21n, 22
Werline, R. A.   158n, 176, 176n, 178n
Westerholm, S.   2n, 4n
Wesley, J.   3n
Wetter, G. P.   72n
White, B. J.   6n, 7n, 8n, 10, 10n
Wilhelm-Hooijberg, A. E.   21n
Wilhoit, J.   130n
Wilken, R. L.   73, 74n
Williams, D. H.   3n, 15, 15n
Williams, R.   15n
van Winden, J C. M.   154n
Winston, D.   81n
Wray, J. H.   141n
Wright, D.   5n
Wright, N. T.   1n, 2n, 126, 126n
Wu, J. L.   112n

Young, E. J.   123, 123n

Zahn, T.   40, 40n, 41, 41n, 45n

Index of Scripture References

Genesis
1:3–4   130n
3:21   136, 137
15   34, 175, 175n
15:6   174, 175, 176, 181
15:15   25
20:17   95
49:10   150
Exodus
15:6   130
15:12   130
Deuteronomy
21:23   176n
27:26   176n
32:39   95
1 Samuel 15:22   27
2 Samuel 19:40–20:1   126
1 Kings 12:16   126
Psalms   131, 131n, 133, 144
2:7   133n
16:10   116n, 145n
17:7   130
18:5   145n
22:1   133n
22:8   133n
22:16   133n
24:20   143n
25:6   144n
27:9   131
30:2   143n
30:3   145n
36:9   95
40:11   144n
44:1–3   130
45:6–7   133n
49:15   145n
51:16–17   27
86:16   151n
95:11   140n
97:7   133n
98:1   130
103:4   144n
104:27–28   95
105:4   131
106:16   123n
110   150, 151, 152
110:1   130n
110:2   150
110:4   150
116:16   151
117   130
117:6   130
117:16   130
147:5   95
Isaiah
40:28   95
43:6–7   95
44   87
45:2   123
52–54   179n
53   179n
53:3   133
66:13   95
Jeremiah
11:14–17   117
11:16   117
Habbauk 2:16   130
Zechariah 3:1–5   136n
Matthew   57n
6:25   96
10:24   134
16:26   98n
19:17   16, 16n
27:43   133n
27:46   133n
Mark
8:31   133
8:34–35   74n
8:37   98n
9:3   134–5
9:12   133
10:45   97n, 99
13:35   122
Luke
6:4   40n
9:22   133

17:25	133	5	92, 96n, 98
24	122n, 154n	5:6–10	96n
24:16	122	5:9–10	65n
24:44	133n	6	32–33, 126n, 127
John	58n, 110, 112n, 150n	6:1–5	125
3	131n	6:5	125, 127
3:16	74n	6:5–11	74n
3:19–21	131n	6:23	93
7:37–9	75	8:18–21	120
8:12	150	8:20–21	113n
8:54	122n	9–11	114n, 158n
9:11–13	95	10:9–10	147
10:7–10	124n	10:10	148n
10:9	124n	13:11	65n
11:50	97n	13:14	136n, 137n
12:28	122n	1 Corinthians	36n, 56n, 177n
13:31	122n	1:20–21	74n
14:6	121n	1:23	56n
17:1	122n	4:4	56n, 60n, 62n
17:4	122n	5	157n
20:25	133n	6:9–10	56n
20:27	74n	7:19	61n
21	46	8:1	78n
Acts		11:1	177n
2:33–34	130n	12:12–13	127
11:26	54	13	56
16:37	120n	15:2	75
22:25	120n	15:8–9	56n
Romans	36n 87n, 102, 158, 158n, 169n	15:9	63
1–11	100n	15:26	145
1–2	87n	15:29	125
2–4	158n	2 Corinthians	36n
2:4	90n	5:14	97n
2:29	179	5:17	120, 136, 144
3–5	33	5:21	69, 101
3:1–2	175n	6:15	74n
3:20	50n	Galatians 36n, 102, 158, 158n, 169, 169n, 170	
3:22	147	2:11–14	50
3:24	147	2:14–15	61n
3:25	92, 100	2:16	50n,147
3:26	147	2:21	71n, 147
3:28	50n, 62n, 147	3	175, 175n, 178n, 182, 187
3:30	147	3:2	50n
4	175, 175n, 176, 182, 187	3:5–9	175
4:7	94n	3:5	50n
4:11	176	3:10	50n, 176n
5–6	185	3:13	97n, 176n

3:27	136n	1:8–9	133n
4:4–6	100n	4:2	127n
4:4	71n	4:3	140n
5:6	61n	7	179n
5:16	137	James	
5:22–23	126	1:12	119n
6:15	61n	1:27	72n
Ephesians	9, 36n	1 Peter	
1:13–14	65n	1:4	119
1:19–21	130n	2:13–17	21n
2:4–7	145	3:18	47
2:5	131	3:19	122n
2:8–9	93	4:1	47
2:8	131	4:6	122
2:9–10	33	5:4	119n
4:4–16	127	1 John	70, 70n
4:24	136n	2:5	70
5:8	150	2:9	70
Philippians	36n	2:11	70
1:20	143n	3:14	70
2:5–11	104n	4:1–6	46
2:6–11	122n	4:7	70
3:9	69	2 John	46n
4:3	19, 20	1:7	46
4:19	96	3 John	46n
Colossians	36n	Revelation	51n, 112, 119n
1	46	1:18	124
1:15–20	77n, 89	2:7	75
1:24	62n	2:10	119
3:16	104n	2:11	75
1 Thessalonians	36n	2:17	75
2 Thessalonians	9, 36n	2:26	75
2:12	144	3	124n
1:5	64	3:5	75
1 Timothy 3:16	62n, 114n, 119, 147n	3:7	124
2 Timothy		3:9	51n
1:13	56	3:12	75
2:12	75	3:21	75
4:8	119n	5:3	112n, 119n
Philemon	36n	11:7	151n
13	97n	12:17	151n
Hebrews	31n, 133n, 141n, 179n	13:7	151n
1:3	130n	19:19	151n
1:5	133n	12	112n
1:6	133n		

Index of Ancient Sources

1 Baruch		61.1–2	21n
4:20	135n	63.3	21
5:1–2	135n		
	135n	1 Enoch	47n
1 Clement	2n, 17, [18, 18n, 19, 20,		
	20n, 22, 22n, 23n, 24,	2 Clement	112
	24n, 25, 26, 28n, 29, 30,		
	30n, 31, 32, 32n, 33,	2 Maccabees 12:44	125
	34n,] 68, 78, 183, 184		
1.1	20n	3 Corinthians	9
5	21		
5.4–5	23	4 Maccabees	41n
5.5	185		
6	21	Acts of Thomas	108n
7.4	23, 23n, 34		
7.7	34	Aristotle, Nicomachean Ethics, 2.2	167n
9	23		
10.1	28	Athenagoras, Legatio pro Christianis	91n
14.1	24		
16	23	The Epistle of Barnabas	84n, 97n, 112,
21.1	21n		159, 159n
21.6	21n		
30.3	24, 29, 30, 31, 184	Cicero, De haruspicum responsis IX.8–9	27n
31.1–2	28		
32	18, 24, 25, 29, 33, 34	Clement of Alexandria	
32.2	25	Strom. 4.17	18n
32.3–4	25, 31		
32.3	26	Codex Argentoratensis Graecus ix	86, 89n
32.4	26, 30, 184		
33	32, 185	Community Rule (1QS)	110
33.1	33n		
33.8	32	Didache	57n
35.1–2	33		
36.1	33, 34	Dio Cassius, Roman History	
36.2	34	67.14.1–2	19n
37.2–3	21n	67.14.2	91n
44.3–5	21		
44.6	23	Diogenis Sinopensis Ep. 10.1.10	98n
47.6	23		
58.2	23n	The Epistle to Diognetus	9, 18, [77, 77n, 78,
59.2	26		78n, 79, 79n, 80, 80n, 81,
60.2	21n		82, 83, 83n, 84, 84n, 86, 87,
60.4	21n		

Index of Ancient Sources

	87n, 88n, 96, 97, 97n, 98,	Eusebius, *The Church History*	82
	98n, 100, 102, 103,] 184, 186	3.15	20n
2	87	3.16	22n
3–4	87	3.36	38n, 40n
3.5	87	3.38	19n
4	87	4.11.8	155n
4.4	87	4.18.6	159n
5–8	88	4.22	22n
5	88n	4.23	19n
5.11	84	4.3	82n
5.12	84		
5.14	84	Hippolytus	
5.15	84	*Philosophoumena*	81
6	88	10.33	82
6.1	88	*Refutio omnium Haeresium*	81
6.6	88		
6.9	88:	Ḥodayot (1QH)	110
7–9	98, 98n		
7–8	88	Ignatius	
7.1–5	82	*Epistle to the Ephesians*	39, 41n, 47n
7.2	77n, 81n	1.2	65
7.4	85	5	65n
7.6–7.7	82	7–8	46
7.7	84	10.1	65n, 66n
7.8	88	11.1	69n, 72
8	89, 92	12.2	36n
8.2	89	14	70
8.6	102, 102n	14.1	56, 69
8.10	92	16.1	56n
8.11	89, 92	18	46
9	78, 92, 96, 96n, 103	18.1	56n
9.1	63n, 93, 100, 100n	19.1	40n
9.2–4	186	19.3	111
9.2	93, 94n, 97, 101, 186	20.1	63n
9.3–5	101	*Epistle to the Philadelphians*	39, 46, 47,
9.3–4	94		47n, 51n, 57, 62, 63, 63n
9.3	101	3.3	56n
9.4	101, 102	5–9	47n
9.5	94n, 97n, 98, 101	5.1	57, 60, 62, 64, 64n
9.6	95, 102n	5.2	48, 57, 58n, 63
10	81n	6.1	45, 47, 51, 52, 54
10.1	102n	7.2	56n
10.8	84	8.1	66n, 72
11–12	81, 82, 87	8.2	47n, 57, 60, 61, 62n, 64,
11	77n, 81, 81n		66n, 67, 68, 75, 76, 185
12.5	78n	9.1	47n
		9.2	48, 55, 57, 59, 60, 111
		10.2	63n

11.1	72	Epistle to the Trallians	39, 41n, 46, 47n
11.2	63n	2.1	66n
Epistle to Polycarp	39	5.2	62n
1.1	63n	6	47n
7.2	63n	6.2	112n
7.3	64n	8.1	56
Epistle to the Magnesians	39, 41n, 46, 47, 47n, 61	9–10	46
		9.2	66n
1	56	12.3	63n
1.2	63n		
4	56n	Irenaeus, Adv. Haer.	80n, 81, 92n
5	74n	3.3.3	20n
6–7	71n	4.20.4	71n
8–10	47n	4.33.9	71n
8.1	53, 54, 71n	5.28.4	40n
8.2	40, 40n, 48n, 71n		
9–10	52n	Jerome, On Famous Men 16	38n
9.1–2	52	Josephus	42
9.1	51	Jewish War	
10	49	2.463ff	50n
10.3	47n, 48, 49n, 55	3.2.4	42n
12	68	7.45	50n
13.1	68n		
14.1	65n	Justin Martyr	
Epistle to the Romans	38–39, 41n	Dialogue with Trypho	9, 92n, [154n, 155, 156, 158, 158n, 159, 159n, 160, 161, 161n, 162, 162n, 163, 163n, 164, 164n, 165, 166, 166n, 167, 168, 169, 170, 171, 175n, 177n, 179n, 180, 181,] 184, 187
1.2	72		
2.2	63n		
4.1	40n		
4.2	62n		
4.3	36n		
5	185		
5.1	37, 56n, 60n	1–9	163n
6.1	66n	3.1	154
7	40n, 73	6	167
7.2	74, 112n	7	167
8.3	65n	8	156, 164, 165, 166, 169, 170, 173, 177, 181, 187
9.2	56n		
Epistle to the Smyrnaeans	39, 47n, 57		
1–7	46	8.1–2	154n
1.1–2	46	8.1	165
2	66n	8.2	159n, 166n, 168
4.2	69n	8.3	166, 166n
5.1	57	8.4	169
6.1	55, 65	10–30	163n
6.2	66n, 72, 72n	10	171
7.2	57	10.1	171n
11.1	63, 64, 64n, 65n, 72	10.3	171n
12.1	70n	11–47	163

11–31		163	
11		179	
13.1		179	
15.7		179	
18		174	
19		174	
23	156, 165, 172, 173, 174, 180, 187		
23.3		173	
23.4		174	
23.5		181	
24		179	
25.6		179	
27		161n	
31–118		163n	
32–110		163	
41.4		179	
44.4		177n	
46.7		180n	
47		177	
47.3–4		178n	
48–107		163	
48–54		170	
92	156, 165, 172, 173, 174, 187		
92.2		173n	
92.3–4		174	
92.3		174	
92.4		175, 179	
92.5		172	
95–96		176	
95		175n	
95.1		176n	
95.3		177n	
96.1		176n	
108–141		163	
111–142		163	
119–142		163n	
119.6		176n	
120.5		161n	
137	156, 165, 180, 187		
137.1–2		180n	
141		162n	
141.1		166n	
142		159n	
First Apology		155n, 161n	
The Martyrdom of Justin		155n	
Second Apology		155n	

Lactantius, Divine Institutes	112
4.12	112n
Laodiceans	9
Liber Legum Regionum	108n
Lucian, "Passing of Peregrinus"	88n
Marcus Aurelius, Meditations	83
1.6	83n
Melito of Sardis	
On Pascha and Fragments	
72–99	84n, 92n
Midrash Rabboth	137n
Odes of Solomon	2n, 9, 15, [104, 104n, 105, 106, 106n, 107n, 108, 108n, 109, 109n, 110, 110n, 111, 111n, 112, 112n, 114, 114n, 117, 118, 118n, 121n, 126n, 129, 131, 131n, 132, 133, 135n, 140n, 143, 143n, 145n, 148, 150, 150n, 152, 153,] 184, 186, 187
1.1–5	106n
1.1	118
1.3	167n
3	106
3.7–9	127n
3.7	111, 127
4.6	132n
4.7	113n
4.13	132
5.1–11	106n
5.3	132, 132n
6.8–18	106n
7.5	132n
7.6	111
7.10	132n, 133
7.13–14	150n
7.22	132n
7.24	111
8.5	114n
8.13	113n
8.17	114n

Index of Ancient Sources — 219

8.18	113n	17.14	125, 126
8.19	114n	17.16	116, 124
8.21	116n	17.17	117
8.22–23	127n	19.1–4	108
8.22	116n	19.4	127
9.5	132n	19.6	110
9.10	114n	20.4	114n
10.3	113n	20.7	132n, 138
10.5	151n	20.9	132n
10.6	151n	21	130, 135n
11	106, 106n	21.2	130
11.1	132n	21.3	130, 135
11.6	112n	22.1–12	106n
12.3	113n	22.11	113n
14.4	113n	22.5	112n
15.2	135	23.2–3	113n
15.7	144	23.2	132, 132n
15.8	111, 132n, 138	23.4	132, 132n
15.9	145, 145n	23.8–9	112n, 119n
15.10	138	23.12	149n
16.1	148	24.1	149n
16.3	148	24.13	132n, 149n
16.4	148	25	115, 127, 129, 130, 133, 135, 135n, 142, 153, 186
17	115, 116, 116n, 117, 118, 118n, 119, 121, 123, 124, 127, 128, 129, 130, 153, 186	25.1	113n, 129, 153
		25.2	113n, 130, 138
17.1–8	116	25.3	131
17.1–4	124	25.4	129, 131, 132n, 141
17.1–2	118	25.5	131, 133, 134
17.1	117, 117n, 119	25.7	134, 135, 135n
17.2–4	113n	25.8–9	138
17.2	114n, 117, 117n, 118, 119, 120	25.8	129, 135, 136, 138, 141, 187
17.3	120	25.9	138, 141, 142
17.4	120, 120n, 121n, 122n, 123, 124	25.10	114n, 139, 139n, 141n, 187
17.5	121n	25.11	129, 131, 138, 139, 140
17.6	117, 118, 118n, 121, 122n	25.12	106n, 114n, 129, 140, 142
17.7–8	116n	26.8	145
17.7	106, 122	26.10	141n
17.8–15	116	26.12	141n
17.8	122, 122n	27	111, 149, 153
17.9–13	122	27.2	149
17.9	122, 123	27.3	149
17.10	123	28	121
17.11	106n	28.3	141
17.12	120n, 124	28.9	121
17.13–17	124	28.17	106n
17.13	124, 125, 125n	29	115, 117n, 142, 143, 143n, 147n, 149, 152
17.14–16	117		

29.1–4	147	42.16	135
29.1–3	145	Codex Askew	106
29.1	147n	Codex Harris	106, 106n, 135n, 151n
29.2–3	143	Codex Nitriensis	106, 135n
29.2	132n, 144, 144n, 147	P. Bodmer XI	106, 112
29.3	144		
29.4	145n, 147	Origen	
29.5–6	148, 153	*Commentary on John* 6.36	19n
29.5	114n, 133, 142, 146, 147, 151, 151n, 186	*Contra Celsum*	16
		Hom. in Luc. 6.4	40n
29.6	117n, 143, 147, 147n, 148, 149, 153	*Pistis Sophia*	106
29.7	143, 149, 149n, 150, 151		
29.8–10	143n, 146, 146n	Plato, *Gorgias*, 515C	97n
29.8–9	150		
29.8	144n, 151, 152	Pliny the Younger, *Letters*	
29.9–10	143n, 149n	10.96	84n, 104n
29.9	150, 151	10.97	84n
29.10	151, 151n		
29.11	151	*Psalms of Solomon*	106, 106n
30.2	141n		
30.7	141n	*Shepherd of Hermas*	41n
31.5	114n		
31.7	132, 132n	Simplicius	
31.12	111	*In Aristotelis categorias*	
33.1	132n	*commentarium* 8.66.16	98n
33.12	138	*In Aristotelis physicorum libros*	
34	132	*commentaria* 10.1350.32	98n
34.6	132, 132n	*Commentarius in Epicteti*	
35.6	141n	*enchiridion* 39.9	98n
36.3	111		
36.5	144	Suetonius	
36.6	114n	*Dom.* 15	91n
37.4	132n	*Nero* 16.2	91n
38.8	112n		
39.7	149n	Tacitus, *Annals*, 15.44	91n
41	121	Tatian, *Diatessaron*	109n
41.3	132, 132n	Tertullian, *Apology*	88n
41.8–10	121	40.2	91n
41.9	113n	Theophilus of Antioch, *To Autolycus*	84n
41.12	114n		
42	106, 121n, 123n, 149	Xenophon, *Anab.* vii, 9, 9	97n
42.1–2	111, 150		
42.6	153, 153n	*Zohar* 1.36b	137n
42.11	145n		

Topical Index

Abraham, see *Justification*
Atonement   34, 47, 59–60, 66, 94, 96–99, 111, 149–50, 179–80, 186
Christology   46–47, 77 n.4, 116–18, 129–30
Descensus ad inferos   122–23, 145
Docetism   36, 45–47, 56 n.76, 111
Election   113
Gnosticism   56 n. 76, 107–09, 111, 122, 140–41 n. 164, 150
– and Paul   7 n.22, 10
– see also, *Docetism*
Imputation, see *justification*
Judaism
– circumcision   50–53, 61, 177–181
– in Antioch   43–44
– Old Testament   48, 57, 61, 87, 159
– Parting of the Ways   44–45, 48–50
– works of the law   50, 87, 164ff, 180–81
– Judaizers   36, 43–45, 47, 50, 54 n.68, 55, 57, 61, 62, 68, 76, 185
Justification
– Abraham, use of   11, 28, 173–177, 187
– and prayer   64–67
– later fathers/medieval   3 n.5, 4 n.9, 5 n.10–11, 13–17
– forensic   115, 119–20, 124, 147

– grace   12–13, 34, 52–53, 70–73, 100, 131–133, 144, 146–48
– Gospel   57–59
– imputation   69, 95, 100–102, 129, 136–39, 187
– Paul and James   31, 184–85
– recent trends   1–2 n. 4
– union with Christ   124–127
– works righteousness (or legalism)   24, 26, 28, 29–35, 67–73, 168ff, 180–81
– by faith   1, 3, 4, 7, 11, 12–18, 24, 25, 28, 29–35, 62, 75, 76, 78, 100, 102, 105, 133, 152–153, 155–156, 172, 176, 183–188
New Perspective   1–2
Paul, Apostle
– center of thought   5–6
– Gospel   58–59, 63
– in memory   19–20, 42, 77–78 n.5, 156–58, 184
– indicative/imperative   32–34
– second century   6–12
Persecution   19–21, 73–75, 84–85, 90–92
Reformation   1, 5
secondary orality   157
Soteriology   18, 34, 36, 37, 55, 65, 67, 68, 75, 86, 98, 103 n.92, 105, 112, 129, 133, 142, 149 n.202, 152, 153, 185, 188

www.ingramcontent.com/pod-product-compliance
Lightning Source LLC
Chambersburg PA
CBHW021353300426
44114CB00012B/1206